Digital Dilemmas

Digital Dilemmas

Power, Resistance, and the Internet

M. I. FRANKLIN

OXFORD
UNIVERSITY PRESS

UNIVERSITY PRESS

Oxford University Press is a department of the University of Oxford.
It furthers the University's objective of excellence in research, scholarship,
and education by publishing worldwide.

Oxford   New York
Auckland   Cape Town   Dar es Salaam   Hong Kong   Karachi
Kuala Lumpur   Madrid   Melbourne   Mexico City   Nairobi
New Delhi   Shanghai   Taipei   Toronto

With offices in
Argentina   Austria   Brazil   Chile   Czech Republic   France   Greece
Guatemala   Hungary   Italy   Japan   Poland   Portugal   Singapore
South Korea   Switzerland   Thailand   Turkey   Ukraine   Vietnam

Oxford is a registered trade mark of Oxford University Press
in the UK and certain other countries.

Published in the United States of America by
Oxford University Press
198 Madison Avenue, New York, NY 10016

© Oxford University Press 2013

[Cataloging-in-Publication Data on file with the Library of Congress.]

9780199982691
9780199982707 (pbk.)

9 8 7 6 5 4 3 2 1

Printed in the United States of America on acid-free paper

For Ngaire Margaret Franklin, my mother

CONTENTS

LIST OF FIGURES

ACKNOWLEDGMENTS

There are many, many people to thank but space is limited and time is up. I have distributed these acknowledgments through the book. Each chapter speaks from a particular research trajectory and with that those people who have been formative in my thinking, granted me time and access to their work, and provided financial and other sorts of support. There are some people I would like to thank here nonetheless. Thanks to Angela Chnapko at Oxford University Press in New York for her support, input into the original idea for the book, and her forbearance over the last months as life and work commitments tripped over one another. Thanks to Nick Couldry, Natalie Fenton, and Jane Powell at Goldsmiths for providing me the time and resources for research leave to work on the book this past year. To Dong Hyun Song and Gareth Stanton my thanks as well for looking after the *Global Media & Transnational Communications* program at the Media & Communications Department of Goldsmiths while I was away. To colleagues Zehra Arabadji, Clea Bourne, Jacqui Cheal, James Curran, and David Morley thanks for the literature tips and attentiveness to how I was getting on, much appreciated. Thanks (again) to Tadgh O'Sullivan for the index, and to Jochen Jacoby, Fernanda Cohen, Toby Van Buren, and xkcd for the artwork. Three people looked after my well-being, helped me through the inevitable bottlenecks in thinking and writing for a book such as this, and kept me human: My warmest thanks to Zeena Feldman for the friendship, moral support, and brain food, to Zab Franklin for lifelong sisterhood and friendship, and Jochen Jacoby for all his love. Could not have done it without any of you. Thanks for putting up with me. Finally, I dedicate this book to my mother, Margaret Franklin, who paid for my education and who has supported me, as she has all my siblings, in more ways than we can ever know. Thanks Mum and with love.

Parts of Chapters 2 and 3 draw on previously published work: "Digital Dilemmas: Transnational Politics in the 21st Century," *Brown Journal of World Affairs*. vol. XVI, issue 11, 2010: 67–85; " 'Wij zijn de Borg': Microsoft en de strijd om de controle over het internet" in *Digitaal contact: het net van de begrensde mogelijkheden*, ed. by Jeroen de Kloet, Suzanne Kuik, Giselinde Kuipers, Amsterdams Sociologisch Tijdschrift, AST-Thema: vol. 30, 2003: 223–253. Every effort has been made to trace and acknowledge copyright for images reproduced in this book. The publisher would be grateful to hear from any copyright holders who believe their images have been used without due credit.

London/Amsterdam, March 2013.

Digital Dilemmas

Digital Dilemmas

INTRODUCTION

Consider the following: an antitrust trial pitting one of the world's most powerful global corporations against the US Department of Justice, homeless people using new media or others doing so on their behalf, and advocacy at the United Nations for human rights online. Participants in all three—individuals and communities, nongovernmental organizations and grassroots groups, governments and corporations—are deploying information and communications technologies in general and the internet in particular as not only means but also ends in themselves. Whatever decisions any party makes, whatever difficulties they surmount or opportunities they grasp—between clear or ambiguous options, in the face of material and digital obstacles, with ample technical and financial resources or on a shoestring—the ways they look to influence the terms of debate and go about achieving their goals inform the multiplex dynamics of power and resistance in an era of technoeconomic and sociopolitical change.

This book's title, *Digital Dilemmas*, points to the allied and antagonistic interests, forces of habit, and socioeconomic aspirations that inform each of the three scenarios explored in this study and alluded to above. To speak of *dilemmas* in this respect is to suggest more than consumers agonizing over which smartphone to buy. At the very least the internet, however defined, operates in all three cases as an ideal of (global) interconnectivity (Franklin 2010) in principle if not in practice. And as these technologies become more embedded in society and wielded as tools of international development, opportunity, and challenge for successive generations of activists, internet media and communications have been undergirding tectonic shifts in world order in terms of the practice of statecraft at home and intergovernmental cooperation abroad.[1] In this context a variety of vested interests are looking not only to entrench but also to extend any incumbent powers they may have over how the internet functions, how it is accessed, and how people make use of the web. These moves include forms of state-sponsored and commercial monitoring, censoring, and various sorts of restrictions on what sorts of content people access and the terms and conditions by which they can engage service providers, exchange information, or interact with one another when online. Policymakers in national and multilateral settings are confronted with conflicting priorities in this respect; for example, ensuring diversity and competition in a sector characterized by market concentration, regulating and monitoring citizens' access and use without encroaching on privacy, pursuing (cyber)crime without abusing civil liberties or consumer or human rights. The idea of the internet being available for everyone, everywhere, and all the time is being countered in practice first by the push and pull between national sovereignty and proprietary property rights that allow a powerful agglomeration of both state actors and corporate interests to control access and terms of use. Second, state actors, unilaterally or in concert, have been reconsidering their respective approaches to regulating the internet as the limits to internet 'freedom' become more pressing for domestic and foreign policymakers. Third, there is an intensification of efforts by all parties to control the narrative, to put forward their versions of what is at stake in a scenario in which the internet plays a leading role as well as provides the decor for other action.

Ordinary people meanwhile have become accustomed to the idea that the cyberspaces they traverse are open, online interactions are transparent in a positive sense, and the web's products and services are more or less "free." In hi-tech, saturated societies, the public is somewhat naive to assume that access to the internet is universal and evenly distributed and that the ways in which it is run are self explanatory. Things have been changing of late though, as these assumptions come under scrutiny for a range of sociocultural, political, and economic reasons. The technolegal intricacies of internet design, access, and terms of use that were once the reserve of expert elites have started to hit the headlines. Now an integral part of contemporary media *and* communications, ownership, and control of the internet by whom, for whom, and on whose terms, has moved from behind the scenes and from behind our screen into public arenas of big power politics (e.g., the United Nations), inter/national media scandals (e.g., the Leveson Inquiry in the United Kingdom or the fallout of the Wikileaks affair), and political revolutions (e.g., in the Middle East and North Africa). In this context the Anglo-American-Euro sense of entitlement to leading decisions on how the internet functions, centered paradigmatically in the United States, has started to wobble. Incumbent powers, from quasi-nongovernmental organizations (*quangos*) to *public-private partnerships*, are being challenged in word and deed. These challenges come not only from longstanding critics from within these societies or rising powers from abroad (e.g., China, India, and Brazil) but also through the cross-border lobbying and mobilizing of other nonstate actors over a decade of the *multistakeholder consultations* that have come to characterize struggles over *internet governance*.[2] All protagonists are staking competing claims in the way the internet, and the web-based relationships and spaces it facilitates, has and will continue to work. And as the lion's share of ownership and provision of web-based goods and services for an increasingly global population of internet users is also largely in the hands of US corporations, challenging this status quo is not an easy task.

In this sense the "internet" has several roles at once: as a contentious object of analysis, arena, and means for action for all parties. However, this is not to suggest a simple technological determinism, to attribute this techno-social-economic "array" with agency in the usual sense of the term. Like all human artifacts, the internet does not stand alone, outside history beyond the reach of societal forces—at least not yet. Automation, simulation, and artificial intelligence have not developed far enough to eliminate the organic social—human—side from the equation. Internet users are still predominately human beings. That said, the increasingly intricate connections between analog and digital social worlds, organic life forms, and "thinking machines" (Quintas 1996; Franklin 2012d), have repercussions not only for conventional thinking about the form and substance of power in analytical terms but also for how new hierarchies and modalities in the exercise of sociopolitical power are shaping public imaginaries, concomitant lifeworlds, and, thereby, the (re)production of knowledge (Latour 2012; O'Neil 2009; Wouters et al. 2012). This enervating tension between the "informatics of domination" and the "fruitful couplings" (Haraway 1990) that emanate from the ways in which humans and thinking machines are increasingly (in)compatible has implications for the intersection of everyday and political life.

Greater than the sum of its parts, the internet's future in this respect "belongs" to everyone, users and nonusers alike. However, this does not mean that everyone has, or can have, a say in how the internet does or could work—let alone to what ends, for whom, and on whose terms. While ordinary users on the whole have limited ability to affect how powerbrokers treat the product of their personal and professional online behavior, others are mobilizing on their behalf, in online and on-the-ground forums of consultation, organization, and (in)direct action. National and regional governing bodies, established intergovernmental organizations, and emerging multilateral institutions have also started to take into account the legal and political implications of these mobilizations on the one hand and, on the other, the "land grab" for ownership and control of the internet that has been intensifying at the intersection of corporate interests and state jurisdictions. With these struggles come equally concerted efforts to control the terms of debate about its future between these competing—and allied—interests and their critics.

This study intends to show how recent, high profile power struggles over *and* through the internet are the more visible aspect to ongoing struggles that have been taking place since the internet's early boom years, at the "back end" (Stalder 2012) of the user-friendly interfaces, gadgets, and services that now constitute the "cyberspatial practices of everyday life" (Franklin 2004: 12, 59 passim) that people take for granted or resent. The three empirical foci that concern Chapters 3–5 explore the implications of these tensions at close quarters and from different vantage points: the Microsoft antitrust trial in light of increasing corporate ownership and control of internet media and communications, homelessness and the internet, and rights-based activism for the online environment at the UN, respectively. Taken together and in turn they provide new insights into what have become internet-facilitated and web-embedded "horizons" of meaning-making and activity (Gadamer in Ulin 1984: 99–102); including contentious discourses of what is at stake that point to competing worldviews, development priorities, and acutely uneven means for taking effective action.[3] These conflicts are crystallizing around *and* through the idea that internet-embedded ways of doing things are indispensable to what counts as the "good society." They also feed into endemic disenchantment with political and economic power blocs at home and abroad along with protest movements on a range of global issues. The popular rise of the web in the 1990s may have gone hand in hand with neoliberal globalization but it also has gone hand in hand with successive waves of local and transnational mobilization around the notion that "another world is possible," that other sorts of globalization are underway, desirable, and sustainable. What remains undereducidated is whether, and, if so, how another internet is also possible, and for whom. This vexing question links the three illustrative cases under study in this book.[4]

In Context

Scholars and pundits still have a tendency to refer to the internet and/or the web in the same breath as "new media," but for the two, if not three, generations of so-called *digital natives* who have grown up with and through its computer-mediated interactions, these media are hardly new. As successive releases in the latest internet-embedded products and services render precursor versions "old" before their time, it is easy to overlook that even in its relatively short lifespan, the internet has had several iterations which coexist. In terms of perception and application, the 1990s' generation of web services, web browsers, and visuals are suffering a fate similar to that of black and white and public service television in the wake of color, cable, and satellite TV last century. In the retelling, however, the brief history of the internet still engenders hyperbolic levels of wonder and excitement, disapproval, and suspicion. Its runaway success in popular and economic terms and in a short time span within the larger history of media and communications (McLuhan 2001 (1964); McLuhan and Powers 1989; Mattelart 1994; Burke and Briggs 2009) has generated its own genus of mythologies and lexicons along with their respective high priesthoods, subcultures and undergrounds, heroes and villains, pioneers and doom merchants. Tales of redemption and despair, of creating and sustaining new sorts of worlds and intimate experiences facilitated and transmitted through the internet are now accessible to people without ever having to leave home, as the saying goes.[5]

Even a cursory look at popular and academic internet-related literature since its heyday in the 1990s shows a sharp polarization between optimistic and pessimistic analyses of the short-term and long-range effects of the internet's global uptake (unexpected) and its global rollout since then (deliberate) for culture, politics, and society. Piggybacking on international telecommunications networks dating from the late nineteenth century, once it emerged from its Cold War generation of US-based industrial-military funded research, the internet both epitomized and contributed to the globalization wave that marked the last half of the twentieth century. After all, the telephone had already made it possible for people to talk to one another at a distance through sender-receiving devices connected by analog networks of copper cables and wires (Standage 1998), so why not computers by way of computer programs and digitized networks?[6]

This first operational problem—how to make computers "talk" to one another—conjoined with a second—how to make computer-mediated defense and strategically sensitive information networks and their data-storage facilities less vulnerable to external attack or natural disaster, to wit the internet's "distributed network" design principle. These two premises then conjoined with a third, making these communicating computers easier to use by developing layers of applications and visuals that are accessible for ordinary people: some for profit, others for the purpose of governing, and others for the "hell of it" (Abbate 2001; Spiller 2002; Blum 2012; Raymond 2001; Vise 2005). The cross-border deals and technical communities that convene for all this interoperability to work have developed in a piecemeal, expert-led, and geopolitically uneven fashion, through informal ad hoc arrangements and increasingly by formalized institutional settings that include setting standards, treaty-making, and intergovernmental resolutions—and when these falter, case law. It is on behalf of communities, publics, citizenries, or consumers that incumbent and emerging vested interests are staking their claim in the changing landscape of ownership and control of internet design, access, and use. Within this larger narrative, including its variations and counternarratives, this study covers a period in which the internet itself has undergone a sea change in the way it looks, works, and how people access and use it.

Caveats

Given the state of flux that characterizes the technohistorical context in which the research for this book was carried out and the book completed, dealing with what this study is *not* about early on is appropriate. This is important because the sociocultural issues, corporate technoeconomic strategies, and statist political projects in play around the future of the internet are gathering momentum and because the ante is being constantly—and consciously—upped by all parties. Incumbent powers are having to deal with familiar and new forms of cross-border resistance as access to the internet becomes framed as not only the sine qua non of economic and human development (UN 2000; World Bank 2002; OECD 2000; UNESCO 2013a, b) but also increasingly perceived as, arguably, a fundamental right (BBC 2010; Jørgensen 2006; UN Human Rights Council 2012a). Efforts are intensifying in all quarters to gain control over the narrative, over which account of origins and destiny in technocultural terms sets the terms of political debate (e.g., Abraham 2012; New America Foundation 2012; Public Voice Coalition 2009; Clinton 2010a) and thereby frames popular imaginaries. In particular a winner-takes-all mentality and predilection for warlike idioms has started to permeate scholarly and media analyses of the interplay between the internet, politics, and society (*The Economist* 2012; Becker and Reißmann 2012; Goldsmith 2012). These "for or against" tropes of Big Power politics further entrench an ongoing polarization between positive or negative evaluations of this interplay and in doing so obscure crucial historical, technocultural, and political-economic nuances. Not only are the issues and practical problems involved irreducible to simple cause-and-effect equations, however comforting these may be in political or cultural terms, but so too are their critical analysis and the alternatives proposed.

What caveats are there? For one thing this book is not agitating for or against the idea that the internet and its so-called *new media* have had an impact on society, culture, and politics in broad terms. This is a chicken and egg argument. Nor is it looking to prove whether said impacts are good or bad, authentic or forms of false consciousness; the internet a passing fad, a tool of domination, or a tool for achieving (digital) democracy and freedom. This is a moral, normative register for analysis. Neither is it about whether or not *this* internet, increasingly synonymous with the *social media* web applications it facilitates, has been the driving force behind globalization and its discontents in general or, in particular, instrumental to spectacular political events in recent years. This is an historiographical and political debate as celebratory readings of these events, where protesters and their media of choice—or circumstance—saw the toppling of authoritarian and oppressive governments, have their flip side in condemnations of how these media have exacerbated protest movements, direct actions, and social unrest elsewhere in the world on the ground and online (see Castells 2012; Barkai 2012; Coleman and Tucker 2012). In all cases the internet and its web-based products, services, and multimedia communicative devices played a role; if not center stage then in the margins, if not for protagonists then for onlookers, reporters, online audiences, or offline publics. Technohistorical breaks are also not being advocated here as such. While some argue that "new media" imply "new politics" (Kern 2012), this study is not about the new sweeping out the old or conversely the old prevailing. Despite their substantial rhetorical value, these notions are not only time sensitive but also specious; one generation's "new" is the next one's "old," and change and continuity are cyclical, linear, and multiplex in varying degrees.[7]

The second caveat regards register. Didactic and rhetorical conventions in the Anglo-American scholarly idioms tend to privilege forms of address, statements of purpose couched in the declarative rather than the subjunctive mode (Sennett 2012): "Don't mess with Mister In-Between," in other words.[8] This book looks to explore just this in between because it is this domain that continues to go begging in critical theory and research on the role successive generations of "new" media and communications play in social movements, political oppression, and its resistance; for example, from the Zapatistas in Mexico in the 1990s to antiglobalization protests around the world from 1999 to 2004, from antigovernment protests in Iran in 2009, to the Occupy Movement in New York, London, and elsewhere in 2011. Overlapping generations of network designs, sorts of access, and uses of the internet combine with real-life and real-time forces that operate not only offline but also in *cyberspace* in ways that are qualitatively and quantitatively different from preceding generations. Having said that, these shifts do not start and stop with the latest software release or globally circulated images of social media brands as graffiti in revolutionary settings. In terms of meaning-making that also frames and coconstitutes the world people live in, this in-between is at once figurative and literal, physical and virtual, practical and conceptual, synthesizing and alternating (Lunenfeld 2000), full of possibility and new opportunities yet also porous to old-school sorts of oppression and newer, more insidious forms of control.

The third caveat is about scale. Although debates about large-scale transformation are germane to these inquiries, the extent of the internet's role in the Arab Uprisings of 2010–2011 or challenges that web-based *user-generated content* or "citizen journalism" raise for the sense of entitlement of incumbent political and media gatekeepers are questions that go beyond the scope and ambitions of this study. This is because the focus here is less on the "why" of competing causal explanations than on the processes and practices at stake, the "how" and, by association, questions around the "who" (or "what"), "for whom," and "when" that can reveal a wider "range of futures" (Ulin 1984: 104) in play.[9]

What this book *is* about concerns the unpacking of scenarios in which incumbent powers and forces of opposition and resistance on the one hand and, on the other, shifts in control and ownership of the internet, in part or as a whole, intersect. From there it theorizes implications for the "haves" and "have nots" respectively. Moving from corporate boardrooms and high courts to the streets, community-based needs and aspirations, and then into UN summits, the book shows how unevenly matched forces come into contact, collide, or cooperate over time in a mixture of online and offline settings. Each case in the book shows actors with different amounts of resources and power, sometimes with very few resources, making a difference in the way people experience the world around them by the way they use (or don't use) computer-mediated media and communications of the day. In the first instance, competing forces look to own and control the internet's underlying architecture, equipment, and other critical resources (e.g., control of operating systems or internet addresses through the *Domain Name System*) and concentrate these resources in fewer and fewer hands (e.g., US-based ICT corporations such as Google, Microsoft, and Facebook, inter alia). In the second instance, those forces, in concert as well as in ad hoc ways, make use of available tools and online products if not adapt the web's spaces as they search out affordable services to provide openings for the disadvantaged and marginalized (e.g., homeless populations and their media). And third, those who mobilize online and on the ground across national and temporal borders to influence decision-making around research and development (R&D) investment, jurisprudence, and regulations that affect internet design, access, and use at the in multilateral settings on behalf of less well-endowed parts of the world (e.g., rights-based advocacy for the internet in intergovernmental organizations). The cases presented here show other ways to think about the material and symbolic implications of the reconstitution of practices of publicness in terms of discourses, spaces, and institutions in an age in which practices of digital (re)production (Franklin 2002) are accompanied by *translocal* (Clifford 1997) and *transnational* modes of address, experience, action, and analysis (Basch et al. 1994; Vertovec 1999; Olesen 2010; Fraser 2005, 2007).

In this respect the larger ambition of this book is to contribute to schools of critical interdisciplinary theory and research for politically engaged scholars of the media-politics nexus. In particular it targets those who are now turning their attention to the internet due to its burgeoning and controversial role in sociopolitical transformations behind the screen and on the street. It speaks to critical theory and research that still struggle to fully take into account the ways in which contemporary power relations can be not only transnational but also computer-mediated arenas of thought and action, freedom and oppression, illusion and imaginings about a better world. Hence its underlying premise is that successive generations of *internet technologies* and corollary social media play a constitutive and not simply a mimetic role in representations of, and changes in, how the world works (Hall 1996a).

It does so by tilting and flipping the viewfinder that is currently locked into the "right here, right now" position in the following ways. First, it zooms in on an important historical moment in current struggles for ownership and control of the internet that took place in US and European courtrooms and legislatures at the turn of this century. The antitrust case brought against Microsoft Corporation's monopoly of personal computing worldwide and its outcome have implications for the subsequent generation of global players—in particular how national and intergovernmental authorities now regard the Google Corporation's domination of the web and burgeoning struggles around control of mobile internet products and services. The discussion then turns to how the internet presents opportunities and costs, openings and exclusions, for specific groups and communities. Here we look at how disadvantaged and disenfranchised "others" have been using or attempting to use the internet, despite substantial material and resource limitations, specifically homeless people as individual users alongside dedicated media and advocacy organizations working on homelessness issues. As a particular sort of subaltern group, homeless internet users look to carve a space to find others or find their voice in online spaces, media outlets, and support services that enroll these technologies on their behalf. Here we see how the internet has been put to use and can be developed in not only noncommercial but also publicly spirited ways. The third and last case study examines mobilization around future visions of—and for—the internet and thereby society from a different angle: human/digital rights activism at UN-brokered multistakeholder consultations around internet governance.

AIMS AND OBJECTIVES

There are historical "conjunctures and disjunctures" (Appadurai 2002) between the rise of the internet as a global phenomenon in the first instance and, in the second, how sociopolitical, political, and economic transformation writ large are rendered in specific contexts. The main empirical aim of this tripartite study is to unpack moments in the way people use internet media and communications spontaneously to serve their immediate individual or community needs vis-à-vis those forces looking to appropriate its critical resources for vested interests. Teasing out these tensions highlights questions around whether "we" are getting the internet "we" deserve. These efforts play a formative albeit unsung role in competing narratives of the internet's past and present as its future role becomes increasingly politicized in both global and local arenas. The cases are elements in a larger set of interlocking contestations that pose challenges for policymakers, scholars, activists, and ordinary people. This challenge begs the question of what sort of future internet, and thereby society, is possible, sustainable, and sociocul- turally acceptable as the internet's Anglo-Euro-American axis is challenged by other uses, visions, and applications (Mendel et al. 2012: 12–13; Farivar 2011).

Doing so requires a mode of research that incorporates the longitudinal in- tensity and rich descriptiveness of fly-on-the-wall ethnographic approaches with the analytical acuity of more macro-level frameworks. This is because the afore- mentioned "digital dilemmas" can indeed be beguilingly mundane. For example, the smartphone you buy matters for more than aesthetic reasons, as your choice can determine what you are required to reveal about yourself when registering for online goods and services. But these dilemmas can also constitute arcane, ex- pert-led debates (e.g., activism around net neutrality in the wake of sophisticated snooping technologies embedded in nonaccountable ways deep within the inter- net's operating architecture) the outcomes of which are local-*cum*-global in their sociocultural implications (e.g., how diasporic populations stay in touch with family and friends back home, and the conditions, legal and otherwise, under which they use the "cloud"). They may also be steeped in post–Cold War geopo- litical shifts (e.g., whether the UN is "taking over" the internet and so threatening state sovereignty, China versus the US models of freedom of expression online), commercially and legally sensitive techniques (e.g., proprietary versus free and open-source software, how search engines work by tracking and storing the per- sonal data of millions of users), or culturally controversial policies (e.g., whether government or self-regulation of web-filtering are an unacceptable form of cen- sorship or the best way to protect minors from obscene material or unwanted attention). These are taking place within the governing institutions of sovereign nation-states but also further "upstream" in older international organizations (e.g., UN agencies such as the International Telecommunications Union, or UNESCO) and younger multilateral institutions (e.g., the World Trade Organization or UN Internet Governance Forum) around the financial and political viability of the dominant paradigm of free market technology-driven development goals.[10]

Theoretically the aim is to provide a conceptually innovative, historically and empirically nuanced reconsideration of the internet's recent past, fast-changing present, and far-from-decided future. It does so by drawing on selected precursor streams of critical thought in light of burgeoning debates about the emergence of the so-called *global information society* (Castells 1996; Gore 1994), dating roughly but not reducible to the end of the Cold War in the late 1980s. Spanning these two poles if not generations of technosensibility is a vast literature of theory and research across the disciplinary spectrum investigating science, technology, culture, and society with respect to particular artifacts, systems, or uses. The specific objectives are first, to link the "technoskepticism" of the predominately dystopian visions drawn by Marxian analyses of the internet's role in the history of neoliberal globalization (see Curran et al. 2012; Foster and McChesney 2011; Fuchs 2007; Harvey 2005; Rupert 2000) with the more utopian tenor of critical "cyber-centric" work on the potential of the internet's facilitating of new sorts of networks as systems and communities (Benkler 2006; Lovink 2012) but also the enhancing of extant ones. This literature concentrates on the ways these technologies can be—and are being—used that challenge incumbent political-economic, and, I would add, cultural powerbrokers (Benkler 2006: 23) in ways that perturb entrenched models of economic growth, social well-being, and political accountability.

In this context the approach is to further develop the notion of *practice* in critical studies of the micro and macro politics of power and resistance in a historical conjuncture that is constituted, however problematically, by the confluence of the internet and neoliberal globalization projects. This means returning to earlier arguments that the microcosms of everyday life and concomitant social relations and cultural practices can inform more macro-level analytical frameworks and abstract explanatory models (see Franklin 2001, 2003, 2004, 2007). A focus on practices of everyday life has never been absent from science and technology studies, media and communications, or work that falls under the rubric of "internet studies" undertaken in anthropology or sociology departments (Bakardjieva 2005 Hine 2000; Miller and Slater 2000; Mansell and Silverstone 1996; Shields 1996). However, the intersection of the macroanalytical modes of reasoning used to apprehend global (for example, cross-border) political issues with micro-level modes such as those preferred in cultural studies remains largely underexplored; alluded to but seldom fully engaged. Chapter 2 develops the ideas and arguments underpinning this ambition further. Suffice it to say that how people use old and newer ICT and media does make a difference for not only local and national but also world politics (Franklin 2009, 2013a; Dahlberg and Siapiera 2007; Davidson 2001; Hakken 2003).

Second, as the research spans at least the last ten years of developments in internet design, web-based applications and uses by ordinary people, and political and economic elites, the book aims to provide a more close-up analysis of trends often treated in macro-level, one-dimensional and ahistorical ways. It does so by conceptualizing these inner dynamics alongside rather than in opposition to their hi-tech and political-economic dimensions writ large. The point though is not to subsume the specificities of these case studies under yet another grand explanatory narrative of hi-tech nirvana or dystopia (Jameson 2005; Franklin 2011). There are enough of those available. In more than a few of those, information and communication technologies in general and various versions of the internet are assigned a key role accordingly. Rather I argue that explorations of the interconnections and interstices that lie between conventional notions of real life (or 'RL') and so-called virtual realities ('RL' online) need to include conceptualizations of the internet as a large-scale "machine" *and* complex ecosystem of microscopic "cybernetic organisms" in ways that can take into account how its constituent morphologies and anatomies wax and wane, through use and nonuses, access and denial of access, and the (global) politics of design. Seldom explored together in critiques of the internet's real or imagined role these studies offer a unique opportunity to look back and look forward as the internet itself undergoes intense transformation in the way it works, is run, and is talked about.

Third, the study considers one way to conjoin the big picture with close-up analysis by way of three particular ideas and their respective theoretical streams. These cases engage scholarly analysis of the large-scale and the intimate dimensions of how the distinct dynamics of technological, sociocultural, and political-economic change intersect, namely through *nation-states, publics/public spheres,* and *governmentality*. In the first two instances, the objective is to move forward attempts to reconceptualize *publics* in ways that account for how they are spliced with transnational and digital formations and articulations of publicness. The silence addressed here is that around how paying attention to nonelite, and by association non-Western articulations, is integral to debates about whether the internet impoverishes or enriches the democratic public sphere.[11] This rethinking of publics (rather than public spheres) calls upon Foucault's critique of modern statecraft as a "*governmentality paradox*" and applies it to political and economic power shifts that affect governance practices and institutions in a global and digital era (Coleman and Tucker 2012; Lipschutz 2005; Walters 2012; Winokur 2003). In this respect the objective is to bring into the frame of analysis more inductive modes of analysis and research that investigate how the intricate modalities of everyday life as proximate, embodied, and localized spatial practices, map onto nonproximate, nonembodied, and translocal ones (that is, beyond national borders). This means taking account of how online practices and computer programming inflect the microfiber of the social fabric as well as the larger weave of multilateral decision-making settings and institutions. Both instances need to take into account how social actors as internet/computer users are objects *and* subjects of power struggles over the internet's design, access, and use that link, quite consciously and strategically, these micropolitics with big power politics. Juxtaposing these cases generates new insights into the subtle yet palpable ways in which longstanding and emerging power hierarchies are being refashioned, exercised, and resisted in an internet-dependent age. They provide other ways to conceive and thereby perceive the object of critique or analysis, in this case the internet-society-politics nexus, in ways that can move beyond conventional dichotomies.

In three illustrative cases we see from closer up the ways in which the internet itself is changing, whether these are by design or spontaneous uses, through the misuse or abuse of its relatively open and decentralized architecture for illicit or oppressive activities, through the efforts of business and civil society groups to influence decision-making on how it functions, and on whose terms. These cases include uses to alleviate isolation, facilitate self-help, and create leverage to help others. In all these respects, developments and indeed controversies over who owns and designs the underlying computer codes, makes the laws, and influences the social conventions (or norms) that affect how people access and use the internet are changing the rules of the game. The studies reveal how power, resistance, and the internet can no longer be regarded through the prism of "old" versus "new" media, "old" versus "new" social movements, "analog" versus "digital" forms of production, transmission, and reception.

Audience

> The sharing you see on sites like Facebook and Twitter is the tip of the "social" iceberg. . . . But most sharing is done via *dark social* means like email and IM (instant messaging) that are difficult to measure. . . . According to new data on many media sites, 69% of social referrals came from dark social; 20% came from Facebook. . . . [The] social sites that arrived in the 2000s did not create the social web, but they did structure it. This is really, really significant. In large part, they made sharing on the Internet an act of publishing, with all the attendant changes that come with that switch. (Madrigal 2012)[12]

The above reference to the "dark social" is telling in a period in the internet's history in which commercial social networking sites and their accompanying cloud computing services have come to define public and scholarly debates around the socioeconomic benefits and costs of transparency, freedom, and open access online. While the larger point is important—the internet was a social medium long before the arrival of services such as Facebook—it positions these older, relatively private forms of online socializing as shadowy, in contradistinction to the assumed user friendliness of today's social media and the "lightness of being" they generate when online. This normative assumption reflects the mood at the time of this book's writing, one that has been changing as this so-called dark social offers a safe haven from being ad-tracked, tagged, or poked, whether these digitalia occur in benign consensual or more destructive ways. Debates on the real and imagined social costs of life onscreen (Turkle 2011; Madden et al. 2012) are a longstanding stream of theory and research including work on another dark side to the internet: illicit and legitimized forms of state and corporate surveillance, crime, and other forms of cybersubterfuge along with violent and abusive uses such as cyberbullying (Lovink 2003; Deibert 2008). To reiterate, the internet as a *social* medium did not begin with the start up of this generation of global brands in social networking sites and microblogs (e.g., Facebook or Weiboo), or *cloud companies* (e.g., Google). The latter, generically referred to as "Web 2.0" (Mandiberg 2012; Everitt and Mills 2009), have been game changers in many respects nonetheless. It is for this reason that a historical perspective is crucial for a context in which the difference between what is regarded as "new" and what is "old" is defined by the shelf-life of corporate product cycles.

The underlying rationale for this study takes its distance from the insidious choice signaled above, top-down or bottom-up perspectives. The net effect is that the analyst either strikes a pose that hierarchizes national at the expense of global perspectives (or vice versa) or so-called RL scenarios on the ground at the expense of paying attention to those occurring online in "virtual" (and thereby implicitly less important) reality (Jurgenson 2012; Shields 1996). While the differences between these two registers and arenas for thought and action do matter, when and how they matter is more to the point than positing an a priori value hierarchy between them. Moreover positing but two alternatives overlooks the existence of more liminal and hybrid forms of computer-mediated/organic-machine interactions, let alone spaces and places for meeting and action.

This book draws analogies from popular science fiction for a readership brought up on and dexterous with multimedia imagery, that makes intuitive, albeit not always well-informed or critical connections between the media they use and the way these frame and represent their world and those of others. In this respect this study addresses what I argue is the ensuing false dilemma between a critique of capitalism and a shared interdependence on the internet, said tool of global capitalism, to mount this critique. This then diverts attention from the way online and offline lives and politics coconstitute one another, albeit in ways that are neither symmetrical nor interchangeable. Without seeking to be characterized as a contributor to a literature that includes influential examples of what Fischbach calls the "pseudo-theological rhetoric" (2005: 17) of "net-enthusiasts" (2005: 13), who he sees as synonymous with apolitical postmodern thought (Fischbach 2005: 17, 49, 61 passim), this book looks to temper ongoing polarizations between those "for" or "against" the web and its cyberspaces as constitutive and so formative of today's sociopolitical realities.

Taking its cue from critiques of the connection between a vision of the internet as an economic instrument and neoliberal ideologies, this book nonetheless argues that socially engaged scholarship on just this nexus still has a lot of work to do in developing ways to counter media centric, techno centric, and state centric accounts of the interrelationship between the internet, politics, and society. Retaining the particularities of each case, yet drawing out the connections between them, involves avoiding taking either a politically convenient skeptical stance (viz., the internet is a tool of global capitalism pure and simple) or a gung-ho optimistic account of this complex technosocial array of communicative devices, infrastructures, and codes as a silver bullet to fix all the ills of the world. Each scenario reminds us of just how complex the issues are but more so as they are now interconnected in literal and figurative terms. As an actor-centered perspective, this approach makes visible the complexity of human experiences with and through the internet in a period that has seen its status in scholarly and popular imaginaries shift from the new to the ubiquitous, from the unusual to the ordinary, from a means for revamping capitalist modes of accumulation and disenchantment in liberal democratic models to a must-have tool of development and modernization for the rest of the world.

ARE "WE" GETTING THE INTERNET WE DESERVE?

One of the major problems affecting contemporary research on communication is amnesia, the absence of a "collective memory," the forgetting of the social and political stakes at issue ... the patterns of implantation of communication and information technologies and the development of their uses as social constructions. They take shape through adaptations, transitions, resistances, and above all through contradictory meanderings where collisions of different actors, ideas, material interests, and social projects are sure to occur. (Mattelart 1994: x; see Hall 1996: 443)

There are several perhaps obvious points to make in light of Armand Mattelart's observation above; dating from the heyday of the (once new) *World Wide Web* ("Web 1.0"). The first thing I want to say is that the internet is a wonderful invention for those who can afford to access and use it. Roughly a third of the world's population and rising have "joined the Internet" (Internet World Stats 2012).[13] The second point is that, at the time of this writing, the internet itself, as a whole or in part, has reached a critical crossroads. To date its technohistorical trajectory has collided and colluded with a number of real and imagined cultural and political-economic transformations. These transformations have been the main focus of attention in scholarly and public debates. The tables have turned recently, however, as the internet itself becomes the focal point. This brings me to the third observation. As a vast computerized "network of networks" (Castells 1996, 2012: 10), not only is the internet a piece of engineering on a grand—global—scale deeply embedded in the Global North, the United States particularly, but it is also a social phenomenon and cultural artifact of material and symbolic proportions. As such it has in practice come to encapsulate life, work, and business on *Spaceship Earth.*[14]

Yet for many users of the web today, indeed readers of this book, the internet "began" in the 2000s, when the two most powerful social media services in use at time of writing emerged: Facebook (the world's Number 1 in social networking sites) and Twitter (likewise for microblogging). In computing terms five years or more is a very long time. The point I want to make in order to ground this book in the here and now, yet not at the expense of a sense of what came before, is that even if for today's digital natives the internet and social media are one and the same, disinterest in the "social and political issues at stake" (Mattelart 1994: x) is no longer an option. As the ability to access the web and your social network of choice becomes increasingly integral to (social) mobility, the globally distributed architecture the internet runs on is also on the move. The web has become a digitally integrated and interoperable whole in ways not possible a decade or so ago, with its professional media, everyday communications services, and inner workings commercialized and concentrated in private and state centric notions of ownership terms in formidable ways. Intentionally or circumstantially, as social, cultural, and political movements make use of the latest web-based goods and services to organize, publicize, and vocalize their respective causes, the politics *of* the internet, as opposed to politics *through* the internet, have been thrown into relief. Whether or not the internet currently in operation and being rolled out to the "next billion" (IGF 2008) is the only option or even the best, that is, the most efficient or the most socially inclusive—(which are not necessarily compatible), is a moot point. Considering the internet's sociocultural, legal, and political-economic dimensions as integral to its strictly technical, that is operational, characteristics is critical to apprehending how as a multiplex object of analysis it operates in ways that are beholden to, yet analytically distinct from, studies of changes in the "media," "politics," "culture," or "society."

This brings me to the next thing to note in historical terms. The web that people access today, whether in Beijing, New Delhi, or New York, looks and feels very different from the one accessed in the 1990s and early 2000s. Stronger still, more than one internet is being made available to users today. The sort of goods, services, and content that Chinese citizens are allowed to access differs markedly (and this is admitted and promoted by the Chinese government) from those on offer to UK or US residents. Likewise, public libraries, schools, or universities filter content to protect minors or prevent users accessing sites deemed unsuitable (or time wasting). If more than one internet exists, then more than one past, present, and future is at stake—a point not lost on authoritarian regimes, one-party states, pluralist liberal democracies; peer-to-peer networks; hacker communities; or those involved in either cyberespionage or criminal activities (Clinton 2010a, b Deibert 2008; Deibert and Rohozinski 2010; Lovink 2003; Franklin 2010, 2011; Morozov 2011). For this reason alone, the way people access and use the internet, the web particularly, is intensely personal and, thereby, political.[15]

What Has Technology Got to Do with It?

> Unfortunately, no one can be told what the Matrix is. You have to see it for yourself. This is your last chance. After this, there is no turning back. You take the blue pill and the story ends. . . . You take the red pill and you stay in Wonderland and I show you how deep the rabbit-hole goes. . . . Remember—all I am offering is the truth, nothing more. (Morpheus to Neo, *The Matrix*, 1999[16])

The above quote is taken from a pivotal scene in the 1999 Hollywood popular science fiction-future fantasy film, *The Matrix*. It is one deeply rooted in Western Cartesian divisions between the mind (consciousness) and body (physicality, organic life) and their countermanding worldviews (e.g., behavioralist versus psychodynamic understandings of the human psyche and behavior). In this scene the speaker, Morpheus, confronts the film's hero, disaffected computer nerd Neo, with the knowledge that the world he thinks is real is a fabrication, a vast all-encompassing computer simulation. Morpheus, the leader of an underground resistance movement as it happens, offers Neo the opportunity to come to terms with this inconvenient truth, show him more of how this "desert of the real" (Žižek 2003; Weberman 2001) actually works. He is offered two choices, two mind-altering means to false or higher consciousness.

The mash-up of Freudian psychology with new- and computer-age sensibilities evident in this scene let alone the whole film has generated its own cult following, as well as a rich scholarly and popular legacy of critical reflections on how contemporary societies' (over)dependence on computerized systems are infused with changes in the locus of material power, political consciousness, and social organization. For societies founded on Western Enlightenment and humanist values, these sorts of scenarios indicate a deep unease with technological futures where all is not what it seems. I will return to this reference later. My point at this stage is to note that as global audiences consume plots and images such as these in which the push and pull between humans and their thinking machines constitute the narrative arc, critical theory and social research to date tend to overlook how popular culture, film, and (science) fiction have been dealing with this interplay between mutual dependence and mutually assured destruction for some time— many generations prior to the release of *The Matrix* in 1999 in fact.

Human-made machines that turn renegade are par for the course in popular culture, from Mary Shelley's gauche *Frankenstein*, written in 1818, to Phillip K. Dick's enraged replicants in his 1968 book, *Do Androids Dream of Electric Sheep?*, immortalized in Ridley Scott's film noir 1982 adaptation, *Bladerunner*, through to Stanley Kubrick's obstreperous HAL in the 1968 film, *2001: A Space Odyssey*, to the lonesome clone in Duncan Jones's *Moon* (2009), or frenetic inner-space commandos in Christopher Nolan's *Inception* (2010). As public telecommunications operations not only computerized but also privatized in the 1990s, concomitant shifts in the form and substance of social relations in so-called RL caught the imagination of burgeoning communities of cyberculture and internet scholars across academe. At the risk of overgeneralizing, mainstream critical theory and research that came of age in the early to mid-twentieth century of social movements (workers', women's, and civil rights) has remained somewhat locked in an analog past. The specter of technological determinism mixed with concern over the corrosive effects of life in capitalist consumer societies haunts debates around whether information exchange and cultural practice in digital forms—how computers work—signals a fundamental deterioration in the way humans think and perceive their world, or in how polities function and rule.[17]

As was the case with critical commentaries on the sociocultural effects of industrialization, mass production and related mechanical forms of reproduction, and consumerism and the "culture industries," theorists, and social commentators today are debating the comparable effects of computer-mediated communications and related digital forms of reproduction (Lunenfeld 2000; Spiller 2002;

Cubitt 1997). This transformation of cultural practices and social worlds, as computer-mediated formations of communication and information exchange, is considered in these analyses as more than a shift in register or means of transmission, or transportation. In computerized media and communications, social texts (written, visual, aural forms of meaning-making and representation) are digitized, by being rendered as "zeros" and "ones." From plasticity to digitality, the net effect for some observers is that this translates once "continuously variable representational relationships" into "binary structures . . . which can then be stored, transferred, or manipulated at the level of numbers, or 'digits'" (Lunenfeld 2000: xii). How to assess the deeper significance of this recasting of the media as massage/message (McLuhan 2001 (1964), McLuhan and Fiore 1967) and the implications for the digital (re)production, circulation, and reception of "representational systems" as "digital information" that "alternate" rather than achieve "synthesis" (Lunenfeld 2000: xvi–xvii) for culture and society preoccupies philosophers and political and cultural theorists still. Meanwhile, artists, activists, and corporate and political representatives employ and adapt these digitized alternations in a plethora of culturally and politically subversive ways for various causes, grand designs, and daily survival, with varying degrees of self-awareness, technical know-how, and want-to.

As these adoptions and adaptations gather momentum, in both developed and developing worlds, nonelite and more powerful strategic users have been making competing demands *on* and *for* the internet. These demands are too often subsumed under analyses concerned with the broad sweep of grand narratives such as globalization, neoliberalism, and terrorism. In these versions of events writ large, critical and celebratory, the internet is a monolithic force that pops up everywhere, wreaking havoc or generating utopian-like euphoria in equally dramatic terms. In this sense as a global signifier of a very contemporary kind, references to "The Internet" can be seen as akin to the visual leitmotiv, the reappearing black column, in Stanley Kubrick's 1968 film, *2001: A Space Odyssey*. Like this monolith, "The Internet" appears in critical and popular commentaries of sociocultural, political, and economic transformations as a foreign object, working its power in opaque ways on humankind as a self-steering agency that appears to stand outside history, ignore physical place, and obliterate social space and other *dispositions* of power, status, and entitlement. As a twenty-first century totem with its own set of media rituals, cultural conventions, and taboos (Couldry 2012; O'Neil 2009; O'Reilly 2012), the internet in mainstream critical and admiring commentaries is defined by its immateriality despite its palpable physicality (Blum 2012; Fischbach 2005). Its effects on human consciousness, social and political institutions, cultural life, and trade, finance, and labor markets have real-life implications for anyone found transgressing at the interstices of older and newer, online and offline jurisdictions that are still in the making. Odder still, as the internet becomes a normalized part of everyday cultural and political life in hi-tech dependent societies, becoming indigenous to advanced capitalist economies and an object of desire for aspiring societies in the Global South, more radically constructivist understandings of its constituent technologies as endogenous, namely as sociohistorically constructed and thereby contestable forces and means *of* and *for* change, get considerably less airplay.

This historical juncture creates a paradoxical situation for critical scholarship, policymakers, and activists, however. The internet is here to stay for the time being even though the terms of its access and use are in flux, its future form under advisement, the ownership and control of its internal design and external physical architecture intensely disputed. Meanwhile, the internet itself remains a volatile and slippery object of research as it works as means and medium for control, consultation, and mobilization. The way we use it—and it uses us according to inbuilt codes, access criteria, and surveillance, for instance—generates a sense of crisis for Western critical theory and research versed in Cartesian splits between mind and body, reality and myth, cultural and political domains, the machine and the organic, public and private. Meanwhile, competing narratives about the internet's past and visions of its future within technical, legal, and policymaking communities center around its constituent technologies, systems, and networks. Taken as a whole or in part, these narratives are generating increasingly public standoffs between some of this internet's pioneering designers and most ardent evangelists and those with other ideas and alternative visions. These conflicts and their implications for apprehending the "brave new world" of not only yesterday but also tomorrow are overlooked by some of its most intransigent critics.[18]

Paradox Dilemmas

The central problematic animating this book is a complex *paradox-dilemma*.[19] By this I mean first that as the internet's nominally global–supraterritorial–transmission infrastructure facilitates more and more person-to-person as well as person/machine-to-person/machine modes of computer-mediated communications in all facets of life, work, and play worldwide, the various ways in which it has developed, works, is used, and has been run are under increasing scrutiny. In legal and regulatory terms, laissez-faire, once the order of the day in the halcyon years of neoliberalism (Harvey 2005, 1990), is becoming less politically desirable. Nor is it efficacious for nation-states, individually or within intergovernmental organizations, to claim disinterest in the internet's future viability and sustainability. Market forces alone cannot ensure its application as a means with "great potential to promote democracy and cultural diversity" (Council of Europe 2012b), "peace and sustainable development" (UNESCO 2013a), or as a tool to facilitate "twenty-first century statecraft" (US Dept. of State 2012) and thereby "expand the role of diplomacy" (Clinton 2010a, b).

Second, the contentiousness of decision-making over the internet's design, access, and use arises because these decisions are not apolitical. They are more than purely technical matters. As I noted above, these once relatively low-profile and arcane matters to be resolved by convention or consensus within their respective technical, economic, or legal forums presided over by business or governmental interests have been thrust under the spotlight of late. This has occurred partly through political events but also by lobbying and media campaigns (Becker and Niggemeier 2012). Once obscure organizations (e.g., ICANN), innovations (e.g., Deep Packet Inspection, mobile web access) and quasipublic decision-making processes (e.g., international telecommunication regulations) have become arenas for a renewed Battle Royale between states and markets, between regulation and free enterprise. While the mass popular uptake of the internet that characterized its heyday in the 1990s was arguably a lucky accident, an intensifying "(geo)politics of design" (Mansell and Silverstone 1996; Vaidhyanathan 2012; Stalder 2012) has been pitting the commercial power of global ICT and media brands against an array of governmental and civic opponents.

Third, looking at how internet technologies and media facilitate and mediate, as well can be wielded as tools of oppression and resistance, domination and liberations, means taking in to account their dual purpose, shared by civic and military capabilities (Holmes 2007). The growing intimacies between thinking machines and humans have an effect on how human history and its concomitant social relations are practiced, archived, and then retrieved for subsequent study. They already affect how businesses target users, state agencies track the same, and people organize themselves in response to these intimacies. Those accessing the web at home, at work, and on the move in between represent a global market, wired citizenries, and emergent publics of *prosumers, netizens, tweeps,* or simply "internet users" (Benedek 2012). Politicians in liberal democracies, authoritarian or one-party states, and multilateral institutions have woken up in recent years to a world that has been reconfigured by the way people have been using, and assume to continue using the internet.

These shifts—some incremental and others more dramatic—boil down to two corollary issues for analysis and action as well as paradox-dilemmas. First, despite the internet's basic design premise that is based on a geographically (viz., global) distributed transmission architecture, its actual functioning and control hubs are increasingly centralized and concentrated in the traditional global political and economic power hubs—the United States in particular (see Mueller 2002; Rushkoff 2001, 2010). New users and access, to landline and mobile internet connections, are gathering pace faster in what was once called the Third World and is now referred to as the Global South. At the same time the economic power is shifting towards China, South Asia, and South America. This conglomeration of not only geographical but also commercial control and ownership of the internet's critical resources (e.g., domain names, transmission routes, service provision) in largely the United States has started to prompt concerted efforts to change the rules of the game, intervene in the agenda-setting as well as organizational cultures at the level of participation, agenda-setting, and decision making. Technically and legally complex for the layperson, such decisions nonetheless have enormous consequences for how people will be able to access and use their internet, their website, and their social networks—and on whose terms.

This one distributed architecture, which coexists more or less alongside of intensifying (state) centralized and/or (private) commercialized ownership and control of key functionalities, is, however, being continually countermanded by any number of ad hoc and organized uses and practices. Some are legitimate—social and political protest by ordinary people, communities, or movements for change—in the larger scheme of things. Some are illicit—the "dark net" of cyber-crime, espionage, and surveillance—and conducted by governments and terrorist organizations. Some are spontaneous, their social or political implications only emerging over time or due to their forming a critical mass at a particular moment. This tension between design and use, strategic intentions and organic spontane-ity, pits policymaking and legal rulings (e.g., on privacy or freedom of speech) against real-time developments; consultations and decisions are not always able to respond to the ICT product cycles or spontaneous, grassroots applications fast enough. The first two uses are not only well-documented and financed, but they predominate academic and popular discourses about the political-economic and sociocultural effects of internet media and communications. The latter, however, is where a lot of work needs to be done to uncover the dynamism and multiplex ecosystem of today's internet, as not only a politically contested cultural artifact if not tool for both forces of oppression and liberation but also as the means to generate wealth and sustain lives, or do the opposite.

This issue dovetails with another question about who pays for the future devel-opment of this technology and its concomitant products and services in the short term and, by implication, who or what agency gets to call the shots in the long term. More complex still is the question: is the "internet" that is at stake the same thing for all parties engaged in these struggles for ownership and control of the material means and the narrative of global interconnectivity and so-called free-dom? As the notion of *multistakeholder participatory models* takes hold in a world premised on computer-mediated and lateral ("peer-to-peer") networking across national times and spaces, protagonists are looking to enroll ordinary users, or their representatives at least, to legitimate a range of competing agendas. While (new) media reform advocates and corporate and political representatives confer and discuss these matters in various consultative settings, social critics within aca-deme and beyond have been preoccupied with another set of questions. These de-bates are dominated by "discourses of loss" that permeate Western social, cultural, and political theory from mid-twentieth critical (Hegelian and post-Hegelian) philosophical traditions. This sense of loss colors the narrative accordingly.[20]

POWER AND RESISTANCE OFFLINE AND ONLINE

Power, as Michel Foucault argues (1991, 2004a, b), amounts to both more and less than conventional accounts. These construe power as an attribute belonging to those (actors or agents) who can dominate by exerting "power over" others. Not a quantifiable property in the Foucauldian view, power needs to be conceptual-ized as something that is "exercised rather than possessed; it is not the 'privilege,' acquired or preserved, of the dominant class, but the overall effect of its strategic positions—an effect that is manifested and sometimes extended by the position of those who are dominated. . . . These relations go right down into the depths of society" (Foucault, in Rabinow 1984: 174). Embedded in existing social relations as well as generating new ones, an understanding of power as a productive force lays the accent on how societies, over time, come to do certain things in certain ways; social forces, discourses, and institutions instill, by violent and nonviolent means, ways of talking about and being in the world along the lines of what is or is not permissible (Foucault 1984a).[21]

In this influential view, power, like society and history, is what people as individuals, groups, and polities make of it; it is both outcome and generator of outcomes. If power and its converse, resistance, coconstitute one another, this does not mean to say that their "overall effect" (Foucault in Rabinow 1984: 174) operates in ways that are equivalent, tit for tat, so to speak. If so, then there would be no conflicts, no histories of victory and defeat, no change as the outcome of long-term struggles or spontaneous mobilization. From a dynamic and critical constructivist perspective of how the social and physical worlds change over time, the history of human societies indicates that power and resistance are not equally distributed nor equivalent in this sense. The politics, however, take shape when incumbents exert power and meet resistance. This brings us to how Foucault's nondefinition (he looks at how power operates rather aims to define it) relates to observations of the internet as either a new genus of power (to be wielded accordingly) or constituent of new power dispositions, namely in computer-mediated domains (Jordan 1999; Toulouse and Luke 1998; Haraway 1997). The emergence of an internet-power nexus occasions new descriptors of power, as if such descriptors are sufficient on their own to capture the way social relations have acquired additional layers and loci as the world goes online in increasing numbers (Nye 2002). As the effects of this shift preoccupy pundits, the question of how we got—or are getting—to this point remains underelucidated. As Geert Lovink points out:

> It is no longer sufficient to complain about network society's dysfunctionalities in terms of usability, access, privacy, or copyright infringements. Instead, we need to investigate that slippery nexus between the internet's reinforcement of existing power structures, and parallel—and increasingly interpenetrating—worlds where control is diffused. . . . we [tend to] read what major news outlets make of the internet phenomenon—not what is actually discussed in forums, exchanged on peer to peer networks, or how people use search engines. (Lovink 2012: 3).

Lovink's immanent critique of both web-shy "old social movement" sympathizers and web-savvy would-be political activists targets the ongoing distaste and high moral ground taken by critical theory and research towards the internet as object of study and means to an end. His is not the only voice concerned with the relative dearth of "appealing critical concepts that will survive as robust memes and transform into socio-technical protocols" (Lovink 2012: 23). By this I take Lovink to mean that there is an elision between Marxian, as well as liberal critiques of the internet and theories that would anchor these critiques into the "hard wiring" of alternative designs and policymaking. Doing so would entail embracing these technologies in ways that include long-term, rather than fashionable commitment to the politics of painstaking institution building and changing norms and values.[22] But it is also about the relative lack of real-time, real-life engagement with the fiddly practicalities of developing and exploring alternative ways of working online, developing or engaging with other sorts of web applications, other design principles such as free/open source software, peer-to-peer networking, or public service provisions for internet access. The irony, however, is that not only are today's easy-to-use social media "invading all aspects of life" (Lovink 2012: 161), but their very pervasiveness makes commercial applications hard to avoid for cash-strapped and nontechie community support networks, activists, or critical scholars.

Within the Foucauldian tradition of critical thought that understands power as relational, reiterative, and so (re)productive, the task here is to integrate radical constructivist understandings of power as also internet-inflected "dispositions" and operations (Foucault 1984a, b, c, 2004a, b; Bourdieu 1998, 2012; Haraway 1997) with materialist understandings of power as something the mighty do and can wield over the less powerful. The Foucauldian approach to power need not dispense with classical understandings of 'power over', an instrument of domination or resource for persuasion. Rather it seeks to adjust the lens through which power relations are experienced and understood, at the time and in retrospect. This is not unproblematic in terms of how these competing traditions tend to be posited as mutually exclusive understandings of what power is and how it works. Whether said instruments can be described as "hard" or "soft" (Nye 2002), networked or virtual, or in any other way (Castells 1996; Jordan 1999; Olesen 2010; Sachs 1993; Trebing 1994) treating power as a possession rather than a practice or relationship pervades mainstream Anglo-American scholarship. Even as this conceptualization has been the point of departure for several decades of poststructuralist, postmodernist, and feminist critiques (Peterson and Runyan 1999; Mitter and Rowbotham 1995), it still tends to prevail in commentaries on the internet's sociopolitical impact on society, thereby eliding how people use these technologies reveals novel ways in which power is reproduced, exercised, and distributed. Critical materialist critiques of this networked and digitally inflected power reshuffle, so to speak, are embedded in conventional understandings of how power (and its imposition) works as Realpolitik and "old social movement" understandings of how domination should be resisted, notable exceptions aside (Hardt and Negri 2000; Dahlberg and Siapiera 2007; Haraway 1990, 1997).

What is relevant here is to note how critiques of the internet and its cyberspaces as democratizing, namely, empowering in principle (see Stallabrass 1995; Ross 1995 (1997)) are most concerned with the historical conjuncture of neoliberal ideology, postmodernity, consumerism, and the rise of the internet as mass media on a global scale (Curran et al. 2012; Schiller 1999; Harvey 1990; Jameson 1984). A fuller exegesis of these debates is not possible here but by way of illustration Peter Sloterdijk (2006), along with others of his generation, including David Harvey (1990), mourn what they see as the loss of physical proximity as a primary form of belonging and community as Western (neo)liberal and capitalist democracies become more dependent on globalized electronic communications and information exchange. According to Sloterdijk (2006: 18–20) there is a yearning for the return of the "real" distance that has constituted Western ontologies of time and space since the industrial-age colonialist project of geopolitical dominion of the planet. Sloterdijk's is one rendition of a prevalent view that sees capitalist globalization, computer-mediated communications, and information networks as intertwined in the production of a "hyper-communicativity" that restricts thought and action (Sloterdijk 2006: 19). Computer networks in this view consolidate the economic realities of globalized capitalist market relations, aiding and abetting their optimization in and as "limitless space." In social terms this results in a sort of mind-meld between those who are near and those further away that amounts to not much more than acquiring the means of "making others unhappy long-distance . . . a possibility once reserved for neighborhood relationships" (Sloterdijk 2006: 20). For this generation of Western *Age of Enlightenment* thinkers, the "death of distance" is not something to celebrate (Franklin 2004: 30–42).[23]

These critiques of the Globalization-Internet conjuncture are diametrically opposed to the celebratory literature that accompanied the phenomenal uptake of the internet and then the World Wide Web, largely emanating from the US West Coast, the home base then and now for the internet's major corporate players. This upbeat literature is rooted in an unmitigated belief in capitalism-as-democracy bolstered by the collapse of the Soviet and Maoist models of communism at the end of the 1980s. From this point of view it is but a small step to construe any notion of cyberspace as a priori "free" from governmental interference, its technical and symbolic faculties limited only by human imagination and ingenuity, its "governance," if indeed there should be such a thing, ultimately subject only to the invisible hand of market forces (Kelly 1994; Shapiro 1999). The metaphysical dimension to conceiving cyberspace in these transcendental terms, of digitally transmitted forms of knowledge and economic exchange as immaterial to power relations of any sort and thereby as inherently "free" by definition, underpins a US-embedded libertarian worldview. This view eschews regulation by central government, is alert to any threat from any claims from intergovernmental organizations to assume leadership in policymaking, and is impervious to any critique of its assumed marriage with capitalism for the most part.[24]

The predominance of free-market thinking, as the synonym of "internet freedom," has continued to operate as the polar opposite to how critical theories treat the sociocultural and political-economic implications of an internet-dependent world. Working within the critical vein of thinkers such as Harvey and Sloterdijk but with a closer eye on how information and communication technologies work and are designed, Rainer Fischbach argues that the assumption that cyberspace is immaterial and the subsequent conflation of this with an unbounded capitalist global economy is not only ideological but also an idealization. In both cases it is a view that overlooks the materiality of the various and variable internet protocols that facilitate web-based spatial practices (Fischbach 2005: 61–62). In this respect

Fischbach's critical conceptualization of cyberspace as a material and socially embedded domain of ideas and action that is not ipso facto "free" meets Anglo-American Marxian suspicions of the circumstantial marriage of the information and communication technologies in general and the internet in particular with late-twentieth century capitalist domination of offline and online spaces, flows, and practices. This is a sophisticated argument within the long-running stand-off between "gung-ho" (Mattelart 1994) accounts of internet technologies as the motor of neoliberal globalization and their critics.

But there is a difference between critiques of the internet's alliance with (global) capitalism from a layperson's perspective and those critiques emanating from within technical and legal communities. Rather than reject the possibilities and future potential of internet technologies or negate the openings that cyberspatial practices of everyday life and peer-to-peer networks have created for challenging incumbent gender power relations and other sorts of race- or class-based prejudice and exclusions, technical practitioners like Fischbach grasp the mettle in another way. Instead of a negation he argues that the way forces of domination do or do not exercise power in and over (cyber)space is not a pregiven. While cyberspace itself is anchored in contemporary science fiction (more on this point in the next chapter), operating there as a metaphor for other forms of consciousness, or parallel worlds, it is also anchored in a material sub-stratum (Fischbach 2005: 63) of hardware and software-based transmission networks, protocols, and organizations that regulate these interactions. In this view cyberspace is a social and technical construction and as such a product of human invention and intervention and, thereby, not devoid of material relations of power and domination.

Resonating with immanent critiques such as that of Geert Lovink (2012) and Donna Haraway (1990, 1997, 2003), although with less tolerance for what he considers to be postmodern "hocus-pocus," Fischbach argues that incumbent powers in RL (real life) can move quite easily in and out of the cyberspatial realm of thought and action facilitated and circumscribed by the way internet technologies recreate and counter domination in a particular formation—in this case a hyper-capitalist one (2005: 63). In considering what sort of resistance can make sense in this very material immaterial world Fischbach first notes that in spatial terms power is exercised, and its forces are articulated in multiple ways. Second, he argues that when considering how powers that be can be resisted in computer-constituted spaces, cyberspace included, such a resistance lies not in construing these spaces in purely technical—but rather in social—terms (2005: 62–63). Here he takes his distance from the high priesthoods of the internet as a technology that transcends the socioeconomic realities, inequalities included, of the Western time-space continuum premised on science and technology.[25]

In short, the operational architecture, traffic flows, places, and spaces that people access and make use of when they go online (to e-mail or check their social networking wall or microblog stream), whatever their purpose, are not equal, level playing fields at all. This is evidenced in the way search engines hierarchize results to how mailing lists work to filter and moderate participation by automated to human means, to the geographical concentration of crucial functions and services in the United States and other parts of the West (see Rushkoff 2010; Introna and Nissenbaum 2000; Fischbach 2005: 64, 189 passim). Power in this sense is not just wielded but exercised, programmed and iterative through sharing in software designs, codes, and their concomitant cybernetic feedback loops. This position is close yet radically opposed to the predominately dualistic albeit astute formulation within critical scholarship that continues to regard the technologies on one side and human actors on the other. Their "interpenetration" (Lovink 2012:3) in this view is not constitutive but episodic.

> In the latter sense power relationships are constitutive of society because those who have power construct the institutions of society according to their values and interests. Power is exercised by means of coercion . . . and/ or the construction of meaning is people's minds, through mechanisms of symbolic manipulation. Power relations are embedded in the institutions of society, and particularly in the state. However, since societies are contradictory and conflictive, wherever there is power there is counterpower (Castells 2012: 4–5).

The issue with this sort of formulation, based on recognizing "constant interaction between power and counterpower" (Castells 2012: 5), is not that this is an inaccurate picture but rather that it presupposes only two ends of the pendulum. The ground covered as this pendulum swings from side to side is where changes in the form, locale, and substance of the practice of everyday life are elided accordingly. In the material minutiae of computer programming, unconscious as well as deliberate, for example, from the point of view of proprietary goals, or "principled decisions" (Lovink 2012: 161) for social inclusion or ensuring open access, for instance, are being enacted every day, from standard-setting decisions in forums such as the ITU and ICANN to those emerging from practices such as those used by Wikileaks, music downloaders and file-sharers, and "snooping" and spying. Fischbach and others have a cogent corrective for both idealizing and demonizing notions of the internet, and more so social media as universally applicable, ready-made tools for resistance in general and in specific scenarios: "the concentration tendencies of the real-world economy are also reflected in cyberspace" (Fischbach 2005: 63).

The immediate response to this paradoxical standoff between so-called old and new media activism and the challenges that organizational and communicative forms of computer-mediated resistance, underground or large-scale, bring to combating socioeconomic and cultural inequities is often couched in terms of how these technologies preface leaderless networks at the expense of vertical leadership hierarchies, for example, the vanguardist movements that arguably characterize the "old" social movements of the early and mid-twentieth century. This discussion is, I would argue, somewhat beside the point in that it is not just a technological question. The history of social and political movements is not simply defined by those based on vertically integrated leaderships; guerrilla and underground organizations are cases in point as precursors to online forms such as Anonymous or Wikipedia (Lovink 2012; O'Neil 2009). That said, recent changes to the scale, location, and tenor of contemporary computer-mediated and web-indigenous forms of organizing are not understandable without taking into account the ways in which "the protocols for human collaboration are up for grabs . . . activists today confront the fact that new media both mobilize as well as deconstruct, disassemble, deschool, and fragment . . . . Instead of counter-power, we have dismantled power entirely. This implies that we have effectively reached—no, realised—the Foucauldian age" (Lovink 2012: 164–165).

In this study I refer to *resistance*, whether passive or active, as a corollary to the above approach to understanding power as intrinsic to social relations. This means that power constitutes the social world and vice versa. Understanding power in relational, practical terms allows for critical analysis into how it emerges, is rendered in spontaneous or institutionalized formations, as fluxus or as sediment (e.g., entrenched hierarchies of access and privilege in decision-making arenas, news production, or academic knowledge production). Hence in this vein, power is understood as a practice in which "in any social relation there is a tension or a negotiation going on" (Edkins 2008: 140) that can be construed as various and variable "interactions of power and resistance" (ibid.), obstinate, dissenting, and broad-based opposition included. Edkins argues in her introduction to Foucault's thought, that to speak of power is to imply resistance, namely tensions and nego-tiations that (re)produce how the world works, or not, for those participating in these interactions. Power "for Foucault, means nothing unless there is resistance" (ibid.). In this sense resistance can be singular, individualized, spontaneous, and organized at the communal and translocal levels.

A key point here is that the "where" and "how" of social mobilization and understandings of leadership within resistance movements have not only shifted but also been enhanced, augmented by digital formations and techniques. There are those who lament or remain skeptical of this turn on principle (Cammaerts 2008; Fenton 2008). Others have been embracing these newer options if not coming to terms with the way internet technologies (for example, internet ser-vice provisions or applications such as the World Wide Web itself) have been game changers for exerting and resisting power on the ground and online (Aslama and Napoli 2010; Barkai 2012; Boler 2008; Lievrouw 2011). And there are those who remain alert if not circumspect to shifts in the online–offline in-duced horizons of possibility (Deibert 2000, 2008; Lovink 2003). Resistance, or-ganized and passive, articulated as individual or communal dissent and forms of public association, now takes place online and so makes use of information and communication technologies in alternative ways that need not presuppose a complete sell-out to global capitalism lock, stock, and barrel. From the point of view of critical theories that are cognizant rather than dismissive of these emer-gent digitized materialities, there is, however, a dearth of internet-age grounded theory and research. Here I concur with Lovink when he notes how close to twenty years of "internet-specific" theorizing across the disciplinary spectrum has seen a plethora of theories [that] effectively describe how networks emerge and grow, and what shapes and sizes they take, but remain silent about how they are being embedded into society and *what conflicts this evokes* . . . . The trouble with current media activist [and critical theoretical] strategies in the age of social networking is not so much their ability to scale up, which they seem to manage quite well, but the absence of a painful setback in the encounter with the powers that be. *Resistance means struggle-with-defeat as a real option—* and this sounds profoundly uncool. (Lovink 2012: 23 and 161, emphasis added, see Fuchs 2012)

Resistance in this respect cuts both ways; it can be an active and a passive process engaged by the relatively powerless in terms of resources and know-how and those with more options at their disposal. State agencies, corporations, and social institutions such as schools and universities can be as resistant to the rise of peer-to-peer networks, instant messaging, and citizen journalism as well as enroll the same for localized and broader purposes (e.g., police looking to tap suspected individuals' phones to monitor mobile messaging networks in the wake of the 2011 London riots). As we shall see in the chapters that follow, these powers that be are well aware and making good use of their own applications and sense of social responsibility (whether adopted from the outset—Google, or required to by law—Microsoft) to enroll and appropriate discourses of freedom and open access as part of their own public relations and marketing strategies.

ORGANIZATION AND CHAPTER OUTLINE

To review, the book is organized around three case studies, each chapter presenting the outcome of the research in its respective timeframe, updating and reconsidering the findings in light of recent developments. The larger themes they address are ongoing areas of controversy, direct action, and policy-based contestations even as the specifics of their respective internet provisions have different technolegal and regulatory bearings. Each chapter shows the aforementioned paradox-dilemmas in a different light, as these pertain to protagonists but also to critical analysis. As these three cases underscore, the history of the internet is still being written; indeed several histories are in the making. This agonistic approach to theorizing (Dahlberg and Siapiera 2007; Laclau and Mouffe 1985) looks to problematize how each case points to passed-over opportunities, would-be closures, and perhaps unforeseen possibilities around the present and future of the internet, as we know it.

Chapter 2 develops the first part of the argument flagged in the above section, setting up the theoretical framework within which these studies make sense, on their own terms but also as parts of a larger analytical whole. The paradigm *reset* I am arguing is necessary here, to distinguish it from the more meta-level ways in which Thomas Kuhn's term *paradigm shift* (Kuhn 1962) has been employed, is in order to reconnect the materiality of "real life" and "virtual" (i.e., computer-mediated) practices within critical, predominately historical materialist analyses, literature that tends to treat all computer mediations as fundamentally the same, in order to then regard them all with suspicion. This reset is long over-due given the way disciplines and respective debates tend to bifurcate along two divergent paths of thought, experience, and action about either the internet and "real life" and the internet and "virtual reality." The chapter lays out the ground-work for reconsidering the theoretical and political implications of taking into account quantitative and qualitative shifts, sea changes in other words, in the "where," "what," "how," and "who" of power and resistance in societies that are increasingly premised on the motilities of *supra*territorial computer-mediated exchanges and communications (Scholte 2000, 2002). These include emerging online and offline relationships, sociocultural geographies, and power relations that in their defiance of traditional state and epistemological boundary markers require rethinking (see Walters 2012; Dany 2012; Lipschutz 2005). As such they entail embodied and nonembodied, nonproximate ways to interconnect, varying degrees of intimacy and/or publicness, and emerging spaces and economies of scale and forms of commodity exchange (Benkler 2006; Marres and Rogers 2005; Raymond 2001; Rushkoff 2001, 2010). That traditional power holders and gov-erning institutions take an ambivalent and contradictory stance to these trends is an undertheorized dimension to how scholars respond to what are now ordinary practices of everyday life online in light of extraordinary practices and uses of the internet.

The primary task of this chapter is thereby to bring mid-twentieth century debates on society, culture, and politics to bear on twenty-first century preoc-cupations, and vice versa; debates that have developed under the aegis of the rise, fall, and rise again of the nation-state along with its respective discontents and miscreants as the container-term of these (post)modern times. I focus on an "older" social and cultural theorist, Michel de Certeau, whose work, influence, and contribution to mid-twentieth century critical thought tends to be overshad-owed by the institutionalized privileging of his contemporaries Michel Foucault, Pierre Bourdieu, and Henri Lefebvre. While quintessentially European, their ideas have travelled far beyond their geocultural points of origin, combining with postcolonial and feminist praxis in particularly fruitful ways for considering the interplay between institutions of *governmentality* (Foucault 1991), the "practice of everyday life" and "capture of speech" (Certeau 1997b). Certeau in particular was aware of the arrival of electronic communications and the role of the media in shaping discourses and arenas of action as these were emerging at the cusp of the prototype internet. Those writing at the cusp of, or perhaps after Web 2.0 (Mandiberg 2012; Everitt and Mills 2009) do not take enough into account the way his thought presages how computational practices and emerging web-medi-ated relations affect not only publics as social and political formations but also the practices of statecraft.

We then move into the cases in point. The first case in Chapter 3 reconstructs a particular episode germane to recent high-profile debates on the question of "who controls the Internet" (Goldsmith and Wu 2006). In 1998 the US Department of Justice took Microsoft to court, charging it with anticompetitive practices. In 2005 and then in 2007 the corporation finally buried the hatchet with the European Union by granting partial access to its source code. Since then attention had shifted to the power of integrated search engines and social networking sites as the response to desktop-dependent internet uses and applications. In the so-called Web 2.0 settings, Microsoft's nemesis, Google, holds the pole position. Google's hegemonic position in this respect as a global brand that champions "internet freedom" and speaks for younger generations of computer users (Google 2012) has put Microsoft on the back foot even as the latter still dominates the global PC and operating systems software market. This chapter reconstructs the Microsoft antitrust case, known at the time as the climax of the "Browser Wars," in light of this next generation of power struggles over computer-mediated communications, or the "googlization of everything" (Vaidhyanathan 2012).

In both scenarios, corporate moves to enclose the internet—its key functions, hardware-software products, services, and "cultures of use" —are indicative of a longstanding standoff on the one hand between vested commercial interests where intellectual property rights and security concerns are fundamental working principles and, on the other hand, advocates of a socially inclusive and equitable internet based on nonproprietary software, peer-to-peer exchange, and low-cost access to the web. Each perspective denotes a particular ethos about freedom, regulation, and openness, and each in turn represents a different view of the internet's future. Both camps, and the various players who shuffle between the two (national and local governments in particular), stake a claim in narratives of which approach governed the internet's past. This longstanding standoff behind the screen, indeed at the user-interface itself, casts another light on the link between the ordinariness of the internet and high-level struggles over its governance and corporate and state-level exertions to extend or maintain direct ownership if not regulatory control of internet design, access, and use. These undertakings are the focus for Chapter 5. As these shift in locus and intensity with the advent of Web 2.0 and concomitant business models, the need to understand that the most recent courtroom battles around the world, pitting new and older ICT corporations against federal or intergovernmental instances as well as against one another in historical context, has never been greater.

But before shifting up-stream into UN-brokered consultations about the governance of the internet, Chapter 4 shifts register and level of analysis. Against the backdrop depicted in the preceding chapter, surviving in between and despite these corporate and judicial battles are innumerable instances of other lives and experiences online and off. These are enabled as well as disabled through the increased embedding of the internet in everyday life and the privatized enclosure of both, far removed from these users yet also instrumental in what they can or cannot do. By way of illustration and in order to concentrate on the microcosm of everyday (non)uses of information and communication technologies in a historical way, this chapter looks at the have-nots from within hi-tech societies of the Global North. Homeless people are amongst the most stigmatized groups in society, the last people who might be seen as active internet or social media users. Nonetheless, as individuals and through the efforts of community-based support groups and engaged researchers, homeless people have a robust and varied presence on the web. In the words of Michel de Certeau, they are "making do" in the face of powerful exclusionary dynamics from standard (at home, or personal mobile) access and uses, ingrained prejudice, and a steady increase in houselessness and structural poverty across the board. Roofless and homeless folk are particularly exposed to the exclusions that arise from commercialization and privatization online as well as being particularly vulnerable to the way inner-city public spaces have become inaccessible and increasingly inhospitable as they morph into quasipublic, commercial business districts; offline versions of the walled garden business models online (Minton 2006; Papacharissi 2010). On the ground and in cyberspace, marginalized groups bear the brunt of these interlocking practices of exclusivity in which cyberspaces and cityscapes become only accessible for those with certain physical, social, and legal credentials.

The focus here is how street papers, editorial teams, vendors, and writers' groups look to make use of the internet for sustenance and networking. While street papers are still largely confined to print, the opportunities as well as the costs of moving online remains an open question for initiatives that aim to provide a space for personal, creative expression; alternative forms of news and pertinent information for readers and general publics; and a form of financial self-sufficiency and social contact for homeless people working as street vendors. The chapter spans a decade, first by looking at how one street paper in midtown New York managed its limited computer and web resources to produce the paper, provide support and inspiration for vendors and writers, and do so at the time that an international network of street papers took shape. An initiative began to facilitate news sharing and support networks between local papers and their constituencies on the one hand and on the other between street papers worldwide by organizing and sharing content online. Second, these earlier insights gained by participant-observation fieldwork with *BIGnews* in New York and interviews with members of its writer group, editor, and members of the national network in the United States are brought to bear on how the *International Network of Street Papers*, run from the United Kingdom offices of *The Big Issue*, has been faring as the 1990s World Wide Web morphed into the social media of today. To illustrate these collisions and collusions, the chapter incorporates insights from interviews, with those working with longstanding street papers and new generations of (once) homeless social media users. The focus here is whether the "subaltern" (Spivak 1985) can indeed speak online; if so, then under what conditions and on whose terms. With answers to the pressing and endemic problem of homelessness in the internet's heartlands on the one hand and, on the other, multilateral and privately funded projects to counter the so-called digital divide (UN 2000; OECD 2001) still leaving a lot to be desired, this chapter aims to put the arcane and high-power struggles over who should control the internet, in theory and practice, into perspective. Moreover, this case underscores an often overlooked dimension to debates about the best ways to combat global poverty, economic, gender, and digital divides between Global North and Global South. As UN agencies put *ICT for Development* and now *The Internet* high on the global development agenda, inequities in its access and use based on race, class, and gender are just as marked within both Global North and South even as more people go online.

Chapter 5 turns to how internet technologies and related media have been affecting changes in how scholars, policymakers, and activists regard publics. Moving from ad hoc and cumulative tactical uses of internet technologies for a longstanding socioeconomic issue such as homelessness to more strategic applications and actions, this chapter looks at an example of how digitally savvy and transnationally astute coalitions are pushing the envelope of traditional notions of real life, direct action, advocacy, and public awareness-raising. By way of a specific example of a "public in the making," the chapter develops Michael Warner's Certeau-inflected conceptualization of *publics* as "self-creating and self-organized" formations that are "conjured into being" (Warner 2002: 49) rather than pregiven citizenries as the object of the disciplinary apparatus of hi-tech practices of governmentality. This chapter speaks, however, to the limits of the ways in which Foucault's "governmentality critique" has been applied to critiques of neoliberal globalization and by association the role of the internet in furthering this political project. Both advocates and critics of the reformative role of "new media" on sociocultural, political, and economic relations in internet-embedded societies tend to take the governmentality critique as one in which "resistance is futile" in any case; more so when articulated or conducted in the computer-mediated domains that increasingly constitute polities. This more pessimistic take on the links between oppressive state apparatuses, corporate power, and digital modes of capitalist production also suffers from the state-boundedness of how publics are theorized and researched. Both thereby overlook the drive, efficacy, and intensity of cross-border and web-based modes of mobilization, collaboration, and co-optation that take place offline and through the internet. While these in the case of homeless groups and their advocacy and media support networks make use of what is available, other sorts of transnational and computer-mediated collaborations have been developing on behalf of the internet itself.

Here the internet features as tool, medium, and object for mobilization. Drawing on over five years of participant-observation research and then direct involvement in work "behind the screen" at the United Nations-brokered *Internet Governance Forum* in particular, the chapter reconstructs the drafting and launch in 2010 of a *Charter of Human Rights and Principles for the Internet*. This is an internet-specific advocacy tool, policy instrument, and focus for raising awareness about the appropriation of the internet to undermine rights encoded in the Universal Declaration of Human Rights and other UN covenants. The *Internet Rights and Principles Coalition*, alongside collaborating and competing groups engaged in rights-related activism and lobbying, illustrate how Warner's argument that "speaking, writing, and thinking" publics and counterpublics are not pregiven but rather "conjured into being" also operates in computer-mediated cyberspaces. This chapter's account of the emergence of a cautious *counterpublic* (see Warner 2002; Calhoun and McQuarrie 2012) from the heart of multistakeholder-based consultations can provide insights into the forms, substance, and loci of twenty-first century contestations of what I argue is the emplacement of a "triangle, sovereignty-discipline-government, which has as its primary target [a computer-mediated and transnational] population and as its essential mechanism the apparatuses of security" (Foucault 1991: 102). Here we see another paradox-dilemma over not only who is but who should be in the driver's seat for an architecture that is defined by its trans-border properties, potentially if not evenly put into practice, shift into struggles over control of the narrative.

The concluding chapter picks up the thread from Chapter 2 in order to theorize our way out of their respective detail. It revisits the three troubled and troubling nodes and objects of analysis (life online and after the nation-state, other publics in the making, and the crafting of internet governmentality) to bring together the themes that these studies share. The aim here is not to simplify or tidy up the conflicts, detours, and contradictions that each case throws into relief. Even as the internet is premised on a centralized yet distributed transmission architecture and increasingly proprietary computer codes that ensure interoperability as a fundamental operating principle of global interconnectivity, the many ways users resist this drive to integrate and standardize has implications for all "stakeholders." The focus of these final reflections is to consider whether it is possible to reconstrue the internet as more than the sum of its technolegal or mythological parts.

SUMMING UP

In this book the internet as a whole and its composite elements is the object of contemporary struggles because of its increasing intertwining with the way power is exercised, resisted, and reconstituted. What does this mean for critical research and political praxis? Whether embedded inside or encountered from outside the human epidermis, through online or on-the-ground access points, internet technologies are now at the epicenter of philosophical, everyday, and geopolitical struggles over the form and substance of human life and society in implicitly hi-tech futures (see Franklin 2011). This is not a new struggle. Looking back, Donna Haraway recalls her own attempt in the landmark essay "A Cyborg Manifesto" (Haraway 1990) to "write a surrogacy agreement, a trope, a figure for living and honoring the shifts and practices of contemporary [global] technoculture without losing touch with the permanent war apparatus of a nonoptional, post-nuclear world and its transcendent, very material lies" (Haraway 2003: 13).

What form would such a "surrogacy agreement" take for those who are concerned about the "very material lies" promulgated by both state-sanctioned and corporate versions of the internet as a harbinger of "freedom" and "democracy" that is best managed by either governments or private enterprise? If this is not just a technical or legalistic question, as some would argue, but a social and thereby a political "Game of Thrones" (to borrow from a recent American HBO fantasy TV drama series) that begs the question of what counts as consensus, coexistence, and dissent in a would-be global and digital world order? Moreover, how to intervene in the very earthly national and geopolitics of the internet itself given the ways in which this term has become a synecdoche for any number of future utopias and dystopias? Those forces with the power to define how the internet features in those (agenda-setting, research and development, regulatory) arenas where some issues are "organized into politics while others are organized out" (Olesen 2010: 4) have considerable leverage on the rest of us. This study does not intend to present easy solutions to simple problems. Recognizing and working with complexity needs to be given more than lip service by critical thought, a point well made by Christian Fuchs.

> Namely, that the media—social media, the Internet, and all other media—
> are contradictory because we live in a contradictory society. As a conse-
> quence, their effects are actually contradictory, they can dampen/forestall or
> amplify/advance protest or have not much effect at all. Also different media
> (e.g., alternative media and commercial media) stand in a contradictory rela-
> tion and power struggle with each other. The media are not the only factors
> that influence the conditions of protest—they stand in contradictory rela-
> tions with politics and ideology/culture that also influence the conditions of
> protest. (Fuchs 2012: 786)

The practices explored here are taking place in architecturally designed, manu-factured, and computer-programmed environments that are lived, endured, and imagined as, and in liminal zones where political choices, social mobilization, and power struggles emerge out of spontaneous and strategic applications of to-day's information and communication technologies and corollary media goods and services. Each case looks at the respective "contradictory meanderings where collisions of different actors, ideas, material interests, and social projects...occur" (Mattelart 1994; x). It does so from the point of view of practice and process rather than the usual emphasis on policy or advocacy outcomes, revolutionary or cu-mulative forms of social impact. The purpose here is to get beneath and behind events or situations that appear to be technologically or market driven, to recon-sider power, resistance, and the internet in terms of these three scenarios where struggles for control, autonomy, and influence take place at and behind people's screens, how these crystallize in online and offline domains.

Grounded in research findings based on the combination of virtual ethno-graphic work, critical literature on new media and the internet from cultural stud-ies and political economy, and direct experience in multilateral policymaking and media advocacy debates around the past, present, and future of the internet and its governance, however defined, the book offers a fresh perspective on struggles over the internet's recent past, contentious present, and still uncertain future. In this respect it engages with other critical scholars looking to apprehend the way computer-mediated and globally interconnected media and communications challenge not only conventional levels of analysis and disciplinary boundaries but also nation-based forms of human experience, social institutions, and political authority. It does so without reifying the technical specifications of so-called converging media, or rather conglomerations of privately owned media industries or emerging business models, from ideational changes in the wider regulatory and geopolitical context. By bringing these three studies together the book also aims to avoid disemboweling the material reach of the internet's infrastructure and political economy of its phenomenological, its larger than life—sociocultural and discursive—dimensions.

Paradigm Resets: Real-Life and Virtual Reconnections

INTRODUCTION: THE INTERNET IS ORDINARY

The internet's World Wide Web and, nowadays, *Web 2.0* "user-friendly" applications have enjoyed an overwhelming success in terms of popular and business uptake over the last fifteen years. Despite a more checkered political career in their governmental rollout and uses there is a rough consensus that the inroads Web 2.0 has made into every facet of people's lives continue to deepen as new populations accessing the internet gather pace around the world.[1] Some argue and do so cogently that this computerized augmentation—coupled with the *assumption* that having access to the internet is in everyone's best interests everywhere—of virtually all areas of human endeavor is actually the converse however. It is everyday life that is being steadily subsumed under the dehumanizing and attenuating tendencies of computer networks as public services, spaces, and sociocultural diversity are squeezed by the internet's corporatized and assimilationist globally networked world order and the predominantly Anglo-Euro-American norms and values that govern how it works, for whom, and on what terms.[2]

According to one strand in this line of argument, the absorption of social institutions, human minds, and bodies into the internet's "network of networks" (see Gore 1994; Castells 1996) is a continuation of a longer historical process in which capitalist social relations and concomitant technical systems exploit and steadily colonize lifeworlds, corroding the integrity of democratic public spheres as they do so (Habermas 1996 (1968); Papacharissi 2010; Fenton 2008). In this view the past, present, and future of information and communication technologies and capitalist accumulation are mutually complicit (Foster and McChesney 2011; Schiller 1999), human agency reduced to a drop-down menu of automatic options, commitments to social justice and engagement undermined by armchair "slactivism," critical thought and journalistic integrity drowned out by the cacophony of amateur opinion-makers and their followers in Twitter and the Blogospheres (Morozov 2011; Curran et al. 2012). In sum, in an age of relentless ad-tracking and surveillance of cumulative databases housed in the servers of predominately US-based corporations and government agencies in conjunction with the way international organizations have been promoting *ICT* (Internet and Communication Technologies) *for Development* programs (Melber 2012; UN 2000; OECD 1997, 2001; World Bank 2002) as the latest technological fix-it for endemic poverty, the options not to (have to) go online, to communicate in other—analog or atypical digital—formats and idioms are fading. And with this so is the "right to be forgotten" (Rosen 2012) as cumulative, nontransparent practices of personal data-retention and automated data mining of the open web become the order of the day. In this doomsday scenario, resistance from within this latter day "Crystal Palace" (Sloterdijk 2006) is futile. Riding the cyborg juggernaut is a one-way ride to the end of the world as we know it and despite the attractive ease of web-based 24/7 communications, the love affair with all things internet should be well and truly over. In short now is *not* the time to "stop worrying and learn to love" the internet (Holmes 2007) but rather to see it for what it really is.

Historically the complex and contradictory role science and technology play, either in metanarratives of progress or as (agglomerations of) commodities, in creating closures and openings for both forces of oppression and liberation is less clear-cut than this bald formulation of ongoing debates would suggest. As Angela Crack points out, "the role of ICT in world politics [and society] is ambiguous: it helps to bolster the prevailing order *and* allows contradictions in the status quo to be exploited by counterhegemonic forces" (Crack 2008: 2, original emphasis). That said, I concur with the pessimists up to a point, particularly at a historical conjuncture in which the internet is being ostensibly redesigned from the ground up (Mendel et al. 2012: 9 passim; cf. Rushkoff 2001, 2010), its foundational myths reconfigured for specific ends and audiences, as we shall see in due course. Hence the philosophical and political impulse animating this study resonates with the underlying critique of capitalism, and of its neoliberal incarnation in particular that informs less than celebratory accounts of the Internet Story writ large. Where I differ is in formulating the subsequent problematic: as the need to get past rather black-and-white arguments in order to gain a greater purchase on just how the above ambiguity operates, online and off. This means shifting the emphasis to the "how" and, secondly, to another "who" than normally feature in critical accounts. In other words, it means exchanging the clarity of condemnation, or wonderment, for that matter, for these ambiguities. By moving in closer to processes and practices unfolding over time, one can gain more nuanced insights into the way in which often imperceptible, unheralded struggles at the intersection of everyday life, big power politics, and various sorts of economic priorities collide and collude behind the scenes to understand how the world works, looks, and feels today.

There is a normative motivation to this shift, and how it informs the theoretical framework presented here. As noted above categorical dismissals of internet technologies as solely a function of capitalism (see Franklin 2004: 218 passim) can severely foreclose alternative visions for, and versions of the internet that have been—and still are—in play. The rather obvious criticism of double standards notwithstanding, these sorts of critiques overlook the inroads these technologies have already made into knowledge production and exchange, epistemic community formation, organizational cultures, and activism on the ground and in cyberspace. This elision and its accompanying politics of reluctance create political and theoretical cul de sacs for several reasons. First, it is a suspicion based on an economically reductionist approach to the technology-politics-society nexus that positions sociotechnological artifacts and their ad hoc institutionalization as if they are exogenous to society, outside history and thereby human agency. The net result is a reiteration of the same critique for all seasons, an unreasonable rejection of all new social forms and relationships constituted by computer-mediated networking (Benkler 2006), spontaneous and diverse practices of web-afforded *onlineness* (Franklin 2004, 2007b) and alternative sorts of social media and/as activism (Lovink 2012). This leads to both an over- and an undervaluing of the incumbent powers and burgeoning dissent respectively.

Second, formal responses to the question "what is to be done?" (Lenin 1902) then become prone to rather romanticized if not ahistorical and self-regarding notions of what sociopolitical mobilization and engagement *should* (not) be in an era in which forces of domination (e.g., state surveillance) and organized resistance (e.g., protest campaigns) operate in domains that are multisited in geographical and computer-mediated respects. The streets are just one of these, newspapers and television have been and still are another, cyberspace—password protected and nominally open-access—is another. There is a lot more to know about social formations and arenas for action that are contingent upon using overlapping generations of (electronic) media and communications, and networking for, often, incompatible purposes in the first instance. In the second, how countermanding forces succeed—or not—when confronting incumbent powers and vested interests looking to assert their hold over respective resources and populations (e.g., pupils, workers, patients, or communities) requires more time and attention than news headlines and impact-driven research programs would allow.

This is not to say that political and philosophical debates about the form and substance of the "good society" in a digital age, including those raging around whether the internet is enhancing or impoverishing democratic ideals and the integrity and independence of incumbent media and political institutions are irrelevant. They are important questions. However, as the internet enters its third decade (at least) my contention is that the time has come within critical theory and research to take more account of how its constituent artifacts, underlying design principles, and operating premises are both determining (e.g., by how computer codes organize how people log on) and are in themselves overdetermined (how court rulings offline create conflicts between service providers, media watchdogs, and users). Also subject to contingencies and larger forces, what look like premeditated designs and policy objectives reveal themselves in retrospect as the outcomes of underestimated or unforeseen factors, for example, popular uptakes can surprise pundits and perplex trend-watchers, courts can make rulings in one part of the world that affect how people access and use the web in another (Deibert 2008; Council of Europe 2012a, b). The ways in which (mis)uses, strategic and spontaneous adaptations and applications of the internet and the web comprise multiple scenarios of power and resistance as well as inertia and disinterest are in turn circumscribed by the effects of these ordinary politics of design, access, and use (Mansell and Silverstone 1996; Wyatt et al. 2002; O'Neil 2009; van Dijck 2013). For every major social success in technological/media terms there are many fail- ures. No application can survive nonuse, disuse, or disinterest for long.

The cases looked at here provide no easy answers to these contentions. Indeed they throw up all sorts of troubling questions in turn. Nonetheless the theoretical underpinning for considering them together draws inspiration from less dismis- sive yet equally concerned critiques of how the internet has been developing over the last decade in conjunction with ideas that predate the web. What is of interest here are contestations *within* the terrain of its past and current development, its past and current applications that show a much less linear narrative of global cor- porate technoeconomic dominance than either advocates of this version of events or their critics would suggest. Uncovering these "murmurings" between the lines of activities in online or across online-offline terrains that adapt, divert, and "poach" (Certeau 1984: 6 passim) these same tools and newish media show that resistance may not be futile, sustainable political solidarity may not be compromised. Rather that both have been shape shifting and with them so have those powers they are pushing against. Indeed the need to move from "no" to "yes but" for engaged schol- arship is becoming imperative in the face of mobilizations from key powerbro- kers in those arenas, (inter)governmental and corporate, that run the internet. In other words the sociopolitical choices and technological means available amount to more than opting to take the "blue or the red pill" between simulated delu- sion, or second-hand reality.[3] Pushing this popular culture metaphor a bit further, these pills can be remixed, indeed are being redesigned as a battle for the hearts and minds of the internet's would be global citizenry has been gathering pace at not only the user interface of web-based media consumption but also further "upstream" in intergovernmental forums and multilateral institution-building.[4]

In this vein, the chapter frames the case studies that follow from a relatively underelucidated historical and conceptual vantage point: that of how the online/ offline dimensions to the macropolitics (viz. global) of who owns and controls the media and the internet pertain to the micropolitics of ordinary usages and users. Lawrence Lessig refers to this difference as one between how "old timers" and "newbies" perceive what is at stake in this respect (2006: 85). By *ordinary* users I am referring to the rising percentage of the world's population who cur- rently spend some if not a large part of their daily lives online (Internet World Stats 2012; UCL 2008; Madden et al. 2012; Millward 2012; Centre for Law and Democracy 2012). This includes burgeoning populations of literal "newbies" now accessing the web from fixed or mobile, freely available or paid-for access points all over the world, that is, those mainly younger populations in China and other parts of Asia, the Americas, the Middle East, and the African continent.

By ordinary I am also referring to those working in businesses, government departments, schools and universities; employees, faculty and students who, while also regular users of the internet and related web-based goods and services professionally and personally, are not conversant with the intricate debates around its ownership and control in technical, legal, or regulatory terms. Nor are they conversant with the subtle but important distinction between digital divide and digital inclusion debates. This broad demographic is, as Lessig points out, "the silent majority of today's Net" (2006: 85). A corollary aspect to putting the accent on ordinariness is to get behind and underneath another set of narratives emanating largely from industry and business literatures. These put the stress on single-minded and single-handed pioneering (largely male) heroes, innovation and design heroics in terms of "creative destruction" and the market's "invisible hand," seen to guide creativity and inspiration in computing terms. As computer programming and software research and development are as much the outcome of teamwork, peer-to-peer sharing of ideas and experience, and long-term collaboration, such tales that stress technological and historical breaks with the past are to the detriment of the role played by precursor innovations as well as other sorts of pioneering thinkers and doers—women and ethnic minorities for instance. They also underplay the role of luck, circumstance, do-it-yourself services for community and other nonprofit motives, and the enabling power of research funding streams. All of these factors have played a formative role in the emergence of the wider internet ecosystem in operation today.[5]

Framing the discussions that follow in terms of the ordinary, that is everydayness rather than exceptionalism, of how laypersons access and make use of internet technologies or conversely are subjected to various mundane pressures and more dramatic enclosures as they do so, means to distinguish these uses and experiences from the aforementioned "old-timers." This latter group is composed of generations of software designers (including professional and hacker technical communities), digital activists, engineers, systems administrators, legal experts, and those "for whom the web is self-consciously a wildly promising location for making life in real space different" (Lessig 2006: 84) and their preferred terrain for work and leisure.[6] In this respect the ordinariness of the internet, and here I am borrowing from Paul Gilroy (2002) in his critical sociology of race and empire, is double-edged as well as historically contingent, imbued with silences that are neither innocent nor golden (Lessig 2006: 340–345; Wajcman 1991; Gurumurthy and Singh 2012).[7]

CONCEPTUAL AND HISTORICAL RELOADS

First, some historical-theoretical grounding is called for to anchor this critical point of entry in a conceptual framework that can also provide an interdisciplinary base for rethinking the (geo)politics *of* the internet. This means cutting a thematic path through disparate literatures that seldom interact yet which are seeing various streams of *intra*disciplinary internet studies emerging. The rest of the chapter will not be attempting to provide a definitive historical account of the internet, nor of its web-based goods and services, and its subsequent cyberspaces in which data, people, and other actors move. There is a burgeoning literature so I will indicate those relevant to this study. Second, nor am I setting out to provide a definitive literature review of the respective debates that specifically derive from each of the three cases. Here too I will indicate those points where these more complex considerations have a bearing on the way each case stands in its own terms and as part of the book as a whole. While each case study is a snapshot of larger standalone inquiries, with its own burden of historiographical and theoretical debates to bear, together they reveal something about why the way we use the internet, and how the internet comes to "use" us matters to contemporary debates around what counts as political economic and sociocultural transformation.

The internet may well be large in scope and complex in design. But unchanging and impervious to other forces it is not. In short what is going on behind our screens at the back end of the web, in the deeper levels of an internet transmissions architecture made up of tubes, wires, and software codes, and between the lines of internet and/or telecommunications legislation and agenda-setting priorities at home and abroad matters not only for designers, advertiser, and lawmakers. What is going on behind the scene also matters in theory and political praxis, to those looking to articulate and facilitate alternative possibilities in particular. How it matters, on whose terms and conditions, and their implications for ordinary users and those excluded from or experiencing declining internet access in the *Brave New World* (Huxley in Franklin 2011) of today or that of tomorrow is being considered in forums where the future of the internet is now top of the agenda. I will return to some more salient historical points in the next chapter. Suffice it to recall that in the second decade of this century, the center of gravity in terms of internet access, use, and manufacturing has been shifting to the Global South, and with that access to growing, younger consumer markets and geoeconomic leverage. This shift from center to margin, from luxury to mainstream commodity, from the internet being for well-heeled elites to undertakings to roll out access to poorer and more remote populations (Kern 2012; ITU/WSIS 2003a, b), has occurred in a relatively short timespan—about a quarter century, though it has been gathering pace over the last ten years (Internet World Stats 2012). This technoeconomic transformation in how the world communicates, makes money, and organizes itself is a result of not only concerted efforts on the part of corporations and governments to "connect the next billion" (IGF 2008) but also the knock-on effects of the spontaneous uptake of internet media and communications around the world.

The thing to note at this historical juncture is the pervasiveness of the seemingly common-sense distinction made between "old" media and communications (newspapers, radio, television, and telephony) and so-called "new" media (all things digital, internetted, mobile). As electronic data exchanges over a computer "network of networks" have been transmitted via cable and satellite connections that piggyback on existing telecommunications networks (digitalizing and trans-forming these accordingly) the consumer-friendly web applications of the 1990s saw a discursive shift that was both marketing ploy and happenstance (Franklin 2004: 19 passim; Lüthje 1997; McHaffie 1997; Mattelart 1994; Mattelart and Constantinou 2008). As a result in popular and scholarly imaginaries the inter-net's computer-mediated communications networks comprising financial data flows, commercial web-based goods and services, and the ever-burgeoning *user-generated content* parted company from conventional telecommunications (voice transmission via cable and satellite). At the same time the primacy of publicly owned telecommunications operations and national media and broadcasting models declined. While business models, policy debates, disciplinary allegiances, and university curricula still make a distinction between the (mass) media on the one hand and, on the other, ICT and the internet, it is one that is increasingly dif-ficult to maintain in practice. This bifurcation between telephony and computing in public and academic discussions belies the symbiotic relationship between the internet's physical backbone of transmission, distinct from the goods and services it carries, and that of precursor and contiguous telecommunications networks. While the day-to-day operations of the former have been dependent on the latter since its inception, intensifying corporate rhetoric and political standoffs at the UN level imply that the two *must* be mutually exclusive domains (more on this in Chapter 6). The perpetuation of this insistence that a priori the "old world" of telecommunications and the "new world" of internet media and communications have nothing to do with one another has high political and economic stakes, as we shall see (Kushnick 2012; Singh 2012a; Feld 2012; Goldsmith 2012).

In the meantime the internet—bearing in mind the operational distinction be-tween infrastructure and the web as a carrier of web-based content, goods, and services—is being brandished as the latest tool for democracy and development (UN 2000; UNESCO 2013a, b; ITU 2005). At the same time, the increasing con-centration of ownership and control of these goods and services is in the hands of larger and more powerful ICT/media corporations, by which major state-actors and private sectors position the internet increasingly as either a state matter or a business first and foremost. The shift from an implicit, albeit politically sensitive, notion of internet communications as an extension of telecommunications and so construed as part of a history of "common carriage" (Noam in Kushnick 2012) to a for-profit, privately owned affair belies, however, a number of alternatives to the assumption that the internet is value-free, or "only an artifact."[8] As this arti-fact becomes the object of power struggles over its constitution, future form, and the way it is run the (dis)connections between the discursive dimensions of its governance debates, the expert communities (legal, technical, political) generat-ing these and their counternarratives, and everybody else, are thrown into relief. Meanwhile generations of "digital natives" regard as entitlements personalized and 24/7 (mobile) access to "free" products and service of an increasingly corpo-rate and privatized internet.

What about scholarly debates? At the risk of overgeneralizing, literatures emerging within and across the social sciences and humanities still tend to bifurcate into the above old versus new media streams, or optimist and pessimist literatures. This tendency is overlaid, even for interdisciplinary projects, by preferences for state centric, media centric, or techno centric modes of analysis respectively: (1) Political science and international studies, where a large part of internet governance research resides, concentrates on the techno-legal policy dimensions of tussles between national sovereignty and would-be global powers. The push and pull between states and/versus markets undergirds these analyses to a large extent. Predictive and explanatory modeling of formal outcomes at the macro-level are favored over the sociocultural contingencies of these processes at the micro-level. Meanwhile the latter is mainly the preoccupation of (2) research into everyday or strategic uses of the internet, for political or cultural ends. These pivot around a priori distinctions between RL and virtual reality, traditional versus "new" media, or analog versus cyber cultural practices.

For those traditions that are interested in the history and sociology of science and technology as the primary empirical object of analysis, the internet and corollary artifacts have generated (3) scholarship into constituent techno-historics, actor-networks, and the (gendered) dynamics of design and use that covers the range of internet technologies to date. The nuance provided by these investigations pay relatively little attention to the wider socioeconomic context and political power plays of these uses as politically and culturally computer-networked artifacts. And then there is (4) an emerging literature from within the internet's heartlands that problematizes the politics and economic consequences of internet design and related networking practices and with that the commercial, private ethos governing its underlying operations, goods, and services that persists at the expense of either public service or open source/open access understandings of these provisions (Rushkoff 2010; Introna and Nissenbaum 2000). These reconsiderations of how proprietarily encoded knowledge exchange compares to peer-to-peer sharing are challenging the liberal economic order. As well they challenge proprietary property rights and regulatory and business models on which liberal capitalist, and thereby hi-tech societies, have been based (Benkler 2006; Lessig 2006; O'Neil 2009; Raymond 2001; Grassmuck 2002).

The coming of age of internet studies in a generic sense and Internet Governance literature in an emergent disciplinary sense aside, the entrenched polarization between more pessimistic takes and wholesale embracing of internet-immersed lifeworlds and research domains create two additional false dilemmas for critical scholarship at this historical juncture. Namely they create the either/or of claims that it is necessary to stake a claim in either offline or online manifestations of everyday life, political power, and economic relations—and thereby that lifeworlds in which humans and machines are coconstitutive are implicitly inferior, if not threatening to embodied, organic worlds. The second is that despite the recognition that *supraterrrioriality* (Scholte 2002), multilateral institutions, and transnational (viz. global) corporations are integral to contemporary world order, political accountability resides in either nation-bound or their self-appointed intergovernmental institutions.

Understanding technological artifacts, singly or operating together as part of larger systems, as socially constructed, time sensitive and thereby not value free, is a philosophical and political standpoint with its own literature (Feenberg 1999; Wajcman 1991; Franklin 2002, 2004: 221–225). Each generation of "new media" or shift in how people and societies communicate has had high political and economic stakes, from the printing press to the railways, telecommunications, film, radio, and television (Mattelart 1994; Mattelart and Constantinou 2008; McLuhan 2001 (1964); McLuhan and Powers 1989). That internet technologies matter at the local, national, and global levels forms the basis of successive waves of advocacy and activism around a host of legal and sociopolitical controversies where the internet and, by association, the web have played a formative role (e.g., increases in and restrictions on freedom of expression, alternative media outlets, government censorship, personal privacy intrusions, new forms of criminality, and so on). Moreover, recent current events around successive revolutions and counterrevolutions or social unrest in which the web and mobile communications were center stage (from Iran, through to Athens, London, Rangoon, Cairo, and Tunisia) alongside public furors over freedom of information, national security, and social justice activism (the Wikileaks and PRISM affairs, the Occupy movement, and *Anonymous* actions) have catapulted into the public domain what were once arcane and expert-led arguments about how the internet works, or should work, and for whose benefit. Ordinary people, more or less accustomed or newer users of the web and by association the internet they access, are now privy to, and the object of these debates.

Cause and effect debates notwithstanding, many from the Anglo-Euro-American critical theoretical traditions have been reluctant to take on board how internet technologies have been not only practical but also theoretical game changers. Political praxis is now an internet affair, unthinkable without the web as venue and a digital toolkit for campaigning and organizing. Yet the seeming disconnect between those looking to understand these developments through old theories of power, resistance, and social relations and those claiming that there needs to be a radical break with the past is paradoxical in that proprietary products and services take center stage in both sets of arguments as a rule. One way to move past this impasse is to embrace these contemporary phenomena in ways that do not presuppose they come ready-made to fit either new or older theoretical paradigms. The cult of the new is actually a very old phenomenon. One reason why this bifurcation persists lies in the way the object and means of analysis, *The* Internet, frames and defines the field of action and reflection. Critical analysis, human agency, and structural powers are mutually informed by the feedback loop of this internet's local and global integrated circuits which are in turn threaded into the tapestry of everyday life online and offline (Franklin 2004: 11–12, 51 passim; Lessig 2006: 85 passim; Bakardjieva 2005).

Nonetheless, the standoff between technoskeptic versus technophile continues. This is partly because for all its recent mundaneness, the internet is still a relatively recent phenomenon. Moreover as a complex, hybrid, and by definition socio-geographically dispersed technological ecosystem that entails things and sensations, machines and codes, automated machine and human actors, it has not yet been entirely domesticated in the way its precursors have been. Film, radio, and television, washing machines, and other consumer electronics have been thoroughly tamed for research purposes, part of academe's intellectual furniture and everyday life, as "we" understand it. But the "internet" is way too big to fit into a living room (like the once new media of radio and TV once did and still do for a large part of the world) let alone a pocket or shoulder bag (although devices that access the web are now small enough). Its constituent organizational and communicative cultures are also not confinable to conventional notions of public squares, town/village halls, or houses of representatives, reading and writing, authorial authority and receiving audiences. It is only elements of this larger amalgamation, or system, that make sense at the experiential level through people being able to connect, log on using devices that can fit into the palm of the hand, onto a screen, or even under the epidermis. The ordinariness of the internet, as rendered by the worldwide spread of its user-friendly applications, booming consumer markets, products, and services is countered by its extraordinary architectural and operational diversity and complexity.

Three nodes within these crosscutting debates have been under particular pressure to take into account the interplay between large-scale and more intimate changes in where and how people interact, experience, and make sense of the world, or worlds today. The first is the role of states, as historically entitled and endowed key actors face data flows and capacity demands that cross over and so defy already beleaguered national jurisdictions every second of every day. The second concerns debates about changes in the constitution, location, and functioning of (national) citizenries as publics, already reconstituted as global consumers or media audiences for some time and now being addressed as digital formations of "netizens" or "tweeps." The third concerns shifts in the form and intentions of traditional and emerging institutional forms of disciplining power as vertically integrated and lateral relations under the aegis of computer-mediated and facilitated modes of multisited and multistakeholder governance, or global *governmentality* (Walters 2012; Foucault 1991). The rest of this chapter critiques, unpacks, and then reconstitutes these three modalities in turn in order to reset the paradigm.

Life on Earth after the Nation-State

The first node to tackle is that of the nation-state, an actor that plays a leading role in the contentious history of modernity and the waxing and waning of its Enlightenment project (Habermas in Borradori 2003; Harvey 1990; Scholte 2000; Sloterdijk 2006; Foucault 1984a, 2004a). But long before both the internet and before that the nation-state (in its twentieth century apotheosis) were invented, the movement of goods, services, people, and ideas were spilling out over various sorts of borders, funded and perpetuated in part in Western contexts by mercantilist, imperial, and then market-ruled routes for traffic in slaves, raw materials, finance, and now digital data. Whether envisaged as ancient cosmologies and made real by photographs from outer space, or in the form of spices, human beings, gold bullion, or financial flows the world has been circumnavigated, networked, and mapped in multiple ways well before now.

However the particular "death of distance" (*Economist* 1997) that the 1990s internet heralded was one that colluded with the end of the Cold War (and with that the "End of History") together with the forecast demise of the modern nation-state as the linchpin of world affairs. This includes an epochal shift from modern to postmodern times, the period in which the internet came of age (Jameson 1984; Harvey 1990; Castells 1996, 2002). References to the rise and fall and rise again of the nation-state operate as a leitmotiv in the narrative arc of "How the World Has Changed" in popular and academic discourses. Information and communication technologies (ICT) are indispensable to the plot. Since then reconsiderations of state centric paradigms in international studies and their corollary in other disciplines, the veracity of the bourgeois public sphere, have made only a dent in the carapace of the modern *nation-state* and the institutions by which it continues to exert real and imagined power over citizens and others within national jurisdictions.[9] Fundamental shifts in how nation-states operate and cooperate over the last century were taking place before but also alongside the emergence of the internet. However decentering the nation-state as a primary actor in this discussion is not to deny the historical achievements of liberation struggles during the first wave of decolonization in the 1960s and since then (e.g., East Timor, South Sudan). Nor is it ignoring how states can and do wield direct power in crucial aspects of how the internet is run and used, within their national jurisdiction and in regional settings. I have argued this point elsewhere and in various ways (Franklin 2009, 2010) with respect to how an overreliance on state centric analyses restricts understandings of the other forces at play.

Notwithstanding the historical and emotional glue of the "imagined communities" (Anderson 1991) that generated and still hold modern nation-state formations together along with statist discourses and institutions (Bourdieu 2012: 58–61) and self-serving political rhetoric, states may well be alive and well. But they are not the only player on the world stage, one that is now online as well as offline. As Fraser and other theorists note there has been an ideational and institutional shift toward a "post-Westphalian mode of frame-setting" (Fraser 2005: 82), one that both generates and emanates from the emergence of "other structures, both extra- and non-territorial" (Fraser 2005: 82–3) that impact on efforts to achieve socioeconomic equity, combat all forms of injustice, and sustain democratic ideals and probity in practice. The contributing factors in this reframing include "global media and cybertechnology" (Fraser 2005: 81; see Braman 2006; Nye 2002; Deibert and Rohozinski 2010). But this still begs the question of how power and resistance regroup in internet-mediated settings given that any "framing" for thought as well as action, "always unfolds with a . . . discursive opportunity structure" (Olesen 2010: 2). The various ways in which these discursive opportunity structures unfold see scholars confronting a double legacy: the historical undertow of the "Westphalian frame" (Fraser 2005, 2007) and the gradual dislodging of its pull by the eddies created by competing interests looking to influence the terms of debate under fast-changing conditions on the ground and online. Whilst politicians debate how the internet should be run from within their inherited Westphalian (i.e. state centric) frame, key decisions on how it is run take place in arenas where other sorts of actors call the shots (Mueller 2002, 2010).

Reframing Publics

This brings us to the second node under consideration, in this case the way in which a longstanding isomorphism between publics and national citizenries is becoming harder to justify in analytical terms, even if judicial realities and electoral systems are founded on this symmetry. "Publics" have generally been thought of in national terms, though since the 1990s scholars in different disciplines have begun to consider the phenomenon of not only "transnational" but also "digital" publics (see Fraser 2007; Olesen 2010; Papacharissi 2010; Drache 2008) given changes in regional and wider political "constellations" (Habermas 2001; Baban and Keyman 2008). This literature has flagged numerous problems regarding the viability of delinking publics in this way from the national on principle. The virtuous circle that is the lifeblood of democratic polities between elected representatives, legislative powers, and publics as voting constituencies raise questions about accountability, representativeness, and legitimacy if publics are construed and addressable in ways that are beyond the purvey of nation-states and ideally democratic institutions (Fraser 2007; Latour 2007, 2012; Marres and Rogers 2005; Aslama and Napoli 2010). In particular, doubts about whether such publics can be fully apprehended as autonomous or sustainable "postnational" or digital formations have stalled these reflections somewhat. Who should or can speak for such distributed constituencies, and in what sort of voice would they in turn (be able to) speak back, and on whose terms? Barring reflections on how the empirical realities of cross-border flows of people as well as media messages and data-exchanges permit hybrid understandings of publics as citizens-consumers-audience (Baban and Keyman 2008; Dayan 2001; Drache 2008) publics that go beyond strictly statist definitions tend to be treated as problematic, volatile and motile. On the other hand national citizenries are treated as stable, quantifiable, and relatively knowable, if not in terms of election or census results then rendered in opinion polls or audience ratings. Yet as social media giants such as Google and Facebook address their registered or tracked "users" as if they were publics of either order, conventional theoretical and empirical framings for these concerns start to creak under the strain.

The reasons for the stop-start characteristics of debates about the form and substance of how publics are or are not changing today, whether they are construed as consensual or antagonistic, national or global mobilizations (e.g., antiglobalization, antiwar, or antiglobal poverty protests), temporary or sustainable social forces lie in the political implications of suggesting otherwise. In the first instance, the idea that publics are not reducible to modern state-forms is, as Fraser reminds us, part of a historical experience and its accompanying framing. This worldview is hard to shift despite well-honed critiques of the andro—and ethnocentrism of public sphere and democratic theory. In the second, researchers argue over the empirical and theoretical limitations to ascertaining publics as observable and legitimate nation-based formations in their own right or viable simply when others speak or act on their behalf (as politicians and activists do). For instance, said other-publics forming as NGO coalitions, transnational issue-networks, or via web-based petition-signing campaigns have, on closer inspection, been less representative, less autonomous, and less legitimate than would appear at first sight. For instance, when they are not being co-opted by power or money, overwhelmed by the persuasive power and superior resources of other players such as corporations, or simply excluded from key decision-making moments (Coleman and Tucker 2012; Lipschutz 2005; Flyverbom 2011; Dany 2012), their moral force is compromised by their transterritoriality. Others note how emerging "global civil society" coalitions have a strong Anglo-American if not Western European imprint, among other things expressed in funding structures, membership, norms and values, and sense of mission (Lipschutz 2005; Guilhot; 2005). Finally, insofar as evidence of digital and/or transnational publics do not coincide with existing national communities, and are not represented in established institutions or recognized through due process, claims that such other-publics can emerge during mediatized global media events (e.g., *The Concert for Bangladesh* in 1971, *Live Aid* in 1985, or *Live 8* in 2005) and campaigns (e.g., *Make Poverty History* in 2005) are considered as fleeting ephemera. This renders these singular moments, particularly when taken out of historical context, as inconsequential to more embedded forces of continuity (viz. nation-states), if not immaterial to larger changes in the offing (e.g., reshuffles in corporate ownership of media and communications, revolutions).

It is a fair point to ask what exactly a transnational public might be in not only political but also cultural and ethical terms; what it looks or sounds like if it cannot be encapsulated by quantitative indicators, or legitimated by presenting its identity papers at the border. Moreover, where does such a public call "home"? Under what rights and obligations does it exist and to whom are its members accountable? Indeed, need such an imagined community best sustain itself as a consensual formation or can it have another sort of predisposition, one that is inherently nonconsensual or even conflictual? Moreover, to warrant the status of a "public" how would this grouping be distinguishable from policy or activist networks, transnational business elites when not construed in even broader terms such as "media diasporas" (Karim 2003), "flexible" citizenries (Ong 1999), or changing sorts of audiences (Dayan 2001)? At the very least, there is a rough consensus that the term needs to account for formations that are not simply an agglomeration of media audiences, consumers, internet users, nonstate defined or subordinated others (e.g., refugees, homeless populations). But if so, how do such publics become a force to be reckoned with over the long-term if they are to matter beyond measurements of their purchasing, voting, or petition-signing power?

I will return to this particularly elastic yet historically ossified concept in Chapters 5 and 6. Suffice it to say that it is not a recent idea that taking publics to be a stable knowable category or containers for legitimacy and powers is a fiction of sorts. In other words a working assumption that publics as synonymous to national citizenries are observable and so to be captured and measured accordingly predates more recent debates about whether the internet has changed the constitution and behavior of not only states (Braman 2006) but also their assumed publics (Drache 2008). One observer, Walter Lippmann, pointed out back in the 1920s how publics were discursive constructs, convenient untruths in that at

> the level of social life, what is called the adjustment of [humans] to [their] environment takes place through the medium of fictions. By fictions I do not mean lies. I mean a representation of the environment which is in lesser or greater degree made by [humans themselves]." (Lippmann 1993 (1927): 15–16)

Taking publics to be one such fiction then, the debates about what internet technologies do or do not do can be put into perspective. How people, in variable groupings and overlapping affiliations, which can include various *sorts* of publics—well endowed or impoverished, consensual or deeply divided—use them come more into focus. It also provides an important caveat to attempts to close the argument by recourse to counting-by-numbers as well. As Lippmann goes on to note, given that any "field of democratic action is a circumscribed area" (Lippmann op. cit.: 272) the stereotype of the "omnicompetent citizen," wherever they may be, perpetuates the illusion that a "complicated civilization" can be apprehended as if it were "an enclosed village" (op. cit.: 273). While villages are complex communities, too, Lippmann's point is nonetheless that evocations of "publics" as transcendent categories that are then rendered as statistical fact or idealized constituencies, assumes that all people are equally willing and moreover able to concern themselves with "all public affairs" (ibid.). These are high expectations for the watchdogs of political engagement, democratic probity, and social justice.[10]

In a would-be global and already internet-dependent era these inquiries have provided philosophical as well as conceptual and empirical complexity for researchers and practitioners working within and across state-bounded formations and spaces. For the purposes of this discussion several elisions need highlighting. First, there is the assumption that to effect change a public has to be large in numbers and consensual in nature. This need not be the case in both instances even as this is a premise for much public opinion research and political polling. Second is the assumption that the only legitimate publics are those that can be seen to act autonomously from governing—be it state, secular or religious—authorities. In this privileged, modernist frame of understanding a public *has* to amount to more than participants in a political rally, more than signatories on a petition, and more than a congregation of believers. Third is the methodological assumption that unless a public can be observed, that is counted, categorized, aggregated, and disaggregated along indices of age, income, gender, race, and so on, it does not exist. How the ontological legitimacy of national publics has developed in tandem with that of the modern nation-state is both a political and an epistemological question. As such it speaks to the development of liberal subjectivity and democratic polities in light of the political economic history of state sovereignty as an idea, worldview, and institutional form (Fraser 2005, 2007; Habermas in Borradori 2003; Foucault 2004a, b; Bourdieu 2012; Shapiro 2004). A cornerstone of mid-twentieth century democratic theory as expounded by Jürgen Habermas, the notion of the public sphere as a historical window, one through which the project of enlightenment could and should be fulfilled (Habermas in Borradori 2003; Habermas 2001) is intimately tied to a particular understanding of the media as independent watchdog—the Fourth Estate. In this respect, debates around the inadequacy of emergent digital or transnational publics to present a substantial challenge or alternative to the malaise in which the twenty-first century democracies find themselves, exemplified in the literature as the fading pulse of the bourgeois public sphere in principle and a "free," independent media in practice. The latter's entitlement to reading and viewing publics confronts web-based and user-generated, nonprofessional news and entertainment as one response to the erosion in journalistic standards and ethics while responsibility for the former malaise is laid at the door of the smartphoning and texting youth of today. There is evidence that in all cases these concerns are well founded. However this is to apply a very narrow, restrictive notion of publicness, publics, and the spaces in which they emerge and re-create themselves.

Daniel Dayan offers a kind of ideal-type of the public against which to assess particular empirical phenomena. In his take, a public involves relative sociability and stability over time, commitment to internal debate, self-presentation in relation to other publics, a shared worldview, the possibility of translating desires and tastes into demands, and a reflexive awareness of the criteria establishing who belongs (Dayan 2001). This definition distinguishes a public from other collectivities, such as clubs, business networks, or professional organizations. Others take this typology further, as I will discuss in due course. Suffice it to say that in this line of argument publics also manifest in informal ways that are transmitted and made real not only by formulas (e.g., voting papers) but also vernacular discourses and cultural forms that bring people together in proximate and mediated ways (Warner 2002; Hauser 1999). The point here is that the line between ideal (and idealized) publics and other forms such as audiences, readerships, constituencies has always been blurry, as are the various political and social ends to which publics (as masses or opinion) have been put by different ideologies. The way internet technologies reconnect, or interconnect these competing understandings in theory and practice has revealed the reification of the notion of publics and, by association, that of the public sphere as the place where said publics "go" or can be "found."

As Gerard Hauser argues there is a "disjunction" between how "most individuals experience their speaking and writing as personal expression" (1999: 5) and how they become rendered as members of a larger "public" as "portrayed by the media . . . [which is] an abstract representation whose needs, thoughts, and responses are extrapolated from survey data" (1999: 5). This search for certainty in quantifiable forms reflects the need to make the fiction Lippmann notes (op. cit.) work for political or social purposes. But it also reflects an historically "chronic ambivalence of democracies toward 'the public'" (Hauser 1999: 5) in a broader sense. Hauser argues that any investigation into how publics work needs to account for how conventional and other-publics are greater than the sum of their rendition as abstractions, with or without the help of statistical evidence, because they also constitute "rhetorical practices and their possibilities shape . . . public lives as citizens, neighbours, and cultural agents" (1999: 6). With this insight into the discursive, dialogic constitution of how publics operate, in tandem with Dayan's more inclusive conceptualization that allows for there to be different sorts of public in play, we can move to conceptualizing social formations in more dynamic and sociohistorically enriched ways; ways that need not dispense with a critical view of how such "publics" can be coerced and co-opted by vested interests, as well as challenge the same in various guises, and at the same time.

Rethinking Governance

Moving on to the third node. That nation-states are not the only actors making and enforcing the rules by which traveling and sedentary citizenries have to live has preoccupied political theorists and social researchers for some time. I will not rehearse these arguments about the form and substance of *global governance* as a historical formation as well as an ideological construct (see Prakash and Hart 1999; Lipschutz 2005; Rupert 2000). In this section I want to signal a more recent shift in how policymakers (elected and appointed) articulate, and researchers investigate longstanding and emerging institutional powers, as they operate as ideas, organizational forms, and legal enforcers in varying degrees of efficacy (Bøås and McNeill 2004). This is a shift away from treating nonstate actors who are not corporate partners in state-sponsored macroeconomic or development projects, so-called "civil society," as antagonists to protagonists.

In the wake of effective antiglobalization mobilization since the late 1990s at least, there has been a shift in how multilateral institutions have come to regard "civil society" as participatory "stakeholders" rather than oppositional forces that have to be kept at bay. For a number of reasons not possible to discuss here, longstanding and emerging multilateral institutions have started to invite "global civil society," a global public by another name, around the table. The depth of inclusion and degree of influence these new arrivals to high-level consultations (on internet governance, global warming) can exert is generating its own research literature (Dany 2012; Flyverbom 2011; Coleman and Tucker 2012). The point is that representatives of this other "public" have taken a seat at the negotiating table, its members having to behave and respond as interlocutors on entering the room so to speak. Once confined to the streets outside any particular event, or observer-status at selected summits, these "social actors" are now fully accredited participants in many UN-brokered consultations, those around ICT and the media since the *World Summit on the Information Society* round (2002–2005) being a case in point.

Debates about whether this is a cosmetic or structural shift in how the business of multilateral—global—rule gets done, decisions taken, put into words, ratified, disseminated and, then enforced, still rage. As do debates about the effectiveness of this sort of incorporation of NGOs large and small into what, for many, are institutions that are part of the problem rather than solution. Ideological and philosophical fault lines aside, as NGOs, single-issue activist platforms, academics, and larger "social movements" have (re)discovered, affinity with and commitment to *multistakeholderism* as a workable practice comes in many shapes and sizes. For example the ITU, World Bank, UNESCO, and WTO have different histories, organizational cultures, and levels of investment in their respective formulations of problem, solution, and the appropriate ways of working with laypersons as full-fledged partners. For critics on the inside and those looking on, options are limited. Formal inclusion and, thereby, shared responsibility and accountability for outcomes, bring familiar and unforeseen challenges for those parties agitating to effect change from within.

This trend in high-level consultations is just that—conversations that take place according to diplomatic protocol, accreditation conventions, and good will of participants with arguably little legal or financial teeth or enforceable commitment by key corporate or political representatives. Meanwhile, as many claim, these latter interests continue to exercise the "real" power and influence, behind the scenes in boardrooms or research and development facilities or up-front as governments ignore or subvert UN resolutions, declarations of principles, and action plans with unremitting regularity. The official record is full of stalled initiatives at the point principle is supposed to become action. For action plans require specifics and, as all regulators and activists know, whatever their ideological or institutional position, this is where deeper divisions take hold in disputes, not about what needs to be done, but how to do it, on whose terms, and at what cost. To further complicate things, these interactions and their practical logistics unfurl now in multisited domains: online (in cyberspace), on the ground (face-to-face settings), and at the interstices between the two, where computer-mediated communications, organizational techniques, and interactive settings play a formative and not just a post facto role. These developments in themselves let alone the implications they have for old and new social and political activism and public awareness of what is at stake challenge existing theory and research into the form, substance, and spaces of twenty-first century society and politics.

EVERYDAY LIFE ON SPACESHIP EARTH

Flipping the telescope and returning to how investigations into the practice of everyday life relate to debates around the local and global politics of the internet on the ground and online, does not make sense without accounting for concomitant changes in *how* people go about their everyday lives, run their businesses, or exercise power. In particular, how do these changes entail shifts in not only *where* everyday life occurs but also in its form and substance, for example, changes in how people apprehend, engage in, and experience their individual and communal understandings of the "everyday" wherever they may reside in formal citizenship terms in (state) capitalist and now computer-dependent or aspirational societies. In these settings diverse cultures of conventional offline (embodied) practices of everyday life are overlaid by online (computer-mediated and web-enhanced) ones in varying degrees and *translocal* and transnational encounters that include for-malized and spontaneous exchanges, cultural fusions, and political power plays that currently take place as online and offline *lifeworlds* converge and diverge (Clifford 1997; Inda and Rosaldo 2002). As I have argued elsewhere, how people use the internet does make a difference to the way the world works, for better or for worse (Franklin 2004, 2013). That said, everyday life and incorporating these sorts of practices into a critical investigation of the internet, power, and resistance writ large need not exclude the extraordinary, the little understood, or the won-drous and fantasy.

In the previous chapter I referred to a key scene in the 1999 film, *The Matrix*, in which the film's hero (played by Keanu Reeves) discovers, with some chemical inducement, that the world in which he lives and breathes, sleeps and works is not as "real" as he assumes it to be. The journey he makes from being in a state of everyday "common unhappiness" to higher consciousness and then politicization is portrayed, thanks to Global Hollywood's use of traditional and computerized special effects, as a physical and psychological ordeal facilitated by analog (tele-phones) and digital (computer codes, monitors) means. Physical matter—flesh and blood as well as the built environment—works, or rather is portrayed in the film in two ways. First, it is shown as an interface between the matrix and the "desert of the real" lying behind its simulation of everyday life; Neo's body is sub-jected to probes in his brain and body in order to transport him to the "other side," his sensory system shocked by reentering a primal (infantile, prenatal) state. Second is the way physical matter (human bodies) and built environments (interior and external cityscapes) figure in the action through their porosity to other life forms. In this case the artificial intelligences (agents of the "Machines" who are actually in control behind Neo's real-life computer screen) take on human form, walk through walls or fly over rooftops as they aggressively pursue trans-gressors and exert retribution in the name of law and order.[11]

This 1999 film and its sequel(s), an unexpected box-office hit at the time and since then global franchise and rich source for philosophers and social critics to extrapolate from may well be a bit dated for audiences today (so "nineties," as some might say) nearly fifteen years after its release. Nonetheless it has come to epitomize both the ambiguities and angst of the late 1990s digital capitalist societies. For public imaginaries in societies in which the Dotcom bubble was about to burst, this film does what its predecessor, *Bladerunner*, did for the high postmodernism of the neoliberal 1980s (see Harvey 1990; Jameson 1984). Since then the themes that animate *The Matrix*, which straddle popular culture (from super-hero cartoons to video/computer games), then emergent science fiction genres ("cyberpunk") and scholarly literatures, have been superseded by other cinematic representations of life on Spaceship Earth, in mainstream Hollywood, and independent productions. My point here is that the way bodies and machines are portrayed, including the contradictions and nonsequiturs in the film's plot and, for some, either its consummate silliness or erudition, take on board the increasing interconnection between physically inscribed practices of everyday life and those operating in fully or semi-immersed computer-mediated settings. The connections and disconnects between "meatspace" and "cyberspace" at the in-dividual level of perception, experience, and activity are no longer, as perceived at the time of *The Matrix*'s release, simply a figment of (science) fiction writers' imaginations.[12]

Between "Meatspace" and Cyberspace

In 1996 Arjun Appadurai first presented an alternative, more holistic conceptu-alization of globalization as a response to what he argues is a surfeit of theoriza-tions that rest on economic reductionist and binary logics of center-periphery or national-international models of world order (Appadurai 2002).[13] With an anthropologist's feel for nuance he looked to complicate what he argued are eth-nocentric and ideological oversimplifications of a shift in world order that com-prises multiplex and multidirectional economic traffic, cultural flows, media content, and their concomitant sociocultural geographies. His model goes a long way in rectifying the state centric and functionalist tendencies of prevail-ing theories of globalization as a singular, unitary transformation of "time-space compression" that affects all cultures and societies equally, flattening out crucial power differentials within and across societies in so doing (Shah 2011; Inda and Rosaldo 2002; Harvey 1990; Scholte 2002). Appadurai breaks this larger picture of an emergent *global cultural economy* down into five descriptors or "scapes" called *ethnoscapes, mediascapes, technoscapes, financoscapes*, and *ideoscapes*. While ana-lytically distinct these scapes are dynamic and porous in empirical terms, but nei-ther synonymous nor reducible to one another. Powerful flows and forces shape as well as traverse these *scapes* in various directions, moreover, some of which trace the deeper grooves laid down by more ancient and more recent forms of imperial rule.

Reservations about what Appadurai's heuristic does to blunt the power analysis of political economy perspectives notwithstanding, the benefit of this re-visioning of key debates at the time, one in which the internet was beginning to make its mark, is that it opened up the possibility of theorizing and researching "globaliza-tion" as more than internationalization by other means or continuation of Anglo-American economic and cultural imperialism that preoccupied scholarly and policy debates in the 1970s (Scholte 2000; Tomlinson 1999; Gerbner et al. 1993). His point is that while these aspects are integral they are only part of the picture. This is a methodological intervention as much as a theoretical reflection in that Ap-pudurai is arguing for the need to incorporate the "deeply perspectival constructs"

(2002: 50) that rationalize but also flow from the material transformations that marked this period—changes in modes of production, distribution, and labor relations and (Harvey 1990; Hardt and Negri 2000) ownership and control of the media. These "perspectival constructs" are however very real in terms of how they inform power relations that are "inflected by the historical, linguistic, and political situatedness of different sorts of actors: nation-states, multinationals, diasporic communities, as well as subnational groupings and movements (whether religious, political, or economic), and even intimate face-to-face groups, such as villages, neighborhoods, and families " (Appadurai 2002: 50–51).

This reconceptualization offers a productive baseline for resetting the paradigm that is the task of this chapter. Two of these *scapes* need closer attention for this purpose, however, *technocscapes* and *mediascapes*. First, for Appadurai the term *technoscapes* refers to technological changes that are singular and cumulative. In other words, the need to account for the "global configuration, also ever so fluid, of technology, and of the fact that technology, both high and low, both mechanical and informational, now moves at high speeds across various kinds of previously impervious boundaries" (ibid.). Second, he underscores the usual distinction, at the time and to a large extent today, between technology as information and communication technologies and "the media" as a distinct sector, public and privately funded, that delivers news, and entertainment. By *mediasacapes* Appadurai recognizes that this distinction is a tenuous one in that he is referring

> both to the distribution of the electronic capabilities to produce and disseminate information . . . , which are now available to a growing number of private and public interests throughout the world; and to the images of the world created by these media. . . . What is most important about these mediascapes is that they provide . . . large and complex repertoires of images, narratives and "ethnoscapes" to viewers throughout the world (Appadurai 2002: 50–51).

As I argue elsewhere (Franklin 2010), these five scapes could do with a sixth one in light of how the above distinction between informational technologies and the media has become increasingly difficult to maintain in the wake of the internet and its "convergent" media. There is a need to take more explicitly into account the specifics of computer-mediated and programmed "perspectival constructs" that are not adequately captured by Appadurai's initial distinction between *mediascapes* and *technoscapes*. Including the notion of *cyberscapes* accounts for the sorts of digital traversals and "imagined worlds" now constituted by, experienced as, and circulated through the internet's cyber*spaces* and places (Lessig 2006: 84; Franklin 2004: 100–101, 232–236). These comprise, indeed cannot exist without, the *cyberspatial* practices of onlineness that are both produced and consumed by participating parties, then received and circulated by others (audiences, users, citizens, professional and lay-producers). Stronger still, these protagonist-participants can no longer be assumed to be organic human beings. They also take the form of computer programs that perform clandestine functions (e.g., botnets), have quasilegal status gaming domains (e.g., those characters populating virtual worlds such as *Second Life* or games like *World of Warcraft*), or stand for physical users in various guises (e.g., avatars and nicknames and other sorts of digital identities assumed for social networking sites).

This extension to Appadurai's critical topology still begs the question of how to critically investigate the ways in which such scapes operate as a whole or in part. For this remains a macro-level analytical framework. What happens at ground level, close up and in a cumulative fashion requires further theorization.

Michel de Certeau Redux

How does one capture both the larger scale and more intimate, indeterminate dimensions of the "perspectival constructs" that Appadurai argues co-constitute as well as frame the world people live in and come to know? As noted above, debates about the interconnection between internet technologies, the exercise of power and forms of resistance tend to bifurcate between macro and micro-level modes of research. In this section I argue for taking on board a relatively "old school" critical thinker in order to consider ways to investigate how a "complex, overlapping, disjunctive order" (Appadurai op. cit.) morphs into another, by force of circumstance or as a result of how both powerful and weaker groups respond to these circumstances. Known largely to cultural studies, social and cultural theory, Michel de Certeau's thought continues to offer a powerful antidote to the techno-determinist undertow that informs both self-serving and critical accounts of how the internet makes a difference.

I have argued for incorporating the work of Michel de Certeau elsewhere so I will not rehearse these arguments here.[14] The point of this "redux" section is to link his more well-known ideas as taken up in cultural theory and media studies (Highmore 2002; Franklin 2004, 2005b) to his more overtly political work (Certeau 1997a, 1997b/1994b). The reason is that it is in his post-1968 writings that Certeau directly addresses the sociocultural implications of electronic communications and precursor forms of computer-mediated supraterritoriality. These writings are also about the day-to-day realities, including setbacks, of effecting change over the long term (Giard 1994, Certeau 1994: 58 passim); of how once captured "speech" can also be recaptured, of how power to effect change also includes taking and holding the floor, figuratively and literally. Like other thinkers witnessing sea changes in how societies interact and represent themselves, to themselves and others, such as Marshall McLuhan (2001 (1964); McLuhan and Powers 1989), Walter Benjamin (in Appadurai 2002; in Franklin 2002), Horkheimer and Adorno (2002 (1944)) or Donna Haraway (1990), Certeau captures both threat and opportunity of unfolding events (in his case those of the 1968 upheavals in Western Europe) and longer-term historical change (1991, 1986).

But first, to recall: As Ben Highmore among others notes, Michel de Certeau (1925–1986), a contemporary of Michel Foucault, Pierre Bourdieu, Henri Lefebvre, and Jürgen Habermas, was a polymath who practiced an interdisciplinarity that is often espoused but rarely performed. . . . (His work is) continually marshalled to the job of finding new ways of articulating the opaque realm of the everyday . . . to invent new ways of bringing into the light (and thereby actually producing) the inventiveness of the everyday." (Highmore 2002: 63; see Bakardjieva 2005: 58)

While his contemporaries were concerned with theorizing how social institutions, labor relations, and capitalist modes of production become "hardwired" into the "DNA" of liberal societies (see Foucault 2004, a, b; Bourdieu 1998, 2012; Lefebvre 1991), Certeau was a theorist of possibility. His thought is that of the "yes, but" sensibility in that he was interested in considering instances of fluidity, movement, and polysemy from the point of view of those who, while subjects of and subjected to the exercises of power (see Chapter 1), are also agents and authors of overlooked and undervalued forms of resistance and dissent. This includes taking account of how the same can become complicit in perpetuating and exacerbating the status quo as well. This commitment to articulating paradox-dilemmas of his times, including research into oral histories, the "unpopular" culture of religious communities, and research ethics makes his work less amenable to being appropriated for political rhetoric even as it became a cornerstone for what later came to be known as reception studies in media and communications.

Certeau is intent on uncovering, indeed recovering, the forgotten or overlooked pasts and presents in which nonelite "users" (of commercial or state-led goods and services for instance, as television or media audiences that "use" various media as consumers) have had, or have a role to play in the eventual outcomes. Not content to posit power as pervasive, self-replicating, or systemic, or its subjects as complicit, docile, or doomed to failure, Certeau looks to conceptualize human agency without reducing it to voluntarist or romanticized revolutionary categories.[15] In essence Certeau's methodological and ethical point of entry is to investigate the

> ways in which users—commonly assumed to be passive and guided by established rules—operate. The point is . . . to indicate pathways for further research. This goal will be achieved if everyday practices, "ways of operating" or doing things, no longer appear as merely the obscure background of social activity, . . . The purpose . . . is to . . . bring to light the models of action characteristic of users whose status as the dominated element in society (a status that does not mean they are either passive or docile) is concealed by the euphemistic term, "consumers." Everyday life invents itself by *poaching* in countless ways on the property of others. (Certeau in Highmore 2002: 64, original emphasis)

This stance has put him in the critical sights of Marxist critics as his work was picked up by apologists for market-led consumerism. The point is, and this is his challenge, to recognize that the "invention" or "making" of everyday life is literal and figurative. It is a production, a *poēsis*—but a hidden one, because it is scattered over areas defined and occupied by systems of "production" (television, urban development, commerce, etc.), and because the steadily increasing expansion of these systems no longer leaves "consumers" any place in which they can indicate what they make or do with the products of these systems. (in Highmore 2002: 65)

If we can construe these "systems" as constituent of the *scapes* theorized in the last section and then consider that the "invention" and "making do" scattered over the areas that Certeau envisages is where the push and pull between strong and weak, endowed and dispossessed, vocal and silent unfold (e.g., television, cities, communities) as ones now mediated and framed by internet technologies, then an accumulation of traditional and emerging "ways of operating" is in operation. This approach, and way of capturing the big picture in the same frame as the microcosms of social change is best encapsulated to my mind in the following quote, addressed to critical researchers and by association activists:

If it is true that the grid of "discipline" is everywhere becoming clearer and more extensive, *it is all the more urgent to discover how an entire society resists being reduced to it*, what popular procedures (also "miniscule" and quotidian) manipulate the mechanisms of discipline and conform to them only in order to evade them, and finally, what "ways of operating" form the counterpart . . . of the mute processes that organize the establishment of socioeconomic order. (Certeau, in Highmore 2002: 66–8, emphasis added)

This passage offers a useful template for the case studies that follow. Certeau's work provides a way into researching the aforementioned constructs as constituent of the still underelucidated ambiguities (Crack 2008, op. cit.) that shape the big power and everyday politics of the internet, as they unfold behind the screen and on the street.

To hone this compass, there are four moves to make through his thought: usages, strategies and tactics, margins to center, and the spatial politics of communication. First is Certeau's understanding of how the media (then and nowadays) is comprised of usages, hence those who use media products, services, and so messages are agents in their distribution and circulation. Usages entail dialogs, conversations as well as processes and outputs, in terms of textual or visual artifacts. Certeau's stress on the vernacular, on the antidisciplinary, agonistic "characteristics of the speech act" (in Highmore 2002: 65) is in order to highlight the extent of, as well as the limits to, power. The "act of speaking" is one form of usage in that it "effects an appropriation, or reappropriation, of language by its speakers; it establishes a present relative to a time and place; and it posits *a contract with the other* (the interlocutor) in a network of places and relations" (Certeau in Highmore 2002: 65–66, original emphasis).

Precisely because ordinary "users make ("bricolent") innumerable and infinitesimal transformations of and within the dominant cultural economy in order to adapt it to their own interests and their own rules. We must determine the procedures, bases, effects, and possibilities of this collective activity" (in Highmore 2002: 65–66). Certeau looks to "restore to everyday practices their logical and cultural legitimacy, at least in the sectors—still very limited—in which we have at our disposal the instruments necessary to account for them" (in Highmore 2002b: 67–68). Hence the second move is to follow his cue in not losing sight of how this "ordinary" creativity is not happening in a social or power vacuum. As Foucault argues (see Chapter 1), power is a productive and destructive force in its exercising and resistance to it. Certeau is interested in how these practices can and do take place for those who are at a disadvantage. This is his oft-cited notion of how the weak have to resort to guerrilla-like tactics in the face of the resources that those in a stronger position can muster. In this push and pull dynamic Certeau posits, loosely, that *strategies* are

> the calculus of force-relationships which becomes possible when a subject of will and power (a proprietor, an enterprise, a city, a scientific institution) can be isolated from an "environment." A strategy assumes a place that can be circumscribed as proper (*propre*) and thus serve as the basis for generating relations with an exterior distinct from it (competitors, adversaries, "clienteles," "targets," of "objects" of research). (Certeau in Highmore 2002; 69)

On the other hand, for those without these means, including proprietary ownership of strategic resources such as software codes (e.g., the source code of an operating system like Microsoft Windows) or a place they can call their own (a home, an institutional legitimacy) a *tactic* works as a

> calculus which cannot count on a "proper" (a spatial or institutional localisation), nor thus on a borderline distinguishing the other as a visible totality. The place of a tactic belongs to the other. *A tactic insinuates itself into the other's place, fragmentarily, without taking it over in its entirety, without being able to keep it at a distance.* It has at its disposal no base where it can capitalise on its advantages, prepare its expansions, and secure independence with respect to circumstances. (in Highmore 2002: 70, emphasis added)

In short, effective strategic power is a scarce resource. Resistance does not come ready-made, off the shelf. It has to be fashioned in situations and contexts over which other forces have control, for example, of agenda setting, terms of access, entries and exits, and of the narrative.

The contrast between tactics (of the weak) and strategies (of the strong) is, as Certeau himself notes, a stark one that could be seen to be implying that the less powerful can never think or act strategically, a point that others have made as well. Critics note that this divests protest movements of any substantive power (in Franklin 2004: 245, note 9). However, the point is more that ownership, if it is nine-tenths of the law, can arguably respond more quickly to changing circumstances than the "inventive sluggish practices" that also comprise the invention of everyday life.[16] The advantage lies then with those who have "proprietary powers," as Ben Highmore argues in defense of Certeau's use of the analogy of guerrilla warfare (2002: 159). The way the internet has provided possibilities for activists, as one form of resistance, to close this gap, however, has not gone unnoticed. The results are mixed and the jury is out as to how long this tactical advantage will be available under the changing context of ownership, control, and use of the internet and alternative media outlets (Lovink 2012; Aslama and Napoli 2010).

As a major contributor to theories of consumption and accompanying shift of attention to how audiences-consumers respond in many different ways to the same message or commodity, it is easy to overlook that Certeau's aim to grant this "silent majority" social and political agency has become overshadowed by increasingly sophisticated and digitized techniques to guide and track people as they navigate or look to negotiate the larger consumer "grid of discipline" in multifarious ways. Looking back with the knowledge of how online our "digital imagination leaves traces" (Latour 2007), how daily millions of individual footprints are stored in huge databases, tracked by service providers and other agencies (such as security forces, state censors, criminal organizations) this hiddenness remains underresearched at the same time as it has become made transparent as the currency of global commerce,[17] subjected to the glare of the digital panopticon's surveillance and control mechanisms (Winokur 2003; Žižek 2006). And as global branding, public relations, and advertising tools have taken the lead in tabulating, gathering, and filtering people's everyday practices (e.g., as they log on and off, browse the web) it is also easy to overlook that positing tactics as the prerogative of those without recourse to these larger strategic resources allows for another perspective. Tactics in this understanding may well

> wander out of orbit, making consumers into immigrants in a system too vast to be their own, too tightly woven for them to escape from it. But these tactics . . . also show the extent to which intelligence is inseparable from the everyday struggles and pleasures that it articulates. *Strategies, by contrast, conceal beneath objective calculations their connection with the power that sustains them from within the stronghold of its own 'proper' place or institution.* (in Highmore 2002: 70, emphasis added)

What this means is that as vested interests assemble and regroup so also do those opposing them.

In this sense Certeau is suggesting that everyday life and cultural practices are not benign, apolitical, or cosy. In this domain, culture (in the singular and plural)

> articulates conflicts and alternately legitimizes, displaces, or controls the superior force. It develops in an atmosphere of tensions, and often of violence, for which it provides symbolic balances, contracts of compatibility and compromises, all more or less temporary. *The tactics of consumption, the ingenious ways in which the weak make use of the strong, thus lend a political dimension to everyday practices.* (in Highmore 2002: 68, emphasis added)

Third, he then moves to establish marginality, the "unimportant stories"[18] as the heartbeat of socially engaged research, in other words, the research ethics of reinserting the vernacular (Hauser 1999) of ordinary conversations and (online) actions of nonelite or marginal actors into the frame of analysis. But, he also makes no bones about what he considers to be the "cancerous growth of vision, measuring everything by its ability to show or be shown and transmuting communication into a visual journey" (in Highmore 2002; 71). What Certeau is actually getting at here, long before the advent of user-generated content and references to produsers or prosumers in the wake of do-it-yourself social media and social networking business models for the web, is that everyday life in Western societies, while largely comprised of written texts, also comprises (fast-fading) oral as well as (ever-increasing) visual practices that move in and out of expanding and contracting (cyber)spaces.

The spatial politics of communication is something that infuses Certeau's policy-based work, political analyses, and sociological research into the practice of everyday life. In a programmatic sense this sensibility is summed up in a report written with Luce Giard for the French Ministry of Culture in 1983, "The Ordinariness of Communication" that has been republished in *The Capture of Speech*, a collection of his political writings on the 1968 events and their aftermath (Certeau 1994, 1997b). What is extraordinary about this particular report is its prescience in terms of sensing the implications of the shift from public service based (analog) telecommunications and media content to privatized (electronic). His focus is on defining communications as not just the transmission of manifest content but, rather, in terms of how its "psychosociological" dimensions render it inherently ambiguous (1994: 169). Clarity of meaning can only be "as good as it gets" in that it is never absolute, unequiviocal, or implicitly rational, as those taking a Habermasian approach would wish to strive for (Habermas in Borradori 2003). Stronger still, this renders all communication as political (1994: 167), neither neutral, nor "innocent" (1994: 167). "[T]here is no communication without ambiguity" (1994: 170), hence Certeau argues against policies that present "technological panaceas" that are, in his view, oversimplifications if not simplistic mindsets that equate the spread of (the mass and early electronic) media and communications with the "miraculous" (1994: 170).

What about the recent globalization (viz. commercialization and commodification) of everyday life, in which the internet and precursor global satellite news and entertainment services have been formative? Certeau recognizes that these changes in the provenance of media messages have an impact on conventional understandings of place, neighborhood, and familiarity (1994: 186 passim). However his is not a static understanding of the media's role in local-translocal interpolations. He is interested in apprehending the local as both parochial and mobile. This is along with his understanding of space as "practiced place" as he looks toward the productive rather than purely destructive dimensions to the then new, changing forms of networking (1994: 187). Neither is he intent on dismissing all new inventions as threats to traditional practices. As is the case with recording technologies new techniques of (then and now) mechanical and (now) digital reproduction can actually revive, "reactivate memories of ordinary things" (1994: 214) that would have been lost with the passing of time and generations. Composers and ethnomusicologists as well as anthropologists have made invaluable use of recording and video technologies, as have latter-day generations with mobile-phones, video cameras, and digital recorders. In this sense his critique of communications policymaking and research at the time is not a dismissal of the new out of hand. He sees radio and television in an optimistic light, opening possibilities for making hidden histories available if undertaken (1994: 214) in ways that provide ordinary people, including dispossessed and disadvantaged populations, with spaces and opportunities for self-expression (1994: 217) that can enable "culture in the plural" (1994: 218).

Certeau puts his finger on the sore point, the elephant in the room if you will, of how technological fix-its continue to be put ahead of sociocultural priorities. The hi-tech, in his time mass media, tail ends up wagging the dog. But his argument is not a simplistic either/or. Here too he takes his distance from those who would romanticize days gone by in the face of technological advances (1994: 166). Instead he argues for a better, more acute understanding and thereby political and cultural agendas that recognize the way in which mediated, enhanced communications make sense first and foremost in terms of the way people *make use of* (new and established) networks within social relations that too are in motion. In this sense communication is paradoxical in that it is the intersection of that which informs and that which transmits, it is where people are anchored in yet also (via various media and nowadays via the web) can leave the local (1994: 165). This intersection points to different "political possibilities, one technological, the other social. . . . We do not have to choose between these two systems . . . or be seduced by nostalgia for the illusion of days gone by. . . . Rather the task at hand is to explicate the political and theoretical stakes that undergird any set of policy propositions" (1994: 166, my translation).

SUMMING UP

To round up this paradigm reset, the following points bear reiterating. First, celebratory and gloomier analyses of the internet's socioeconomic and democratic implications have accompanied its advancement step by step. Instead of indulging in the propensity to either demonize or idolize a reified notion of "*The* Internet" there is a need to repoliticize this internet by unpacking cases where we can see how practices of power and resistance through and over parts of its design, access, and use unfolding over time and in specific ways. This means unpacking how the internet operates as the object, means, and medium for politicized contestations in each case, the outcome of which have both an immediate and longer term influence on the practice of everyday life and ordinary internet users. This connection is not self-evident however. As Bakardjieva notes, ordinary people, or civil society as a "stakeholder" in multilateral institution-speak remain "marginalized subjects in a technocratic society. They are excluded from the governing of a society steeped in technology because they have no voice in the process of designing and implementing technical systems. Like women in a patriarchal order ordinary users represent objects of seduction in the name and through technologies" (2005: 57). Hence the need to move between the outer and inner limits of this "dispersed, tactical, and make-shift creativity" (Certeau op. cit.) without overlooking how the latter can itself adopt the mantle of power, become in turn a vested interest. To wit, while these

"ways of operating" constitute the innumerable practices by means of which users reappropriate the spaces organized by techniques of sociocultural production . . . the goal is . . . to bring to light the . . . dispersed, tactical, and make-shift creativity of groups or individuals already caught in the nets of "discipline." (Certeau, in Highmore 2002: 66–8)

Second, acknowledging the cogency of immanent critiques of (digital) capitalism as well as overt mobilization against blatant forms of oppressions, the theoretical grounding of these case studies draws on social constructivist analytical frameworks of technology, culture, and society albeit in such a way that the broad canvas of world politics is not held at arms length from the minutiae of everyday life or cultural practices. The political question that undergirds this study is about how "we" get the media, the internet "we" do, or do not deserve (Franklin 2004, 2007, 2010, 2012a), likewise for the power we endure and impose and thereby the sorts of revolutions "we" engage in, with and without access to the latest media and communications. My aim here is to draw a provisional line in the sand between ingrained pessimism from without and informed protestation from within that target contemporary capitalism and its deployment and derailment of information and communication technologies. This is a fine line to walk given the bifurcation between condemnatory and celebratory literatures around the internet and society. It is more so in the face of how web-based marketing and consumerism have managed to colonize large swaths of the planet's physical but also digitally constituted lifeworlds, personal lives, and public spaces.

These changes have been incremental and dramatic, spontaneous at a specific and global level as well as programmed. They have been socially engineered by state-run projects within national borders and commercially pushed across the globe by powerful corporate players. So, third, the chapter has argued how despite increasing public and scholarly attention to the internet's perceived effects in market terms, for example, how a mobile phone brand's messaging system came to symbolize the 2011 riots in the United Kingdom while the political uprisings in Tunisia and Egypt appear to have been fortuitous public relations for a couple of global brands—and a public relations disaster for others (Franklin 2013)–little attention is being paid to processes and practices that constitute these events *avant la lettre*. Whilst some usages have been used to good effect, by activists and advertisers alike, for research purposes, process and outcomes are, however, not the same. Unchallenged, this conflation, usually made in hindsight by those who stand to benefit (e.g., "Facebook Revolutions") continues to both reify and underestimate the way the internet as now ordinary, taken for granted, and so apparently apolitical, belies underelucidated tensions around its role, and enrollment in perpetuating and refashioning structural power, and with that, its ultimate role in exacerbating seemingly incorrigible socioeconomic and cultural exclusions respectively. In this case I am referring to exclusions that are not only circulated as content (the medium is the message/massage) but also perpetuated and resisted beneath the silky silicon surface of the user-friendly interfaces of consumer electronics, articulated and dissimulated in "freely available" online advertising-speak or "access for all" and "internet freedom" policy- and advocacy-speak.

Fourth, the focus on resetting received theoretical frameworks, changing political mindsets, means developing a conceptual lexicon that can inform and engage with an empirically grounded ecological understanding of how the internet and its global cultural political economy constitute particular sorts of artifacts, cultural practices, material power hierarchies, symbolic rituals and codes of meaning, traffic, and renetworked "things" and "publics." A focus on practices—everyday (non-, mis-)uses, access issues, as well as programming, standard setting, and legislative "creep" toward or away from more overt control by states or markers—rests on the question about how *other* ways "we" use the internet could make a difference. This difference could be situated in the sociocultural, political or economic spheres of endeavor. It would be written deep into the internet's functional codes, or based on how ordinary people get past software gatekeepers or governmental surveillance to make use of the internet for a range of purposes. The way that its design facilitates lateral interactivity in principle, along with real-time synchronicity across clock-time and physical space has been enhanced, if not challenged and critiqued because of the way people develop its informal and formalized design characteristics, and exploit the suppleness of its governing software. At the same time these uses are restricted or enhanced by the internet's physical properties and the consumer goods and services that have accumulated since its mass uptake in the early 1990s. However, the kind of society implied in these overlapping and (in)compatible designs, accesses, and usages is not reducible to them. Conversely competing visions of the sort of "world we want" imply different understandings of how these technologies can facilitate or hinder these visions.[19]

Rebooting the paradigm in light of this discussion and the three case studies that follow will be the task of Chapter 6. To conclude and segue into the next chapters, it bears reiterating that the entry point for this chapter's critique is my contention that to date theory and research on the internet-society-politics nexus tends to follow ethnocentric, mediacentric and technocentric lines of thought. By taking practices seriously, and the power hierarchies comprising them, also in motion, the internet presents less as an immovable, ahistorical object than a complex set of cultural practices, hardware and software connections, communities, and a politically charged geography. Space, as Certeau notes, is a "practiced place" (in Franklin 2004: 165). Likewise is cyberspace.

The point is that internet technologies are products of sociocultural and political economic forces that are also undergoing historical change. The world and these media and technologies are, however, intricately connected even though this interconnection is not a fait accompli. More importantly, as powerful state actors wake up from twenty-five odd years of self-induced slumber during the period of "laissez-faire" at home and abroad, we find that the internet as we know it has become the provenance of increasingly powerful commercial forces. In this time, however, ordinary "users," singly and through mobilization or specific organizations indigenous to the web, have been continually looking for ways to use internet technologies for social betterment, improve the conditions of local or disadvantaged groups through specific applications, or simply provide culturally appropriate and affordable ways for people to get in touch with family and friends while abroad, to find their roots, or have a room of their own online.

Who Rules in the "Internet Galaxy"? Battle of the Browsers and Beyond

INTRODUCTION

> "Don't be evil." Googlers generally apply those words to how we serve our users. But "Don't be evil" is much more than that . . . it's also about doing the right thing more generally—following the law, acting honorably and treating each other with respect. . . . Sometimes, identifying the right thing to do isn't an easy call. (Google 2012)

In early 2013 the US Federal Trade Commission cleared the Google Corporation of anticompetitive practices despite "some evidence (that) suggested it was trying to remove competition," (FTC Director Liebowitz cited in Arthur 2013; Federal Trade Commission 2013). The main protagonist in the FTC investigation has become a household word in this century's "internet galaxy" (Castells 2002), based on the overwhelming dominance of its homonymous software programs that enable people to find things on the web quickly and effectively, Google Search and its many spin-offs (e.g., Google Scholar). The decision was based on a two-year

> extensive investigation into allegations that Google had manipulated its search algorithms to . . . unfairly promote its own competing vertical properties, a practice commonly known as "search bias." In particular, the FTC

evaluated Google's "Universal Search"—a product that prominently displays targeted Google properties in response to specific categories of searches. . . . Similarly, the investigation focused on the allegation that Google altered its search algorithms to demote certain vertical websites . . . however, the FTC concluded that the introduction of Universal Search, as well as additional changes made to Google's search algorithms—even those that may have had the effect of harming individual competitors—could be plausibly justified as innovations that improved Google's product and the experience of its users. It therefore has chosen to close the investigation. (Federal Trade Commission 2013)

In so ruling, however, the commission stipulated that Google must make changes in how it displays and links search results to its own products or those of advertisers (Federal Trade Commission 2013; Arthur 2013). While Google did not get off completely scot-free, its competitors in web computing and mobile telephony, Microsoft, Samsung, and Apple in particular, were vocal in their publicized disappointment in this outcome. As the FTC puts it, "Google is a global technology company with more than 32,000 employees and annual revenues of nearly $38 billion" (Federal Trade Commission 2013). This description is an understatement in light of how anything to do with, or about the internet today is linked in some way or another to Google since the early 2000s (Vise 2005; Vaidhyanathan 2012; Lazuly 2003).

But this chapter is not primarily about Google. It is about one of these main competitors, Microsoft. Having made its mark in personal computing and corollary software for computer operating systems in the 1980s–1990s, a market which it still dominates, Microsoft was to become the leading provider of crucial software for navigating the web in the late 1990s, its house-brand web browser *Internet Explorer.*[1] Seemingly eclipsed by the Google-led next generation of consumer electronics, web-based communications, and computers since then, in recent years the corporation has become a renewed force to reckon with as it too has shifted its attention to the (mobile) products and services that characterize the *cyberscapes* of today (see Chapter 2). For example in 2011 Microsoft bought the Voice Over Internet Protocol (VoIP) company Skype, for $8.56 billion—in cash, pipping Google and Facebook to the post (Bright 2011) with the immediate effect of discontinuing its still widely used instant messaging service. One reason for this "extreme makeover" is the effect of antitrust litigation that the corporation was embroiled in between 1995 and 2002. In contrast to Google a decade later, Microsoft *was* prosecuted for anticompetitive practices in this period. These protracted court battles along with new players and concomitant sea changes in the wider context in which all these actors are operating have obliged Microsoft by law and circumstance to change its approach to the internet, not only to keep in business but also to reposition the corporation as a global brand in light of these changes in computer-age zeitgeist.[2]

In computing terms, the 1990s are a long time ago, virtually prehistoric for generations weaned on broadband mobile multimedia devices. Nonetheless it bears repeating that the internet and the web do not date from the mid 2000s (when Facebook, Wikipedia, Amazon, YouTube, Skype inter alia took off in global terms). Nor are "social media" a recent invention. The initial design of the World Wide Web was premised on sociability from the outset, as I have argued in the previous chapter. Today's global brands are in this sense more recent colonizers of cyberspace as they expand out from the internet's heartland in technological and geopolitical terms, the United States. But neither are governments or multi-lateral institutions new arrivals to the "digital economy" arena that the internet enables. Having taken a backseat as a policy priority in the laissez-faire frenzy of the neoliberal 1980s, twenty-five years on and in the wake of the 2008 global financial crisis, state actors unilaterally and in unison have woken up to the regulatory challenges raised by the way citizens, at home and abroad, use the internet. The first instance involves domestic concerns about its effect on social cohesion (e.g., China, South Korea), for the health and safety of the nation's youth (e.g., the United Kingdom, United States), or challenges to the power executive by rebellious citizens' uses of the web (e.g., Egypt, Iran). The second instance relates to how the supraterritoriality of computer mediated interactions and transactions surpass incumbent national—legal and regulatory—jurisdictions, rendering longstanding intergovernmental treaties and covenants obsolete as they do so.

With another sort of sea change underway in terms of the geopolitics of internet design, access, and use (see Chapter 5), a reconstruction of the *US Department of Justice v. the Microsoft Corporation* trial is an invaluable way to put into historical perspective contemporary power struggles over and through the internet. This first case study is thereby a historical reconstruction, in itself a disputed narrative. It is also a complex scenario involving a myriad of technical standards, expertise and legalese, the secret lives of computer hackers and software visionaries, and the double standards of public-private partnerships to finance the world's communications alongside the intertwining of private lives on screen with vitriolic corporate wheeling and dealing and political lobbying behind the scenes. The backdrop is two-tiered, one the fast-changing consumerization of the web and the other a more glacier-like embedding of internet technologies as strategic and economic resources in the Global North and Global South. High finance and high politics, everyday life and popular culture are all imbricated in this story, which is one reason this account draws analogies between these power struggles and the TV science fiction series *Star Trek*, more specifically the *Borg* storyline.[3]

Making Sense of Hi-Tech Legalities through Popular Culture

In *Star Trek: The Next Generation*, and *Star Trek: Voyager*, the two sequels to the 1960s original *Star Trek* series in the 1980s and 1990s, one of the richest narrative clusters involves the relationship between the crew of the *Starship Enterprise* and an alien species known as the Borg. The Borg are *cyborgs*; cybernetic—machine and organic—organisms whose battle cry is, "We are the Borg, you will be assimilated. Resistance is futile." This species functions as a highly integrated and efficient hi-tech social whole with a division of labor represented as a sort of bee colony, sets and costumes reminiscent of Fritz Lang's silent movie classic, *Metropolis*, and many a reference to Cold War–inspired stereotypes of communism. The Borg are not individuals in the usual sense of the term. Each Borg—or drone—is but a part of the greater "collective" and only operational within it. They speak and act as one voice. While a Borg is no longer functional, indeed cannot survive, if disconnected from the collective, as a unit it must be retrieved. As a society, and an aggressively colonizing one at that, the Borg is dogmatic and totally single-minded in its mission to take over all other species and their accumulated knowledge in order to furnish their own inexorable march forward. This process and mission of *assimilation* is accomplished when Borg forcibly "interface" with another life form, a process that initiates a physical and psychic metamorphosis and integration into the collective's communications infrastructure, knowledge base, and consciousness. And what motivates the Borg to assimilate everyone and everything it meets? It's not just a lust for power but also the simple belief that they are by definition technologically and socially not only more efficient but *superior*. In the *Star Trek* series it is quite clear that it is the Borg who are the bad guys and the crew of the Enterprise who are the good guys, valiant defenders of freedom and individuality on behalf of the "United Federation of Planets."

Whether or not real life is more complex and less scripted than a television series, the aim here is not to draw a simplistic analogy between the Borg and Microsoft, or indeed between the Borg and other powerful global players. The analogy I want to draw is about the assimilationist mission and how it is resisted, mutated, and reiterated in this storyline. These nuances in and underlying ambivalence of successive generations of Borg storylines in *Star Trek*—this is not the place to go into detail about the show's narrative or production genealogy—serve as a useful metaphor for the Microsoft case and its relationship to later developments.[4] Nonetheless, the immediate parallels between the Borg and Microsoft in terms of attitude, behavior, and intent are quite striking.[5] For many different reasons, other software houses, US administrations, lobby groups, state legislatures, consumer groups, and media activists agree about one thing. Microsoft has been an unbearably aggressive and overbearing firm. For opponents, the corporation consciously exploited its market dominance as leverage in its exclusion of competitors in key developments in software encoded products and services. For others, the antitrust trial encapsulated a long-simmering divide between competing sociotechnological ideals, working cultures, and everyday communicative practices, all of which have come to reside in divergent notions of what constitutes the way forward for information and communication technologies in general, and the internet in particular.

So the Borg storyline, in its various permutations, is used here to highlight the subtle historical, technical, and social dimensions to this corporate courtroom saga. Even in *Star Trek* renditions, it serves as a metaphor for an intense and incomplete struggle between the ethos of different societies and how they go about achieving their respective technological and sociocultural goals; the Borg have become a symbol in popular culture for any juggernaut against whom "resistance is futile." The period in which the Microsoft trial reached its climax brought to light the underbelly of a burgeoning internet-society-politics nexus. The moot point for key players in this scenario, then and now, revolves around questions that are at once ethical, political economic, and technical; for whom, and by whom is the internet being developed and on what principles? Is it by way of openly shared or exclusive copyright-protected software? Are those making key decisions about how people access and use the internet doing so in transparent ways, and how can they be made more accountable? If the internet is that important, that indispensable for the good of society, then are its core functions and architecture being put in place and run on democratic principles such as the public interest? At the time, these larger questions murmured between the lines as technical community subcultures and pioneering generations of digital activists, along with a number of budding entrepreneurs (e.g., the founders of Google, Wikipedia) were preoccupied primarily with how copyright laws and licensing put restrictions on their ability to develop new, expand, or improve existing (proprietary) software applications.

This reconstruction is divided into four sections. In light of the previous chapters, the first fleshes out some historical points to put this case study in the context of significant shifts in ownership, control, and regulation of telecommunications operations, the infrastructures and privatization of which still constitute the internet's transmission backbone. The second section reconstructs the key moments in this antitrust trial and its spinoffs. It introduces the political and corporate protagonists along with those who would now be regarded as falling under the rubric of "civil society"; advocates and adepts of "free and open-source software," as user networks, prototypes of political movements and their flagship response to the corporate power of Microsoft inter alia, the Linux operating system. The third section considers the role and characteristics of a core element in these struggles, "software," computer programming and the codes that make the internet and the web happen, and accessible to laypersons. This section highlights software's double-edged, paradoxical nature. Precisely because it is infinitely flexible and malleable there is a tension between commercial and noncommercial, libertarian and statist understandings of what "free" and "open" mean in this domain. The fourth section puts this historical reconstruction into contemporary perspective, that of the recent "battle of the search engines" in a burgeoning web-embedded and mobile context of design, access, and use.[6]

FUTURES AND PASTS

Since the 1980s there have been major shifts in the political, economic, and regulatory landscapes governing information technologies, telecommunications, and the media, one which also heralded the arrival of Microsoft in the information technology (IT) sector. Simply put, these years saw the integration of "pre-internet" media (print, radio, public broadcasting) and "old" telecommunications sectors with information technology (see Drake 2001; Ligtenberg 1998).

The academic/defense locales of the early internet, and then its popularization through the World Wide Web crystallized over these two decades; the 1980s and 1990s respectively. The *socio*economic significance of the rapid uptake of the web was unevenly, grudgingly acknowledged in national, regional, and intergovernmental quarters. Most accounts date the *political* arrival of the internet/World Wide Web from the oft-cited position statement given by Al Gore, then vice-president, in 1994, a speech that presaged later iterations of how the US at least looks to position geopolitically its technological superiority and sense of entitlement to being a major broker in internet governance debates (Clinton 2010a, b). This announcement of a US government strategy for the *Global Information Structure—Global Information Society* (Gore 1994; Lüthje 1997) intersected with moves by intergovernmental organizations to institutionalize free-market principles through these "global" networks (OECD 1997; Grassmuck 2002: 196–197; European Commission 1997; World Bank 2002; Castells 1996; Schiller 1999).

What came first, the technoeconomic or ideational, are part of ongoing political and scholarly debates about the demise of the Bretton Woods international liberal economic order as it imploded in the 1970s, to be replaced by the monetarist doctrines of the Reagan (in the United States) and Thatcher (in the United Kingdom) era of neoliberal politics (Rupert 2000; Scholte 2000; Harvey 2005). "Natural monopolies" such as telecommunications, energy, water, and public transport systems were targeted one by one in this new mood wherein such services and infrastructures were no longer deemed the responsibility of elected governments to keep afloat (Trebing 1994; Bauer 1994; Schiller 1999; Foster and McChesney 2011). Instead these core activities were to become self-sufficient, for-profit enterprises with a "global" as opposed to "national" mandate; accountable to "stakeholders" and valued in share-market terms. Public telecommunications operators, flag-bearers for first colonial might and then national independence, were transformed into privatized corporations overnight as quasi nongovernmental organizational watchdogs (*quangos*) simply monitored competing service-providers.[7] With hindsight it would appear that all these changes were causally linked, down to the inevitability of technological development, "creative destruction" brought about by ongoing automation, digitalization, and then informatization processes all put down to computer programming. However, this sort of teleological reasoning overlooks the equally important power dynamics of policy agenda-setting, both national and multilateral, and the massaging of public imaginaries that go hand-in-hand with programs of socioeconomic engineering of any order. The history of the internet in particular did not emerge out of a political or sociocultural vacuum, nor can successive power convolutions be reduced to one causal factor alone.[8]

There are several aspects to these broad brush strokes that need more delineation. First, there are the aforementioned changes in structural power, organizationally (in labor and production relationships) and in public and private accountability. Second, there are specific technical developments—unexpected or designed—and research and development (R&D) investment strategies for *internet*-related technologies. Third comes the constitutive role of image-making and circulations of meanings about globalization, economic restructuring, liberalization of public sectors, and such like. Although ideational shifts are harder to pinpoint in historical analysis, with evidence partial and fickle at best, the power of advertising and marketing is undisputed in modern consumer societies. Even before "global branding" became common currency, image-making—and breaking—has been a powerful ally, change agent, and strategic tool in corporate restructuring, social engineering campaigns, and private lives. By the end of the 1990s and into the new millennium the gung-ho globalization mood was becoming more subdued in the wake of a series of globally felt stock-market crashes, the bursting of the Dotcom stock-market bubble at the turn of the century, and as antiglobalization protests on the ground grew in size and vehemence (Deibert 2000; Eschle and Maiguashca 2005; Van Aelst and Walgrave 2003). Widening poverty gaps within and between regions, along with an awareness of the need to close an emergent "digital divide" intersected with these ideational and organizational changes in the convergence of once separate IT, telecom, and media sectors (World Bank 2002; UN General Assembly 2000).

In the first instance, new management strategies led to the demise of the vertically integrated firm as a model for corporate success. Instead, companies had to be "lean and mean," "flat," or horizontally organized into clusters of smaller, affiliated or allied firms, all operating with a drastically reduced workforce thanks, again, to automation.[9] The 1990s then saw a wave of corporate-level buyouts, takeovers, and, in particular, strategic alliances in telecommunications equipment manufacturing, transmission, and services as well as the IT and traditional heavy manufacturing sectors. The irony is that despite the aforementioned downsizings and disinvestments, by the end of the twentieth century, the—still powerful— "dinosaurs" of yesteryear in telecommunications, IT, and media had regrouped to form even larger, albeit no longer vertically integrated, global corporations. The host of smaller IT-service and software development companies that sprang up in the wake of the internet boom were either swallowed up in the process, or came into their own in this time. As Microsoft's star was rising in this decade, critical observers were already noting how these newly converged and privatized multimedia sectors were dominated by an ever smaller number of huge conglomerates, predominately American (e.g., Time, Warner Brothers, and CNN) but not exclusively (e.g., Rupert Murdoch's News Corporation in the Asia-Pacific region, Bertelsmann in Germany, and Dassault and Lagardère in France). The policy of deregulation and liberalization of "natural monopolies" encapsulated in telecommunications legislation in both the United States and Europe has resulted in less—not more—competition (Ligtenberg 1998; Lüthje 1997; Curran et al. 2012). A handful of the once public telecommunications operators, now privatized mobile and landline service providers and networks, dominate the worldwide flow of telephony: Verizon, Deutsche Telekom, and Orange in particular. At the time of writing, attention has started to focus on the predominance of US corporations who own and control the lion's share of web-based goods and services: Google, Microsoft, Facebook, Yahoo!, Wikimedia, and Amazon.[10]

In the second instance, crucial moments in internet technology include the arrival of PCs and distributed server-based networks at the cost of the larger mainframe, along with consumer items such as laptops and all the rest, as digitally integrated artifacts and systems replaced analog ones. Increases in computing power and capacity went hand in hand with increasing miniaturization.[11] By the mid-1990s the Dotcom gold-rush was on, with the establishment of a powerful global financial market for technology stocks and shares, the NASDAQ, and the now familiar stories of boom-and-bust around companies such as *America Online* (AOL), *Napster*, and many others.[12] Despite the collapse of the Dotcom phenomenon by the turn of the century the user-based and relatively free-for-all internet of the 1980s and early 1990s had become the domain of big business and object of increasing regulatory interests from national and international bodies. Its history has been (re)written accordingly.

In all this computer-mediated communication flurry, where long-distance phone calls became affordable, computers talked to each other, people hung out or played in cyberspace, emails took over the working day, and hackers became part of the establishment, one thing did stay constant. By this I mean the interlacing of geostrategic interests on the part of political and military establishments vis-à-vis interesting or unexpected technological innovations and popular uptake, both the United States and China being cases in point here. As noted in the last chapter, the internet's infrastructure, transmission pathways, and server distribution follow the underwater and overhead lines of communication laid down by the British Empire and then post-World War US satellite communications, concentrating the aggregate traffic flows in and round hubs in the Global North and its cities—London and New York linking the Atlantic, and twentieth century Asian hubs such as Tokyo linking the Asian East with the American western Pacific seaboard.[13] As emailing and computerized mechanisms constitute more of the hi-tech and industrialized parts of the globe's communicative and economic apparatuses, scares such as the *Millennium Bug*, the "I Love You" virus at the start of this century and contemporary scares around the use of viruses and malware for cyberterrorism or state-sponsored forms of (counter)espionage such as *Stuxnet*, have become integral to increasingly polarized public and scholarly debates about the limits to either internet freedom (in terms of free enterprise) or governmental regulation (Deibert and Rohozinski 2010; Deibert 2008).

Issues around the changes in the local-global "circulation of meanings" (Franklin 2004: 19 passim; Kleinsteuber 1996; Mattelart 2007), some historically contingent and others marketed, are also germane to the way the legal intricacies of the Microsoft antitrust battle and those of the next generation are interlaced with changes in public imaginaries about ownership and control of media and communications in a postneoliberal era, one also marked by major geopolitical and technological shifts. What the FTC ruling in favor rather than against Google shows (Federal Trade Commission 2013), is that times—like the internet—have changed somewhat. The origins of these wider shifts can be tracked back to the 1990s, a decade that also saw expensive marketing campaigns launched by once national, now privatizing and globalizing, telecommunications operators in search of a new image, new clients, and "green fields."[14] All the usual techniques of advertising and marketing were put into play to sell communication as a global commodity. And as the internet continues to commercialize, IT developers and/ or service providers have all made use of these well-honed services (Blankesteijn 2002; van Amelrooy 2003; Stielstra 2002; Rushkoff 2001; Rogers 2000; Le Crosnier 2008). Microsoft was no exception. Neither was the web as banners and pop-up ads proliferated. Since then blogging, and its successors microblogging and social networking sites, have gone hand in hand with the development of increasingly powerful search engines, tracking, and user data-collating software. Advertising as the primary way to generate revenue in an internet galaxy that is ostensibly "free" and "open" ups the stakes as ordinary users and their (reconfigured) rights become the new currency of social status and commodity exchange. While in 2002 the eventual ruling against Microsoft appeared to make little impression on the corporation's de facto monopoly of the world's PC and related software markets, by the end of that decade several other species—equally powerful players—were looking to redesign the internet in their own image, as young, hip, and global.[15]

Consumer fashions and global marketing campaigns aside, one reason for this sense that the 1990s web is a thing of the past is the way its look and "feel" have been overtaken by those "Web 2.0" based principles. This term, designating not only a sense of historical break but also a shift in thinking in web design and, by implication, internet access and use, epitomizes a generalized sense in public and scholarly debates of profound rather than incremental change within the short history of the internet. As noted in the previous chapter, academic discourses of historical rupture alongside the role that the strategic maneuvers of corporate actors play in shaping global markets belie how the internet is made up of older and newer applications and operating layers. These continue to coexist, albeit not always harmoniously. Ordinary users are caught between ignorance of other options and the ease of what comes with the package. Moreover, the notion that all of the latest "buzzword-addicted start-ups" in web-based goods and services are Web 2.0 by definition is also arguable (O'Reilly 2012: 33; Mandiberg 2012). The term, Web 2.0, itself is self-consciously ephocal and fuzzy. As Tim O'Reilly, one participant-observer well positioned to comment on the before-and-after of the internet in Anno 2001, notes, the applications and business models that emerged in the ensuing decade have been increasingly based on the premise that the web itself is origin and destination for all new applications. With a space-age metaphor firmly in place he argues that:

> Like many important concepts, Web 2.0 doesn't have a hard boundary but rather a gravitational core. You can visualize Web 2.0 *as a set of principles* and practices that tie together a veritable solar system of sites that demonstrate some or all of these principles at a varying distance from the core. (O'Reilly 2012: 33, emphasis added)

The point of this reconstruction, however, is not to ascertain where Web 1.0 ends and Web 2.0 begins. It is a term that will be superceded in due course. Nonetheless as a discourse of evolution it has entered the public imaginary, relegating previous albeit still viable sets of "principles and practices" online to bygone days.[16]

THE MICROSOFT ANTITRUST TRIAL

Set up by Bill Gates, computer nerd extraordinaire and former employee of both IBM and Macintosh Apple, over twenty-five years ago in Redmond, outside of Seattle, Microsoft epitomized the global ICT corporation of the 1990s. Between 1993 and 1998, the peak years of not only the internet boom but also the public battles between Microsoft and its (former) allies and rivals, the company's share value rose by 560%. The company has been well known for its tightly organized, introverted, and highly motivated company culture and infamous for its aggressive sales and marketing techniques that are anchored in getting the most profit out of the propriety ownership principles of patents and intellectual property rights and closing access to its strategic codes. It did this as its operating system started to link computer users to the burgeoning World Wide Web, premised on being a relatively "open web" (O'Reilly 2012: 44–46; Benkler 2006: 434–436; Lessig 2006: 146–149). Its infamy is also partly down to all but total control of basic PC-software packages, respective operating systems (which are the "engine" of any computer), and related hardware through early alliances with companies such as Intel, the world's leader in computer chip manufacture. Gates, who started out as the Magician's Apprentice of Apple, the firm that launched the "click-here" icon on PC-desktops, is one of the world's richest men, a best-selling business guru and philanthropist. But this is not the first giant corporation to be prosecuted by the US Department of Justice (DOJ) under American antitrust regulations. Nor is it the only IT or telecommunications company to stand accused of behaving like a monopoly by "abusing its market dominance."[17] IBM, AT&T, and Intel were all in this position before Microsoft. IBM, erstwhile strategic ally and later coplaintiff, had its monopoly of computer chip manufacture (more than 85%) challenged in 1982 in a case that took fifteen years of litigation before it was effectively dropped. In the AT&T case, one of the world's largest telecommunications operators (Ma Bell) was split into eight smaller companies (the Baby Bells) in 1984, followed in 1995 by a further three-way, voluntary split of the holding company into three separate ventures. In the final instance, that of Intel, the judge ruled that the company had to share strategic information with competitors in order to temper its comparable dominance of microprocessors.

   In this latest case, four sets of actors lined up against Microsoft. The first was the DOJ, from officers serving under the Clinton and George W. Bush administrations respectively. Next was a range of smaller and larger software companies, former business allies or companies that had done deals with Microsoft, who attested to the corporation's highly aggressive way of doing business. The third set of actors overlaps with the latter group from the IT sector. This group will be treated separately for they had a major role in the development of key internet-based software and what came to be known as the "Browser Wars" between Microsoft's *Explorer* and Netscape's *Navigator*.[18] The fourth group was a loose conglomeration of free and open-source software developers and computer programmers (which include computer hackers). The popular success of the considerably cheaper Linux Operating System in the 1990s (see below), developed largely through the online information-sharing of computer programmers, brought the longstanding working practices of "amateurs" into the public gaze. This alternative ethos behind the development of Linux and its good repute among technicians contrasted sharply with a groundswell of dissatisfaction with Microsoft's Windows operating system; nonetheless, it looked good, but its functionality was to be called into question with every new release.

Microsoft versus the US Department of Justice

At the time, with its dominance of global consumer software for personal, institutional, and corporate computing—90%, 95%, and 80% respectively—Microsoft was operating de facto as a monopoly for some time. Bill Gates' unapologetic stance to this dominance was becoming problematic for US federal agencies as well as intergovernmental organizations such as the European Commission charged with monitoring and regulating the fast-changing telecommunications and internet sectors (Harmon 1998; *The Economist* 1998a, 1999, 2000; NRC Handelsblad 1997a, b; Volkskrant 2002a). Initial moves from the DOJ against the corporation began in the early 1990s, during Janet Reno's term as attorney general in the Clinton Administration. A key moment was in 1994 when Microsoft received an official reprimand for uncompetitive behavior. The company managed to avoid penalties through a settlement in 1994.[19] Nonetheless, a year later saw these two parties again locking horns as a result of Microsoft's reneging on this commitment by its insistence that Explorer was an in indispensable feature of the Windows operating system rather than a separate product. It is from 1995 onward, in the same year Gates announced that Microsoft would now be pooling its resources into internet R&D that formal complaints and evidence against the software house start to accumulate. For instance, Netscape faced litigation if Microsoft's terms and conditions were not complied with; America Online charged the company with having unreasonably restrictive licensing agreements that allowed only Microsoft products and services to be installed; and various consumer-interest groups claimed that Microsoft either overpriced Microsoft products and updates or undercut products of other companies with threats of legal action against those users deemed to be acting illegally.

Two parallel issues emerged as these concerns about the company's way of doing business were being aired. The first of these was the *technically unnecessary* functional incompatibility between Microsoft software products and those from other sources (both commercial and noncommercial). Symptoms of this sort of incompatibility range from the large number of unpredictable "bugs" that come with every new generation of off-the-shelf Microsoft software to incorrigible hardware conflicts between the latter and equipment from non-Microsoft affiliates. Another intractable issue is that of the unavailability of the all-important source-code for Windows to non-Microsoft entities. Without full access to this code, programmers can only develop compatible programs up to a certain point. Both these sides to the incompatibility conundrum are put down to the corporation's somewhat draconian responses (see above) to any signs of resistance to or noncooperation with the software house's rules of the game.[20]

While 1998 marked the official start of the antitrust trial between Microsoft and the US DOJ in the courtroom, a number of pertinent legal rulings and their respective appeals had already been lodged. In the wake of the outcry caused by the automatic linking of the standard Windows desktop to Microsoft's internet browser, Explorer, in 1995 (and then its Media Player), a judge ruled in late 1997 that the software house must allow other browsers—Netscape's Navigator namely—onto the Windows desktop without the fear of computer crashes or legal retaliation. Microsoft promptly appealed even as it agreed in the interim to delink Explorer from Windows and grant visible access to others (more about this shortly). As the annual profit margins of the company jumped by 30% in 1997, and the "new and improved" Windows 98 package came with both Explorer and Netscape's Navigator, the latter started to lose ground.[21] Microsoft went on to win the appeal against this enforced delinking as well as its five-year legal battle against Apple, a copyright case over who had exclusive rights to the "click-here" icon, a concept developed at Apple. The figures for the last quarter of 1998 saw a further increase of 72% in Microsoft's profit. One of the first significant decisions was in 1999. Despite a series of delays, ongoing appeals, and settlements, Judge Jackson ruled that Microsoft was in legal terms a monopoly, with punitive measures to be enforced. Meanwhile, the corporation proceeded to launch its new, improved (meaning with more automated default settings) operating system, Windows 2000, with a huge marketing campaign. In the same year, Judge Jackson announced that a two-way split of the corporation's business was on the table: an internet/operating systems division and a software division. In addition, he ruled that all company correspondence pertinent to ongoing litigation had to be made available. Microsoft immediately appealed.

In 2000, Bill Clinton's administration was replaced by that of George W. Bush, a well-known supporter of Microsoft's standpoint. In 2002, the appeal case was terminated and the *Final Judgment* released in November of that year. Thanks to the less hostile atmosphere on Capitol Hill and among Republican High Court judges, this judgment came down in favor of the corporation, endorsing its argument that it had a right to make as large a profit as it could and in as proactive a way as it deemed fit. Not only was the mooted divestiture off the agenda but, better still, the composition of a supervisory committee to monitor activities was handed over to the company to decide. Nonetheless, the court also ruled that the corporation did need to comply with demands to make its source-code available to other parties as well as to relax the more draconian elements of its licensing agreements and contractual relationships with clients. At the time, with the threat of antitrust litigation from the European Commission hanging over its head, it still looked as if the wind had been taken out of the corporation's sails. A number of out-of-court settlements with a range of litigating consumer groups ensued (NRC Handelsblad 2002; Volkskrant 2003a).

Microsoft versus the Rest (the "Federation")

The DOJ was not the first in the queue to line up against Microsoft in that a number of computer manufacturer and software companies were well underway with law suits in the 1990s; all grist to the DOJ's mill as the case hinged on numerous internal memos, email correspondence, and affidavits from disgruntled former business partners. After the Dotcom boom years, which saw a wave of buyouts and mergers in the IT and Telecom sectors, DOJ preparations offered both old friends and enemies an opportunity to settle scores. This decade heralded the intensity of attempts by parties, large and small, to stake a commercial claim in the growth in internet products and services across the Global North, and in concentrated parts of the Global South. Microsoft's working relationship with established IT—now ICT—giants along and the way national and regional R&D strategic planners viewed the same were very much in flux. Somewhat inchoate at the time, albeit more palpable in recent years, these private sector repositionings and shifts in governmental thinking about direct foreign investment and R&D funding presaged a key issue for the coming debate, the fate of the personal computer itself as web server-based computing started to gain ground. This seesaw relationship between the PC and PC-centered internet functionality—the foundation of Microsoft and its allies' dominance to date on the one hand and, on the other, web-based activities and internet-dependent functionalities that would make the PC and its related array of off-the-shelf proprietary software obsolete lie at the heart of the next generation of power struggles. More on this is below but, first, a brief look at who the opposition was in the 1990s.

A major reason for Microsoft's success in dominating the global PC market was its longstanding relationship with IBM and Intel, the world's largest PC and microprocessor manufacturers respectively. In this period Microsoft and one of its other arch rivals, Macintosh and its Apple Computers, was also a strategic ally in software development. It has become legendary as to how the tripartite working relationship between the first three, whereby all IBM computers are fitted with Intel processors and Microsoft software, effectively excluded Macintosh from a large slice of the global pie.[22] In this respect, Macintosh/Apple was one of the first and most high-profile victims of Microsoft's Borg-like assimilation strategy from the mid-nineties on. A second protagonist in this period was *America Online*. AOL was then the largest internet service provider (ISP) in the United States, with 35 million users—half of the total market at the time. In 2000, AOL was acquired by Time Warner, also a major player in the conglomeration of ICT, media, and telecommunications corporate ownership.[23] In the 1990s AOL and Microsoft had an agreement whereby AOL got to be on the Windows 95 desktop, and Microsoft's browser software, Explorer, was the default browser for AOL clients. In 1997, however, AOL accused Microsoft of overly aggressive negotiating tactics; Microsoft stipulated that AOL completely drop the main competing browser, Netscape, from its services. By 1998–1999 things had gone truly sour as Microsoft proceeded to offer "free" internet access directly through Windows (bypassing the need to use AOL at all) along with "free" instant messaging options. With 77% of its revenue coming from membership, both AOL and Netscape's viability were at stake. In 1999, AOL attempted to offset this by buying the failing Netscape (for US$10 billion) and signing a strategic alliance with *Sun Microsystems* (*Economist* 1999a; de Beer 1998). Other firms joined the fray by 1997, IBM, Novell, and Oracle to name three, with similar accusations. Together with Netscape and Sun Microsystems, these corporations combined to challenge both Microsoft's market dominance and its business tactics. Apple Computers (alongside the ongoing Apple v. Microsoft case mentioned above) added their voice, along with Compaq (another computer manufacturer), to the chorus, accusing the corporation of bullying; for example the refusal of access to crucial software codes that would facilitate said agreement, threatening to withdraw the Windows license agreement if the company's Explorer icon was not visible on the desktop provided by the manufacturer. Finally, consumer groups also started to take action against prohibitively expensive off-the-shelf Microsoft consumer software.

At this juncture a brief background note is warranted on the aforementioned antagonism between Sun Microsystems and Microsoft as it has a bearing on future generations of these power struggles. Alongside these major and smaller court cases, tensions between the two firms were growing over Javascript, a cornerstone computer language developed by Sun Microsystems that facilitates communications between various (generations of) computer codes lying behind the hyperlinking operations of day-to-day web-browsing.[24] Microsoft was pushing its version of Javascript, declaring it to be a superior product. Sun Microsystems not only disagreed but also pointed out that this rival version was designed in such a way as to hinder Sun's version from functioning on Windows. This would affect over 90% of the world's PCs and thereby be a serious problem for Sun. In 1998, Sun won its case when a Baltimore court ruled that Microsoft had to permit full operability on its then latest version of Windows, Windows 98.

This litigation overlaps two other, equally crucial developments in internet-based software technology; HTTP (*Hypertext Transfer Protocol*) and HTML (*Hypertext Mark-Up Language*).[25] Not only is software that enables *hyperlinking* the sine qua non of the web but it has become an ever-important feature of PC software packages, ever-important for desktop and online practices per se. It is important to bear in mind that, at the time, these core functionalities were based on *open-source* computer codes, available in the public domain—not protected under copyright law—and thereby accessible to anyone with the desire and ability to make use of them.[26] The tension between the aforementioned PC triumvirate (IBM-Intel-Microsoft) and developer-proprietors of these emergent internet—browser—technologies not yet under the aegis of the latter was to sharpen. Together with what are commonly called *web browsers* proper (Netscape and Explorer as cases in point), these three sets of codes—Javascript, HTTP, and HTML—are cornerstones of internet-based interactivity: hyperlinking, searching, tracking. Something much taken for granted a decade later but that at the time was exemplified by what came to be known as the *Browser Wars* between (Netscape's) Navigator and (Microsoft's) Explorer—the struggle for pole position, influence over, and by association proprietary control of not only the aesthetics but also onlineness as an everyday practice. The next generation, or Battle of the Search Engines, emerges about a decade later. But first we need to step back a moment in time to the 1990s.

The Browser Wars

In 1994, or thereabouts, approximately 90% of web-surfing was done from the PC desktop through Navigator, owned by Netscape. At the time only about 7% was done with Microsoft Explorer. Within four years, the market-share of Netscape had plummeted by 50% and was continuing to fall, with all the usual consequences, not least for the company's workforce (NRC Handelsblad 1997a; *The Guardian* 1999). It is in 1995, however, that the first signs of a direct face-off between these two, albeit under the watchful eye of the DOJ, started to crystallize in light of Bill Gates' much publicized announcement that Microsoft was shifting focus from PC software to internet R&D. The boom in internet use, web-surfing, could be harnessed by integrating the hyperlinking operations of an internet browser directly into the operating system. Rather than being a separate—gratis or bought—downloadable item users install later, the browser was to become an indispensable element to the design of the Windows operating system. Conversely the former could not function unless it is enabled to do so by the latter. This business decision is at once a software design imperative and a strategic move with huge consequences for others given the size and market reach of this corporation (Kehoe 1999; Foremski 1999; Benkler 2006: 434 passim; Grassmuck 2002: 197 passim).

After years of studied disinterest, Gates' pronouncement pushed internet-based software R&D onto center stage with 1200 software designers put to work. Explorer was offered "free" using the rhetoric of *freeware* or strongly recommended as an accompanying element to Windows 95. At the same time, Explorer was simply integrated into the latter's design features by way of the *user default* function. The argument here, according to Gates, was that Windows 95 could not function properly without either Explorer or its twinned email function, Microsoft Outlook. In other words, attempts to delink them would lead to a systems malfunction; a claim that was loudly contested, and apparently disproved in trials by many parties rejecting this on technical, ethical, or commercial grounds. It was in 1995 that Netscape took Microsoft to court for allegedly making threats along the above lines in a secret meeting of the same year, refusing to cooperate in divvying up the global (and ever-growing) browser market as a result. Amidst protests from within and beyond the industry, the *default* (automated) linking of Explorer with Windows saw the corporation's share-price soar as part of the wider

Dotcom boom, with service providers (such as AOL), university, governmental, and other public institutions welded to Microsoft products through exclusive licensing and terms of use (NRC Handelsblad 1999a). Through these exclusive agreements Microsoft seemed to have achieved its assimilationary aims.

How much things have, or have not changed since then are not explained by unfettered market forces alone, however. Other actors, including states, and consumer groups made up of technically savvy activists had a role to play. While each browser is developed as an integral part of its respective operating system, for example, Safari with Apple, Explorer with Microsoft, each manufacturer now has to make it functionally possible for others' browsers to work. The "default setting" needs to be changed by the user for sure but that it can be changed has been the result of these judicial outcomes, in the United States but also in the European Union. In this respect, the term Browser Wars means not much more than which product is the fastest, or can be branded the most successfully as a component of larger search engine functions. For example, a survey by New Relic (2012) revealed that in terms of popularity, Microsoft's Explorer has had to cede place to its major rivals within its own operating system on PCs and laptops; Internet Explorer has barely a third of user preferences. In the current boom in the mobile market of internet access, however, the roles are reversed: Apple predominates in much the same way as Microsoft once did, its devices and their Safari browser making up 61% and 87% in the PC and mobile interfaces respectively. To recall, Google's Chrome browser is making inroads into the desktops of both these corporations, used by 21% of Mac users and up to 41% of Microsoft ones (New Relic 2012). With Apple's Safari completely dominating the current mobile market in ways reminiscent of Microsoft's dominance of nonmobile "desktops" in the mid-1990s how to influence both perception and practice remains moot for corporate players and their critics. As one industry watcher notes rather ingenuously "at the end of the day it's the end user's experience that can make or break how your (application) is perceived" (New Relic 2012). Thirteen years after Netscape's demise Google's dominance in today's internet galaxy sees all other browsers, including Firefox, the open-source response to proprietary products, losing significant ground to Chrome; it was the global market leader in 2012 at 32.8%, which was a twofold increase from the previous year.[27]

The Linux Phenomenon: Open-Source Life Forms

In the meantime, a different sort of contender was emerging to challenge these corporate players; a trend that also caused concern at Microsoft headquarters by some accounts (van Jole 1998). The unexpected and widespread success of the Linux Operating System as not only viable but a cheap and, moreover, nonproprietary (free/open-source) alternative to Windows made explicit an often overlooked dimension to the Microsoft case: the competing ethoses around who owns, or has the right to control access to the deeper layers of the internet and web's functions. Linux represented an alternative vision and set of working practices of how the internet itself could be a medium and means for lateral, open-sourced sorts of knowledge development—R&D without a corporate logo (Benkler 2006) or state interference (Lessig 2006), or ligitation threats from copyright holders (Grassmuck 2002). As opposition to market-driven ideas about the globalization—an information society dyad started to crystallize, broaden, and mobilize toward the end of the 1990s, Linux—as an alternative product and way of life—came to the fore based on longstanding communities of practice allowing access to the underlying codes of a software program to facilitate cumulative and collaborative development for all comers. These communities are integral to the internet's developments, their mobilization thereby embedded in these corporate standoffs. Linux, as a high-profile exponent of the "free and open-source software" ethos from which it stems, was in this respect not a new phenomenon; hence, a brief overview of the Linux story is integral to this narrative.

Linux is the name given to an operating system developed in 1992 by Finnish informatics student, Linus Torvald. With an eye to improving his system, Torvald made use of internet newsgroups and other sorts of peer-to-peer networks (O'Neil 2009; Raymond 2001), some of which have come to dominate the global hit list of top websites and services such as Wikipedia, or on the wanted list of governmental authorities such as Wikileaks. What this amounted to was to make the codes underwriting this prototype completely available online and to ask the newsgroup community of computer programmers/hackers and other users for ideas and suggestions. The success of this approach and the Linux OS as such is now a well-known story of how the predominance of Microsoft Windows came to be technically and ethically questioned in the form of a serious not-for-profit alternative. At the turn of the millennium, public institutions such as universities and government departments (in parts of Germany for instance) were starting to move over to Linux, in part or completely (NRC Handelsblad 2002b; Grassmuck 2002: 9–12). During the height of the Microsoft antitrust trial, the Linux success story presented a real, as opposed to fictional, alternative to the technocorporate imperative taking hold in the 1990s generation of ICT. But it also stood for another set of online practices, software-hardware relationships, and communicative cultures of use.

The notion that the software programs that govern how various generations and standards in information and communication technologies can work together as an internet can emerge, indeed can be improved, in an atmosphere of collaboration and information sharing runs completely against the grain of how intellectual property rights are currently managed and institutionalized (Benkler 2006; May 2009; Lessig 2006). Important legal differences between software programs that can be accessed and changed by anyone, or that which falls under more open, flexible sorts of licensing than is normally the case aside, what is at stake is more than a legal-technical question: "it's not about the software but about what sort of society we want to live in" (Stallman in Grassmuck 2002: 29, my retranslation, see Cerf 2012). The popular success of Linux, particularly at this juncture, underscores the paradox-dilemmas lying at the heart of the Microsoft antitrust case. On the one hand we see the suspicion and discontent of Microsoft's longstanding and upcoming competitors at the corporation's whole project: working practices, marketing, and hard-ball negotiating style. On the other hand, we see a multivariate array of independent computer programmers and media activists who object in theory and principle to the corporatization of products and services.[28] At various points along this spectrum lie wannabe corporate magnates (the still-young founders of Yahoo, Google, Facebook, inter alia) and resolute activists allied to the other-globalization, World Social Forum, and media and social justice movements. All of the above made it their business to resist Microsoft's assimilatory mission. Somewhere in between, and often unwittingly, lie ordinary users, and by association nonusers (Wyatt et al. 2002).

What about these everyday users? Most people, the silent majority signaled by Lessig (2006), have little time or interest to delve into such intricacies. The technical and legal details are complex, debates arcane and expert-led. To all intents and purposes these corporate reshuffles, legislative maneuvers, and marketing rhetoric have little direct influence on internet users' daily habits. Most people in the workplace use the machines and software they are provided with, still predominately based on Microsoft software and its partners, Intel for instance. Dominance of the global PC market for this amount of time, as has been arguably the case with web-based goods and services that Google commands online (Federal Trade Commission 2013), means that interoperability, having things work together and so minimalizing incompatibility, is 9/10ths of the law. It takes time to switch systems, machines, and services, and people on the whole tend to stick with what they know. However, it is not until things go wrong—for example, the latest release of a new MS Operating System (from Windows 98 through to Vista through to Windows 8)—and reveal bugs, leaks, or simply rendering previous generations of installed programs or competing software no longer functional or awkward to reboot that some people may pause to think.

THE DOUBLE-LIFE OF SOFTWARE—FREEDOM FIGHTERS?

The two terms (free or open-source software) describe almost the same category of software, but they stand for views based on fundamentally different values. Open source is a development methodology; free software is a social movement. For the free software movement, free software is an ethical imperative, essential respect for the users' freedom. By contrast, the philosophy of open source considers issues in terms of how to make software "better"— in a practical sense only. It says that nonfree software is an inferior solution to the practical problem at hand. For the free software movement, however, *nonfree software is a social problem*, and the solution is to stop using it and move to free software. (Stallman 2012, emphasis added)

What exactly is "software" and how does it work? A basic definition of software will suffice here: "Software programs tell a machine what to do. The term contrasts with 'hardware,' which refers to the actual physical machines that make up a computer system. The hardware by itself is of little value without the instructions that tell it what to do" (*Barron's* 1995: 291). As Lawrence Lessig argues, computer codes are socially constructed in that code "is never found; it is only ever made, and only ever made by us" (2006: 6). This property means that code can be designed, and in turn can govern other designs in a variety of ways, to serve a variety of ends. And as "codes constitute cyberspace; spaces enable and disable individuals and groups" (2006: 88), they thereby matter. They matter because in formalized legal, de jure, and informal, de facto ways "code regulates, then at least in some critical contexts, the kind of code that regulates is critically important" (Lessig 2006: 139). Lessig considers that software and hardware together need to be seen as code because together with the hardware (the things we can touch and feel) software comprises the larger and smaller networks of "thinking machines" (Quintas 1996) that cohabit more and more of the world's waking and sleeping lives every day.

For most people this term commonly refers to consumer—off the shelf— products that are either already installed in PCs or offered as upgrades. Nowadays these products are being offered more and more online as services, relatively affordable or as "free" downloads. In this latter scenario, advertising is the key revenue as opposed to the sale of software packages in retail outlets. All computers and ICT systems are comprised of both software and hardware. Software is the computer—digital—code; built up over successive generations ("versions") and computer "languages," all requiring variable degrees of know-how and use specifications. Hardware, on the other hand, is all the "nuts and bolts" of the actual machinery: plastic, silicon, metal casings, and such like that make up the object itself. Hardware and software are mutually dependent; software cannot function without the physical machinery (even when this is microscopic or organic matter as in the latest microprocessors and "botware") and likewise for digitally based consumer electronics and, increasingly, large-scale apparatuses and machines such as mobile phones, washing machines, cars, airplanes, nuclear power stations, stereo systems, supermarket cashiers, banks, and so on. Drawing a line between the software and hardware components of today's electronic goods, entertainment units, and larger systems such as telecommunications or airport traffic control is difficult. The intimate and intricate working relationship between computer codes and machines as usually understood has become intrinsic to late-capitalist societies across the board, from telecommunications, household appliances through to transport systems, border controls, credit cards, and online banking, and the barcodes on supermarket items.[29]

The way in which the internet specifically operates notwithstanding, to have more complex machines and systems workable, computer codes need to be able to communicate according to the twin principles of *interoperability* and *compatibility*. These are at the very heart of the World Wide Web/internet concept as well as debates about "who controls the Internet." Technical standards— de jure and de facto—have been the traditional form of enabling compatibility and interoperability since the early days of telecommunications, a whole issue area and history in itself.[30] In short, software cannot be regarded simply as a politically or socioeconomically autonomous realm of knowledge production in that it lies at the heart of small, medium-sized, and large-scale "virtual machines" that now characterize and drive hi-tech industrialized societies—and conversely. While software, by definition, is malleable, adaptable, interchangeable, and thereby inherently fluid, new computer-based developments are based on an accumulation—layering—of old and later sets of code. In this way, software's intrinsically flexible—"soft"—nature transmutes into complex and opaquely rigid thinking-machineries. Larger, older, and more complex systems such as telecommunications (including the global internet infrastructure per se), transport systems and, increasingly, national defense infrastructures are particularly prone to rigidity in this sense—unintended system-crippling computer viruses, and deliberately deployed forms of "malware" of every ilk. Attention has now shifted to real and imagined forms of cyberterrorism, online security issues for electronic commerce, or concerns over "spyware" that trace and increasingly constitute web-based interactions. Whatever the scenario, these instances underscore this double life of software, that is, its plasticity, malleability, and accessibility, which coexists with the way in which it can become ossified over time into static, complex mazes of computer codes.

Another characteristic of this doubleness, in function and application (see Holmes 2007), is the socioeconomic motility of those working with or creating software; moving quite easily between the corporate private sector of proprietary R&D from the (once) underground, activist or "grassroots" habitats of amateur computer programming, ranging from the (usually male) at-home DIY enthusiast to computer hacker/gaming communities in various social and political guises. Everyday users can also be included under the amateur rubric. Without needing to be particularly au fait with computer programming or intending to bring public or private systems to their knees by sending out viruses, and within clear inbuilt design parameters (the user default and source code questions dealt with above as cases in point), anyone is effectively reprogramming their own virtual—thinking—machine when changing any aspect of the look, operations, and interaction between parts purchased. How many, and how far the ubiquitous user-default options go determines the height of the hurdle ordinary users may have to straddle. A feature of PC production and marketing, generic to Windows and nowadays to the notion of predictive texts in mobile telephony, is the way in which basic word-processing programs have become increasingly automated. They are more user-friendly, so the saying goes, but also take the very act of writing along a preordained set of criteria about how, and what textual production should be—let alone look like. Free/open-source software advocates and media activists recognize software's double life as integral to safeguarding certain notions about openness, laterality, and, by implication, democratic uses and applications of ICT. Computer programming is not, in this view, the sole preserve of IT experts, professionals or commercial interests by definition. As digitalization makes deeper inroads into everyday life, cultural reproduction, local and global politics, and economics, software has acquired strategic significance as a critical internet resource.

Attempts to either halt or insist upon the slippage between the terms "free" (see above) and "open-source" software is in this context an exemplary example (Greve 2002: 13; Grassmuck 2002: 19). Both commercial and not-for-profit interests, proprietary copyright-owners (individual, medium-sized, and corporate) and peer-to-peer communities lean on both the distinction and the ambiguity of the term "free." Companies offering so-called free services and products are not necessarily offering open-sourced ones. The next generation of browser wars—that of the search engines—in a Web 2.0 universe pivot on this ambiguity, one in which advertising revenue takes on a whole other dimension. The above slippage has taken on increasingly overt political connotations. The positions taken, business tactics, and public relations rhetoric of all the corporate players in the Microsoft antitrust case operate according to commercial understandings of the term "free."

This standpoint is far from being a case of wishful thinking or political idealism. As the Linux success-story and its integration into operating systems and web servers "at the expense of Microsoft systems" (Lessig 2006: 147), along with less socially acceptable spam and viruses show, free/open-source ways of working with software are not only pragmatic or a lifestyle choice. There is enough evidence that this approach works to pose a serious alternative to extant business models and assumptions about knowledge and creativity (Benkler 2006; Lessig 2006; Introna and Nissenbaum 2000). There lies the rub. While some may wish to relegate these sentiments and working practices to computer countercultures, youthful idealism, or malice in the case of malware and such like, they position themselves as the antithesis of proprietary cultures and business models with a long tradition of other ways of exchanging knowledge and economic value, providing philosophical and political traction (May 2009; Barbrook 2006; O'Neil 2009).

THE NEXT GENERATION: BATTLE OF THE SEARCH ENGINES

> Communication and telecommunications are not synonymous. . . . Many of the problems we face today arise from our desire to create a "society of convenience." (Friedman 2000 (1975): Preface, my translation)

To recapitulate, with fact imitating fiction, developments in internet browser technologies have seen a new arrival on the scene. What Species 8472 came to mean for the Borg in later *Star Trek* series, is what Google has come to mean for Microsoft.[31] Stronger still, search engines have taken on the role that the browser wars of the 1990s had in terms of battles for ownership and control of the web, de jure and de facto. To all intents and purposes, Microsoft won the browser wars by default; high court rulings were trumped by either the company ignoring fines and rulings or using appeals to protract final settlements. While the company has the financial resources to do this, there is more at stake here than share prices or shareholder expectations. An ethos, a way of working, design-ing, and using ICT in general, let alone the future of PC-to-internet functional-ity, continues to be played out for high stakes, from the intricacies of who calls the design and emplacement shots to high-level agenda-setting and consultative practices.[32]

Time now to return to the main protagonist in the 2012 FTC ruling that found Google not liable for prosecution for anticompetitive practices. Set up in 1998 by two Stanford grad students, the Google search engine is a quintessentially inter-net-based development. Unlike its predecessor and most popular search engine at the time, Yahoo!, the algorithm that governs Google's search techniques is based on sweeping the web for the "key words" entered, filtering the results in a partic-ular way, and ranking them for the user as "top hits," usually in multiples of ten. Instead of compiling a list of results that then have to be browsed, the index-based system employed by Yahoo! and indigenous to early-generation web-searches, Google does a certain amount of the legwork through this preselection. Seductive, hierarchical in terms of assigning status, and extremely effective, this fundamen-tally different design principle, grudgingly admired and rapidly deployed across the board, has been attributed to the company's commercial success. Other prod-ucts and services rapidly followed. Most preexisting search engines have fallen into relative disuse, dropping off the global statistics radar as the very meaning of searching the web by using software dedicated to this purpose came to be syn-onymous with the company brand. By 2004, Yahoo! was trailing behind in terms of user figures, share-value, and advertising revenue despite attempts to regain ground by acquiring Alta Vista in 2004, along with moves to cozy up to Google and then resist Microsoft's advances in 2008.[33]

It is the way in which Google incorporates principles of "preferred placement" (see Rogers 2000; Marres and Rogers 2005), exploits the laterality of hyperlinking (billions of websites) and then combines these with advertising revenue that marks it apart. The latter, built into the actual algorithm which, like Microsoft's source code, is a closely guarded secret, is also what has led to criticism and increased scrutiny by federal and intergovernmental regulators (Federal Trade Commission 2013). The principles have far-reaching implications in terms of linking up data-bases, data-mining techniques (national security and commercial agencies alike), and neurological dimensions (Bénilde 2007). Furthermore, this successful com-mercial and computing formula has generated a whole parallel universe in terms of the way in which the Google search "hits" become indispensable to the political economy of citation indexes, online public relations and marketing, knowledge production, and NGO advocacy activities (see Lazuly 2003; Franklin 2007c). In-ternet mapping techniques, policy networks in both online and on-the-ground domains, and visualizations are increasingly intertwined with Google-based modes of onlineness, circulation, and production. The upshot is that Google—Species 8472—has been able to resist assimilation, and has colonized according to its own modus operandi in turn. As Microsoft was in the 1990s, Google is to date a young, vibrant, and innovative company. However, unlike Microsoft, cur-rently repositioning itself as a guardian of online security and stability, Google has been successful in becoming a global champion of "internet freedom" and in one sense has been able to position itself as the Federation's saving force in the face of the Microsoft hegemony, the latter having become synonymous with old-school applications where the PC ruled and internet design, access, and use were a stationary affair. Google's different style and lobbying powers have not gone unnoticed, its spending on lobbying in Washington, DC, and other parts of the world (for example, its German-based think tanks and recently established Google University in Berlin) are two cases in point (Becker and Niggemeier 2012; Becker and Rosenbach 2012). Its well-honed ambitions to want to "googlelize everything" has also generated a burgeoning literature of Google watchers and critics, as did Microsoft in its day (Vaidhyanathan 2012).

Microsoft's attempts to join forces with Yahoo! in 2008 would have led to a global duopoly of search engines, their larger portals, and spinoff services. Antitrust regulators and parts of burgeoning media/ICT social justice networks (Volkskrant February 16, 2008: 7) see Google's predominance as worrying enough, let alone this sort of merger, instigated on Microsoft's part to offset the dominance of Google online. By the same token, Google's cries of victimization have been greeted skeptically by most pundits; its politicization of the issue is regarded as cynical given its own monopolistic status. Despite its recourse to tropes of openness, transparency, and online "chic," Google too is a corporate juggernaut albeit with a different modus operandi. Full access to the algorithm that governs Google Search is not available and, as this chapter noted at the outset, its ongoing refinements of preferred placement and generating advertising revenue through, and by guiding users to Google-embedded products and services have mobilized US and European antitrust watchdogs (Federal Trade Commission 2013; Arthur 2013). More recently, Google's power has taken on an overtly geopolitical dimension. For instance in 2010 its claim to "do no evil" saw it falling from public grace in the wake of it permitting the Chinese authorities to censor content, and potentially allowing the Chinese authorities to track down perceived political subversives in mainland China (Franklin 2010; Becker and Niggemeier 2012; Vaidhyanathan 2012: 115 passim).

Summing up, there are three broad technohistorical dimensions to the way these behind-the-screen struggles constitute and also frame debates about the way the internet is used, perceived, and experienced by ordinary people, corporate players, and regulators around the world. First, we have now seen twenty-five odd years of technoeconomic and organizational changes in the once-discrete telecommunications, information technology, and media sectors. Second, the internet saw a swift and unprecedented takeoff in the 1990s as World Wide Web technologies superseded those of its 1980s precursor and, later, Web 2.0 applications became dominant. And third, a plethora of plaintiffs turned to the law across legal jurisdictions (from the United States to the European Union). These legal battles pitted longstanding IT corporations against one another and newcomers at the height of the 1990s Dotcom boom, along with an array of individual software developers, hacker communities, and user groups.

CONCLUDING COMMENTS: BATTLE OF THE CLONES?

Technological innovation now requires major investment and has become
a collective, institutionalised process. The evolution of a technology is thus
a function of a complex set of technical, social, economic and political
factors . . . is socially structured and culturally patterned by various social
interests that lie outside the immediate context of technological innovation.
(Wajcman 1991:24–25)

Despite its global and universalizing ambitions and cosmopolitan outlook,
Google's search functions are not effective in connecting and unifying a
diverse world of web users. Instead, its carefully customized services and
search results reinforce the fragmentary state of knowledge that has marked
global consciousness for centuries. . . . Just as important, the Internet itself
does not simply or automatically universalize experience, knowledge, or
communication. Although it connects along certain axes, it severs along
others. (Vaidhyanathan 2012: 138, 139)

The deeper implications of exclusive and proprietary business strategies encoded in the latest software releases and persuasive power of global branding
campaigns (e.g., as was the case with Apple's successful marketing campaign in
which the iPod cornered the MP3 market at the end of the last decade), meta-
level regulatory debates in seemingly obscure UN bodies like the International
Telecommunications Union (ITU) or Internet Governance Forum (IGF), or
successive "culture wars" (Ross 1995 (1997); Everitt and Mills 2009) between,
for example, Microsoft or Apple afficiandos, pass over most people's heads.
Meanwhile, the nature of everyday computer/web use—habit and the high entry
threshold for most new products (hence the need for heavy marketing)–means
that the inexorable process of assimilation is well underway. As computers,
phones, and internet technologies become more integrated, more interoperable and so increasingly intertwined with people's working and everyday lives,
the tension between who does and who should run the internet becomes more
acute. As I have argued in the previous chapter, the ordinariness of the internet and its computer-mediated communications belies the extraordinary way
in which nation-based and supraterritorial vested interests can reach out of
people's computer screens to affect the way they contact friends and family
(e.g., Microsoft deciding to discontinue its still popular online texting service,
Microsoft Messenger, on buying out Skype), or write and submit an essay for
class (now submitted online and archived in various constellations of commercial cloud services such as Turnitin).

   Concerns about the degree and depth of both commercial and state-sanctioned
forms of internet-based surveillance and data-gathering of ordinary people's uses
and preferences when they are online have started to gain momentum, at least in
wider, as opposed to specialized, public arenas. This change of mood is providing longstanding mobilization around digital privacy and freedom of expression
online with some popular traction, as these legal and business complexities start

to unfold closer to home. As observers argued in the 1990s, the global economy is comprised of informational flows and digital modes of capitalist accumulation (Castells 1996; Hardt and Negri 2000; Schiller 1999) and this means that software is part of this emerging currency. As the Borg-like tendencies of Microsoft appeared to be tamed in the face of these prosecutions alongside the rise of equally single-minded and effective rivals such as Google or Facebook, their strategic power to decide how people think, remember, and make sense of the world is embedded in their command of the terrain, if not owning then at least controlling access to online services and transmission, that is, circulation, of "user-generated" content. In this respect, the Microsoft and Google cases, separately and together, are indicative of the technopolitical and ethical "mother ship" in which internet-dependent societies find themselves. As users and institutions continue to use and need to use Microsoft products and services along with Google ones by either force of habit, circumstance, attraction, or financial imperatives, past and pending litigations have made but a dent in their profit margins and respective market dominance. In this respect resistance appears to be futile indeed. The 2002 Final Judgment between the US DOJ and Microsoft and the 2007 settlement with the European Commission have done little to change the broader context in which Microsoft, let alone Google, are currently able to operate and prosper. The emerging standoff between internet-based services and personal computing products affects these two giants as both are contending with the challenges of new rivals, and court cases, in the mobile telephony and, by association, mobile web applications and operating systems.[34]

What is being decided in these courtroom struggles is the literal and figurative future of the internet itself. The arrival of Google is a timely reminder that this story is not just about one corporation striving to control the gates to this new kingdom. The deeper embedding of internet technologies as an operating principle in all aspects of life, work, and government in computer-dependent societies sees corporate and political powerbrokers colliding and colluding with one another. In between these two nodes of power and control are ordinary individuals, communities, and citizenries. Both corporate and state actors in these various power struggles regard access to this "silent majority" (Lessig op. cit.) of everyday users, and nonusers whether by choice or default, as their entitlement; they are courting, grooming, socializing, and institutionalizing their visions of a would-be "global civil society" of prosumer-netizens respectively.[35]

To sum up and move on to the next two chapters, the following themes emerge. First, back to Microsoft. With a case resting on the "right" to be as aggressively competitive as possible in a global-market economy, and to make as much use of intellectual (private) property rights legislation as far as it can go, this not-so-natural monopoly has not been divested, as with AT&T. It has not been brought to its knees, as with IBM, nor has it showed itself anywhere as willing to comply as Intel did in its turn. Even bearing in mind the realignment of anti-Microsoft lobbies in both the search engine and social networking realms that characterize the "internet galaxy" of today, Microsoft Windows and strategic partners (IBM and Intel) still run and control the majority of individual and institutional PCs and internet servers. The assimilation of the desktop with internet browser—by aggressive sales tactics, licensing, and stealth, for example, default settings that can "eliminate a nascent competitive threat" (Federal Trade Commission 2013) has not seen the demise of the competition. Neither has Google's rise spelled the end of Microsoft's monopoly of personal computing software. The strategy remains an assimilationist one even as the tactics have changed. Considering whether another internet, or web, is possible requires knowing about and considering what else has been, or still is possible. It means reversing the process: not a straightforward one as Jean-Luc Picard and, conversely, a later addition to another starship, the former Borg, Seven of Nine, discover in TV science fiction terms.[36]

A second theme is that of the political and social question of whether open, public-based, and noncommercial forms of R&D, technological rollout and public-private partnerships can be even countenanced in the ongoing focus on economic well-being defined by corporate profit-margins and share-market indexes, for example, Yahoo! stakeholders' annoyance at their CEOs' refusal to take Microsoft's final offer in 2008 (Volkskrant May 5, 2008: 1; Le Monde May 17, 2008: 12). This is as much a question of ethics—about norms and contestations—as it is about economic orthodoxy and political will. ICT corporations as/and conglomerations dominate in a universe populated by fewer and ever more consolidated corporate players. Ownership and control resides here while public bodies, be they governmental, intergovernmental, or multilateral institutions, behave more like hands-off middle management or watchdogs—all bark and little bite. On the other side is an array of groups who see diversity, transparency, socioeconomic inclusion, if not redistributive ICT configurations being squeezed out by these vested interests, the political laissez-faire in which they operate, and multilateral consultations that put the stress on a technical fix-it understanding of *ICT for Development*. It is a truism to note how internet technologies are well and truly integral to the daily life and economic rhythms of hi-tech societies. They are also being promulgated as the latest silver bullet for addressing global poverty, socioeconomic inequities, and democracy.

In light of recent developments in a Google-determined matrix of everyday usages, what can get overlooked is that free/open-source ways of working with computer codes have been around as long as the internet has been.[37] Somewhere along the line the not-for-profit version of the internet was folded into the for-profit ethos, another sort of collective. The overt struggles instigated by Microsoft, Google, inter alia to gain market share are thereby the tip of the iceberg of underwater overt and covert forms of resistance—online, on the ground, and in the interstices in between. Seemingly technically neutral in nature, computer codes are, as Lessig argues, "law" (Lessig 2006). This makes arcane and expertise-dependent convolutions around the technical standards, transmissions, and provision of crucial services comprising the internet also inherently political and with this sociocultural questions. As open-source software activists and social justice and human/communication rights activists argue, not always in unison as it happens, the free-market ethos of the contemporary corporate-industrial and political axis upon which recent and future developments in ICT currently turn is not adequate. So a third theme running through this story is how the Microsoft case is illustrative of competing policy and agenda-setting visions about the future information and communications landscape in local, global, and transnational terms. Governments, traditional UN-based institutions and emergent activist/policy networks also have a stake in the outcome of locally fought patent litigations. Overlapping the proprietary versus nonproprietary, public versus private, state-society dividing lines are different notions about what the internet is, let alone what it means from the point of view of the "prospects for a global civil society" (Vaidhyanathan 2012: 134). Bearing in mind that this goal is in itself a contentious one, based on assuming that culture can be rendered in the singular, with multilateral institutions such as the United Nations, the Organization for Economic Cooperation and Development (OECD), and World Bank framing development, growth, and progress around the internet in global terms, the issue is more about who pays; should internet access be premised on commercial interests or primarily state (national) self-interests? Should it be publicly or privately funded? Based on universal, multilaterally decided criteria or developed according to local-national needs? Are these decisions reducible to technical standards, ideas about political sovereignty vis-à-vis internationally negotiated agreements, or should the invisible hand of the "market," the pull of consumer "demand" ultimately decide?

Fourth is the interlocking between fact and (science) fiction, real life on the ground and real life online. The Borg analogy is instructive here; science fiction permits both reflexivity about the here and now but also about possible futures (Franklin 2011). The Borg and other life forms are not only embroiled in a deeper, existential struggle over the nature of community and coexistence but also have to reluctantly acknowledge that each other's survival as distinct societies are mutually dependent. It can be discomforting to acknowledge just how deep the "Microsoft Way" or the practice of "Googling it" has infiltrated daily life, let alone academe, and how limited the access still is to influencing the deeper codes of either. Both Microsoft and Google have assimilated billions of computers and shaped the daily habits of internet users. In liberal societies premised on individual autonomy, freedom of expression, and free choice, this state of affairs still barely raises a ripple in the cyber-waters of the twenty-first century. This paradox, irony perhaps, is the final underlying theme I would like to draw out at this point. Like the Borg, Microsoft—and nowadays Google—is highly regarded for its corporate work culture and effective way to get what it wants. The ability of the Borg to adapt to any new sort of attack, weapon, or species' self-defense mechanisms is what sets it apart in the Star Trek populace of alien species. Microsoft, at least by its own accounts, prides itself on similar qualities. Another feature both actors have in common is dogmatism. Adaptation is not a two-way street in an assimilatory frame of mind. Microsoft has been quick to identify potential threats, moving to acquire or defuse them accordingly.[38]

The Borg in the *Star Trek* series, and corporate forces in the recent past and soon future internet galaxy examined here, are exemplary for their combativeness and effectiveness in achieving their goals. From top-down to bottom-up, internet uses and architectures are dependent upon and infused with Microsoft integrated circuitry. The Googled operations of the next generation add another layer to this array. In short, at all points of the internet matrix we see corporate ownership and control predominating, ostensibly as competitors but also as shape-shifting strategic partners. In the meantime, the moral of this story is that "we" are already more or less assimilated. If the collective is indeed everywhere, then is resistance indeed futile?

Can the Subaltern Speak in Cyberspace? Homelessness and the Internet

INTRODUCTION

> Reality is reality no matter what form it takes. . . . [The] true way to know yourself is to live alone in a very sick house. (*BIGnews* Writers' Group member, New York, June 26, 2002)

> The Internet has been a blessing for homeless people to communicate for free with loved ones. (Michael Stoops, National Coalition for the Homeless, interview 2012)

> I want to give [homeless people] a voice. (Helmut R. Brox in Wirth 2012: 4)

This chapter shifts perspective and register for the topic in hand, homelessness and the internet. The idea that this is a connection that warrants further investigation has incited strong, at times negative, reactions if not disbelief during the initial fieldwork, and since. There are two sides to this mixed response. On the one side skeptics consider the internet to be completely *irrelevant* to homelessness issues (as one effect of losing your job, eviction, or forced displacement) because more immediate physical and emotional survival needs far outweigh what access to the internet could possibly offer; to suggest otherwise is technologically determinist or elitist thinking. On the other, critics contend that unemployed, destitute, or displaced people wherever they may be cannot possibly be *informed about* or *interested* in the internet for similar reasons. In short, computer-mediated communications are at the top end of a human being's "hierarchy of needs" (Maslow 1943) if they belong there at all.[1]

The immediate answer to these criticisms is that they are not entirely unfounded on both counts. First, poverty—of which homelessness, however defined, is one symptom—sees people in a crisis situation, a state of temporary if not chronic precarity that puts more immediate priorities like shelter, food, and water ahead of other concerns. Second, when in this predicament it is correct that many do not have the wherewithal to engage the latest in internet media and technologies meaningfully—for example, the requisite equipment, computer skills, or access credentials to even begin browsing the web let alone keep up email accounts, find more "friends," or set up and sustain a website or a blog. By the same token, rejection of the idea that it is worth exploring this relationship rests on three faulty assumptions: (1) that homelessness is primarily a personal rather than a political problem, (2) that any technology on its own is either a cause of, or solution to a particular constellation of problems, in this case homelessness, poverty, and other forms of social exclusion, and (3) that homeless people's communication needs, media literacy, or computer skills, and desire to keep informed and stay in touch are somehow "special" or radically different to those of the general populace.

The point is that many homeless people have been using the internet *despite* the exigencies of their situation, and have done so since the early days (Civille 1995; Davidson 2001; Wirth 2012). Moreover, nowadays, as is the case with the general populace, homeless internet users have been becoming increasingly "internet savvy" (Tim Harris interview 2012). Hence the underlying premise of this chapter is that homeless internet practitioners constitute a longstanding constituency in cyberspace albeit a diffuse, unevenly sustained, and geographically skewed one. Their online presence, whether it is through user generated or third party sorts of content production and corollary online traversals form an undervalued and relatively underresearched dimension to how the internet is also comprised of sedimentary layers of open access, low-cost, and low-tech applications, and gradations of itinerate usages if not disuse. As would be the case generally speaking, looking back over the last ten years at least we can see how all sorts of online spaces and networks created by and for homeless people have come and gone. As the clean, well-ordered, and automated platforms of the commercialized social media that have colonized the web of today are at the vanguard of this "tidying up" trend, more informal, spontaneous and nonprofessionalized inventions by people accessing the internet under difficult circumstances are swept into corners. That said, caches from bulletin boards, discussion forums, and websites set up for, or run by, homeless individuals are still accessible and leave their own digital footprints and content, sometimes abandoned in terms of defunct websites, blogs, or Facebook pages that are no longer maintained, but still there in their original formatting, 1990s-styled web designs, based in free web-hosting domains. Others have ceased altogether as domain name registrations are no longer renewed. Others have looked to provide specific information for homeless user needs (Brox in Wirth

2012: 4), and others have embraced the literary opportunities that blogging has offered to many others. While Web 1.0 interfaces still persist, the rise of social networking sites and then microblogging in the last seven to eight years has provided a fresh impetus to these earlier undertakings; presenting an updated layer of opportunities for homeless people to make contact or generate a room of their own online within these "walled garden" designs. What all these activities have in common is the foregrounding of homelessness as an unnecessary, cruel, and debilitating situation. Working to exit this situation, to generate more awareness and counter prejudice about being homeless is another line of continuity. In this respect online media for and by homeless writers and readers reflect preceding (multi)media projects.[2]

These organic, "tactical" usages (see Chapter 2) are now represented by the increasingly adept uses of the web by support and advocacy networks in this domain. They are developing their own set of counterstrategies to stake a claim for and on the internet in combating homelessness. In the same period, over the last decade at least, the web has become increasingly integral to how government services, including housing and other support services, community/alternative media, and campaigners work with, and on behalf of homeless people around the world. Again this uptake mirrors trends in society at large. After a shaky start in the late 1990s, often with limited resources and not without some misgivings about the implications that going digital has for work premised on face-to-face relationships (e.g., by diverting time and resources away from needing to respond to the physical and emotional needs of people in extremis) they too have been enrolling the internet and more recently social media applications more consciously for fundraising, advocacy, and mobilization at the local (shelters, inner-city streets), regional (policy and research), and global (networking and sharing information, publishing and distribution) levels.[3]

While the combined hardships of penury, physical deprivation, and social stigma delimit many homeless people's experience with the media—and now the web—their "digital imagination" (Latour 2007), content (user-generated and otherwise) and online traversals (Franklin 2004: 100–101, 204–206) are also part of the internet story to date, generating other sorts of cyberscapes in and out of transborder population flows as they intermesh with localized experiences of marginalization and exclusion. These experiences remain undervalued and underelucidated given the "huge amount of mythology out there" about homelessness itself, and homeless people as a stigmatized group, or as individuals (Tim Harris interview 2012). The variety of organizations and initiatives that form around combating homelessness as a pressing social problem and political issue on the one hand and, on the other, projects looking to empower homeless people themselves engage successive generations of internet media and communications in different ways. Some remain consciously "old media" by predilection but also because internet connections presuppose computers or mobile devices, accounts, software applications, skills, and access points. Dedicated—alternative and independent—media outlets for and by homeless people have been an established pre-internet and the digital age platform for such efforts of which street papers are the primary example. Closer examination of these experiences are pertinent to policy discourses (see Chapter 5) and business decisions (see Chapter 3) being made further afield, for example, seesawing debates over public internet access, the pros and cons of inner-city renewal for local populations and poorer neighborhoods, how to address structural poverty and the *digital divide* in the Global North as well as Global South through (digital) inclusion and (computer) literacy programs, and the geo- and personal politics of ICT manufacture and distribution where companies make use of cheap labor markets.[4]

In light of wider debates at the international and domestic level about the form and substance of said digital divide (UN 2000, OECD 2001, Dabu 2002, Dimaggio and Hargattai 2001, Warschauer 2002), and ways to counter it through a range of "digital inclusion" policies, e.g., media literacy and computer skills programs in local communities, technical support for cash-strapped organizations and foreign direct investment to provide computers in schools or IT "capacity building," this chapter takes as its starting point the observation that homelessness and the internet is a domain that bears closer attention. This case provides a way into examining the push and pull between those with resources and those without, between those who enjoy strategic control of the terrain in light of how those without these entitlements "make do" (Certeau 1984) in creative ways with what is available. The ambiguity entailed in positing that there is a positive, productive relationship between homelessness and the internet underscores how on the ground socioeconomic and cultural divides and perceptual "disconnects" in how the issues are framed and debated, are becoming overlaid with comparable ones online. For critical analysis the ethical and political economic ambiguities of defining and combating homelessness (more on definitions in due course) are intertwined with how homeless users take advantage of all available public media and internet access points for a range of needs and desires. These are not reducible to those media organizations, think tanks, or community-level support groups enrolling internet technologies in the ongoing work of combating homelessness.

To speak of there being a positive relationship between homelessness and the internet belies, however, a more fundamental disconnection in a world premised increasingly on private home and media ownership, access, and use, personalized access and user preferences when online, and global mobile phone and computer brands. Being (made) homeless delinks you in one fell swoop from all this. The majority of housed and employed people now take as a given having access to internet-based communication and information services; the boom in internet cafes for backpackers and low budget tourists around the world simply underscores this gap. If you have been homeless for a long time, having to sleep rough for instance or not able to use a computer or mobile phone for a while, you can become deskilled, lose confidence quite quickly given the fast-changing context in which media literacies and computer competencies currently evolve (Dimaggio and Hargattai 2001; Warschauer 2002; Allen 2009; Schneider 2012). As more social interactions and relationships shift online into the microblogosphere, through fixed and mobile computer-mediated networking and web-based news and entertainment in everyday life, those who are not "linked in" this way by force of circumstance (having and making an informed choice is one matter, not being able to exercise said choice is another) stand to be disadvantaged even further. Like it or not mobile phones and/or email addresses are increasingly indispensable for employment, social services, and social contact. Stronger still, once registered as homeless you are particularly vulnerable to the ways public and private agencies can harness the same technologies to track, monitor, and possibly discipline your behavior, production, and movements online and offline.

ORGANIZATION AND ARGUMENT

Bearing in mind the limits and pitfalls to researching underprivileged groups or vulnerable people as a socially responsible and ethical research practice (see Kerr 2003; Allen 2009; Butchinsky 2013) this chapter is organized around two ways of considering this interaction. It first considers street papers, or, in this case, writers and vendors and their support groups involved in generating dedicated media and forms of independent income in settings of production, distribution, and socioeconomic interactions. These are becoming increasingly defined by the need to move more consciously into online publication on the one hand and, on the other, digital forms of vending and distribution. In mainstream media sectors these shifts are a mixed blessing if not negative trend, auguring the death of print. How these shifts affect alternative and "minority" media such as street papers goes beyond the digitization of content, given the central role that face-to-face exchanges and conversations play in street paper vendor-reader relationships (Harris interview 2002, 2012; Stoops interview 2012).

The second axis is conceptual and perceptual, namely in terms of how homelessness on the ground in tandem with its online iterations relate to changing power hierarchies of ownership and control of public spaces and services in both domains and at their intersection. Indeed what now counts as a public access is at stake in both. This tension can be observed in the trend for local authorities to hand over the ownership and maintenance of civic spaces to private enterprise, railway stations for instance, or in the way that global social media brands delineate and circumscribe the way people congregate online and access their production and material as a default setting (see Chapter 3). In the United Kingdom at least Closed Circuit Television (CCTV) provides authorities and security firms with 24/7 surveillance facilities. Google Streetview and other sort of geo-information systems (now linked to mobile telephony and web access) plot and divulge public and private activities. These respatializing politics cover what are now familiar sites in towns and cities (parks, squares, shopping malls, and railway and subway stations) and in cyberspace (websites, discussion forums, and news and information services on the open web). This is where I look to draw some provisional parallels and make a careful analogy between homelessness and the internet in two directions. I first consider literature that has characterized the privatization of inner cities and urban spaces as a form of "disciplining urbanism"

(Meert and Stuyck 2008: 153; Minton 2006; Munger 2002; Sahlin 2008). This notion captures one dimension to the "grids of discipline" that thinkers such as Certeau and Foucault theorize in order to understand how incumbent powers contain and control vulnerable populations in ways that are both direct (antiloitering or panhandling laws for instance) and indirect (railway closures for security reasons at night time, funding cuts). Second, I draw this line to the politics of internet design as these power struggles gather pace under the aegis of the UN and other multilateral institutions, and make their presence felt at the front end and back end of people's computer screens—a pattern of public-private partnerships that both look to enclose and exploit (cyber)spaces and (city) places for vested interests.

While all city dwellers and internet users are exposed to these twinned processes, those who are particularly squeezed are thereby the less well off. Without the requisite material or symbolic resources, disadvantaged, minority, or peripheral populations online and on the ground are rendered bereft of the requisite purchasing or agenda-setting power that can make a difference in spaces that are increasingly marketized and monitored. That said, drawing these sorts of parallels is not to equate the hardships of being homeless to figuring out which smartphone or gadget to buy. Nor, on the other hand is it to imply that being evicted from your home is on a par with being locked out of your email account because of a default password reset. These very different scenarios of distress are being made comparable for the purposes of critical reflection, and reflexivity on the part of readers for whom a real life home and an online homebase are self explanatory. However, power struggles around ownership and control of the codes that govern the ways users interface with their personal devices (see Chapter 3) and those whose rights and obligations should be primary in online domains (Chapter 5) have a direct impact on ordinary access and uses of the internet along with its publicly accessible and pay-for-view goods and services. The squeeze on public spaces and affordable places in inner cities around the world to which disadvantaged and marginalized groups are particularly susceptible has its counterpart in the more arcane legal, technical, and policy-formative struggles around who should control the internet.

If these street-level forces of "disciplining urbanism" can be viewed within the same analytical frame as those programming and institutionalizing forces that look to control how the internet is run then what comes to light is that in all cases less well-endowed or articulate populations are particularly exposed. What also comes to light on closer inspection is how these populations manage to find room to move, to live, and interact with others in self-respecting ways online and on the ground against all odds. Dedicated media based on community media working practices (Howley 2005: 2) as part of support networks for homeless populations are having to deal with not only the challenges of digital modes of media reproduction but also do so within an "increasingly privatized global media environment" (Howley 2005: 7). These developments present analytical and ethical challenges to engaged researchers and funders. One reason is because of the way the stark realities of homelessness and its social stigma belies how here too there is a "complex and dynamic relationship between people, places, and communication technologies" (Howley 2005: 7).

The empirical focus in this case is on not only how advocacy and community support initiatives around helping homeless people out of their plight have perceived or made use of the internet in the last decade but also on how homeless people have been grasping the digital mettle of the age on their own terms; at the very least to alleviate the "cruellest part of homelessness . . . invisibility and [social] isolation" (Anitra Freeman interview 2002). In the former case I look at how a form of "old media," street papers, have been working to maintain their mission by keeping their ears and eyes close to the streets but also move with the digital times. How successful a balancing act this can be depends on time, place, and circumstance, which is why the focus here is the experience of New York City's second—and to date last—street paper, *BIGnews*. In the second instance, I look at an example of individual experience of homelessness and the internet in its current Web 2.0 iteration; the "digital natives" that recent studies focus on can and do experience homelessness. The focus here is on Nadia, who ran the "Once Homeless Girl" Blog, whose approach to and use of the latest social media reflects that of her generation. Both angles throw into relief longstanding disconnects as well as more recent openings as changes being rung in internet design, access, and usages present new challenges in projects dedicated to "providing a context for people to have relationships with each other [that] can be transformative" (Tim Harris interview 2012).

Methodological Note

The rest of this chapter develops findings from fieldwork carried out on the ground, mainly in New York as well as in Amsterdam between 2002 and 2004. This earlier period provides the historical framing for this discussion, fleshed out since then by periodic visits back to the New York base, and more recent interviews with former and new contacts since then. Retracing these steps and looking online for remnants of precursor initiatives to use the internet as an empowering tool or space for disadvantaged communities—usually done in the days before social networking and microblogs with free hosting services for developing a website or blog—is a form of cyberarchaeology; picking up online trails that have gone cold, retrieving old mailing lists entering the remains of defunct, text-based discussion forums and then piecing together these traces from an arguably "prehistoric" internet in light of recent shifts in how the internet looks and works. However, I would expect there to be similar issues for someone in the future looking back to these sorts of usages, now largely contained in Facebook pages, Twitter accounts, or blogs as these applications have been taken up by homeless individuals or enrolled for outreach and sales by support organizations and street papers. If "friend" and "like" counts matter for how successive digital generations see themselves, and are seen by others online, then at first sight the tendency for Facebook pages set up by homeless people to fall into disuse underscores how social isolation and media uses are in an ambivalent, indeterminate relationship. However, being homeless does not necessarily deny a person from developing a successful online profile (in terms of traffic, links, friends, followers) even if exceptional uses of the web by homeless "media celebrities" tend to overshadow everyday inventiveness and needs (Brox in Wirth 2012). By definition this is an account of episodic research that is inherently what George Marcus calls multisited research, based in an initially "single-sited" encounter around an issue that has global, and electronic dimensions (1995: 113–114). In lieu of presenting findings from a comprehensive, formalized survey of either websites or designated users (of web-based resources or other media relevant to this discussion), the account that follows extrapolates from this initial fieldwork in 2002.

The terrain here in temporal terms has changed considerably since I first started, as have the web-based idioms and internet technologies in play. As Marcus notes, multisited ethnographic research is distinct from both "self-defined" activism or disciplinarily circumscribed anthropological fieldwork (based on lengthy, full immersion in one fieldwork site) in that it is "quite specific and circumstantial to the conditions of doing multi-sited research itself. . . . [e.g.,] one finds oneself with all sorts of crosscutting and contradictory personal [and professional] commitments" (Marcus 1995: 113). Recognizing how data gathering and analysis in the case of participant-observation work, and more so in the case when observation morphs into fuller participation, the intertwining of researcher and researched, episodic, over the longer term or lifelong is an integral element to the knowledge produced. Conducting research on homelessness and the internet, in face to face or computer-mediated domains, underscores quite sharply that in "certain sites, one seems to be working with, and in others one seems to be working against, changing sets of subjects" (Marcus 1995: 113). As an impressionist rendition of these multisited fields and multiple levels of analysis and experience, this case study is not an exhaustive one. Nor does it intend to be.

Stipulations and Context

Before continuing with an investigation that gives rise to more political, philosophical, and methodological questions than this chapter can possibly answer, let me make the following stipulations and then some contextual points.

The first thing I want to say is that in Western societies being homeless, legally and figuratively, is more than sleeping on the street. "Rough sleepers" are only part of the visible (i.e., counted and monitored) and invisible (moving between friends and family without access to assistance) homeless. As homelessness becomes an endemic feature of hi-tech industrialized societies, city centers particularly, the second thing to say is that homelessness in all senses of the term has been on the rise across the developed world over the last twenty-five years—more on this in due course. Thirdly, as noted above, homeless people have been using internet media and communications (email, the web, the latest social media) from *public*, *low-cost*, and *donated* access points and equipment, mobile and fixed, since its earliest years, on their own accord. These spontaneous do-it-yourself instances emerge alongside a plethora of projects looking to provide and engage homeless people in all sorts of traditional and new media (TV, radio, print journalism, the spoken word, video, photography, creative writing) as a form of personal empowerment, computer skills/media literacy training, confidence building for generating more chances of employability, and political mobilization. Finally, a more complex point—precisely because the exigencies of being homeless restricts access to and use of these goods and services as they become institutionalized, commercialized, and privatized, vulnerable groups are particularly exposed to the knock-on effects of changes in the design, accessibility, and costs of internet use through changes in the technoeconomic and political power struggles around media ownership and control.

Now for some contextual delineations: Homeless people constitute one of the most disadvantaged groups in Western societies, their circumstances making them palpably "out of place" (Wright 1997) in physical as well as symbolic and civic terms. This *subaltern* position arises because of the way homelessness confines people within a physical, institutional, and emotional "space of difference" (Spivak 1985, in De Kock 1992: 45). Access to public amenities (e.g., public conveniences that now charge money for use in many cities), goods and services (bank accounts) that the majority take for granted are limited if not closed when homeless. Physical mobility and rights become restricted, physical and emotional well-being compromised, and rights to speak and be taken seriously severely curtailed; "We've edited ourselves silent" as one long-time advocate points out.[5] In societies where having a fixed address is a marker of effective citizenship as well as a prerequisite for gaining access to the gamut of public and private services, homelessness tends to be positioned in the media and public debates as exceptional, the personal misfortune of others.[6]

This visceral as well as figurative "space of difference" as many (once) homeless people will testify, includes becoming inarticulate, invisible to passersby or, when noticed, treated with suspicion or distaste. As noted above, those who are sleeping rough represent only the tip of the homeless iceberg in official statistics even as they have the highest profile in debates that pivot on stereotypes ("bag ladies," "bums," "hobos," or "vagrants"; crazy people, junkies, or petty criminals) and polarized positions about the cause and effect of poverty in general and homelessness in particular—more on these definitional politics in due course. While homelessness takes multiple forms, is measured and responded to in a variety of ways in different parts of the world in urban centers, there has also been a trend toward its criminalization, in US cities in particular through, for example, laws against begging ("panhandling"), spending time or gathering in public spaces ("loitering"), and sleeping outside (see NCH 2002, 2009; Meert and Stuyck 2008; Fooks and Pantazis 1999). Rough sleepers and those using shelters are also subject to overt forms of discrimination on a daily basis that include physical harassment, violent assault, and verbal abuse. In short, as homeless figures rise so does public intolerance and the increasing intrusiveness of regulations and preventative measures around the risks to "health and safety" or "security" homeless people are seen to bring with them. On the other hand how people end up without a home of their own, cope, and also find ways out of this situation continues to generate a rich and nuanced policy and critical research literature, within and across the various institutional, cultural, and social geographies in which homelessness and poverty are constructed and responses developed.[7]

Without suggesting that rough sleepers are able to counter those who regard their presence as undesirable with equal force (indeed how could they), the point here is to note that they persist nonetheless. By staking a claim, regularly and defiantly, these groups who are rendered "out of place" (Wright 1997) illustrate how tactically their resistance and persistence "also show the extent to which intelligence is inseparable from the everyday struggles and pleasures that it articulates" (Certeau in Highmore 2002: 70). Processes of privatization, gentrification, and commercialization have been putting increasing pressure on who has the right to move, stay put, or live in urban and also rural areas designated for renewal. Such strategies "by contrast, conceal beneath objective calculations their connection with the power that sustains them from within the stronghold of its own "proper" place or institution" (Certeau op. cit.). The movements of homeless people are particularly subjected to increasingly interventionist forms of monitoring and control that move individuals, groups, and shelters out of sight, away from city centers but not out of homelessness. In recent years, researchers in Europe have been debating these developments in terms of "revanchist" urban planning, whereby middle-classes are moving back into city centers after several generations of suburban living bringing with them priorities about public spaces (health and safety concerns such as noise levels, local facilities for double income families with young children, playgrounds, and so on) all of which demarcate various sorts of street-based groups as nondesirable. In both cases rent controlled, lower income areas and homeless groups in those neighborhoods undergoing forms of "renewal" suffer inordinately as a slew of developments that critics have termed a form of "disciplining urbanism" see certain groups gaining as less advantaged others become targets, for cleaning up or clearing out (Meert and Stuyck 2008, 154; Tosi 2007; Kerr 2003; Minton 2006). In recent years debates have focused on the underlying reasons for this intransigently upward curve in homeless statistics around the world, for example, rising property prices as inner-city areas gentrify and social housing decreases, increasing unemployment through job cuts as businesses restructure, soaring levels of personal debt in consumer societies, the effects of urbanization, war, and famine on internal and cross-border population displacements and migration flows. As such these are germane to not only the technoeconomic but also the "cultural conversations" that underpin the intensifying local and global "battle over the institutional ecology of the digital environment" (Benkler 2006: 277)—an environment that is now infused with online and offline lives and spatial practices that include flesh and blood human beings, including their social media profiles and avatars.[8]

Whether becoming homeless is down to individual misfortune and mismanagement, underlying structural socioeconomic inequalities, or systematic forms of injustice however, recent analyses confirm that business-driven urban development along with the 2008 global banking crisis exacerbate the situation. Here over-inflated housing markets and foreclosures have played no small role in increasing homelessness statistics (National Coalition for the Homeless, 2002, 2003, 2009; Minton 2006). That said, evidence of "new" forms and contexts of homelessness have been documented since the neoliberal turn of the 1980s, giving rise to a new underclass of "working poor" (Munger 2002; Kennett and Marsh 1999; Sassen 2002). In the first instance, ethnic minorities, families, women with children, and young people make up these statistics. In the second, the combined effects of inner-city gentrification and decline in publicly funded, affordable housing along with the consequences of personal debt have had a direct impact on the rise in personal bankruptcy, evictions, and repossessions that follow. In the third, shifting immigration policies and ensuing restrictions on asylum and residency provisions in the European Union, the United States, and Australia for instance have seen many who are facing deportation move onto the streets in recent years. These changes in the political economic context and local-global crossovers that now constitute homelessness fuel longstanding debates about the socioeconomic effects of free-market thinking (viz. *neoliberal globalization*) in macroeconomic and local governmental policymaking circles across the board (Munger 2002; Bingham, Green and White 1987; Glasser 1994; Meert et al. 2008; Wright 1997; Schiller 1999). In any case, defining, alleviating the effects of, and looking to prevent homelessness, as is the case with unemployment, poverty, and underdevelopment, are politicized and culturally embedded exercises. Like the internet, homelessness is a global issue.[9]

In this wider context, the entry point for this chapter and corollary dilemma-paradox from which any number of analytical and policy dilemmas arise is that the number of homeless people around the world has been increasing during the same period in which internet access and use has taken off globally, since the late 1980s and particularly since the 1990s. These trends are interwoven with projects, a decade later on, that have been linking increased internet access to poverty reduction and international development under the aegis of the United Nations' *Millennium Development Goals, World Summits on the Information Society* (WSIS) and Internet Governance Forum (IGF) (UN 2000; Jørgensen 2006; see Chapter 5). On the other hand axiomatic shifts in the global geography of internet access and usages among the rising middle classes and younger populations of the so-called BRIC countries (Brazil, Russia, India, and China) are currently changing the Anglo-Euro-American domination of the *ethno-cyberscapes* (see Chapter 2) of internet design, access, and use to date; Asia (e.g., China) along with parts of sub-Saharan Africa (e.g., Kenya, Ghana), the Middle East and North Africa (e.g., Egypt, Tunisia) have seen the fastest-growing group of new, predominately young internet users (Barkai 2012; Mendel et al. 2012: 12–13). Mobile telephony itself along with web access and applications once reserved for at-home, fixed access are gathering momentum in this regard and preoccupying theory and research accordingly. Those who are digitally disadvantaged and/or homeless in the internet's heartlands tend to fall between the cracks.

HOMELESSNESS SUPPORT NETWORKS AND THE WEB

> There are lots of homeless on the Internet—go look at the public libraries.
> (*BIGnews* Writers' Group, June 26, 2002)

It is an everyday truism that first impressions matter. For those who are homeless over any length of time, keeping up appearances becomes a daily struggle, personal hygiene, dress standards, and self-confidence start to diverge markedly from the wider populace. Making contact first by email for job searches or accommodation is in that respect a relief and an opportunity. If we were to translate these contingencies into a cyberspatial setting—namely website management, registration fees, and the labor-intensive activities of updating content, outward and internal linking, and nowadays social media services that in turn required maintenance—some comparable "conjunctures and disjunctures" emerge. First, for organizations dedicated to supporting people in need on the ground, work that is based on face to face relationships, running a website, or nowadays the indispensable Facebook page (Tim Harris interview 2012) remains an ambivalent priority. This is the case not only in political terms, given the nature of the work, but also because funds and person-power are not regularly available to set up and maintain websites let alone Facebook pages or Twitter feeds (Stoops interview 2002, 2012).

Nonetheless, over the last decade, having an online presence has become a must for any organization working with and for homeless communities. Once considered a luxury, in the second decade of the internet's social media incarnation, being accessible and visible online has become a necessity. Nonprofits in the United States and variously funded charities elsewhere, in the United Kingdom and the European Union at large have been devoting time and resources into upgrading and (re)designing their online offerings of late. The audiences for whom these websites, Facebook pages, and Twitter feeds are intended differ however. While supporting and informing homeless constituencies (e.g., families, domestic violence victims forced to flee their homes, rough sleepers) is the backbone of these organizations' work, their websites and social media outlets are primarily aimed at raising public awareness, or engaging funders, informing and supporting social workers, and educating policymakers (Harris interview 2002, 2012; FEANTSA 2012a). This target audience, for the most part not those who are homeless themselves, is an increasingly important part of these organizations' work. As is the case with international NGOs such as Greenpeace or Amnesty International, having a substantive and dynamic web presence and incorporation of internet technologies for fundraising and campaigning alone have become an integral dimension to the work. For homeless organizations in the United States at least, ten years ago the web was still a new space to consider, web-designing skills were for technical experts, and the point of being online was less self-explanatory. Partly through the internet's normalization and partly due to changing expectations that the web is the place to find information about anything these days, homelessness support networks have become increasingly cognizant of how the internet can serve their needs in terms of funding and awareness. This observation requires a fuller historical and web-based analysis that is beyond the scope of this discussion. That said, based on my own observations the last ten years have seen a clear growth in the depth and breadth of basic information, research, and outreach via websites—and, more recently, via social media.

These resources, however, are not always available in equal measure in any case for any NGO, charity, or grassroots organization with web-presence ambitions; the means often lag well behind the ends. These differences, in commitment and resources, are quite palpable in terms of website design, currency, and updating of material, and in the extent to which the latest social media tags (e.g., Twitter, Tumblr, Facebook inter alia) are integrated into the website or actively used. More to the point, in many cases the face-to-face interactions and direct forms of support to people sleeping rough and needing food or shelter outweigh the commitment needed to set up and sustain a virtual presence for the purposes of informing others about homelessness. Ten years ago there was a nascent awareness of the positive applications and wider implications of the internet for work around homelessness. For one, and this is a basic that still holds today, for those without a conventional address or telephone, public internet access points are invaluable. While internet cafes are a common sight in poorer neighborhoods, a first stop for backpacking populations in major cities, free access to the web provides openings and access to information, family, news, and entertainment. These access points, largely provided in public libraries, do not come without restrictions for those who are sleeping rough or in shelters. The local knowledge of which libraries are most congenial, how long access is allowed (e.g., a half hour, more or less), and identification criteria (such as having a library membership, again predicated on having a fixed address) includes how to get between access points, by bus or on foot, to cobble together enough sessions to write an article, send emails, run a website or social network presence. Libraries have become de facto drop-in centers for the many people who cannot afford (or do not have) a computer and internet connection, which is one reason why library facilities and librarians have been at the forefront of conserving public access to the internet in this regard (Kahin and Keller 1996; Winkelstein and Cortez 2010).[10]

With support organizations and advocacy groups around homelessness increasing the time and effort they put into maintaining various sorts of online profiles, from simple lo-tech websites, to more up-market informational and resource-based formats, or mixed formats incorporating live Twitter feeds, blogs, and everything else in varying degrees of up-to-dateness and activity, how websites in this genre provide the sort of information that help homeless people help themselves, directly or indirectly, remains a moot point. A longstanding form of self-help, advocacy, and alternative media has been provided by street papers (otherwise known as homeless newspapers or magazines), a common feature on the streets of the world's cities as they are sold in various formats and prices by vendors who themselves have been, or are homeless. As traditional media confront the challenges of online publishing and user-generated content that dispenses with the traditional gatekeeping and professional journalism of print media, so do street papers. If the disconnect between those who have a

home and those who do not correlates in any way to those who have access to the
internet and those who do not then this larger digitalization trend in the media
at large has repercussions for the working premise of the street papers. These
include individual, often small-scale and lo-tech, print publications and larger
well-known brands such as *The Big Issue* in the United Kingdom (Swithinbank
2001) and around the world, or established community stalwarts such as *Real
Change* in Seattle (see below), *Streetwise* in Chicago (Green 1998), *Street Feat* in
Halifax, Canada (Howley 2005), or *Z!* magazine in Amsterdam, the Netherlands
(Torck 2001).

STREET PAPERS: ON THE STREETS AND ONLINE

> Because of its very concreteness, people tend to confront technology as an
> irreducible brute fact, a given, a first cause, rather than as hardened his-
> tory, frozen fragments of human and social endeavour. (Noble quoted in
> Wajcman 1991: 23)

> [A] life that is closed upon itself needs doors and windows: authori-
> ties that can be heard, points of reference that allow a sociocultural
> "exchange." Some credible signs are needed because they are also an *outlet*
> of experience; that is the condition of its possibility. (Certeau, 1997b: 12)

All street papers are based on the premise of helping homeless folk help themselves, mainly as vendors and variously through contributing copy or input into
editorial decisions.[11] These publications are, by definition, locally embedded and
usually city based so their relationship with each other beyond the immediate
urban environment where their respective constituency (as vendors, potential
writers, subjects) is located is not a given; networking occurs within countries
and across spaces and often between different legal systems, for instance between
federal political systems (e.g., the United States or Germany) or regions such as
the European Union (with support and financing for collaboration and comparative research based in Brussels). Financial limitations, small and volunteer based
workforces, and the particularities of the main constituency as both object of attention and means of distribution means that street papers and community, on the
ground support organizations (e.g., drop-in centers) are interconnected, sharing
staff and buildings. Many rely on a transient, volunteer-based workforce of writers
and editors who can include professionally trained journalists, students (on in-
ternships or research projects), and community activists. Looking at street papers
as a particular media genre, whether defined as community media (Howley 2005)
or social entrepreneurship (Swithinbank 2001), they are made up of publications
with production values, journalistic experience, and political views that range
from the do-it-yourself forms of underground media and creative writing to professional nonprofit and for-profit publications based on high production values
and professional journalism.

If all street papers are based on the premise that they can provide a legitimate form of income for homeless vendors, not all of them are premised on content being primarily the production of homeless writers. However, there is an implicit normative commitment to street papers being about providing (creative) writing outlets and opportunities for their respective constituencies: to generate spaces for people to express themselves and to find a voice (of their own) to speak with through writing. As the North American Street Newspapers Association (NASNA) puts it, most "street newspapers also provide homeless and/ or those living on the margins of society the opportunities for expression by publishing their articles, letters, and artwork. These publications build a bridge between the very poor and the wider public by helping people to understand the issues and the personal stories of those on the lowest rung of the economic ladder" (NASNA 2013). Traditional creative writing techniques have been integral to how street papers, singly and as national or regional associations, see their work. Writing as a form of empowerment is a core principle in street papers; social media in another sense of the term means that the open web, its successive offerings in online formats and spaces, lends itself readily, at least in theory, to this undertaking.

These sorts of publications are extremely varied in terms of where they lay their emphasis; whether creating employment through vending and distribution or focusing on providing journalistic or creative writing outlets, those (once) homeless writers of bestselling books become in this respect the benchmark (Stringer 1998). They tend to fall into two broad genres: creative writing and reporting or news and information with some creative writing. For instance, one of the longest running papers in the United States, *Real Change: Seattle's Homeless Newspaper* (http://www.realchangenews.org) provides a mixture of news, views, creative writing features, and political advocacy. In the Netherlands, the Amsterdam-based *Z! Magazine* combines reports and news items by professional writers with the work of homeless poets, columnists, and illustrators. In Berlin two street papers, *Motz* and the *Strassenfeger*, provide news and commentary by staff writers and are predominately print-runs. Other, smaller papers are not much more than pamphlet length, based on stories, poems, and personal testimonies of their constituency. Most publications are linked to drop-in centers and other sorts of self-help or support initiatives on the ground that provide support for city residents struggling to make ends meet, find a place to sleep for the night or enough to eat, or deal with rent and debt-related crises. Amongst this variety of editorial policies around variable content and production values, intertwined with differing business models, street papers look to sustain themselves past the initial burst of enthusiasm, volunteer-based human resources, and the literary ambition of editors or contributing writers. There needs to be content that people want to read, publications that can sell for more than reasons of charity.[12]

While nonprofit versus for-profit business models are a major distinction in global terms, splicing through, yet also underscoring, this distinction is another one; those publications focusing on culture and art adopt a magazine format and content on the one hand and, on the other, those looking to provide a more journalistic-oriented form of news coverage and features. The most successful publication based on the for-profit business model, commercially and in terms of its relatively high public profile is the United Kingdom-based *The Big Issue*. While its ethos is firmly based in providing alternative forms of employment and thereby income to its teams of homeless vendors, *The Big Issue*'s content and format follows the formula of inner-city weeklies in the mainstream media such as London's *Time Out*; it includes music, culture, celebrities, and entertainment news with a selection of homeless columnists, poets, and vignettes. Based in Glasgow, Scotland, but prominent in London and now a brand name for other street papers around the world (from Australia to sub-Saharan Africa) *The Big Issue* has been a formative presence in the establishment and growth of a global street newspapers movement. This twenty-five-year-old street paper (in 2012 *The Big Issue* celebrated its jubilee) is based on a for-profit business model, publishing news and entertainment content written by professional staff and sold by homeless vendors. Currently it hosts and runs the online web portal for the *International Network of Street Newspapers* (INSP) and arguably dominates the online and offline public face of street papers for and by homeless populations around the world.

This approach and format to raising awareness about homelessness that distinguishes between production and content of these media and the constituency whose needs it aims to serve is not without its critics (Torck 2001; Kerr 2003; Wright 1997). But that is a political and philosophical debate that goes beyond this discussion. Suffice it to say that it is distinct from the other nonprofit and self-consciously advocacy-based content model that characterizes US street newspapers on the whole (Stoops interview 2002, 2012). The aforementioned advocacy umbrella network, the National Association of North American Street Newspapers (NASNA), which works closely with the National Coalition for the Homeless (NCH) based on Washington, DC, generally adheres to making explicit in both content and ways of working that "the problem of homelessness, like all social problems exists in a stream of conflicting representations, it is not possible to change social reality without challenging its simplifying overlaid images" (Rosler, quoted in Hislop 1998). In both scenarios, there is "a reason our vendors aren't selling apples or t-shirts or telephone plans, all of which could, perhaps, be more lucrative in a world where reading is increasingly out of fashion," (Lisa Maclean cited in Suri 2008). Whatever their political and editorial differences, another objective of all street papers is to provide "a very immediate response to a human need; both a dignified employment opportunity and a way to integrate back in society" (Young, INSP cited in Suri 2008; Tim Harris interview 2002, 2012; Wirth 2012). Given this undertaking there is an ongoing tension between what a street paper can offer given huge differentials in skills and resources to produce a professional level journalistic or literary publication, on the one hand and, on the other, what it should offer if homeless writers, vendors, and populations at large are considered their primary constituency. Here there is a longstanding political and normative distinction between street papers that aim to produce content by and for homeless writers and readerships, with the general public supporting this by buying the papers, and those that aim to be a legitimate publication that can stand its ground in a highly competitive world of print and online news and entertainment media.

However, this begs the question of third line of division, one that is pressing in on street papers as primarily print media and their sales as necessarily face to face (Tim Harris interview 2012) in the face of the digitalization of media production, distribution, and consumption; the 2012 demise of the print edition of *Newsweek* is a case in point. In the same month, *The Big Issue North* (the Scottish-based affiliate of *The Big Issue* in the United Kingdom) announced its first fully digital edition. Not only are mainstream print media having to restructure their production and circulation models, along with how they attract and keep readerships in open access digital rather than subscription-based domains, but so too are street papers. The difference is that the latter are premised on a particular sort of vendor relationship that is an ethical and an economic one; going digital in content terms has implications for how vendors can sell; visibility on the ground looks to be replaced by digital payment systems that delink vendor, paper, and buying customer from each other. The paradox is that while street paper editorial desks have been developing websites, and increasingly using social media such as Facebook (mostly) and Twitter to good effect and in more concerted, and self-aware ways than they were being greeted a decade ago, the shift to digital formats is undermining this fundamental relationship, and with that the core mission of street papers to "offer a positive experience of self-help that breaks through the isolation that many homeless people experience. They offer the public a means to reach out with their dollar to help a homeless person directly and, over time, form a caring relationship" (NASNA 2013).

On the Streets in New York: The Case of *BIGnews*

In the past twelve years (1999–2010), the National Coalition for the Homeless (NCH) has documented one thousand, one hundred eighty-four acts of violence against homeless individuals by housed perpetrators. These crimes are believed to be motivated by the perpetrators' bias against homeless individuals or their ability to target homeless people with relative ease. The documented violence includes everything from murder to beatings, rapes, and setting people on fire. (National Coalition for the Homeless, 2012: 9)

At the time I bought my first issue of *BIGnews* in the summer of 2002 and then took part in the weekly writers' group, this publication at the time was being purchased for 10 cents by vendors and sold for a nominal $1. As with all the publications based on this principle, the goal, according to its (now offline) 2002 webpage entry, was to make "selling a valuable employment opportunity."[13] This model is not without its critics, for example, it provides only sparse earnings for publications no one reads or takes seriously, changes little in structural terms, and fails to deliver convincingly on various claims to be empowering homeless writers (see

Torck 2001; Wright 1997: 323–4). However, many vendors I spoke to at the time attested to the power of being able to earn some money without having to beg. As noted above, others earned some income by copy-typing the work of other writers for uploading and layout.[14]

In the late 1990s and early 2000s, New York City, one of the "meanest" places to be if homeless or on the streets (NCH 2003), officially had two street news-papers in circulation. The first (and for its editor, John Indio Washington, the only New York city street newspaper) was *Streetnews,* which began in late 1980s. As a for-profit newspaper with homeless people and related issues as its main focus, *Streetnews* (*The Big Issue* in the UK notwithstanding), was the exception in an area of nonprofit grassroots journalism and social justice activism. *Streetnews* officially folded in 2007 though it had not really been viable for some time before then. A passionate advocate of the for-profit model and outgoing editor of this, the "oldest street newspaper on the planet" (Indio Washington, NASNA Annual Conference, Boston 2002), Indio is an iconic figure in the history of the US street newspapers movement and seen, along with people like Tim Harris (founder of *Spare Change* in Boston, and *Real Change* in Seattle) as one of the "wise men" of this sort of grassroots advocacy (Michael Stoops interview 2002; Knipfel 2000 Duffy 2000; Mickey 2006).

The second, *BIGnews,* and its sister magazine, *Upward,* began in the late 1990s. Like most other publications of this nature, it operated under an um-brella social services nonprofit organization and aimed to create a space for "possessors of unique ideas that deserve to be voiced."[15] Based in midtown Manhattan, in the neighborhood around Grand Central Station, *BIGnews* and *Upward* were published monthly under the auspices of the Grand Central Neigh-borhood Social Services Corporation and its outreach arm, the Mainchance Drop-In Center, originally operating out of a church before moving to East 32nd Street. *Upward,* distributed to New York City shelters and social services centers consisted of articles, news stories, and features written for the most part by (formerly) homeless people. Changes in bylaws affecting roofless read-erships, local politics, and accounts of violence against homeless people were the main fare; it was a publication by, for, and about New York's populations for the most part. *Upward* was an insert to *BIGnews.* It was designed to provide a "monthly newsletter . . . that consists of short stories, poems and pieces of advice written by homeless or formerly homeless men and women. Our em-phasis is on offering advice for getting by these days—survival tactics for both the body and mind."[16]

In 2002 *BIGnews,* which changed its title in 2003 to *BIGNews: The Art and Liter-ary Monthly,* had a circulation of about 15,000, while *Upward* had a circulation of around 10,000 (Ron Grunberg interview 2002). They were both printed together at a printing firm outside the city. All nonprofit newspapers face printing as their biggest expense. Both these publications at the time were being laid out at manag-ing editor Ron Grunberg's workstation. Ron, a professional typesetter when "he [was] there," did the layout for each month's edition and sent it to the printer as a camera-ready copy. All other transactions to deal with the paper were also to be found at this desk: petty cash payments, a file containing up to 600 potential stories, poems, and items (Ron Grunberg interview 2002), scanned images, email correspondence, and so on. It looked like chaos as papers and folders dripped all over the equipment. But it was not. This work is labor-intensive as well, as many texts come into the editorial room (which doubles up as informal meeting-place and office) handwritten. The (not necessarily homeless in the strictest sense of the term) writers themselves either had PCs/laptops or access to one through contacts or they used the public library access points; the public library on Madison Avenue had 36 terminals at the time. For those I talked to, half an hour is ample and prints are free if you have your own paper. Others submitted handwritten text and artwork to Ron, who scanned or copy-typed them himself or employed others part-time to do this work.[17]

At the time, *BIGnews* (see Figures 4.1, 4.2, and 4.3 for three Black and White examples of the colorful artwork used for *BIGnews* covers) had a relatively large annual budget as part of the Mainchance initiative, some $2.8 million provided by the city and local businesses. But there were always shortfalls as the money would come through late, a cash-flow issue that was exacerbated in post-9/11 New York (Ron Grunberg interview 2002) and which in turn led to chronic staffing shortages as neither the paper nor outreach program could afford to hire enough full-time staff. As is the case with people struggling to make ends meet in cities (like New York or London) where rents continue to rise, the Drop-In Center and *BIGnews* production were dealing with a looming 100 percent rent increase at the time. Ron was responsible for running *BIGnews* and the weekly writers' group. He and his coworkers divided their time between outreach activities, fundraising events, and the newspapers' production. In terms of editorial decisions, these resided squarely with Grunberg; a former journalist, his baseline was "Do I want to keep reading the story?" Here Ron was referring to creative writing and reportage and the ability to sustain the writing of those members who showed ability or perseverance. Writing one's way out of misfortune, turning your life story into a best seller was an ambition that more than a few members of the group then, and people since, have reiterated in conversations. Ron's aim was to stimulate writing and, where possible, pay for the contributions; at the time this was at least $5–10 per article, sometimes $20. In this respect homeless people could earn money not just by selling but also by contributing to the paper in various ways (Van Buren 2006). Getting people to come up with new material and ideas was a continual struggle, as was the lack of time to revise and hone a piece. The issues are the same for maintaining a minimal website. As is the case with grassroots and community work based on voluntary labor or minimal staffing, "everyone in the team has to wear several hats" (Grunberg interview 2002). The website was maintained in this sense by everyone and no one at the same time.

For Ron, the priorities were clear in terms of how *BIGnews/Upward* fitted into the larger context of street papers. For him it was part of a wider project of social inclusion in practical rather than overtly political terms. In the extract below from

Helping the Homeless Help Themselves

Figure 4.1 *BIGnews* Cover, vol. 3, No. 28, November, 2002 (by Fernanda Cohen; http://www.fernandacohen.com/).

an early bulletin board, *The Homeless People's Network*, Grunberg takes his distance from the more politicized discourses around the causes of, and solutions to homelessness, on this discussion list and in general:

> Do we join causes? Address issues of social justice, etc? Not really. I've been on the job for a couple of months [as editor of *Upward*], but I have not sensed anything other than knowledge of what is going on out in the world. There are poignant comments and knowledgeable personalities . . . but there is no call to action, or ever discussion of joining rallies here or there. Perhaps that will change. We only have a few people in our group. And our center has either clients who are trying to get back into the flow of things, and are very near "ground zero," just in off the street . . . or who are working on our staff, on outreach or in drop-in center business . . . and that is their "political

statement," I suppose: they are working full time hands on to help those who pass through our doors, people who they once were . . . weeks or months or years ago. (Ron Grunberg 1998b)[18]

In the case of how observers at the time assessed these two publications in journalistic terms and as an effective means to achieve the above aims, some were quick to note the

> differences between the readerships. On one hand, there is a large, professional-looking paper full of entertaining stories and articles, which is aimed at the general public. On the other, there is a small paper full of lesser-quality writings and aimed at the city's homeless or formerly homeless groups. As an observer, this serves to highlight and possibly even to perpetuate contrasts between the readerships. It seems to almost underscore the differences between homeless and the general public without making any moves toward erasing the dissimilarities. (Sackmann and MacKay 2003)

Journalists and gifted writers can be homeless too so this isomorphism misses the point. The point here is that ambitions to achieve high quality content and the ways in which others, including researchers, assess this quality in terms of its journalistic or literary integrity is one thing. Concerns about the role producing media of this sort plays in alleviating and ultimately combating homelessness is another criterion. This tension has been evident from the outset. For instance:

> Although they could very successfully measure their effectiveness in qualitative terms, the New York City street newspaper collaboration measures their effectiveness in terms of the number of homeless people they have helped to get off the streets. . . . the priority is making sure that homeless survival is assured. This is a very realistic approach because it capitalizes on the fact that things such as artistic expression are made irrelevant by the always impending necessities of food and shelter. (Arellano 2004)

This push and pull between creating exit-openings and creative opportunities for homeless populations, who is writing for whom, and power hierarchies between editorial desks and homeless writers and vendors is carried over to how street papers have been greeting and using the web as opportunity and challenge (the case ten years ago) and as lifesaver as print media outlets increasingly move online. As mainstream media shift online, looking to stay afloat in the face of falling subscriptions, so do street papers albeit with fewer resources to make full use of online publishing and digital distribution. Indeed as the web moves content and access upstream in one way the distance between those running websites and those selling the papers (with hardcopies being the meat in the sandwich) is arguably greater; those "impending necessities of food and shelter" (Arellano 2004) do appear to trump mobile phones, computer usefulness, or internet access.

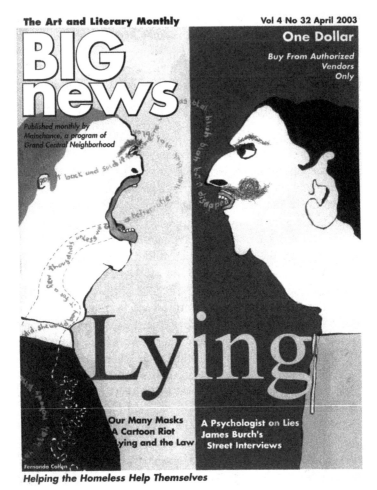

Figure 4.2 *BIGnews* Cover, vol. 4, No. 32, April, 2003 (by Fernanda Cohen; http://www.fernandacohen.com/).

The *BIGnews* Writers Group

The Writers' Group that I was able to sit in on for two months in 2002 had a lifespan of six years (1998–2004 approximately). As the now unavailable Mainchance website noted, it was a regular group of participants who "meet weekly to sit down together, speak their minds, and put their thoughts to paper. . . . We see the Writers' Group as an integral part of our social services program, something that encourages self-reflection and self-reliance. Both magazines act as morale boosters, for they contain the voices of a population so used to feeling insignificant and invisible." According to Ron Grunberg (Interview 2002) the aim of a regular meeting focusing on writing for *BIGnews* and *Upward* was to generate copy. But not just any copy, as Ron hastened to point out; he worked by keeping a file of stories ready for the next month's edition, and he was prepared to be "ruthless in so far as *BIGnews* was not supposed to be "just about homelessness." While he was prepared to allow more literary leeway in *Upward*, he was clear that he wanted "more than complaining." This larger ambition is one shared by street papers generally, to provide an outlet for people to express out of this particular experience but also to create content that goes beyond these exigencies; misery does not sell well after a while.[19] The time I spent there underscored this aim but there was a lot more going on besides as such a group also provides a regular, noninstitutionalized, meeting place, a regular point for socializing in the week in what is a "very lonely city" (Personal comment, Writers Group member July 2002).[20]

A fuller account of these weekly sessions and conversations I had with participants before and after each session warrants its own treatment. Suffice it to say that after some initial hesitation the group made me more than welcome, people were keen to share their stories, talk about writing options, and took a polite interest in the project itself even though the internet at the time was hardly a major preoccupation. The dialogues I managed to transcribe at the time constitute a narrative, or set of recitatives, in themselves that call for a different approach to their retelling than simply inserting extracts into this discussion. What was clear, looking back at my notes, was that this was a period in which the group was under some strain due to interpersonal tensions (these crystallized into a conflict between one regular contributor to both publications, and close to Grunberg, and another, more aggressive and provocative participant). Ron's primary aim to have discussions generate content, ideas, and photographs or transcripts of conversations was trumped by the way these conversations took on a direction, and tenor of their own. As far as facilitating style is concerned, the most remarkable thing about Grunberg's handling of a group comprised of strong personalities and people living in varying conditions of housing precariousness along with budding writers looking to *BIGnews* to provide an outlet for their work was his approach. His was in effect an approach out of the leaf of the radical pedagogy manual in that his was a very hands-off, non-interventionist approach to facilitating a group discussion. It was also a wry and witty one that relied on a range of running jokes between him and group members. Only once did Ron take a clear stand against the tensions emerging in the latter weeks of this summer period, turning his back on the group and then leaving the room in one dramatic meeting. It was an effective gesture for deescalating what was a potentially explosive situation as a disruptive member threatened the continued participation of longer term members showing signs of distress; Ron admitted later that these tensions had undermined the project (Interview 2002, 2004).

Since this initial period I met Ron Grunberg twice more. The first was in 2004, when I revisited the group again, though in a very different atmosphere and location. Then in 2007 we met at a Burger King outlet on 7th Avenue. At this meeting Ron introduced me to someone he described as "another writer." We met at the back of an almost empty restaurant. This was when I heard that *BIGnews* was in trouble; the Grand Central Neighborhood Business association had withdrawn the funding and Ron had fallen out with his brother Jeff, who had been the higher profile figure in the drop-in center (a very different character, more hands on to

Figure 4.3 *BIGnews* Cover, vol. 4, No. 34, June, 2003 (by Toby Van Buren).

Ron's diffident demeanor). The aim at the time was to set up a web-publishing outlet for a *BIGnews* online version, but it was clear that Ron was struggling with motivation and direction. The other guy fit the profile of other *BIGnews* writers, having literary ambitions. In 2009 I was unable to get in touch with Ron to set up a meeting. It took me a while to find out that he had died that year after a long fight against cancer. Figure 4.4 shows Ron in hospital, a sketch by Fran Cohen an artist he helped when she was starting using her work on *BIGnews* covers (Figures 4.1 and 4.3).[21]

Now that *BIGnews* and *Upwards* have folded, they and other street papers are cultural artifacts, palpable examples of the liminal zone between analog pasts and digital presents and futures, only available in part because of the archiving efforts of librarians working with physical and digital archives. Thumbnails of covers and a list of the tables of contents of *BIGnews* are still available in index form, however access to the content is not.[22] For how long these cultural productions will

Figure 4.4 *New York Blue:* Sketches of my good friend Ron Grunberg [editor of *BIGnews*] who is going through Chemotherapy at Beth Israel Hospital in New York, May 5, 2008 (by Fernanda Cohen; http://www.fernandacohen.com/content/images/editorial_206.htm).

still be accessible as the web tidies itself up, gets real in commercial terms, and disciplined by state and corporate interests is anybody's guess. This kind of research does not leave one untouched, not at the time and not since. We scholars who move in and out of these multiple sites, with the ability to come and go as we do are inevitably in an ambivalent position in ethical and political terms toward our research subjects. In this sense I would underscore Marcus's point that the "circumstantial activism involved in working in such a variety of sites, where the politics and ethics of working in any one reflects on work in the others" (Marcus 1995: 113) are only ever "resolved . . . ambivalently" (ibid.).

Online: Local-Global Networking and News Services

The two most prominent uses of the internet to promote information exchange between street papers, raise the public profile of these publications as part of wider projects of social engagement, and promote high quality press services for papers that are often in need of copy and support, are based in the United States and the United Kingdom respectively. The North American Street Newspapers Association (NASNA) and the International Network of Street Papers (INSP) emerged in the late 1990s and early 2000s as the networking potential of the web started to gain traction among some editors, support organizations, grassroots advocates, and librarians (as noted above, at the forefront of developing ways to provide public access and catalog street papers). The main focus at the time was to set up an online news service for papers to pool stories from and so boost their journalistic content. Originally run from the NASNA offices in Washington, DC, under the title "Homeless News Service," what is now the "Street News Service" is a full-fledged and funded service based at the INSP. This early enthusiasm for the internet, as a way to link up geographically disperse and widely diverse sorts of street papers, as a means to educate and reach potential donors (Tim Harris interview 2002) was already underway in the 1990s. The project crystallized at the 2002 Annual Conference of NASNA (still predominately an on the ground association) in Boston. Looking back from a web-saturated news and entertainment vantage point it may seem odd that at the time not everyone shared this enthusiasm for what the internet could do, for a range of reasons. For instance there was hesitancy about the practical and social implications of replacing face-to-face support with emails or websites. As some noted, for people who are already highly marginalized and whose social networks are limited, email accounts (and Facebook pages) can exacerbate isolation, for emails and social media presume respondents and social networks already formed (Paula Mathieu interview 2002; Curly Cohen interview 2002). These reservations were coupled with a commitment to creative writing, as an empowerment and mobilization activity for disadvantaged groups, that need not, indeed cannot be reduced to computer access.[23]

In 2002 the International Network of Street Papers listed twenty-two member countries and around fifty different papers. In 2012 this had grown to over 120 editions. Over the last decade street papers, many using *The Big Issue* title (this street paper has become effectively a global brand) have sprung up all over the world, and at least these publications are made visible through being listed in the INSP website. In North America street papers are an integral part of homeless support networks and cityscapes, thriving or combating the economic and print media down turn in varying degrees.[24] The genesis and rollout of street paper networks as national-international online undertakings embedded in internet technologies, and nowadays incorporating social media more and more, is a story in itself (see Swithinbank 2001). As the INSP was brought under the wing of *The Big Issue* organization in 2005 the for-profit, reader-centric business model of the latter publication and the not-for-profit, homeless vendor based models of the US-based network remains a subtle albeit clear distinction (Stoops interview 2012). It is a fine line to walk between retaining sales while remaining

> strongly committed to empower local street newspapers to develop leadership among poor people, while cultivating journalistic integrity and sustainable street papers. NASNA supports non-discrimination and values a diverse and inclusive street paper movement. We strive for high ethical standards and require financial accountability from its members. (NASNA 2013b)

So what has changed and what has remained constant over the last ten years of media for and by the homeless? While there are divergent views about how much time and money should be committed to being digital in this kind of work, there are several shifts that bear mentioning, political and cultural contextual differences notwithstanding. First, what has remained constant are the time demands, and given the face-to-face nature and urgency of the work, constraints of maintaining any sort of web presence coupled with the downsides of mobile telephony, onlineness, and digitalia for this populace and work (Michael Stoops interview 2012). This applies to when papers and support organizations set up ad hoc websites for individual publications or devoted time to setting up more sophisticated pages or extended web portals. The tension is clear here for homeless constituencies and their cash-strapped and understaffed advocacy organizations. Namely, while the "Internet has been a blessing for homeless people to communicate for free with loved ones" through email accounts and public (library or drop-in center) access, the downside is that "we are becoming enslaved to the Internet" (Michael Stoops interview 2012).

Along this spectrum is the recognition that computer-skills courses, social media accounts, and networking opportunities between geographically dispersed agencies and street papers have been beneficial, but only if there are people and resources available to maintain and update websites, blogs, and now increasingly Facebook pages and Twitter feeds. Full use of any of these elements let alone all together is a "time suck" (Tim Harris interview 2012) so choices are being made even now. Second, these decisions bespeak what has been changing in terms of web media uses and mobile applications (Harris interview 2012). The most recent casualties in cyberspatial terms are blogs and websites as the main axis. Street papers with a long history of working with internet technologies, such as *Real Change* in Seattle and *The Big Issue* in the United Kingdom, are visibly moving from extensive website offerings to concentrate on Facebook and now Twitter, or moving to online archives of past issues. Blogs are now old new media, and websites are being pared back to the bare essentials (Tim Harris interview 2012). As for who these various media are intended to help, the practical distinction between looking to maintain a web presence that can draw in funders and readerships on the one hand and on the other provide access and support online for homeless people's immediate informational and support needs remains a constant.[25]

This brings us to some of the latest developments as digitalization of content production has affected how street papers distribute and sell their publications. As noted above, initiatives at *The Big Issue* and *Real Change* to set up online editions or digital sales are cases in point (Harris interview 2012, INSP 2012). Selling a digital issue on the street via a code or access card is one thing; in the case of *Real Change* vendors sell up to 75% of the paper's print-run, and have done so for the last eighteen years. Digitalizing the transaction itself, in essence, employing vendors as digital access points, or "human service providers" (Michael Stoops interview 2012) has produced a highly publicized furor. This experiment in "human hotspots" (Price 2012) has implications for the vendor-reader relationship as well as public perception. Donors supply computers and internet access, use of which have become part of the daily work at drop-in Centers and street paper offices. Offices that were a once a "geek fest" are now used by increasing numbers of "computer savvy" visitors (Harris interview 2002, 2012). The deeper issue is not so much about the passing fads and vagaries of investing time and energy into making an application or web space or tool work for the business, even as important as these decisions are to economic viability. Rather, as summed up by Tim Harris and echoed by all those I have spoken to over the years, the core mission remains one that can "provide a context for people to have relationships with each other . . . that can be transformative" (Harris interview 2012). This requires that at all times the approach is "relationship-centred" (ibid.).[26]

HOMELESS WRITERS AND WEB 2.0: THE "ONCE HOMELESS GIRL"

> [Those] of us who are not homeless . . . are faced with complicated feelings, frustrations, and choices about homelessness, and our empathy can be easily over-ridden when facing the difficult questions about whom to help, how, and at what cost to us as individuals and as a society. (Passaro 1996:2, see Torck 2001)

In this section we move into the current era of web design, access, and use, mobile web access and social networking sites such as Facebook and Twitter. As noted above, homeless internet users and their media have taken the emergence of social media goods and services in their stride; once focused on email accounts and websites and then setting up blogs, street papers and individuals have carved out their own places online in Web 2.0 settings, albeit with varying degrees of linked-in success and longevity. Developing a web presence these days is, for anyone, increasingly defined by interactive, multimedia formats (embedding video for instance) and cementing links to social media applications. If the "digital natives" of today are growing up with these latest goods and services then so too are their contemporaries living in conditions of housing precarity; young people feature in the rising statistics of homelessness (Centrepoint 2010), hence their lack of internet access exacerbates the social and economic consequences of homelessness in internet-dependent societies. Nadia is one example of the openings and exclusions that occur when encountering homelessness at a young age—education, employment opportunities, and social contact all suffer as a result. Yet at the same time, taking to the web by creating a blog, getting on to Twitter and/or Facebook, if access can be negotiated, can generate opportunities of another sort. I came across Nadia, as one of the people interviewed by Mark Hovarth in his *Invisible People* TV project, http://invisiblepeople.tv/blog/. Nadia's appearance on this series of films about homelessness around the world was striking.

Twenty-three-year-old Nadia and I met up face to face in late 2012 in a city outside of London. Her story, how she and her mother became homeless after losing their house in the wake of the 2008 subprime mortgages scandal has been documented by others. Nadia herself has narrated her experiences of being homeless as a teenager many times (Hovarth 2012). The story that she tells in the rest of this section looks at the media and communications (dis)connections that are interwoven through her experience. As Nadia is a natural storyteller, the interview, which she recorded on her new iPhone (it was a gift), works as a narrative in its own right. Between 2004 and 2011 Nadia and her mother were homeless twice after their house was repossessed. The details of how this happened include getting into debt by being overcommitted financially and unable to grasp the consequences of not making mortgage payments, exploited by unscrupulous real estate agents, and then becoming dependent in the longer term on the care of friends and church members. Nadia's largely absent father footed the bill for her schooling, but the cost was a major financial burden in any case, and without a home or regular employment Nadia's mother could not cope. Nadia had to quit school. She was happy and enjoying the chance to get a "good education" in a subsidized boarding school, but everything changed when she and her mother found themselves on the street in 2004. They found themselves forced to spend the night anywhere from Paddington Station, to cheap hotels, or other people's spare rooms. Since 2012 both Nadia and her mother have found homes, separately now, after years of shuttling between various cities, dealing with her mother's health problems and the increasing stigma and isolation that arises from having to rely on other people's kindness for a long period of time, outstaying their welcome in more than one instance. In Nadia's own words, her relationship with her generation's mobile and web-based media and communications underscored as well as emerged from her pathway in and out of homelessness.

In brief, Nadia's first mobile was an Ericksson "brick." A cheap Skype phone with a free Twitter app came next, which is what got her onto Twitter. She then moved to an HTC Wildfire in 2010 and then received her current iPhone as a birthday present. She joined Facebook in July 2012, setting up a page so that she could enhance the links between her other accounts. But Nadia's main activity on line was her blog, which she began in 2008 and kept up "on and off" during the tough times. At the time blogging appeared as a cheap, easy way to success, and social contact. At the time we met she had had her Twitter account (@HomelessGirl1) for two and a half years and had also experimented with videoblogging on YouTube. She established her *The Adventures of a (ONCE) Homeless Girl* (the "once" was inserted as Nadia exited homelessness) blog with WordPress.com when she was 19, at a cost of around £10 a year.[27] In 2010 Nadia bought the domain name and hosting service, which increased the cost tenfold. Nadia has been a dedicated follower of blogs from an early age. She reads other people's blogs (around 200), the bulk of which are either on fashion or US politics; the gladiatorial gamesmanship of the US political blogosphere is a feature Nadia enjoys. In blogging terms, Nadia's big break came when she became a regular contributor to the Impact section of the *Huffington Post* after one of her blog entries (on how homeless people are abused and exploited on a daily basis) was noticed by one of its editorial staff. More than happy to contribute to this high-profile web publication, as a "proper avenue to have your voice heard," Nadia became a weekly and then fortnightly contributor. Her experience with Facebook is more recent and more the result of finding that people were adding her to their Friends list even though she had not at that time made her personal details available; at the time she was blogging as "Homeless Girl" rather than in her own name (more on this below).

There was more to her decision to join Facebook, however. She set up the page in order to "reclaim the space"; unsolicited friending requests required her to take action online in order to exercise control of her own public persona. "Quite private about a lot of things," Nadia had her own Facebook page for family and friends but the power of the hyperlink led to her decision to keep her two online lives distinct with two pages, one for herself and one for Homeless Girl. Her blogging persona was not connected—at least not actively by Nadia herself—to her real name between 2008 and 2010. Nor did she use a photo. She "came out" after realizing that she no longer felt ashamed of her circumstances, no longer cared so much about what others, for instance, old school friends, thought of her becoming homeless. However, making herself visible online, in real-name and visual terms was a gradual process: she started with her picture and first name and then began using her full name about six months later. This process was also based on her increasing conviction that the time had come to legitimize her claims about homelessness as something that can happen to someone from a relatively well-off background. Moreover, given the so-called network effect of how social media service providers tag, index, and link up their users in automated, nonconsensual, ways, Nadia also realized that she needed to differentiate her online self from other claimants (e.g., another blogger called "I am Homeless Girl"; having her blog clearly associated with a real person also preempted accusations of insincerity). By 2010 Nadia had completed her online metamorphosis. At the same time, she and her mother were once again without a home.

Seated in a global chain of cafes in a shopping mall that could be anywhere, no longer homeless and studying to get her high school diploma (interrupted by her having to leave school) what did Nadia think about her cyberspatial timeline? First, while blogging had "given [her] more than [she] wanted," she had an ambivalent relationship with the Homeless Girl blog, cryptically likening it to a naughty child that "exceeded expectations." As is the case with start-up street papers, she began writing as a form of personal testimonial, or an online diary, but quickly realized that those stories were not what people really wanted to read. The "most popular things I write are not about homelessness" but rather topics like "how to help a homeless person" and other sorts of advice and opinions. These pieces in the *Huffington Post* are what generate the most attention. So, second, despite her literary and social advocacy intentions, her success in the blogosphere pivots more on topics that confirm preconceived stereotypes of homeless people; she says "people aren't that interested in me," rather they are more intent on positioning her as an opinion-maker. What has made her more cynical, however, is the ongoing rise in endemic homelessness.

By early 2010, Nadia and her mother had moved back to stay with the woman who first put them up. By now, "praying less and learning more" during the course of her Twitter conversations, Nadia started to realize that she had had enough, and that it was time to do something. Challenged by her brother about whether she wanted to live the rest of her life in a hotel room with her mother, Nadia took the chance of having a more stable home environment (their hostess offered them a more permanent house-share arrangement). By 2011 Nadia had met her current boyfriend, and she moved in with him in March 2012. This change of circumstance for both her and her mother has made a "huge difference." Based in the public library Nadia has since then completed studying for her high school diploma qualification ("A-Levels" in the United Kingdom) in sociology, economics, and English.[28]

At the time I met Nadia she was getting a bit tired of it all; thinking increasingly about quitting the blog (she had also tweeted to this effect). Moreover, her own version of her story is available online under a pseudonym. Many of the facts are still "quite raw," so she was not so sure about how she felt about these personal details being available "out there" or how her family might react (she is very protective of her mother). While the piece has enjoyed a modicum of online success, and she enjoyed it at first, she began to feel increasingly ambivalent about the attention. As she felt she needed the blog a lot less, she posted on it less frequently—once a week, if not less often. More to the point, she was feeling increasingly that she was "yelling at an empty room" with "nothing left to say"; perhaps the *Adventures of a (ONCE) Homeless Girl* were over. I asked her how ending the blog would make her feel. She replied that it would make her feel "quite happy—I've achieved what I wanted to . . . I think I've changed perceptions of homelessness and what homeless people look like," by which she means that even privileged people can end up homeless. Not unlike writers for *BIGnews* and other street papers I met ten years ago, Nadia's original dream of perhaps landing a book deal by virtue of her writing on homelessness was not so alluring any more. Indeed she commented that she would actually be "happier if people were to know less about me," feeling currently "overwhelmed by it all" in a social media spiral of connectivity that left her with the feeling that she had less and less control of her online life. Since we met, Nadia has not renewed the domain name registration for her blog, persuaded the *Huffington Post* to take down her articles (at her insistence), and changed her Twitter handle. On March 26, 2013, Nadia tweeted "I deleted my blog last week. This is the place to find all my previous work and some new content. http://bit.ly/Zs66II."

Counterintuitive as it may seem, and transgressing the academic rules of superimposing the authoritative voice of scholarly analysis over personal accounts like this one, I will desist in this instance. Nadia's story does, and should speak for itself in the context of this case study. While she has taken a clear step back from what was quite a high profile online existence in the domain of commentaries and social networking around homelessness, Nadia has confirmed on reading this version of her story that she has no regrets about letting it be part of this study nor of taking a stand and being counted.[29]

DEFINITIONAL MATTERS

> Homelessness . . . depends on the formation of a socially shared image of the absolute poor. . . . This socially shared image contains other images that convey social distinctions between housed and unhoused people, and judgements about who is deserving . . . and who is undeserving . . . displacing questions about the impact on the very poor of city redevelopment policies and land-use decisions. (Wright 1997: 17; see Tosi 2007: 229)

> The prevention of homelessness or the re-housing of homeless people requires an understanding of the pathways and processes that lead there and hence a broad perception of the meaning of homelessness. . . . Homelessness *is a process (rather than a static phenomenon)* that affects many vulnerable households at different points in their lives. (FEANTSA 2012a, emphasis added)

Moving from on-the-ground fieldwork, cyberarchaeology, and personal accounts of life online as a (once) homeless blogger, this section shifts register again to address the vexed issue of definition and categorizations of homelessness within the United States and European Union primarily. In light of the above more experiential-based explorations, these policy and thereby political and economic considerations need to be unpacked, for not only do they have a bearing on how governments and communities perceive and respond to homelessness but also any connections made from homelessness to internet access and uses come with their respective political loadings.

The very category itself begs all sorts of questions. To recall, for many onlookers homelessness is simply a synonym for rough sleeping. All agencies, and the testimony of people in this predicament hasten to note, however, that while homelessness "means not having a home, some people have no roof over their head and sleep on the street, in doorways or on night buses. But much more homelessness is hidden—on a friend's sofa or spare room, or in squats" (Shelter 2013c). As noted earlier, not only is homelessness one of the more pressing local and national social issues in Western societies over the last twenty-five years but it is also an international—global—phenomenon; endemic poverty is on the increase in the wake of the economic crisis and as a result of war, famine, and civil conflicts. Here too the race, ethnicity, class, and gender dimensions of different sorts of homelessness, some recognizable and others less visible, bring their own weight to bear on the statistics, with political refugees and other migrant populations forming a significant part of recent figures. Moreover, different ways of measuring and defining homelessness makes comparison difficult. In social and political terms these issues are reported and experienced at the local (neighborhood and municipal) and national levels primarily. Hence compiling figures on homelessness across national and legal jurisdictions raises issues around having the adequate resources and methodology to do so. "By its very nature, homelessness is impossible to measure with 100% accuracy. More important than knowing the precise number of people who experience homelessness is our progress in ending it" (NCH 2009b). In this sense keeping track of how many people are homeless and who they are—as individuals, family groups, their gender, ethnic and educational background—is a partial and politically charged undertaking (FEANTSA 2012a; NCH 2009a; Wright 1997).

With this caveat in mind and for the purpose of anchoring the discussion above, the following snapshots should suffice to underscore how homelessness, as part of endemic poverty or the effects of circumstance in the short term, is more than a sidebar to the local-global politics of the internet as such, or to the recalibrations of center-periphery models of global cultural and economic flows (Appadurai 2002; Castells 1996, 2002). Some facts and figures should suffice to illustrate these indices over the last decade: In 2002 nearly half of "literally" homeless people in the United States were African American males. By 2006, 68% of registered homeless populations were African American (42%), Hispanic (20%), and 6% other ethnic groups. Only 38% were white. These indicators vary in the United States from state to state, and between urban and rural areas (NCH 2009). The main thing to note, however, is that ethnic minorities are disproportionately represented in homelessness statistics the world over (NCH 2002, 2009b, c; Glasser 1994). While poverty and low-income work histories and lack of formal educational qualifications figure largely in the demographics of homelessness, women and men with university degrees can also find themselves in situations of housing vulnerability. Soaring rents and mortgage overhead creates housing difficulties that often fall off the radar. Unaffordable housing makes those who lose their jobs, also part of a rising statistic of recent times, particularly vulnerable; "homelessness is only one paycheck away" (a comment made during a *BIGnews* Writers Group meeting, July 3,

2002). While there are more single homeless males in the United States than there are women, domestic abuse and the number of women—with children—having to find shelter with friends and relatives is often a hidden dimension to statistics. Again, in the wake of the global financial and housing crisis, monitoring agencies have been signaling that the numbers of homeless women, young people, and indeed whole families are on the rise in the United States, United Kingdom, and the rest of the European Union (Shelter 2013a, b; NCH 2009c; FEANTSA 2010). For instance in 2012 the United Kingdom charity Shelter reported a marked increase in the number of families living in bed and breakfast accommodations in 2012, an increase of 51% (Shelter 2012). Similar trends have been signaled in the Netherlands and other parts of the European Union.[30]

Simultaneously, the disconnect from internet access, mobile, and social media resources experienced by these populations—indeed to live as full-fledged members of the generation of "digital natives"—becomes more acute. These figures beg the question, however, of conceptualizing homelessness. These definitional concerns are not immaterial to considering how, where, and on whose terms homeless people use internet technologies. Neither are they irrelevant to wider debates about who pays for and who provides the requisite access, goods, and services to growing populations of would-be internet users. In the United States legal definitions frame homelessness mainly around economic criteria, that is, home ownership or living in "adequate" housing, differences between federal and state definitions notwithstanding. For example the Washington, DC, based *National Coalition for the Homeless* (NCH) defines homelessness according to US federal law; namely as the lack of a

> fixed, regular, and adequate night-time residence; [or someone who] . . . has a primary night time residency that is: (A) a supervised publicly or privately operated shelter designed to provide temporary living accommodations . . . (B) An institution that provides a temporary residence for individuals intended to be institutionalized, or (C) a public or private place not designed for, or ordinarily used as, a regular sleeping accommodation for human beings. (NCH 2009c)

The NCH goes on to note that there are other parameters in force for other federal agencies. These would "include only those persons who are on the streets or in shelters and persons who face imminent eviction (within a week) from a private dwelling or institution and who have no subsequent residence or resources to obtain housing" (2009c). While this definition accounts for "large, urban communities where tens of thousands of people [would then be rendered] literally homeless" the NCH goes on to make an important distinction, one shared by other support and monitoring agencies. Namely, that in rural areas and also where people have family and friendship networks available people "experiencing homelessness in these [respects] are less likely to live on the street or in a shelter, and more likely to live with relatives in overcrowded or substandard housing" (NCH 2009c). Another DC-based lobby group, the *National Alliance to End*

Homelessness, sums these legal precisions up in a sentence; homelessness comes about when "people or households are unable to acquire and/or maintain housing they can afford" (National Alliance 2013). The causes for this situation are firmly situated within wider issues of poverty according to this definition: "It is the scarcity of affordable housing in the United States, particularly in more urban areas where homelessness is more prevalent, that is behind their inability to acquire or maintain housing" (ibid.). In this formulation, appropriate responses to homelessness "requires a grasp of several social issues: poverty, affordable housing, disabilities, and others" (National Alliance 2013).

On the other side of the Atlantic, Shelter, a major charity in the United Kingdom notes that legal differences within the United Kingdom in how homelessness is defined affect the sorts of financial support and legal entitlements available for those living in different jurisdictions, being homeless in England or Scotland for instance. The charity's website, whose form of address is to readers in these situations first and foremost, stresses that while homelessness "means not having a home—most people who are homeless don't sleep on the street." Moreover "if you have a roof over your head you can still be homeless. This is because you may not have any rights to stay where you live or your home might be unsuitable for you due to severe overcrowding or other reasons" (Shelter 2013c). In this more expansive understanding of homelessness as a more pervasive state of precariousness rather than "night-time residency" alone, the web page then goes on to note that if "you don't have a place to live, your local council may have a duty to house you. But dealing with the council can be difficult and not everyone is entitled to emergency housing" (Shelter 2013d). In other words, emergency housing is a legal entitlement in the English context at least (being homeless in Scotland falls under different provisions). But eligibility for these provisions goes beyond homelessness itself, into the legally complex and politically fraught area of immigration policy and citizenship.[31]

In the larger European Union there is a move to regard homelessness in more dynamic terms: as a process along a spectrum that allows for a range of temporal and physical sorts of homelessness. To this end the European Commission-funded *European Federation of Organizations Working with Homelessness* (FEANTSA) and its Observatory has developed a typology in which the notion of "home" is not defined solely in instrumental or economic terms (namely renting or owning a "house" or simply having access to physical shelter in physical or ownership terms). This way of thinking about and so dealing with homelessness incorporates conventional notions of having a "home" in the physical sense of ownership or occupancy with the legal and social dimensions that go along with this (FEANTSA 2012a; Fiske 1999; Edgar, Doherty, and Meert 2003).

> Having a home can be understood as: having an adequate dwelling (or space) over which a person and his/her family can exercise exclusive possession (physical domain); being able to maintain privacy and enjoy relations (social domain) and having a legal title to occupation (legal domain). (FEANTSA 2102a)

This dynamic, process-based approach underscores the unarticulated dimensions to what it means to be deprived of not only a legally recognized physical domain but also the civic (e.g., identity papers) and personal (e.g., privacy) entitlements that go along with this in Western societies where the two are intertwined. This

> "home"-based definition . . . uses the physical, social and legal domains to create a broad typology of homelessness and housing exclusion . . . according to their living situation: rooflessness (without a shelter of any kind, sleeping rough); houselessness (with a place to sleep but temporary in institutions or shelter); living in insecure housing (threatened with severe exclusion due to insecure tenancies eviction, domestic violence); living in inadequate housing (in caravans on illegal campsites, in unfit housing, in extreme overcrowding). (FEANSTA 2012a)

The analogy between having a home vis-à-vis being homeless on the one hand and, on the other, (not) having internet access is in this respect less counterintuitive than first appears. What all these definitions point to is that homelessness today is understood not simply in terms of an economic lack but increasingly articulated as a form of economic and sociocultural *precariousness* that is not a given. Rather it is time sensitive and fluid and thereby implies that homelessness has a timeline. However, what constitutes "adequate" housing becomes more acute in the case of traveler communities, those who take up residence in caravan parks and camping grounds for instance. Long term residents in these places designated for holiday or short-term accommodation include Romani populations in Europe. They too along with established communities of rough sleepers confront housed residents and cash-strapped local authorities directly as land and urban renewal schemes become political and financial targets for politicians and property developers alike. To recall Certeau, the politics of space and strategic resources that landowners and local residents can muster to combat those who are considered disturbances to the peace, who give rise to "health and safety" and security issues such as rough sleepers or communities staking out a space in public parks or squares for instance, are played out nightly in the internetted streets and gentrifying neighborhoods of the world's global cities. Bridges and other structures frequented by rough sleepers, temporary shelter provisions, and railway stations become sites where the tension between the strategic powers of those with resources and leverage and those who have little is put into visible and visceral relief.

DISCUSSION: "MIND THE GAP"

> Although numerous experts have demonstrated, eloquently and convincingly, that homelessness is due primarily not to mental illness or other personal problems but to large-scale social and economic inequalities, many people still resist acknowledging such a cause. . . . As more and more

homeless people [have] appeared in public spaces, and people with homes [have grown] less tolerant of seeing them, the gap seem[s] to be widening. (Golden 1992: 9,10)

The title of this chapter, borrows from the phrase made famous by Gayatri Spivak, "can the subaltern speak?" (1985). Spivak argues that the term, *subaltern*, needs more restricted conceptualization in light of its use in Gramscian and postcolonial theories as a generic term for the economically and culturally dispossessed in capitalist and colonial societies respectively. Michael Kilburn (1996) notes that Spivak's point in the original essay (Spivak 1985) is that voicing and speaking is not the same thing. It is not that "the subaltern does not cry out in various ways" but that speaking is "a transaction between speaker and listener" (Kilburn 1996 citing Spivak). In this sense Spivak's distinction echoes the tension, tradeoffs, and co-optations that are entailed in the "capture of speech" at moments of social or political upheaval and its recapture as things return to "normal" that concern Certeau (1994: 40 passim) as well as the self-awareness (organic but also nurtured) of counterpublics when they are positioned through a "conflictual relation to the dominant public" (Warner 2002: 85). The difference between talk and action, keeping and taking power that makes a difference by staking a claim literally and figuratively is where the politics of resistance and power of incumbents are in tension (Certeau 1994; 70). The distinction between having or using one's voice and being able—or rather being allowed—to speak and actually taken notice of, vis-à-vis interventions by others acting or speaking on behalf of those whose voices are not heard, who are unable to take the floor as it were, is a longstanding dividing line within the various organizations and media working for, or with homeless people around the world.

We need to pause for a moment to consider what exactly Spivak means or rather maintains what it is she does *not* mean by whether the subaltern can—or cannot—speak. For Spivak, being able to engage in dialog and so heard is more than making sounds; the context and conditions for dialogue based on behavioralist, or rationalist models of "communicative action" (Habermas in Borradori, 2003, 1996 (1968)) circumscribe these engagements, define them as more than lip service, or "noise" while other forces set the agenda, "capture" the floor, and so the narrative and right of reply (Certeau 1997a, b). Spivak makes this political and historical distinction as what transpires when

you say cannot speak, it means that if speaking involves speaking and listening, this possibility of response, responsibility, does not exist in the subaltern's sphere. . . . [The] only way that that speech is produced is by inserting the subaltern into the circuit of hegemony, which is what should happen, as subaltern. . . . No activist wants to keep the subaltern in the space of difference. To do a thing, to work for the subaltern, means to bring it into speech. . . . [you] don't give the subaltern voice. You work for the bloody subaltern, you work against subalternity. (Spivak, in De Kock 1992: 45–46, emphasis added)

Without presupposing that one sort of "subaltern" has replaced or is more
excluded than another, a spurious distinction that Spivak also puts in its place
(De Kock 1992) my point here is that when considering homelessness and the
internet Spivak's rhetorical and political point is instructive. In this scenario, as
is also the case for the most acute debates in internet governance arenas, definitions are not just a question of semantics. They are imbued with the political. I am
positing this notion here as it pertains to disconnects and overlaps between these
uses and how others deploy the internet on their behalf.

ENTRIES AND EXITS — PATHWAYS

In light of the conceptualization of homelessness in terms of pathways (FEANTSA
2012a), and the variety of entry and exit points and trajectories that this understanding allows for, we can see how going online, looking to connect and be heard
through social media networks, is not incompatible with the mission of street
papers, in their traditional and their convergent media forms. Breaking down this
large and scary category into more accessible domains for thought and action
begins by delineating between the physical, social, and legal domains of homelessness, as an experience and an increasingly pressing political issue. There is,
however, another dimension that has yet to be taken fully on board, one that this
chapter hopefully has been able to make visible. This is the nascent dimension
to homelessness in a digital, to wit social media context. But it is not a new insight. In a very early discussion forum, Ron Grunberg has this to say about social
movement-based advocacy, media (in this case on homelessness issues), and
social enterprises within any

> industry that grows around a social problem should offer as many of the jobs
> as possible to the people affected by that problem. However, a person does
> not qualify for a job merely because they are homeless. That is only one of
> the qualifying characteristics. He/she must also be "job ready," meaning they
> possess the traits one normally looks for in a candidate. They must have job
> references. Our program [Grand Central Neighourhood Services] has been
> designed from the start to develop potential candidates. . . . In this way, being
> hired full-time by us is an achievement, not a pandering act on our part. Our
> staff of 90 is 50% drawn from the people we serve. Our goal is that they move
> on from our program to jobs "on the outside" where they are not defined as
> "ex-clients."[32] (Ron Grunberg, 1998)

The way people access and use the internet encompasses and also rearticulates
the physical, legal, and social domains of everyday life (FEANTSA 2012a). In so
doing they point to a fourth dimension: the cyberspatial domain and its accompanying practices and cultures of onlineness that are in the process of being (re)
constituted as either public or private spaces (and by implication places) in terms
of what goes on there, who accesses, and who controls these interactions. But this

dimension is also where enclosures and the rise of quasi-private/public spaces are occurring with exclusionary dynamics. The three dimensions to homelessness conceptualized above in the ETHOS schematic (FEANTSA 2012a) have acquired in a digital age an additional dimension. This is pathways that designate comparable issues around having adequate access to, rights of use and privacy, and ability to form sustainable relationships in online spaces that presuppose digital indicators of use and "occupation," points of access, rights of reply and data retention for being part of social networks, discussion forums, listservs, and virtual communities. Under commercialized or exclusive (memberships—paid or not, password entry-requirements) conditions of online communications, disadvantaged groups look set to be excluded twice over. If they are included, then it is under highly specific and intrusive conditions. But, as I say that, the openings that remain, and the very porosity and permissive nature of cyber-homeliness also offer some countertactics.

For those in various sorts of housing precarity attitudes to and aptitudes for the opportunities, latent and active, of web-based networking, information sharing, and social contact cover the same spectrum of pessimism and enthusiasm as in other sectors of society. These too are tempered by generational shifts in know-how and want-to, behavior and attitudes, norms and values. The contradiction between the ideal of comprehensive internet interconnectivity in purely functional terms on the one hand and, on the other, the socioeconomic, cultural, and political practicalities of making this ideal work in real life for all members of society is at its most stark when considering homelessness and the internet. As Yochai Benkler argues, the deeper question is what sort of internet, access, or interconnectivity is being envisaged here:

> We cannot, however, take for granted that the technological capacity to participate in the cultural conversation, to mix and make our own, will translate into the freedom to do so. The practices of cultural and countercultural creation are at the very core of the battle over the institutional ecology of the digital environment. (Benkler 2006: 277)

The battle Benkler is referring to above looks back to the last chapter and forward to the next case in Chapter 5. For the purposes of this case, we need to invert the telescope by concentrating on how a particularly disadvantaged sector of computerized societies, and those who advocate and work on their behalf, engage the internet in "ways of operating" [that] form the counterpart . . . of the mute processes that organize the establishment of socioeconomic order (Certeau, in Highmore 2002: 66–8). The paradox-dilemma at stake in this respect is that while in the Global South *ICT for Development* undertakings, to which UN member states make their contribution within national or multilateral international development programs such as the Millennium Development Goals continue (UN General Assembly 2000), what remains underaddressed are burgeoning issues closer to home around how "new media" (social networking, mobile phones, web-based services and information, digitalization of public records) can relieve as well as exacerbate other forms of overlapping exclusion. In short, the knock-on benefits that are seen as accruing from having access to the internet and their converse are issues that permeate the internet's heartlands as well.

RETHINKING THE PROBLEMATIC

> There is a difference between the imaginary world and the practical world of the computer; *if* [the Internet] is a way to make relationships happen then it is useful.[33] (Paula Mathieu interview 2002)

As this chapter suggested at the outset that there is an analogous "disciplining" dynamic that affects homeless populations on the ground and online (Meert and Stuyck 2008: 53; Harris interview 2012), as spaces on the ground become increasingly inaccessible, even more inhospitable, and in many cases openly hostile to those who have no "home" to go to once office, shops, and railway stations have closed for the night, activist-advocacy organizations and engaged researchers have been mobilizing. A comparable dynamic has started to gather momentum online. While not necessarily the target of these corporate-led and state-endorsed enclosures in terms of the politics of the internet's design, content, and access points, poorer and vulnerable populations such as the homeless (or those in the Global South) are particularly exposed to the effects. On the ground and in cyberspace, marginalized groups bear the brunt of these interlocking practices of exclusivity in which cyberscapes and cityscapes become only accessible for those with certain physical, social, and legal credentials.

In terms of a notion of *public*—or open, nonprivatized—cyberspace the debate shifts to how to (re)create or at least maintain these sorts of access points, online spaces and practices in the face of encroaching privatization (commercialization and corporate ownership of means and media) of ICT and related multimedia sectors. Offline—on the ground—this commercial trend is well underway in downtown business areas, in the Central Station area of Amsterdam, Potsdamer Platz in Berlin, and parts of New York, Grand Central Station in particular. In highly desirable urban areas homeless groups, including street vendors, have been targeted as undesirables, eyesores by local residents and powerful retail lobbies—and city hall, and considered as bad for tourism too. Public offline spaces are decreasing in New York City and all over the USA (NCH 2003). Homeless folk are the first to feel the pinch as they get told to move on from, or are put in jail for being in, public toilets, railway stations, street corners, park benches and so forth.

This squeezing of public areas is related to local populaces' perceptions of insecurity in the presence of people who live on the streets (those in shelters or couch-surfing are out of sight and so out of mind). CCTV, database initiatives to track and place homeless folk, and business coalitions' lobbying to clean up inner-city areas are also linked, if not causally then by association, to increasing privatizations of urban space in the name of commercial urban renewal or tourism. As Talmadge Wright argues, policies that focus only on "the individual empowerment of the very poor and homeless" are not sustainable if they refuse to address

> a system that reproduces poverty and homelessness, locking out output from the margins. . . . The celebration of democratic self-realization and self-management without the necessary public and cultural spaces that allow that to occur merely reinforces systemic inequities required by the reproduction of capital. (Wright 1997: 324)

There is the distinction between blurring of genres and blurring of intentions; that is, being "homeless" is not a literary genre, journalism by homeless writers or creative writing may well go beyond "misery" (Kantlijn Writers Group, Amsterdam 2004), yet the circumstances of extreme poverty and distress do circumscribe attempts to bring content past this cutoff point. Street papers also reflect two, not always reconcilable, intentions: to provide outlets for homeless people's creativity (writing, art, theatre, or music) as well as a form of alternative income and independent media outlets.

CONCLUDING COMMENTS

> Between two forms of unconsciousness—one that refuses to see the damages and one that avoids the responsibility of reconstruction, one that denies the problem and one that refuses to seek any solution—we must look closely at the issues of lucidity and action. There is a relation between the discredit that must be challenged and the work that needs to be taken up. (Certeau 1997b: 3, 4)

My aim in this case study, one that spans a decade, is to start thinking in different ways about how access and use of the internet by homeless people and those organizations working on their behalf sheds some light on the contradictory stakes in the politics of the internet. While the last chapter focused on struggles for ownership and control of the user web interface, this chapter is about the politics of access and use in terms of what can be made available and what has been possible to date for and by those who are digitally and civically disadvantaged. This has not been to posit a spurious cause and effect, that the internet causes homelessness or indeed can solve it. Rather the intent is to note a particular socioeconomic, technohistorical, and scholarly conjuncture around suppositions concerning the politics of internet design, access, and use on the one hand and, on the other, normative debates about the role these media and communications *should* play in society. As the disconnect between the internet as a means and medium premised on either an "access for all" or "user pays" principle becomes increasingly marked in policy and academic debates (see Chapters Three and Five), consideration of the way disadvantaged, "atypical," or disenfranchised individuals and communities use these media and technologies for their own needs, and on their own terms, remains off the radar.

Learning more about these usages, and nonusages, in specific and comparative terms is not only instructive per se. It can also provide an antidote to the more myopic and reductionist conclusions of the "Internet and Society" debates that emanate from utopian and dystopian schools of thought alike. For a start, this case study aimed to challenge the perception (quite prevalent in the 1990s and early 2000s) that homeless people accessing and consciously using the internet for their own needs, via public access points or even through mobile phones, is a "waste of time," their aspirations superfluous to requirements or looked on with suspicion. In short the assumption that homelessness and the internet are mutually exclusive is not correct. Second, this case shows how analysis of disenfranchised, disadvantaged, or minority usages (of the media of the day) can contribute to critical thought on the tensions between the global technopolitical economy of today's media and communications on the one hand and experiences of communicative imaginaries and lived realities of everyday life in a digital age on the other. Like the rest of us, how homeless people, for themselves or as represented by others, use the internet makes a difference too, even when these uses underscore the ambivalence and uncertainty of homelessness and access-for-all as a lived reality. Third, the chapter does look to draw analogies between how people are subjected to forms of enclosure and exclusion from public spaces on the ground as compared to public and quasipublic cyberspaces and related ways of communicating and sharing. But it does not claim that homelessness online departs markedly from experiences on the ground. Being web savvy may well exacerbate as well as alleviate social exclusion, and being visible and public about being homeless may generate unwanted attention of all sorts. By the same token as disadvantaged users, like the general populace around them, might look to go online (e.g., hang out in virtual realities, find out things, connect with others, be creative, mobilize, or make themselves heard), the openings to do so in an affordable and equitable way are also under pressure as cyberspace becomes squeezed by powerful commercial and political forces.

The chapter aimed to put these sorts of "subalternity" as they may pertain to the distinction and blurring of the online/offline distinction center-stage by treating them as legitimate and integral to the (geo)politics of the internet. Becoming homeless remains a social taboo in hi-tech Western societies. As such, homeless people are seldom regarded as active internet practitioners or social media participants in their own right. And when doing so they are presented as heroic exemplars, mavericks, or objects of corporate benevolence (Civille 1995; Davidson 2001; Ogles 2006; Schactman 2009; *San Francisco Chronicle* 2011; Rott 2010; Wirth 2012). The point is that despite the exceptional circumstances of these uses and applications there is no universal pattern or relationship; homeless people have as many ways and motivations to experiment with the internet as reasons they have for desisting, or consciously "exiting," as in Nadia's case, for example. While still a textual medium at heart, engaging online can mean being able to articulate one's situation on one's own terms to start and so play a role in undoing the "cocoon of ignorance" many homeless people find themselves in (Julia Tripp, NASNA 2002 Conference Keynote Speech), but it also underscores the "influence of the written word and the power of the spoken word" (ibid,) for populations who spend most of their time being "ignored and not counted" (*BIGnews* Writers' Group, March 10, 2004).

When talking about the internet and "the poor" (Civille 1995), a closer look suggests a multidimensional and double-edged correlation than initial dismissals would suggest. These cover a spectrum of views and approaches to what the main priorities should be, spanning applications of internet technologies as a "low-tech, low-cost tool for the homeless" (Taglang 2001), to projects that look to engage the latest applications as ways of "creating one's own media" (Wright 1997: 323), or longer-term commitments to develop international networks and advocacy tools through web portals, news services, and archiving. A closer look shows a highly uneven, largely unarticulated set of dynamics; between the web's lateral—global— connectivity and the parochial geographies of home-based access and use, from public via landline or mobile phones. Whether online or offline, the core aim of all these pro-internet activities is to allow this group of people a place to have their say, and in an enabling space/place to boot. To illustrate, in traditional (commercial and academic) publishing scenarios, editing is a powerful gatekeeping force that applies strict rules to what is appropriate in terms of form, style, and content. In blogs, literary and journalistic publications, and writers' groups the main focus is thereby to learn to "exercise influence" in a nondestructive way (Julia Tripp, op. cit.) for people who often find as they come out of homelessness that they have literally "lost [their] voice" (Tripp op. cit.). Writing—online, by hand, or with a computer—is one way to counter the "cruellest part of homelessness . . . invisibility and isolation" (Anita Freeman, NASNA workshop, July 20, 2002) for many who have become physically "unpresentable" (ibid.). However, the potential of internet technologies to circumvent geography or alleviate circumstance only really operates for those who are virtually mobile even if they remain actually grounded. Homeless folk, to varying degrees and lengths of time, while actually mobile are virtually grounded by being physically present yet effectively invisible in social and perceptual terms as the rest of us step past them in order to get on with our lives online and on the ground.

Let me make some final points to bring this chapter to a close and in light of the depressing emergence of homelessness as an endemic feature of the *scapes* that constitute today's global cultural economy in meatspace (face to face encounters) and online, in cyberspace (see Chapter 2). First, the many successful and stalled self-help and organized applications of internet media and technologies by and on behalf of various sorts of homeless populations take place in the face of an entrenched diffidence if not hardening of social and political attitudes toward homelessness itself. Ongoing debates about structural or individual causes notwithstanding, the point remains that defining and combating homelessness, as is the case with other (gender, racial, or nowadays digital) divides, is a *political* issue that spills over national borders. The politics here pivot around agenda-setting and spending power as well as deeper differences in how to go about achieving well-being at the individual and societal level as populations move with difficulty, money moves with ease, and everyday life online takes to the road through mobile devices. Second, highlighting how the internet can be a positive thing is not to say that throwing a computer or smartphone at the problem (or disadvantaged person for that matter) will make the problem go away. But refusing to acknowledge that homeless populations can and do make use of the media of their age, indeed may well jump at the chance to do so, as well as throw into relief those who have little interest in the latest gadgets (just like the rest of us), is disingenuous at best given the trend toward digitalization in all aspects of life, work, and politics that the majority of us enjoy or resent in varying degrees. Enabling people in these situations to have emails and voice mails can—and does—allow them to break the cycle of stigma and uncertainty, give them some "turf" they can call their own and present themselves to others. Yet such services can also accentuate isolation and frustration when they don't work, when there is no social network already in place, or no anchoring in broader long-term changes for the better. When already disadvantaged if not stigmatized, already rendered voiceless and invisible, negotiating life between offline and online realms for the purposes of (self-)empowerment, however defined, can only make sense when there "has to be a relationship,"[34] if not broader relational context in which computer skills training and learning to use web applications for job hunting or access to services take place in a meaningful way. Just as in offline scenarios, online communication is not a solo affair. However, and this is the dilemma-paradox facing street papers today, changes in the medium within which this relationship takes place moving to digital sales for instance, has implications for the form and substance of this primary relationship.

This sort of research undertaking puts the accent on how, paradoxically, changing media practices and domains collude with yet also contest entrenched issues of socioeconomic marginalization, within hi-tech liberal democracies in particular. What is a truism, if not a fact of life for those experiencing short-term or long-term periods of homelessness as well as those who work in this area, is that homeless people are dealing with a double burden, the exigencies of everyday survival where the "oppression of the here and now" (Certeau, in Franklin 2004: 48) is particularly acute alongside the ignominy of everyday prejudice. As the world goes online and resources from multilateral and local governmental institutions are being poured into e-projects (of government, education, medical care, and so on) then what happens to those left out in the cold literally and figuratively becomes more pressing. So third, while equitable internet futures and affordable housing are not mutually exclusive neither are they interconnected in a straightforward way. Providing support and shelter in cyberspace is one thing, in *meatspace* (e.g., by offering a couch or bed for the night, buying an issue of your local street paper and then reading it) is another. That said, policies that can marry principles around affordable internet access and public service with affordable housing and public spaces for all to access and enjoy would be a giant leap in a human-led technological direction. For those looking to find voice, to speak, in visceral and symbolic ways in order to be heard, the internet, social media, print, theater, prose, and poetry are all means to an end.

AFTERWORD

> We need to pause and ask—are our normative frameworks—infoethics
> and info-civic imaginaries—adequate to ensure that every person, the
> last woman, can be a global citizen in the interconnected global world
> (Gurumurthy 2013)

A final footnote: In 2007 I met Ron Grunberg for what was to be the last time. We arranged to meet in New York at a Burger King outlet somewhere on 7th Avenue, quite a ways from where I was working at the time. I was coming from downtown, was running late, and unfamiliar to the neighborhood. On arriving I encountered someone standing in the entrance holding out a street paper, high up so that I could not miss it. In fact he was all but thrusting it in my face. Normally (at least since this research project) I would have stopped, looked at the vendor, considered buying it, or declined. But as I was late I wasn't paying attention. I didn't stop, just kept going. The vendor was insistent through. He stepped forward, I hesitated. It was Ron selling the latest *BIGnews*. I had looked right through him.

Who Should Control the Internet? Emerging Publics and Human Rights

INTRODUCTION

> [E]xperience has shown that authorities will always strive to maintain their hold on the national narrative and undermine any proposed alternative. (Barkai 2012: 21)

> [The argument that] access to the Internet makes revolutions more possible is not necessarily [correct]; many Internet-rich access countries saw no change but lo-access countries like Egypt or Libya did see change. . . . [The main point] is actually about who wins in creating the narratives and discourses. (Emin Milli, Azeri Blogger, IGF 2012)[1]

From looking at how people access and use the internet when experiencing the physical and psychological deprivation that arises from homelessness, an acute and overlooked form of disenfranchisement in the internet's heartlands, this chapter moves upstream, to where policymakers, ICT technical communities, corporations, NGOs, and more than a few academics gather to confer and argue about policy priorities for the future of the internet itself. In its more narrow definition, the term *Internet Governance* designates the technoeconomic and legal issues arising from any decisions, de facto or by law, that affect the design, access, and use of the internet as a specific sort of communications network architecture.

Incorporating an understanding of the sociocultural dimensions of decisions taken around the internet's design, access, and use is an underresearched aspect of this domain. Yet for those mobilizing to raise awareness of how freedom of expression, women's and indigenous peoples' rights, and endemic socioeconomic divides are increasingly an internet affair, decisions about the long-term as well as day-to-day running of the internet amount to more than the sum total of their technical specifications. In these understandings the question of who *should* run the internet is intrinsically political because it is a sociocultural concern (Gurstein 2013; Gurumurthy 2013; Gurumurthy and Singh 2012; Jørgensen 2006; Hamelink 1998; WSIS Civil Society Caucus 2003, 2005).[2]

At the macro-level, which is where much scholarly analysis still resides, the annual summits and periodic meetings that fall under the rubric of *global internet governance* are an exercise in contemporary institution building (Flyverbom 2011; Brousseau, Marzouki, and Méadel 2012), imbued with a sense of the global and digital accordingly (Drache 2008; Franklin 2009, 2010; Mueller 2010). As an emerging set of multilateral institutions and their accompanying framings of the world (Bøås and McNeill 2004; Dany 2012) global internet governance consultations based on multistakeholder participatory models (see Chapter 1) have been gathering pace over the last decade in different locations, brokered by UN organizations such as the International Telecommunications Union (ITU), UN Educational, Science and Cultural Organization (UNESCO), UN Conference on Trade and Development (UNCTAD), and the UN Development Program (UNDP) for the large part. Elsewhere private quasi-public organizations such as the US-based *Internet Corporation for Assigned Names and Numbers* (ICANN) or the *Internet Society*, or intergovernmental organizations such as *the Council of Europe* and *Organization for Economic Co-operation and Development* (OECD) preside over other sorts of meetings.

Anchored in the UN Millennium Development Goals (UN 2000), the timetables and wide-ranging agendas for UN-brokered meetings on internet governance are indicative of a change of mood; namely one shifting toward a supraterritorial rather than an implicitly state centric framing for decisions about the future internet, and with that a recognition of the need for wider participation (in this case, from "civil society") in the agenda-setting and decisions taken. On the one hand, visionary resolutions, declarations of principles, and action plans render these ambitions to forge a so-called global consensus in a format intended for a wider consumption among UN member states and their respective citizenries (ITU/WSIS 2003a, b; ITU/WSIS 2005a, b; UNHRC 2012; OECD 2001). On the other hand, and in another register, a panoply of highly specialized issues and legal decision-making are emerging as case law, technical standards, international treaties, and trade agreements (e.g., Abraham 2012; OECD 1997, 2000, 2011; Council of Europe 2012a, b). Even getting this far in both respects is easier said than done, however. There are powerful vested interests who regard UN-led attempts at "global consensus building" with ambivalence if not suspicion; in the first instance as evidence of a "global internet governance movement" that challenges national sovereignty or smacks of neo-imperialism given the predominantly Anglo-Euro-American genealogy of the internet to date. Or in the second instance, allow governments a license to undermine civil liberties by overregulating what companies and individual people do in cyberspace and thereby threaten "internet freedom" itself.

From a practice-based, actor-centered perspective, the embedding of an open-door policy for convening high-level policymaking meetings on the ground, as well as through online consultations and organizing, has been a game changer for all concerned, including participants, pundits, and politicians. As such these twenty-first century encounters mark a shift in organizational cultures as they allow participation by all comers in principle, reluctantly (e.g., the ITU and ICANN) or at full throttle (the UN Internet Governance Forum, and more recently UNESCO). A pioneering example of UN-led "multistakeholder participation" was the ITU-hosted *World Summit on the Information Society* (WSIS) between 2003 and 2005, initiated with an eye to generating a baseline for considering information and communication technologies as, essentially, a global rather than a purely national concern, to wit the engine of a would be "global information society" (another contested notion that has engendered its own critical literature). Its successor, the Internet Governance Forum (IGF) has managed to continue to date as a fledging autonomous organization within the larger UN system: eight years old in 2013, it is but a youngster when compared to the UN itself (nearly seventy-five years old) and older agencies such as the International Telecommunications Union (almost 150 years old). The WSIS and especially the IGF have been exceptions to the rule of high-level summits in this respect, as they are relatively uncomplicated to attend for those with time, money, and interest in either monitoring the process or influencing the outcomes. In short, grassroots groups and lobbyists, laypersons and small businesses can be on the official record of proceedings once reserved for career diplomats, politicians, technical experts, or accredited NGOs. Other sorts of gatherings where the regulation of the mass media, telecommunications, and now the internet have been on the agenda are not like this however. These meetings are more arduous for nonaccredited participants to get access to, based as they are on technical or business credentials, or diplomatic accreditation protocols where only limited observer status is granted if at all.[3]

Despite the best of intentions, these exercises in multistakeholderism as a working principle for decision-making but more so for agenda-setting remain somewhat removed from how ordinary people use the internet in their everyday life. Moreover, being a layperson in this domain is a relative term given that taking part costs (a lot of) time, and money. It also entails moving from broad ranging, expert-defined topic areas to single issue–based and highly technical conversations, being able to engage the idiom and "work" the (virtual and physical) room alongside professionals and old hands. It also means working within a reformist mood, dealing with the glacial pace of protocol-saturated organizational cultures, the tedium and stiffness of formal deliberations (e.g., plenary sessions) and exigencies of producing coherent and diplomatically correct "policy-relevant" output under extreme time constraints (Franklin 2005b). Hence these settings are not particularly amenable to more organic forms of face-to-face mobilization (see Chapter 4) or high profile enough to warrant traditional forms of direct action, sloganeering, or public demonstrations. That said there were echoes of "old social movement" mobilization during the WSIS years, and have been since the IGF meetings.[4]

Even as meta-level narratives, accumulating conversations about norms and values, as well as technolegal regulations, around who should control the internet with their own intricate subplots, the institutionalization of internet governance as a process that takes place in multisited online and offline domains warrants more than passing attention. Open access to IGF events, and the official record, belie the intensity of the struggles involved, the attrition aspects to debates that have long tails into precursor events (Singh 2012). It requires tenacity and where-withal to see an idea, resolution, or principle through, and all in the spirit of open consultation. Intertwined and underscoring the minutiae of these institutional cultures, competing *grand narratives* of the internet's past, present, and future are increasingly jostling for attention. Cross-border and online-offline mobilizations to influence these narratives are the case in point for examining how *publics* are being addressed, if not redefined and reinvented in digital settings that are, as I argue in Chapter 2 and return to in the next chapter, part of an emerging internet governmentality paradox. These narratives have a substantive and ideational role in both the big power and ordinary politics of the internet in that all protagonists are looking to influence if not change the conversation about how the internet and its assumed role in promoting a greater public good are interconnected; for example, in combating global poverty (UN 2000), promoting democracy and freedom of speech (Clinton 2010a), or as the latest tool for "peace and sustainable development" (UNESCO 2013a).

This third case study looks at how the IGF has been emerging as a focal point for mobilization around a particular "transnational frame" (Olesen 2010: 2) that addresses and engages a different order of internet governance issues than hitherto; namely it looks at a project to put human rights at the heart of internet design, access, and use and to do so as a global public issue. The chapter examines these behind-the-screen mobilizations as an example of, what I argue, is a transnational public in the making, by and large a cautious counterpublic (see Chapters 2 and 6). A specific example of how these transnational and digitally inflected social formations (Warner 2002) unfold over time is evident in the process of drafting and launching a *Charter of Human Rights and Principles for the Internet* (IRP Coalition 2013; Hawtin 2011; Centre for Law and Democracy 2011) as a self-conscious, cross-sector and trans-border initiative for promoting internet governance as an inherently human affair. Drawing on over five years of participant-observation, and then more direct involvement with the IGF and earlier work on civil society interventions at the preceding WSIS (Franklin 2005a, 2007b, 2011), this final case study examines human rights-based advocacy for the internet in the arguably "post-national constellation" (Habermas 2001; Fraser 2005, 2007) that underpins the multistakeholder in-stitutional settings in which internet governance narratives are being formed, and contested.[5]

The primary paradox-dilemma underscoring this case study is that all parties in the emergence of internet governance as an intrinsically "open-source" consultative decision-making process based on *multistakeholder participation* have reservations about the point of the exercise as an effective way to leverage change or, if preferred, protect the status quo.[6] State actors such as the United States, China, United Kingdom, South Korea, or India, for instance, have markedly different ideas about who should control the internet, however defined, and on whose terms web-based goods and services are to be made available to their citizens. Transnational corporations, particularly those US-based companies who currently dominate the global market for web-based goods and services, or who own and control the strategic hardware and software that make the internet or the web function (see Chapter 3) inevitably focus on maintaining their market-share. But they are also engaged in taking a moral high ground in successive face-offs with governments looking to control, indeed demanding that global internet service providers (e.g., Google, Facebook, Yahoo!) tailor their provisions to comply with national jurisdictions. There are hearts and minds as well as new consumers to be won, if not by direct confrontation then by stealth. Meanwhile, for those "stakeholders" participating as members of "civil society," relative newcomers to high-level settings such as the UN, being full-fledged participants on the conference floor but also behind the scenes has provided an important platform for promoting alternative views about how the internet is being, or should be run and to do so from *within* the process.

By and large though the exercise of power and resistance in these multistakeholder institutional realms is a level-headed, meticulous affair where every word, comma, and full-stop is considered in full, if for no other reason than that these outcomes become written record (uploaded and archived online to be indexed, searched, and circulated accordingly) and can have legal and political import. For the purposes of this case the main point to make at the outset is that from the outside looking in, these sorts of settings are not very romantic in a period punch-drunk with the revolutionary fervor of recent mobilizations on the streets and online. Moreover in practice they tend to operate as meta-level deliberations that waft over the nitty-gritty of the technical and commercial *business* of rolling out basic or enhanced internet access and web services to homes, businesses, government departments, and public services (from schools to hospitals to highways to airports). What the IGF, as a digital age genus of global institution-building and norm-setting does do, however, is bring parties together who normally gather in parallel settings: technical people mix with philosophers, activists with corporate representatives, researchers with diplomats. Whatever the outcome, this is in itself unusual. It has also presented new practical and political challenges (Franklin 2005a, 2007a) for groups accustomed to the persona of Critical Other. The flip side to this opportunity, however, is that despite the seductions of being invited to sit around the table, in these ostensibly inclusive participatory models here too "visibility can be a trap" (Foucault, 1984b).

Before proceeding with the case in hand, some background is warranted to provide first, the discursive (human rights) and second the wider institutional (the UN) context in which the study has taken place. Alongside its formative role in formulating and furnishing international human rights standards, the United Nations has been active since its earliest years in brokering international consultations around media policy (Frau-Meigs et al. 2012, MacBride 1980), crystallizing into three, and potentially four historical phases and respective media debates (Gerbner et al. 1993): the late 1970s, early to mid 2000s and the last decade.[7] After a long hiatus, the ITU-hosted *World Summit on the Information Society* (2003–2005) and Internet Governance Forum (2006–present day) have looked to shape the debate at the global level though not exclusively. After this scene setting the chapter turns to what has been happening in one area of mobilization at the Internet Governance Forum, the case of the *Charter of Human Rights and Principles for the Internet* (here on in *IRP Charter*). It focuses on the initial debates about underlying principles, format, and how to collaborate and *collabowrite* in a suitably transparent and accountable "multistakeholder" manner to resolve disagreements about terminology and audience for the charter. The main period I focus on here is the one between the production of the initial draft (IRP Charter 1.0) in 2010 and eventual launch of the "Beta" version (IRP Charter 1.1) and accompanying *Ten Principles* in early 2011, which was disseminated to the "international human rights community," regional intergovernmental organizations, and hopefully publics back home.

Producing a document that had its skeptics at the outset—and since—meant conjuring up a particular sort of public in advance. It has had to take into consideration that such an undertaking was at the time considered a reinvention of the wheel (e.g., any rights based issues for the internet are already dealt with under national or international law) if not a sidebar to more pressing technical considerations. The drive and wherewithal to produce a document, and do so in a computer-mediated mixture of old new media and new Web 2.0 tools, also meant mobilizing minds and pens—or keyboards—to collabowrite not only a "tangible" but a legally coherent text (it was not clear at the time whether for use as a policy and/or advocacy tool) that would put human rights issues squarely on what had been predominantly technocratic and techno centric agendas. Precursor initiatives from the WSIS period notwithstanding (more on this below), between 2008 and 2012 this and many other charters, declarations, and bills of rights emerged as a result. For some observers this represented an "explosion" (Hawtin 2011) in rights-inflected initiatives. In this case, however, we see the IRP Charter emerging as a rhetorical device, laying out an alternative vision for the future of the internet as explicitly anchored in precursor UN treaties and covenants. The chapter concludes by discussing the implications of the IRP Charter case and its multistakeholder, multisited setting for apprehending how (counter)publics are forming around internet governance as social formations specific to this domain and time.

This chapter cannot deal with all of the facets to this reconstruction of a project that is very much "under construction"; a fuller analysis of the substantive content of the IRP Charter in the context of other rights-based initiatives that have been emerging is one case in point. Another is an analysis of how the coalition itself relates to established "policy networks" and advocacy lines of affiliation and focus.

This chapter is thereby a partial account (in all senses of the term) as it looks to capture the essence of the genesis, genealogy, and process of writing and legitimating the IRP Charter process as an experiment in multistakeholderism. This reconstruction also straddles a period in which working practices, in this already novel multilateral institutional domain, were colored by the availability of Web 2.0 tools, cloud computing services as well as what is a very old form of new media nowadays, an email list. For the purposes of this chapter this case is an illustrative example of how publics can and do form beyond the legal and imagined confines of nation-state discourses and jurisdictions; and as such need considering in terms of their multisited and hybrid manifestations that emerge in real time and computer-mediated circulations.

The objective here is not so much to posit the *Internet Rights and Principles Coalition* and the production of the *Charter of Human Rights and Principles for the Internet* as some paragon of multistakeholder virtue. It is rather to pin down, for the time being, the shifting goal posts (see Chapter 6) and my own role in the process changes, through the prism of the initial stages of the IRP Charter project. In any case I am not claiming that the IRP coalition, made up of diverse organizations and individuals, constitutes some quantifiable, verifiable new "public" as conventionally understood, and critiqued (Warner 2002; Hauser 1999; see Chapter 2). Rather the aim is to start unraveling how rights-based mobilization around the internet constitutes emerging, self-creating counterpublics within the burgeoning "transnational discursive opportunity structure" (Olesen 2010: 2) of mainstream internet governance institutions. For civil society groups who traditionally have fewer resources or political leverage to influence agenda setting in these arenas as do corporate and governmental actors, the trend toward multistakeholder participation is also a concrete opportunity to make a difference as policy is being created, and norms established, in real time so to speak.

This sort of engagement, as a recognized interlocutor in official proceedings and so full signatory to the outcome, is for some a double-edged sword, in that it shifts the political axis from voicing dissent to defending consent (see Lipschtuz 2005; Coleman and Tucker 2012). For others, multistakeholder participation in forums that are primarily about agenda-setting, circulating preferred narratives and established terms of public debate, is a chance to publicly call governments and corporations to account for policy and business decisions that can be detrimental to ordinary people, the most disadvantaged members of society in particular (see Chapter 4). In this sense the IGF participatory model, and its limitations as a non-recommendation-making body (ITU/WSIS 2005c), is an important forum and access portal for civil society participants mobilizing in the aftermath of the "Another World Is Possible" tenor of the antiglobalization protest in the early 2000s (Hardt and Negri 2000; Rupert 2000). This reconstruction also bears in mind a more recent development that will concern Chapter 6, namely a spate of fierce antigovernment/antiregulatory rhetoric that crystallized in 2012 at meetings where both the internet and international telecommunications were on the agenda. This was a moment that arguably heralded preparations for a "global battle for governance of the internet"— and thereby one for the hearts and minds of internet users around the world. In one fell swoop, the question of who *should* run the internet found itself center stage after years spent in the wings, even if as the result of a global public relations exercise. Internet governance had "arrived," becoming a global and publicly political affair.[8]

This then is a reflexive critical reconstruction, from a relative insider's view, of how publics and counterpublics form within an agonistic model of democratic politics (Laclau and Mouffe 1985; Dahlberg and Siapiera 2007).[9] As such and without second-guessing whether these publics in the making are (as yet) successful, sustainable, or desirable, this study treats them as emergent publics that are intrinsically though not exclusively transnational or digital, that engage in different sorts of vernacular and formal discourses and actions, online and off. Indeed, the object of the exercise—rescuing the internet from vested political and economic interests that would undermine universal rights and civil liberties—demands and facilitates radical rewritings and reframing of word, thought, and deed.

HUMAN RIGHTS AND INTERNET GOVERNANCE: ANOTHER OXYMORON?

> We aspire to build information and communication societies where development is framed by fundamental human rights and oriented to achieving a more equitable distribution of resources, leading to the elimination of poverty in a way that is nonexploitative and environmentally sustainable. To this end we believe technologies can be engaged as fundamental means, rather than becoming ends in themselves, thus recognising that bridging the digital divide is only one step on the road to achieving development for all. . . . It must be remembered that the Internet is not a singular communications "platform" akin to a public telephone network; it is instead a highly distributed set of protocols, processes, and voluntarily self-associating networks. Accordingly, the Internet cannot be governed effectively by any one organization or set of interests. (WSIS Civil Society Caucus 2003: 3, 22)

> The Internet provides an open, decentralized platform for communication, collaboration, innovation, creativity, productivity improvement and economic growth. (OECD 2011: 3)

As an illustration, these two quotes encapsulate the contrast in articulating the role envisaged for information and communication technologies (viz. the internet) in furthering broad sociocultural, political, and economic ends. The first quote above dates from the first WSIS meeting in 2003, part of a dissenting statement civil society participants in this ITU-hosted event issued at the end of the proceedings (see also WSIS Civil Society Caucus 2005). The second is from the OECD, an organization that joined internet governance consultations at a later date. In the first we see how references to information and communication technologies are predicated on a human rights "discursive frame" (Olesen 2010) first and, second, on their being a means rather than an end in themselves. Direct references to the internet per se were less prominent in the WSIS period in that the object of critique revolved around the limitations to framing ICT for Development agendas within a notion of the "information society" (Franklin 2005a, Jorgensen 2006). A decade on, the situation had been reversed; foregrounded references to the internet have proliferated and in these framings it has taken center stage as both ends and means for any number of global and nation-based aspirations. This shift is encapsulated by the second statement from the OECD, first from framing the internet as something that is "not a singular communication platform" (WSIS Civil Society op. cit.) to being just that, "an open, decentralised platform. . . ." (OECD op. cit.). A second shift occurs from human rights as a central principle by which to launch any *ICT for Development* policymaking and investment decision, to human rights as an implicit element in that "any policymaking associated with [the internet] must promote openness and be grounded in respect for human rights and the rule of law" (OECD op. cit.: 3, 5).[10]

In the case of digital/human rights activism, these are initiatives based on a conviction that the outlook for an equitably accessible and affordable internet is one that incorporates human rights and principles at all levels: within its computer codes and protocols, terms of use, points of access, and available content. At the very least, developments in the way the internet, and by association the web, functions, oversight over key operations (e.g., allocating domain names, transmission and retention of data), and provision of goods and services (email accounts, social networking services, content like news and entertainment) should not evolve in ways that can harm ordinary people inadvertently or by intent (e.g., poor privacy controls of personal data or forms of censorship and surveillance online). However, for most of its users, the internet is "just there," and the political implications of the subtleties of placement and articulation in a burgeoning body of internet governance *hypertextual* discourses are far removed from daily web-based work habits and socializing.

But awareness of the politics of the internet and its governance had started to crystallize downstream well before the events in 2012; inequities, imbalances, and injustices around the way ICT can be used to track, monitor, repress, and entrap are only now coming into popular (viz. public) debates. This change occurred in the wake of the Arab Uprisings, the *Wikileaks* controversy, *Occupy* movement, and corollary actions by the *Anonymous* collective of direct digital activists that gathered pace from 2010. These events and the role played by social media (those goods and services premised on Web 2.0 platforms) put the internet squarely at the epicenter of public and political debates about the role of old and "new" media in social transformations, revolutionary and otherwise. By force of circumstance, historical events, the internet had become a public issue, at home and abroad.

In this view the notion that the internet and its governance are not mutually exclusive ideas is closely allied to the idea that the internet is more than an artifact or a business matter (Cerf 2012). Instead it is a communicative means and ideal that should by rights belong to everybody (WSIS Civil Society Caucus 2003, 2005). Official civil society participation since the WSIS in the 2000s and, before that, the *New World Information and Communication Order* period of the

1970s and 1980s (MacBride 1980; Gerbner et al. 1993; Frau-Meigs et al. 2012) took on an intrinsically holistic stance to the technoeconomic and political policy debates that impinge on the ownership and control of the "mass media" of the day. Partly as a result of governmental and corporate strategies but also various forms of social mobilization from grassroots groups and NGOs large and small, the (global) politics of media policymaking and with that internet governance (Freedman 2008; Mueller 2010) have been increasingly polarized. The problem for those mobilizing around this more qualitative, normative premise in internet governance arenas large and small is the disconnect between the way people around the world use the web and so the internet, take it for granted in their everyday and working lives at the "front end," and the opaqueness of ad hoc and (de) regulatory decisions being made at the "back end" of the internet's transmission and access architecture (Stalder 2012: 249; Deibert 2008).

The case of the IRP Charter within the IGF meetings is instructive for considering the way internet media and communications have become a coconstituent of contemporary power relations and their resistance in two respects. First, it offers a fruitful way of examining in real-time and over time, rather than through archival reconstruction or episodic visits to events, the way in which these sorts of publics and, by association, counterpublics take shape; as discursive and physical social formations that create "vernacular" and formal "rhetorical exchanges" (Hauser 1999) these publics look to propel themselves as "self-creating and self-organized" (Warner 2002: 50) actors in settings in which these sorts of efforts are not indigenous. They are required to behave as fully accredited protagonists in debates and outcomes while embedded in longstanding traditions of grassroots and NGO activism and advocacy networking and mobilization that also predate the cyberspatial turn in these domains. The case here unpacks a notion of publics that sees them "move from spectatorship to active consideration of issues" (Hauser 1999: 274). It is one that illustrates how publics that are not preconceived or polled in national citizenry or public opinion terms are "conjured into being" through "texts and their circulation" (Warner 2002: 49–50). This case points also to the literal-digital dimension of these circulating "texts" in that rights-based initiatives (as literal texts in document form such as charters, declarations, compendia, and so on) have become a prominent way to raise consciousness of how state and corporate deployment of internet technologies can undermine human, social, and economic rights. In so doing this public is becoming palpable as digital, audio, and visual footprints online. In UN meetings at least the digital archiving of all proceedings, verbatim and official output, on the open web is now coupled with the increased use of remote participation applications that record proceedings. These publics can be heard if not seen, as well as read in the expanding online archives and audio archives of these meetings.[11]

There is a second reason for spending time with a specific formation and project that has emerged within the wide purview of the IGF period; indeed there is an inexhaustible range of concerns that are arguably more prominent, more pressing in terms of internet governance agendas. This snapshot of an ongoing process permits a purchase on one of the many issues jostling for attention on the internet governance agenda, so complex in itself that the wood is quickly lost through the trees. The case of the Internet Rights and Principles Coalition (IRP Coalition henceforth) and its Human Rights and Principles Charter (IRP Charter) allows a peek into emerging practices and thereby codes of behavior in exhibitions "of publicness with a forward-looking concern for constructing the future from an interpretation of the present" (Hauser op. cit.). In this case we will look at how a digital and transnational public in the making self-creates and self-organizes in conventional and novel ways that fit the times. In this respect the IRP Coalition, as its participants ripple outward to other, overlapping and contentious constituencies is treated here an aspiring public in a context defined predominately by technoeconomic paradigms (OECD 2011). As such it is a public of a particular order. Like its institutional home base, the IGF, the IRP Coalition, as a whole and among its various members, is emerging from, and engaging in and with the computer-mediated and supraterritorial domains enabled through and by the internet. To do this the coalition has had to invent itself as a viable party in the proceedings, navigate and negotiate its way around the local, national, regional, and transnational interests of its membership, and establish its own way of doing things (online and on the ground) in a variety of arenas.

There is more at stake however as the changing political landscape in the world and mobilization of the two other official IGF *stakeholders*, UN member-states and corporate actors, upped the ante considerably. Once considered purely an advocacy ("soft") platform in the precursor WSIS meetings and first five years of the IGF, the idea that how the internet is run and human rights are interconnected, if not hardwired into issues around the internet's DNA, its code as a form of regulation (Lessig 2006, appendix) has become a hot topic. It is a topic upon which powerful actors, political and economic, have started to stake claims of their own. As a loose coalition working within a "multistakeholder participatory model" premised on consensus-building rather than direct action or confrontation, I argue that the IRP Charter project actually reveals a *cautious* counterpublic emerging; one moreover that is rendered by deeper ideological and cultural divides in terms of how participants perceive and articulate the point of the exercise. By working within the UN system, accepting full participation and thereby sharing responsibility for outcomes, this public is having to learn ways of negotiating and navigating a twenty-first-century "triangle, sovereignty-discipline-government, which has as its primary target populations and as its essential mechanism the apparatuses of security" (Foucault 1991: 102). I will return to Foucault's governmentality paradox in due course.

GLOBAL MEDIA AND COMMUNICATIONS: WHOSE PUBLICS?

Internet governance is also about who gets to participate in decision-making about Internet policy and technology, and how. Since its infancy, the Internet has benefitted from a lightweight, decentralized, multistakeholder approach to governance that combines targeted government regulation with various formal and informal multistakeholder organizations to help guide its global development.... To be sure, current implementation of the multistakeholder model remains imperfect and there are still challenges to address—we must find ways to democratize global representation and expand participation, particularly from the global south. But in general, the open, transparent, multistakeholder model is what has made the Internet the robust, global platform for human rights, development, democratic participation, and commerce it is today. (Llansó 2012)

I noted earlier that the above characterization of how the internet is run, in principle at least, encapsulates what has become the dominant narrative of internet governance, one based on the twinned rhetoric of cooperation, equivalence, participation, and openness on the one side and, on the other, that of democracy, human rights, and commerce. What it does not mention is that all these ideas, separately and as bundled ideals of the good society that is inherently computer-mediated and facilitated at a global level, are contested spaces. The politics of internet governance as a "lightweight, decentralized, multistakeholder approach" to the technoeconomic and legal practicalities of "who rules?'" on this domain are elided.

Media-focused NGOs working on a variety of issues concerned with press freedom, freedom of expression, and affordable access to news and information predate the arrival of the internet and these information society framed efforts by the UN to monitor and steer agendas in the early twenty-first century. Nowadays, activists and policymakers focus on these longstanding concerns (and political standoffs) coupled with digital age specificities such as electronic privacy, internet filtering, public access, cyberterrorism, and so on. The UN's own prehistory of principled declarations of intent and action plans that linked questions about the ownership and control of the media as a matter for international cooperation are notwithstanding (see MacBride 1980; Gerbner et al. 1993). NGOs, journalists, and media activists in earlier generations operated as external critics or observers rather than full-fledged participants. From an organizational and communicative point of view, these more recent consultations depart from usual UN practice embedded in closed shop, diplomatic protocol.

At the United Nations: From Global Media to Global Internet Debates

The United Nations has its eyes on the Internet. A summit next month could lead to a telecommunications treaty granting a UN agency jurisdiction, and control, over the online universe. The issue is being furiously debated and lobbied in advance of the summit. Companies, technologists, free speech advocates, and national governments must now consider the relative merits of the current decentralized, US-centered governance of the Internet, versus a more equitable, multinational (but possibly more restrictive) system. (New America Foundation, 2012)

To get a sense of the legacy, and in many cases the longstanding commitment of certain NGOs, and activists based in the media reform movement (the United States in particular), press associations, and nowadays internet-related issues around Freedom of Expression, privacy, and education, but also academics, a quick overview of how the latest round of agenda-setting came about is warranted. In brief we can divide these international, now multilateral, initiatives into three generations. The "First Generation" was hosted by UNESCO, during which calls for a *New World Information and Communication Order* emerged, along with two cornerstone publications, the UNESCO "Mass Media Declaration" (1978) and the *MacBride Report* (1980). The titles alone indicate the mood, hopes, and struggles at the time between competing media models and their concomitant political systems.

While diverse in practical terms, ideologically and in the debates of the time the contenders split into two opposing camps. On the one side were defenders of the "free world" and their respective media freedoms based on hybrids of public service broadcasting media (exemplified by the British Broadcasting Corporation) and privately owned print media. In the other corner were state-owned and controlled systems that characterized the Soviet Union, Maoist China, and various dictatorships allied with these two powers or other countries within the Non-Aligned Nations. Spread out between these two extremes of how the media of the day should be owned and controlled, however, were a number of UN member states with other ideas, newly independent former colonies included, who were looking to reconcile these two extremes for diverse political and social agendas. These earlier "global media debates" have since been superseded by not only geopolitical realignments, the end of the Cold War and the events of 9/11 in particular, but also those debates wrought by the rise of global (satellite) news media and entertainment, neoliberal policies that deregulated and privatized public services (railways, telecommunications, power utilities) in the Western world, and the rise of the internet itself (see Chapters 1 and 3).

It took some twenty-five years for the "Next Generation" to get going, this time hosted by the International Telecommunications Union and the aforementioned *World Summit on the Information Society* (2003–05). The third host, based in the Web 2.0 generation of internet media and communications, is a self-contained organization within the UN's purvey, the Internet Governance Forum. As noted above while it is early days there is a fourth phase unfolding in the wake of an ITU meeting scheduled to revise outdated international telecommunications regulations (ITRs) in Dubai in December 2012 (the WCIT-12, see Chapter 6). This was a meeting in which the diverging interests from the internet and telecommunications regulatory and business sectors and their nation-state avatars confronted each other head on. At the time of writing the dust was still settling after the United States, United Kingdom, and others refused to be signatories to the eventual agreement. This was a rerun of what had happened in the 1980s at the UNESCO hosted events (Frau-Meigs 2012). Then, even as the Cold War was entering its terminal phase, the West versus East rhetoric was still ferocious. The same two major powers walked out, one withdrawing from UNESCO. This had severe repercussions for this agency's credibility (JP Singh 2012).

Largely forgotten, if not deliberately sidelined, this early period of global (viz. intergovernmental) media debates was one in which a generation of media reform and community media activists cut their teeth in multilateral institutional arenas such as the United Nations. The role, positive and negative, of either nation-states (members and building blocks of these very institutional settings even as they were not the only major players) or private enterprise, remains a contentious one to this day. As noted in Chapter 2 and underscored in Chapter 3, it is this most recent period of laissez-faire capitalism that arguably ushered in the internet as the mass media of the day. As such its design and terms of use have also become synonymous with the private sector, a paragon of freedom understood as free markets and governmental nonintervention. Here is not the place to argue the historical veracity of this easy-to-use bifurcation between the "bad old days" of state media ownership, relatively underdeveloped in the United States despite an underground history of public service broadcasting ethic and activism (Aslama and Napoli 2010), and the utopianism of internet freedom discourses based on corporate self-regulation and government regulators who can stay obedient to the disciplining of market mechanisms. The point to note here is a historical one. While scholars of internet governance today, predominately but not exclusively US-based, debate the pros and cons of who should control the internet (Goldsmith and Wu 2006; Goldsmith 2012; Singh 2012a), leaving broadcasting media models or telecommunications provisions to others, the burgeoning "battle for the soul of the internet" (Mueller 2010: 1) has its political economic and sociocultural roots in these earlier battles for the soul of the world's media.

Twenty-first Century Interventions

Full participation by civil society representatives, in the form of larger and smaller NGOs, grassroots groups, and academics in UN-brokered consultations around contemporary media and communications have been taking place since the inaugural summit exercise in the early 2000s: the WSIS between 2003 and 2005. The successor to the WSIS consultations is the IGF (2006–2010), now entering its "second generation" phase since its first mandate ended in Vilnius, Lithuania. The second phase opened in Nairobi, Kenya, in 2011 followed by the IGF 2012 in Baku, Azerbaijan. The 2013 IGF takes place in Bali, Indonesia.[12]

Based on an organizational model that loosens the usual accreditation protocols of UN gatherings to allow individuals and organizations other than governmental representatives or the business sector to participate, the WSIS initiated and the IGF institutionalized the principle of opening up access to discussions to all comers with the express aim of "global consensus-building," as an earlier version of the IGF's homepage put it. More recent versions state that the IGF is "an open forum which has no members. . . . Its UN mandate gives it convening power and the authority to serve as a neutral space for all actors on an equal footing. As a space for dialogue it can identify issues to be addressed by the international community and shape decisions that will be taken in other forums"

(IGF 2011). As such this is an organizational form that stresses agreement and consensus over overt controversy or confrontation as public (state), private (corporate), and all others (civil society) participants come to the table to establish principles and terms of debate that in principle "feed into" policymaking, and standards-setting arenas that affect how the internet operates, is accessed and so eventually used. Funded and endorsed by the UN General Assembly (ITU/WSIS 2005), the IGF has been a new addition to the wider ecosystem of "interconnected autonomous groups drawing from civil society, the private sector, governments, the academic and research communities, and national and international organizations . . . who work cooperatively from their respective roles to create shared policies and standards that maintain the Internet's global interoperability *for the public good*" (Wikipedia 2013, emphasis added). While it may not be more than a paper tiger, a "talk-shop" to its detractors, the Internet Governance Forum is, like the internet itself, in a state of flux. The IGF's leadership is under pressure within the UN where other agencies have historical claims to being better equipped to take the lead in this domain, the ITU and UNESCO being two cases in point. The centripetal forces of powerful state actors within the UN General Assembly and Security Council looking to keep these sorts of gatherings in their place, the United States, China, and Russia for instance, also makes the sustainability of the IGF over the long term, particularly if UN member states withdraw support and funding for this effort after its second mandate passes and all efforts to date are reviewed in 2015.[13]

In the meantime, IGF meetings have become a relatively convivial arena where both powerful and less well-endowed participants converge on the ground look to shape the agenda, official and informal, for a range of competing as well as overlapping ends. It is one arena in which its own stakeholder communities are both vying and colluding with forces within and outside the IGF itself for control of not only the internet's future agenda in technoeconomic and legal terms but also the terms of debate, if not now, then for posterity. This includes control of a larger narrative, the internet's "creation myth," and, ultimately, the outlook for experiments such as these within the wider UN ecosystem where the issues at stake are implicitly of transnational and supraterritorial political and economic importance. Geopolitics, regulatory priorities, and the cultural politics of global norm setting collide and intertwine on the conference floor and behind closed doors (Flyverbom 2011; Dany 2012). Like wider debates that flow from and inform UN-brokered consultations on how to tackle global warming, global poverty, or nuclear arms, those around who controls the internet engage business, politicians, and the rest of us (viz. civil society). The relatively inclusive participatory model of the Internet Governance Forum is a radical shift in the way intergovernmental organizations perceive their own roles, and regard their publics at large (implicitly international or global) as interlocutors.[14]

However, *civil society* as one of the three official "stakeholders" in these meetings, participating in an individual or organizational capacity, comprises highly diverse and thereby contentious constituencies made up as they are of competing political ideologies, worldviews, funding streams, and allegiances. As the most recent participating party in international diplomatic meetings, it is also one with the least experience, least traction in institutional, financial, or lobbying terms. Moreover, participants in the multistakeholder settings that are now the trademark of international meetings around internet governance are there wearing multiple "hats": as members of technical communities (engineers, programmers for instance) and engaged in various advocacy or activism platforms, as academics engaged likewise and/or working as government and/or business consultants.

While government representatives can claim to be political representatives and corporate sector participants are unreservedly there for business purposes, civil society participants thereby have a range of mandates and claims by which they speak for and intervene on behalf of others, are open or prone to co-optation by other parties. Taking part is not the same as engaging in protest action from the outside. Accepting stakeholder status means becoming complicit, contributing arguably to both problem and solution. The Internet Governance Forum has set itself the task, currently endorsed by the UN General Assembly in principle, of working on behalf of a transnational (viz. global) public for whose good it aims to find common ground around the optimal way to run the internet.

For this reason alone the IGF is worth a closer look, particularly from the point of view of a multiplex and dynamic constellation of contesting publics and by association counterpublics that are formal and vernacular social formations embedded in the particularities of internet governance cultures, discursive and organizational. As these groups appeal to larger publics as well as specific constituencies from a range of perspectives and crisscrossing investments, what were arcane debates confined to arenas of expertise relatively far removed from the headline grabbing actions of street-level, "tweeped" mobilizations have become in themselves the source of increasing media attention. For this reason, the question at stake of who *should* control the internet, how and for whose benefit has become a wider debate, particularly as lobby groups and public relations strategies of corporate and political powerbrokers collude and collide with multiplying multistakeholders.

As the IGF seeks to find its niche in the larger UN system and hones its role as one of the above "interconnected autonomous groups" combining multiple and competing interests rather than represent a singular one, it faces a number of challenges. This is the case over a decade after the UN's International Telecommunication Union won the toss to host the WSIS. These challenges come from within as the leverage and input of the diverse groups that constitute civil society participation in the IGF process waxes and wanes over time. Not unlike the shifts in commitment of time, resources, and person-power during the WSIS phase among civil society groups (Franklin 2005a, 2007a), those still working on IGF-related events and agendas are having to contend with questions about legitimacy, purpose, and strategy from within and from without. Critics looking on, those who advocate state-centered approaches and traditions to any sort of media regulation as well as those who object to any regulation at all point to the IGF and related venues as a nascent "Internet Governance Movement" putting forward an internationalist, if not corporate-led, agenda for moving governance of the internet (viz. media) out of the remit of representative democratic institutions.[15]

These activities in situ, action-plans and declarations produced by meetings, and mobilization in between planned events are aimed at intervention in high-power politics around ownership and control of the constituent parts of the internet. They constitute largely invisible layers of decisions taken by governments, regional organizations and large corporate players that also impinge on how the rationale for these decisions are *framed* for public consumption (see Fraser 2005: 81). The point here is that contestation around governmental and private (corporate) sector plans for how people connect, interact, and go about their daily lives, work, and study by these groups working on behalf of local, national, and also "global" publics have been largely unfurling behind our screens. Multilateral meetings such as the IGF are the decorative tips of a much larger iceberg. For any initiative looking to reframe these diverse agendas toward a certain end, or intervene in these settings on one particular platform (privacy or freedom of expression issues online for instance), this shift in institutional context has required a change in tactics, indeed signals a political change in strategic terms. For those NGOs speaking for constituencies, or issue-areas as civil society representatives, the WSIS and IGF means interacting with governmental or corporate participants as peers. In principle even if in practice the means and access to key decision-making is uneven.

THE UN IGF AND ITS DYNAMIC COALITIONS

The Internet Rights and Principles Dynamic Coalition (2008-present day) is, exactly as the name implies, a coalition, not an organization. The term "dynamic coalition" was coined in the first IGF meeting (Athens 2006) as a move away from the traditional "silo" categorization of participants as governmental, private sector, or parallel groupings of civil society that characterized its precursor, the WSIS, and indeed the UN as a whole. The descriptor "dynamic" indicates the intention behind the idea of generating "informal, issue-specific groups comprising members of various stakeholder groups allow collaboration of anyone interested in contributing to their discussions."[16] Whilst falling short of working group status, in this respect the IRP Coalition has managed to achieve a modicum of broad-based participation as well as dynamism in that it is recognized as an "active coalition" by the IGF Secretariat.

The *Internet Rights and Principles Coalition* emerged out of the first round of Internet Governance Forum meetings (2006–2010) establishing the organizational structure and approach to working across geographical borders and time zones in 2008 at the IGF in Hyderabad. Drawing on a number of previous efforts to codify disparate issues around the politics of design, use, and access of the internet at the intersection of social justice, media reform, and ICT for Development advocacy platforms, the coalition crystallized around mainly civil society but with some private sector and government representatives from the Global South and

Global North (Brazil, India, South Africa, Europe, and the United States). The IRP Coalition membership is currently comprised of NGOs (e.g., the Association for Progressive Communications, IT For Change, the Centre for Internet and Society [India], and the Electronic Frontier Foundation to name but a few), academics, (inter)governmental organizations (e.g., the Council of Europe), digital campaigners (e.g., Access), social enterprises (e.g., Global Partners), business representatives (e.g., from Google, Tiscali, and Orange), and private sector interest groups (e.g., the Internet Society, Global Network Initiative).

Despite crisp differences in political ideology and rights-based priorities based on different understandings of human, civil, and economic rights, the basic premise held by all members of this coalition, in their own right and in relation to others on the IGF floor at the time (e.g., the Freedom of Expression and Gender Coalitions) was that internet governance in all possible permutations is first a social and second a technical issue. At time of writing it was part of a push by a number of diverse initiatives looking to take pole position in the anchoring of "human rights as a prism to assess internet governance policy-making."[17]

It is an ad hoc and therefore fluid coalition that the IRP Coalition can be seen as an example of a Web 2.0 social actor, in so far as it is not housed in a physical headquarters under a particular legal jurisdiction. Rather it operates mainly through an email list and periodic meetings, of which the IGF as an annual global meeting, regional internet governance meetings (in the United States, Europe, Asia, India, and Latin America, for instance) are the main moment of face-to-face interaction in organized and ad hoc ways for participants. The IRP Coalition has proved to be one of the IGF's success stories for this reason. This is largely due to its longevity and sustained actions between IGF meetings but also because it has managed to achieve a palpable output that is greater than yet beholden to the sum of its constituent members' individual projects and campaigns. For the most part other coalitions have stagnated or sprung to life just prior to each IGF, only to lie dormant again shortly after until the next year.

There are multiple and contesting narratives entailed in this cursory summary. They fold backward and sideways into precursor and contemporaneous initiatives and declarations, some from earlier UN forums (see section above) and others upon which the charter is based and in turn have piggybacked off the charter. This reconstruction, partial and from a fully immersed observation point, looks at how the coalition undertook to lead in drafting and mobilizing the energy to launch (online mainly and modestly by professional standards) the *Charter of Human Rights and Principles for the Internet* (IRP Coalition 2013a). Based on the *Universal Declaration of Human Rights* and subsequent UN covenants, the key purpose was to devise a document that would articulate where and how the online environment that the internet supports, including web-based products and services, raise specific issues that need more explicit articulation than the UDHR currently provides. This is the case even as existing laws and covenants are currently under review and being adapted for the online environment at the international, national and regional levels, such as data-retention laws, privacy rights, freedom of information and freedom of expression. All these are being reconsidered in internet-dependent and internet aspirational societies. The IRP Charter (1.0) was launched and opened for consultations in late 2010 at the IGF meeting in Vilnius just as the Wikileaks controversy was peaking and the events of the Arab Spring were taking off. In early 2011, a fresh draft (Charter 1.1 or Beta Version) alongside an abbreviated version of the charter, the "Ten Punchy Principles," was launched as events in Tunis and Cairo were peaking. Active members in the coalition at the time were involved in these events directly (e.g., several Tunisian activists such as Slim Amamou were taking part in discussions) or working to support the movements through technical expertise, web proxies, or as media intermediaries, spreading the word around the world via social and conventional media.[18]

HOW THE IRP CHARTER CAME ABOUT

Reconstructing this process highlights how internet-based and web-embedded this project was. While the coalition itself was not an organization indigenous to the social media of today's Web 2.0, indeed it would be safe to say that the coalition's daily business is based on a rather old new medium—email—it is unthinkable without the internet. More on these particulars in due course but first, an overview of the timeline.

Between 2008 and 2010 the coalition undertook a collaborative writing-exercise of a full charter that was based on the UDHR. The aim was to make explicit relevant sections of the UDHR in such a way that IT and telecommunications technical communities, policymakers, and user groups could use it as a "policy instrument," or "template" for assessing whether existing rights-based principles and practices adequately account for the way the internet has been changing the rules of the game. These groups looked at how people access and use information and communicate with each other as well as at state and corporate responsibilities and obligations in internet-dependent environments.

Between 2010 and 2011 the need for a more accessible advocacy and educational version of the Charter became clear so the coalition drafted and launched in early 2011 the *Ten Principles*. These "ten punchy principles" distilled the larger more legally complex document into a digestible form (IRP Coalition 2013a, b).

Between the 2011 IGF meeting in Nairobi, Kenya, and the 2012 IGF in Baku, Azerbaijan, raising awareness of the IRP Charter beyond its UN-based environment as an educational and debate-raising tool (the point of the "ten principles" initiative) and the coalition's work stalled somewhat. Events and more powerful forces took over in this period in the lead up to a major ITU-hosted meeting in Dubai, which was scheduled directly after the Baku meeting. As corporate lobbying around the notion that the UN was looking to "take over the internet" in general but particularly at the Dubai meeting (more on this in the next chapter) intensified, and major players such as the United States, United Kingdom, China, and Russia took opposing positions on the limits to multistakeholder approaches to running the internet from the point of view of national sovereignty, the IRP coalition was undergoing an internal rethink. By the end of the Baku IGF in 2012, the coalition had renewed its intention to continue, albeit with a clearer aim of furthering the charter itself as well as supporting corollary projects looking to put human rights and principles on internet governance agendas.[19]

I will leave to others, and another discussion, a more detailed assessment of not only the content of the charter, but whether these efforts are needed, or have made or will make a difference. A number of analyses have already emerged over this timeline that consider these questions (Murray 2010; Musiani 2009; Center for Law and Democracy 2012a). Suffice it to say that multistakeholderism (or open-source discursive productions) such as the charter can be enrolled for any number of agendas. Hence such undertakings can be a double-edged sword if in the long run there are not substantive and sustainable changes in how (state, corporate, and individual) human rights transgressions in the online environment can be brought to account and redressed. For these arenas are also places where powerful vested interests with little interest to part with substantive power look to deploy the working practice of multistakeholderism as they have evolved to date for their own ends; to "manufacture consensus" by having the endorsement of civil society-based organizations. For some observers there are more than enough legal instruments to achieve this goal (see Musiani 2006; Council of Europe 2012a, b). For others it is about changing the terms of debate, changing the conversation that would put human rights and internet governance in separate domains.[20]

With these caveats in mind, there are four domains in which the IRP Coalition or its members have succeeded in getting human rights and the internet onto the radar and onto the UN human rights agendas. This has occurred through outreach as well as active participation in respective initiatives, including the United Nations Human Rights Council, major rights-based initiatives in Latin America (the Brazilian Marco Civil [Bill of Internet Rights] project in particular), the Council of Europe, and the first stock-taking event of the WSIS + 10 review (UNESCO 2013a, b). These overlap with the more nitty-gritty work of drafting the IRP Charter and Ten Principles in these years, online (in the list) and off-list (in working groups) and on the ground (at official venues).

Taking each in turn: First at the UN, the IRP Coalition was active in advocating the IRP Charter principles in light of the work of Frank La Rue, special rapporteur for the UN Human Rights Council, whose attendance at the Vilnius IGF 2010 was part of the coalition's outreach during the charter drafting phases. The upshot was a report that framed human rights in light of changes being brought about by how people use the internet and the arising need to cope with privacy abuses, freedom of expression, and censorship issues. La Rue's report explicitly mentions issues around the censorship of online content, the need to ensure access to the internet as it becomes integral to basic information needs, the "criminalization of legitimate expression" online (La Rue 2011: 33; Shah 2011), and other issues. In the first paragraph this report makes clear that there is a connection between existing international human rights, that is, the core units of UN treaties and covenants that fall under the rubric of the "International Bill of Rights" and corollary treaties and covenants that make up the larger UN-based "human rights system" (Clapham 2007: 49; Smith 2012: 37 passim) and the need to protect these online. Careful to stress that this connection applies to existing rights and principles, the tenor of this report is clear from the first paragraph. It emphasizes "the applicability of international human rights norms and standards on the right to freedom of opinion and expression to the Internet as a communication medium, and sets out the exceptional circumstances under which the dissemination of certain types of information may be restricted" (La Rue 2011: 1). The stress on continuity in rights despite the recognition that the internet marks a quantitative and qualitative shift in how people access news and information and communicate as internet access is rolled out as a global project (UN 2000) was underscored in the resolution that accompanied this landmark report. Specifically it said that "the same rights that people have offline must also be protected online" (UNHRC 2012: 2).

At the same time as the IRP Charter was taking shape, in Brazil coalition members were mobilizing around a consultative process that generated a civil rights framework for the country's 77.8 million internet users (Knebel 2011), a major ICT market in the region. The "Marco Civil" was launched at the Vilnius IGF in 2010 in tandem with the IRP Charter.[21] It was held up as an example of how governments can work productively with as opposed to against the interests of their citizenries, with the Chinese authorities' tight control of internet users posited as the other extreme. The bill suffered a major setback in late 2012 when it failed to get majority support in the Brazilian parliament. While the Brazilian consultation process, resultant resolution and accompanying internal debates have their roots in a national and regional context, the implications of the success or failure of this regional experiment for discourses of multistakeholderism as the modus operandi in principle for internet governance (Kern 2012; Souza 2012) are wider.

The above two arenas are ones in which coalition members have been active, through which the IRP Charter as an opinion-shaping initiative has had an indirect influence (indirect in so far as the charter itself is not cited as a source document). A third one in which coalition members are present, and the charter itself is an explicitly visible element in the planning is the European Union, its Council of Europe in particular. A recent initiative, the *Compendium of Existing Rights of Internet Users* has on its committee several IRP coalition members active in the drafting of the charter (members of the coalition's "expert group"[22]). They are currently engaged in developing a "compendium of existing rights for internet users" that anchors the desiderata of the IRP Charter, and concomitant initiatives (see below) in existing human rights and consumer rights (Council of Europe 2012a, b; Miriri 2011). A fourth domain in which the coalition has been recognized is in the round of UN-brokered meetings to review the WSIS (and with these the Millennium Development Goals) Action Plans that kicked off in February 2013 (UNESCO 2013a, b) and will end in 2015. Being present and counted, on the record and so part of the UN's online archives is in this respect a marker of existence and evidence of persistence. Whether it is a marker of success is another matter, and moreover dependent on how success is defined and measured.

Collabowriting a Charter of Human Rights and Principles for the Internet

> To address a public we don't go around saying the same thing to all these [different] people. We say it *in a venue of indefinite address* and hope that people fill find themselves in it. The difference can be a source of frustration, but is also an implication of *the self-organization of the public as a body of strangers united through the circulation of their discourse.* (Warner 2002: 59, emphasis added).

This approach to linking media policymaking and human rights together at a multilateral, meta-level did not come from nowhere. Those groups and individuals behind this particular project were aware, albeit in different measures, of the legacy of preceding and contemporaneous efforts to articulate in a concrete way undertakings to keep social concerns at the heart of internet governance agendas. This legacy of "previously existing discourse" (Warner 2002) reaching back to the early days of the UN as outlined above was a refrain in early discussions in meetings, and online. Earlier attempts and publications were evoked as not only forerunners but also a working template.

Another distinguishing feature in this case, one that for some created obstacles to getting things done, and for others was intrinsic to the legitimacy and effectiveness of the eventual outcome, was the stress on multistakeholder participation. To this end the coalition's mission statement and steering committee is self-consciously comprised of NGO, academic, government, and private sector representatives and their interests. The charter and coalition behind it, while largely civil-society based, rests on creating tangible ways to persuade wider publics, at home and in multilateral settings, so that this is a reasonable attempt at being geographically and socioculturally representative. This is not an easy matter in practice and discussions continue as to the limitations; this is so in terms of personnel, time, money, and other resources to sustain a project of this kind as a bridging initiative between diverse NGO, governmental, and corporate interests in their respective visions of the future for the internet.[23]

Charter 1.1

How to start writing a document of this sort? Where to start, which format to use, indeed what would be its role and purpose given the large body of legal casework within national jurisdictions but also the treaties and covenants that constitute the UN's International Bill of Rights?[24] At the outset some of these questions needed immediate attention; for example, who indeed is the "target audience"? What sort of format should the drafting process take, and how many people and what sorts of people should be involved? These practical issues dominated the early discussions on the IRP mailing list; some issues operational and practical, others more complex and politically charged (e.g., whether there should be an attempt to draft "new" rights or not, whether access to the internet is thereby such as new right). Once it was clear that the charter would follow the organization and order of appearance of the Universal Declaration of Human Rights by opting "for the approach of saying that everything in the charter derives from Human Rights standards contained in the UDHR" (comment from the IRP Discussion List 2010), the next step was getting started. This initial phase proceeded by coalition members self-selecting themselves to commit to one-to-three clauses from the UDHR. Each drafted a few sentences that would bring the clause up into an internet context and then committed to further consultation.[25]

This inductive, Do It Yourself approach created a document that for many within the coalition was untenable on legal and technical grounds. However, it did create a clear draft from which to work. With the chair based in London (Lisa Horner and then Dixie Hawtin from Global Partners UK) and the coalition's founding chair (Max Senges who took up a position with Google Germany shortly after work began) monitoring progress closely, the next task was to shape the content of this draft into a more legally coherent, and workable document. Here conference calls underpinned the email-based interactions. At this point one of the first major debates took place. That is, how to keep the project serious in the eyes of the larger "international human rights community" (i.e., Amnesty International, Human Rights Watch, UN Human Rights agencies). By late 2009 this rough draft, as a "Wiki" version, emerged as the IRP Charter 1.0, its next round of revisions animated and commented on by the wider coalition after being drafted by the aforementioned "Group of Experts" based in France, Austria, Brazil, Denmark, China, South Africa, and Sweden. The next major debate that emerged was on how to promote the charter, to whom and with what means. The issue of whether to keep this consultation (and thereby legitimation and outreach) process close to home, within the wider UN Human Rights community for instance, or whether to go completely public was resolved by not deciding either way. Resources for a full public launch were not available but neither was there a clear consensus that "going for it" in this respect was wise if the charter itself was still in draft form. Other schools of thought considered that this was exactly the moment to go public, and engender more support for the project from wider constituencies (linked to coalition member organizations). The upshot was at the time a lack of publicity for the coalition's efforts as well as the braking effect generated by the emergence of competing projects and understandings of where rights and principles in general, and human rights in particular fit into the mainstream of internet governance debates.[26]

The range, scope, and indeed ambitions of this process are immediately apparent in the table of contents. Noting that the order of appearance was in itself the source of extended discussion—what comes first matters, these are as follows:

1. Right to Access to the Internet
2. Right to Non-Discrimination in Internet Access, Use and Governance
3. Right to Liberty and Security on the Internet
4. Right to Development through the Internet
5. Freedom of Expression and Information on the Internet
6. Freedom of Religion and Belief on the Internet

7. Freedom of Online Assembly and Association
8. Right to Privacy on the Internet
9. Right to Digital Data Protection
10. Right to Education on and about the Internet
11. Right to Culture and Access to Knowledge on the Internet
12. Rights of Children and the Internet
13. Rights of People with Disabilities and the Internet
14. Right to Work and the Internet
15. Right to Online Participation in Public Affairs
16. Rights to Consumer Protection on the Internet
17. Right to Health and Social Services on the Internet
18. Right to Legal Remedy and Fair Trial for actions involving the Internet
19. Right to Appropriate Social and International Order for the Internet
20. Duties and Responsibilities on the Internet
21. General Clauses

(IRP Coalition 2013).[27]

Those familiar or new to the content of the UDHR[28] will note that the IRP Charter includes clauses and issues that move beyond those in the original declaration (e.g., clauses 12, 13, and 9) in significant ways. The order of appearance has also been changed. In short, the process of drafting, debating, revising, consulting, and rewriting has created a self-contained document rather than a carbon copy of its source document. A lot more remains to be said about the way these clauses were written in light of their legal implications if (and here prominent members were very careful not to get ahead of themselves) the charter were to take on a higher profile role in the upper echelons of the UN. Suffice it to say that in successive IGF meetings and preparatory events the aim was to engage key addressees in the UN system rather than offend.

COLLABOWRITING AS POLITICAL PRAXIS

Now for a brief word on the actual practices of collaboration, or "collabowriting"; facilitated in palpable ways by the use of social media tools, the actual writing of the central document and accompanying briefs, guidelines, declarations, and reports to the IGF secretariat was more or less shared. While the fine-tuning of the main text resided in the Expert Group, a complex and vibrant debate on whether or not this initiative was, or should attempt to be about creating new rights emerged. The outcome was a decision to ensure that at no point would the document claim to be promoting *new* rights. This was considered a tactical necessity as well as a practical and legal one given the political realities that these covenants themselves were "fragile" and often abused instruments by UN member-states of all hues. Second, and as fine-tuning on the wording of the hot topics predominating IGF agendas at the time (e.g., internet filtering and privacy issues) continued, discussions about the underlying values, objectives, and eventual form of any formal statement took shape.

That said, and this trope has remained a vibrant one to date, there was an acknowledgement from the outset that access to the internet (see clause 1 above) would by definition, and intention "be the only new right that we establish in the Charter, as . . . everything in the Charter derives from . . . the UDHR" (IRP List 2010, op. cit.). Opinions about whether access to the internet is or is not a new right continue to be divided, but it is worth noting that since these discussions took place the notion itself has become a more familiar, less foreign idea within IGF settings at least. In short, with the Arab Uprisings in full swing and Tunisian coalition members prominent in these discussions (and the coalition in turn joining the chorus of Western voices urging the former Tunisian authorities to comply with the protesters' demands) the idea of access to the internet took its place at the top of the charter if for no other reason than without it the rest of the charter made little sense. For if the internet "as a new space or domain is considered important enough to write a new charter of rights, the right to that domain/space is a prior right" (IRP List 2010).

A further discussion point was organizational, developing an accountable and representative working model, where (if anywhere) on the ground the coalition would be based, and how to proceed for an undertaking comprised largely of geographically dispersed (relative) strangers. This was coupled to a growing awareness that certain aspects of the emerging charter were more developed than others. This was important if the UDHR was to remain a strict template. A related axis for discussion, some of which were intense debates about the nature of consultative processes as either expert-led or by intention open to all parties was how best to improve the draft versions in practical terms for participants spread around the world. Based on a website and its evolving set of Googledocs and presence on Facebook (the use of both not self-explanatory for some participants, including myself), it was decided to keep these initial and important revisions within the immediate vicinity of the coalition and email-based discussions; other mailing lists created a zigzag of crossing correspondence but also indicated a wider constituency in email terms at least. The eventual decision to adopt a tripartite approach emerged in order to create a way of handling a document that was growing in density and complexity from a legal and technical point of view, and length: (1) a preamble couched in more upbeat language and the succeeding clauses of the charter proper as listed above; (2) a technical, more applied set of implementation guidelines written by and for a more specialist audience; (3) a commentary. It is at this point that the current charter has remained for the time being.[29]

Who Is Talking to, and for Whom?

Recalling the initial rethinking of publics beyond a priori categorizations as either citizenries/voters, or media audiences, or consumers from Chapter 2, according to Michael Warner publics other than political forms are recognizable as "different from a crowd, an audience, or any other group that requires co-presence" (Warner 2002: 53). In this understanding the "idea of a public, unlike a concrete audience or the public of any polity, is text-based" (op. cit.: 51, emphasis added). In other words, as an idea shared by a self-organizing "body of strangers united through their discourse [comprised of] indefinite and impersonal address" (Warner 2002: 60) publics exist "by virtue of being addressed" (op. cit.: 50; original emphasis). I will return to this discursive, practice-based conceptualization of publics in the next chapter in light of this case. Suffice it to say that for undertakings such as the IGF as an internet-focused and web-based endeavor to generate discourse of a particular kind, this understanding of publics as comprised of those who are (writing and speaking) subjects in the process, and addressees for its outcomes is valid.

Nonetheless, to speak of publics as text-based only, or as "a space of discourse organized by nothing other than discourse itself" (Warner 2002: 50) need not exclude some basic enumeration or attempt to ascertain who is actually taking part in the "body of (relative) strangers," that is the IRP Coalition. The outward ripples of other publics that coalition members may be representing (as is the case with NGOs or governmental bodies) make this enumeration but an anchor point. Communicating principally by email, on a mail list, the IRP Coalition conforms to Warner's understanding of a public in terms of membership being open, participation invited rather than demanded, content and terms of address comprising internal and external issues, formal and informal terms of address and a sense that there is a larger "public" at stake. Those who sign up to the IRP Coalition mailing list are addressees and protagonists in this regard because "merely paying attention enough to make you a member" (Warner 2002: 53); emails constitute the principle means of communicating, disseminating, and mobilizing accordingly.

At time of writing the total membership of the coalition based on the mailing list stood at 309. Its Facebook "likes" were a total of 1583, and Twitter followers 617. These numbers are not exactly a cast of thousands, but numbers can be deceptive here. To recall, the coalition exists as much as an email listserv as a set of overlapping circles of memberships (and their respective social media links, websites, and personnel) that convene elsewhere online or on the ground. Questions about what counts most these days, social media followings or "like" totals aside, the mailing list is where the coalition resides at the practical, everyday level. Face to face meetings notwithstanding, this is a public that is literally "text-based" in digital settings. A cursory roll call underscores the difficulty of pinning down categories in a setting in which participants have multiple affiliations. Hence the following overview is based on the "stakeholder" categories that accompany certain email address suffixes. Breaking down this membership in this way, whereby the email address supplied is an approximation of affiliation at least (members often opt to use personal rather than professional email addresses, while others from the business or government sectors are there primarily for that purpose) shows that membership is fairly evenly spread between first individual and/or company email addresses from the main internet service providers such as Google or Yahoo! (39%).

The second largest group is made up of ad hoc groups and NGOs using the. org or .net suffixes (24%) along with (inter) governmental and other sorts of organizations (research institutes or think tanks) using either country domain names (of which Italy and Brazil feature prominently) at 26%. The third cluster, one that straddles civil society, government, and private sector affiliations, is that of academics; they make up 12% at last count. The choices members make about whether to use a work or private email address for this list are personal and professional, for example, some opt to be members in an individual capacity (and they say this) while others are there in an official one. Some companies are relatively well represented on this roll (e.g., Tiscali in Italy), as are lobby groups such as Access, the Electronic Frontier Foundation, or larger international NGOs such as the Association for Progressive Communications (APC) or Human Rights Watch.

There is a question of whether in this period (mid-2009 to mid-2011), the period leading up to the launch of the first draft in 2010 and then Version 1.1 and Ten Principles in 2011, the coalition could be seen to be operating as a transnational public in the making, at least in terms of its modes of address, self-awareness of this role, and composition of known and unknown strangers (Warner 2002). Categorizing the posts into either internal or external sorts of conversations, a provisional typology of the sorts of subject matter and internal concerns on the mailing list (1098 in just over two years) emerges. The number of members registered on the listserv in 2011 stood at 201; this number increased by a third two years later. At this time 57% were actively participating (based on the number of posts per named participant/signature provided). This implies that the rest were either "lurking" or ignoring these posts; whether these addressees were paying attention all of the time is not possible to prove categorically though people will indicate at the time of their first post that they have been "lurking." Others make their participation known in bilateral emails around specific issues. What this snapshot shows, without unpacking the content, themes, and debates within the message headings, is that those posts designated as "internal," namely those concerned with organization and the charter itself, composed 64% of the total posts. Those designated "external" were 36%. In this time period the events of the Arab Spring where members of the coalition were engaged, some imprisoned (e.g., Slim Amamou in Tunis who was active on the list at the time) and other issues (member organization campaigns, links to other events, or relevant meetings) are grouped together. The point here is that over these two years this listserv was not simply talking to, or about itself.

New Entrants: Collaboration 2.0 and the Ten Punchy Principles

The people formally known as the audience wish to inform media people of our existence, and of a shift in power that goes with the platform shift you've all heard about. . . . The people formally known as the audience are simply the public made realer, less fictional, more able, less predictable. (Rosen 2012: 13 and 15)

This modus operandi, to be accessible and do everything in the open, making the charter accessible too, crystallized during the Vilnius IGF in 2010. As newer

participants got involved in the coalition from the "Digital Activist" generation, the need to make this charter more palatable to newcomers and laypeople
took shape. In Vilnius an action group set itself up to translate the charter into a
"punchier" version, expressly for advocacy, education, and consciousness-raising.
Less concerned with pedigree issues around parallel and precursor initiatives, this
working group came up with what the coalition recognizes, and launched, as the
"Ten Punchy Principles" underlying the charter itself.

As the charter itself took shape, so did the sense of the coalition's aims and objectives for this document. A source of ongoing discussion about what the primary
objective of this drafting process was, along with what to do with it once it was
ready for public consumption, opinions divided roughly between those looking
for it to be an advocacy tool, in which case the charter document could serve as
an inspirational and resource base for shorter, more accessible, and so "punchier"
statements. The other school of thought was to shape the, by now, expanding core
document, with its own preface and tail of legal and other commentaries, into
a coherent policy tool. In this case the charter itself needed to be able to stand
on its own feet as a legitimate document in legal terms. With the UDHR still as
the source code, so to speak, and other core documents that codify social and
economic rights, women's, children's, and indigenous people's rights, the charter started to take a more substantial, lengthier, and more legally and technically
complex form. Not only were its parameters growing but so was its usefulness
for advocacy. Consciousness raising was at the time still lagging behind the way
participants in (and scholars of) internet governance perceived the importance of
these issues. At thirty-five pages and growing, this text hardly made easy reading.
A change in tactics was needed, a new impulse in terms of outreach as attention
shifted from activism and advocacy on the ground to online, digital renditions.

The twenty-one clauses listed in the table of contents above were distilled into
ten Big Ideas: Universality; Accessibility; Neutrality; Rights; Expression, Life, Liberty and Security; Privacy; Diversity; Standards and Regulation; and Governance.
The public launch of the Ten Principles, making as much use of social media
(Facebook, Twitter, and so on) was at the end of March 2011. Coalition members
volunteered or found others to translate this shorter document into over twenty
languages, from Dutch to Khmer to Swahili. A poster (the Ten Punchy Principles
Flyer with a quite "retro" design, Figure 5.1) campaign, and formal presentations
of the charter itself in various UN and intergovernmental venues took place at
the same time. It was a modestly resourced and modestly successful campaign
for a project increasingly conscious of its digital dimensions. Its 1003 "likes" by
individuals/organizations on the charter's very own Facebook page was considered "not bad" under the circumstances.

Critiques and Commentaries: The IRP Coalition 2012 and After

Before considering in more theoretical terms how this case illustrates, if not
underscores, the paradox-dilemmas that concern this book, some points about

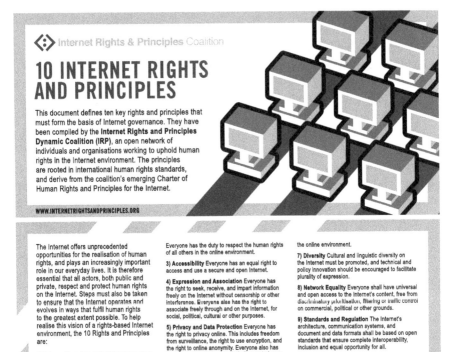

Figure 5.1 *Human Rights and Principles for the Internet: Ten Principles* (IRP Coalition; http://internetrightsandprinciples.org/wpcharter/).

internal debates, critiques, and ongoing developments warrant discussion. These are germane to how the coalition, as a whole and in terms of its membership, operates as a self-aware public in the sense Warner puts forward (2002, see Chapters 2 and 6). First is the point that the exercise is in itself an unfinished project. This goes back to the initial impetus for getting the charter off the ground, at least as evidence in the early years that the coalition's email discussion list was to generate a concrete project that could focus the fledging coalition's energies. As various rights-based platforms and advocacy organizations were attending the IGF for a multitude of single-issue concerns, the charter, as an initiative that looked to propel precursor ones forward, was one way to put these diverse and diffuse concerns into a single frame. It provided a more inclusive view to a plethora of rights and principles issues around the internet that were to date emerging in a piecemeal, national-level, and uncoordinated manner.

In this sense the charter project was a bottom-up approach within the top-down idioms of the IGF working model (Musiani 2009: 514–15). Commentaries on the charter itself as well as interventions that draw on the charter from coalition members are a burgeoning, albeit diffuse literature. During the drafting process and launch of the IRP Charter, coalition partners with legal expertise played a key role in providing commentary and critique of the draft (IRP Charter 1.0) and its current version, including raising questions about utility, relevance, and sustainability in a domain suffering from "Charter overload" (Hawtin 2011: 51–54, see Figure 5.2) if not a surfeit of information law-making (Musiani 2009). A commentary on the charter from a legal perspective by the Centre for Law and Democracy (2011) is currently one of the most thorough critical analyses of the IRP Charter itself and a cornerstone document for any further work. Meanwhile coalition members from the Global South have also made critical interventions on the role of rights-based initiatives and their tendency to be dominated by Western governmental and/or corporate readings of human rights as either consumer or civil rights (Singh 2012c).

Second, where this sort of work and the specific and wider publics it seeks to address if not influence fits into the wider institutional context. It bears reiterating that the IRP Charter did not emerge from a historical vacuum, as it took its cue from earlier initiatives to codify a Bill of Rights for the Internet that go back to the WSIS period if not before.[30] However, during these email-based and traditional sorts of conferrals, picking up as the IRP Charter and its Ten Principles campaign was launched in 2010–2011, a plethora of like-minded declarations started to mushroom, taking their place on the web alongside older ones, still present though inactive websites. These complementary though not necessarily synonymous initiatives require separate treatment in that they point to the deepening and widening terrain of vernacular and formalized public discourses about how rights, however defined (and this too is a political bottleneck) and the internet are not mutually exclusive. As written text is the primary form of output, policy consists of written texts produced in traditional and online settings. These

Figure 5.2 *How Standards Proliferate* (by xkcd; http://xkcd.com/927/).

sorts of speech-acts warrant, and lend themselves to a range of textual analysis and other interpretative techniques, legal included. Like literary and popular culture productions, these hypertexts are also how digital publics in this sense are "made flesh" once in circulation. But the apparent "mainstreaming" of human rights within internet governance bodies along with emerging differences in style and substance between coalition members suggested that the IRP Charter's self-conscious institutionalist approach was being perceived as too "old school" in a fast-evolving context in which threats to internet freedom were seen to warrant an approach of another sort.

A new arrival to the coalition at that time, Access, a DC-based campaigning organization with a successful track record in digital activism and behind the screens support on the ground in parts of the Middle East and North Africa, threw these different paradigms into relief. They also provided the impetus and campaign skills to mold the longer, dense IRP Charter into the sharper, shorter Ten Principles. Even as they were not intended to be mutually exclusive, the latter began to overshadow the larger charter. A year later, the emergence of a campaign based on a *Declaration of Internet Freedom* (Access 2012) modeled on the Ten Principles generated a different sort of debate within the coalition as "old timers" took exception to this campaign's initial positioning of itself as a new, and more consultative initiative. The outcome of four months of list-based, and off-list debate (37% of four months postings on the list were posted within a month on this topic) threw into relief the markedly different ways in which internet "freedom" (versus regulation or in conjunction with regulation) is understood between US-based members and those elsewhere. It also highlighted differences in advocacy style and target audience, a more general global public on the one hand or, on the other, government ministers, human rights bodies, and UN agencies. Riding high on other successes, a number of US-based activist groups (rightly) observed that "the Charter was just too dense for advocates, many policy makers and most users [who were] (rightly) taking a long time to get it right" (IRP List 2012). Here the preferred approach was to mobilize and gather demonstrable evidence of public support through a range of campaigning techniques, such as online petitions (Access 2012, 2013). However for those in the coalition working at the legal and politically substantive level, relying on oversimplified declarations (here the object of critique was the aforementioned *Declaration of Internet Freedom*) was counterproductive in the long run; such declarations are "a form of McPrinciples; they are sugary and calorific enough to make the reader (and signer) happy for a while, but soon you'll find that you're still hungry (and that Internet rights are still unprotected)" (IRP List 2012).

Since then, a more civil society–focused coalition has been formed within and around the IGF-ICANN-ITU nexus (thereby breaking with the principle that all coalitions have to be formed of all stakeholders). The inaugural *Best Bits* meeting at Baku took place the weekend prior to the 2012 IGF Meeting (November 3–4, 2012). With members of the IRP Coalition active in this meeting, this initiative marked a coalition of coalitions within the IGF willing to take a stand to present a more self-conscious and organized "civil society" standpoint. They were "calling on the IGF to draw from the 'best bits' of various Internet rights statements including the IRP Charter and the Declaration of Internet Freedom in order to develop a multistakeholder statement on Internet governance" (Bankston 2012, Best Bits 2012). With a sense of being at a crossroads already evident in the Nairobi IGF of 2011, of how the "IRP must adapt in order to remain useful and influential" (IRP List 2011), at the 2012 IGF Meeting in Baku, Azerbaijan, the IRP Coalition met on the final day to take stock and elect new officers. The main issue on the agenda was how to proceed, if at all. Discussions about what the next steps should be occurred in light of the success of the IRP Charter in raising awareness within intergovernmental forums and increasing prominence of human/civil rights-based internet initiatives and discussions within IGF meetings and in wider public debates in the wake of the anti-SOPA/PIPA mobilization earlier in 2012. There was a robust attendance at the meeting (around thirty attended, a threefold increase from the previous meeting in Nairobi) and a clear mandate, to be ratified by the larger constituency on the listserv who were not at Baku, for the IRP Coalition to continue within the IGF. The meeting also voted to continue supporting the rollout of rights-based initiatives within respective IGF stakeholder organizations where appropriate, and more importantly to promote the IRP Charter more vigorously to a wider public.

DISCUSSION

> While we can take the position that "the public" is a socially constructed category, . . . as all categories are, this does not mean that such a category isn't worth retaining. . . . There are, in short, many ways of signifying the "public": the issue is how one inscribes the public within political discourses. (Lewis, 2001: 19)

To summarize, the IRP Charter, in its full, written form, emerged through overlapping drafting, consultation, and outreach (publicizing) phases in this time (Center for Law and Democracy 2011, 2012, Hawtin 2011). Looking back, the outcome and decisions, and the many debates that constitute these (non)decisions appear straightforward. But they were not. Even before it got started the very idea that the coalition should even set out to write such a document was contentious. This charge, that such a charter of human rights for the internet is simply reinventing the wheel, or as an aspiring transnational rubric is superfluous to local needs and national jurisdictions is still a potent criticism. It stands along with other reservations, in particular that as such the IRP Charter stands "no chance" of ever being ratified by UN member states in the UN General Assembly. Even if it were to reach the acceptable level of legal legitimacy or moral weight required for this sort of political consensus, doubts about the point of the exercise remain from within the coalition and beyond; the hazards of appearing to be promoting new rights when "old" rights remain vulnerable to abuse by UN member states and other perpetrators being a case in point.

These reservations are not the focus of this discussion. Rather how this experiment in seeing how the documents comprising the International Bill of Rights, with the Universal Declaration of Human Rights (UDHR) as the linchpin, could provide a template for an internet-focused document. This template would enhance the larger body of human rights instruments (international treaties and covenants that articulate economic, social and cultural rights in the first instance and, in the second civil and political rights) that have evolved since (Clapham 2007: 48–52). Given how the "international human rights agenda" (Clapham 2007: 49) has been, and continues to be colored by the history of ideological, political, and economic struggles within the UN General Assembly and Security Council that straddle the Cold War, decolonization, and New World Order eras of the twentieth century, this experiment in applying these already contentious covenants to the online environment was a bold one. The drafting and then refining of the document that currently carries the name were organic processes, driven by the energy of individuals as well as supported indirectly and directly by larger NGOs within the coalition interested in having a critical mass form around human rights and principles for internet governance as a global and public interest issue, not simply the domain of corporate or big power politics.

For all the diversity and unevenness that constituted the broader email-based efforts, limited financial and human resources (drafting documents like this is fine-tooth comb, time-consuming work), and access to requisite levels of legal and technical expertise, the IRP Charter has taken its place within the circulating discourses that constitute the IGF's working culture. In this sense, the Version 1.1 of the IRP Charter is recognized, by coalition members at least, as the coalition's touchstone for any future endeavors, its own set of "Talmudic documents" as one member put it.[31]

Whether the current version of the IRP Charter, and any further work on it, has anything substantive to offer to "existing" human and consumer rights law as they apply to the internet (Council of Europe 2012a, b; Benedek 2012) is a moot point. What is relevant to this discussion, however, is that as a process embedded in web-based and multistakeholder understanding of collaboration as a public performance of participatory democracy, the charter's journey through the larger Internet Governance Forum process is one that encapsulates competing understandings of the internet itself as a synecdoche for either the "world we want" or conversely the "world we do not want." The jury is still out in both respects. However, as this chapter is about resistance not being futile but also needing to shape-shift and navigate multiple domains for action in the fast-moving terrain of internet governmentality (see Chapter 2), this analysis is less concerned with whether this has been the definitive effort to put human rights on the internet governance agenda (there are other claimants to this role). Here the coalition as a whole is but one actor in this production. The main concern here is to show how publics and counterpublics are being conjured into being in this domain. This makes efforts such as this also open to being appropriated, speech and actions captured under the aegis of those who can command the space and places for decision-making (Dany 2012; Lipschutz 2005; Coleman and Tucker 2012). But it also offers a look into ways in which resistance, of a reformist inclination, can also unfold with relatively few resources and to date no direct funding, or sponsor affiliations.

Countering Publics

In considering whether the Internet Rights and Principles Coalition conforms to the notion of publics conceptualized as self-creating, discursive formations that are not duty-bound to either statist or market-based understandings (Dayan 2001; Warner 2002; Hauser 1999) as argued in Chapter 2, the question arises as to whether internet media and communications are causal factors in these nascent Web 2.0 social movements. This will have to remain an open question in this case. Moreover, historically how people mobilize on behalf of others has taken place not only within but also across physical, sociocultural, and media geographies that have not been and are still not reducible to the territorial confines and jurisdiction of nation-states. Political leaders, community organizers, revolutionaries, and social reformers throughout modernity's imperial and postimperial orders have all looked to forge alliances, broaden support-bases, and evoke empathy beyond their immediate arenas for action.[32] Struggles to forge and legitimize any "imagined community" all require physical effort, the mustering of symbols, and historical resonance as participants deploy all available resources and powers of persuasion to achieve their ends. In this regard, discourses, as literal and visual texts, circulate as well as bodies.

That said, the IRP Coalition and its affiliations within internet governance domains is by focus and predilection a product of the digital age; its transnationality is thereby also digitally encoded and located. More to the point, in terms of how the IRP Charter operates as a counternarrative and the coalition as a counterpublic we see an example of what Gerard Hauser notes as how "our standard of reality is a function of how we talk and write about it" (Hauser 1999: 273). For participants engaging in public undertakings by their own volition the success of any outcome lies in which version of events and whose claims become the most legitimate in the eyes of others. Which standard of reality is talked and written about, whose speech is "captured" (Certeau 1994) in official archives or media messages, and which idea goes "viral" in today's social media-speak demarcate public matters today as much as their geographical coordinates on a map.

In this respect Michael Warner's 2002 essay, "Publics and Counterpublics," throws down the gauntlet in the first sentence when he writes; "This essay has a public. If you are reading (or hearing) this, you are part of its public. So, let me first say: Welcome." (Warner 2002: 49). In this opening salvo he exposes the porosity of distinctions between audiences, consumers, or subcultures on the one hand and notions of publics as nation-based political formations on the other. By pointing out how "in speaking of the public, . . . whenever one is addressed as the public, the others are assumed not to matter" (2002: 49). To speak of or situate *a* public allows for the possibility of singular and multiple publics coexisting if not overlapping in time, place, and space. Addressing *the* public is an all-embracing rhetorical device, implying a pregiven cohesion and shared identity of purpose. Warner is looking to examine what he terms this "intuitive understanding" (2002: 50) of publics understood in terms of a singular and compound "sense of totality" (2002: 49) by asking how this idea actually works from a Western cultural perspective. To do so, Warner incorporates a third key ingredient into the mix with these two notions of unbounded and bounded publics: that of a public as something that "comes into being only in relations to texts and their circulation" (2002: 50). He then goes onto to present a six-point schematic pivoting on these three premises in order to unpack some of the "rather odd" (ibid.) rules by which publics and social worlds coconstitute one another in ways that are not reducible to measurable indicators alone.

The first principle for Warner is that rather than being presumed, a "public is self-organized . . . a space of discourse organized by nothing other than discourse itself. . . . It is self-creating and self-organized, and herein lies its power as well as its elusive strangeness" (2002: 50). In other words a public is aware of itself as such and generates "discourse" (conversations, written texts, images, and other material) in organic and organized ways. Second, in order to distinguish these formations from more intimate, interpersonal relations Warner then notes that a "public is a relation amongst strangers . . . that organizes itself independently of state institutions, law, formal frameworks of citizenship, or preexisting institutions such as the church" (2002: 53). This is where his schematic resonates with but also departs from political theories of publics as functions of either democratic public spheres or the populations that produce public opinion. Third, he then takes his schematic into another domain of endeavor. A public is "also . . . the self-organization of . . . a body of strangers united through the circulation of their discourse . . . [as] . . . indefinite and impersonal address" (2002: 59). In other words, discourse here is open-ended, impersonal, and based on its movement in time and space, in whatever venues or formats these movements may take—bound books, blogs, Twitter-threads, face-to-face or web-conferencing.

Turning to what makes a public a distinctive formation—more than, yet not excluding, lobby or interest groups, smaller and larger organizations—Warner argues that, fourth, a "public is constituted through mere attention. . . . [It ceases] to exist when attention is no longer predicated" (2002: 61). This insight is a crucial point in Warner's distinction of publics as active, reflexive, and formations of interlocutors, one that relates to theorists such as Hauser (1999), who explore publics as informal, vernacular discourses and gatherings in contradistinction to those concentrating on larger entities as the primary characteristic such as masses, national citizenries, and public opinion polls. Publics, other than bilateral, familial, or kinship-based interactions, are based on others wanting to, and actively listening. No attention, means no publicness. So publics here are not butts-in-seats or ticks-in-boxes. The fifth aspect is thereby more complex in that here Warner is positing that while discourses and publics are interdependent, texts do not work as exogenous forces. Publics here are social, not static formations for a "public is the social space created by the reflexive circulation of discourse. . . . It is not texts themselves that create publics. . . . Only when a previously existing discourse can be supposed and a responding discourse be postulated, can a text address a public" (2002: 62). In other words, these conversations/discursive practices (as speech, writing, listening, reading, blogging, or tweeting) work with and address what came before, that is earlier articulations, historic documents, or current ones—"live" discourses. The temporal qualities also matter then in this formulation so, sixth, to move past being a group of experts, or insider groups (networked, distributed, or contained by time and territorial space) defined solely by their own jargon or timeline to be publics, these formations also need to be considered as they act "historically according to the temporality of their circulation. . . . All publics are intertextual, even intergeneric . . . [yet] put a premium on accessibility" (2002: 68). The internal communicative practices, idioms, and intentionality of a public include a desire, indeed requires conscious attempts, to communicate to others.

The last part of Warner's argument looks at the flip side of these formations: counterpublics as subordinate perhaps even subaltern voices and tendencies that regard and present themselves in terms of distinctions. Sometimes, as is the case with ethnic or sexual minorities, this is the result of disenfranchisement or discrimination. Sometimes, and these can overlap, this is through a countercultural or dissident persuasion. Two additional points in his argument are germane to this case. First, a "counterpublic maintains at some level, conscious or not, an awareness of its subordinate status. The cultural horizon against which it marks itself off is not just a general or wider public, but a dominant one" (2002: 86). Here power hierarchies, singular or intersectional, impose a structural obstacle to inclusion yet also an opening for mobilization and affinity. From here, we see how Warner's schematic takes his more sociocultural countercultural approach to meet those from political science and critical social theory. Namely, counterpublics include the production of "spaces of circulation in which it is hoped that the poësis of sense-making will be transformation not replication merely" (2002: 88).

Contesting Narratives

Inequalities that women face in terms of economic power, education and access to resources also affect access and participation in shaping the Internet, its debates and policy. This explains why the Internet has become an increasingly critical public sphere for the claiming of citizenship rights and civil liberties, including women's rights. For those who have little access to other kinds of "publics" due to the multiple forms of discrimination faced— including based on gender, age, economic status and sexual identity—it can be a particularly important pace for the negotiation and fulfillment of their rights. (APC 2012)

Looking back over these four–five years of online and face-to-face collaboration and drafting a document that could stand up to legal and political scrutiny in an atmosphere of entrenched cynicism about the status of the UDHR in light of UN member-state abuses, what we see are a number of meta-narratives about the internet itself. These splice through differences in how coalition members, and commentators on the charter drafts regarded the point of the exercise. The IRP Charter as part of an emerging group of discourses and actions around various notions of "digital rights" or "Internet rights" in this respect is a contested and evolving cultural artifact within a context that regards the internet simultaneously as a means to an end and as an instrument for state power, or market-share. In the second, the internet is an idea, if not an end in itself for future visions of sustainable development, poverty-reduction, social equity, or increased civic participation. However all these ideas imply different internets. Third, this case reveals the IRP Charter process and the wider rights-based activist ecosystem in which it is nestled as content-production, discursive practices, power relations, and ad hoc and preplanned interventions in official settings that are intrinsically digital. By association these have also acquired supraterritorial—transnational— qualities alongside their face-face and localized renderings. Drafting a document across physical space and time zones by using cloud computing services (in this case Google.docs) rather than exchanging attached documents in emails was not self-explanatory. At the same time the listserv emerged as the main hub for online commentaries, and debates, intersecting with Twitter feeds and email exchanges with coalition members in Tunis and Cairo. All these venues overlapped more conventional ones on the ground.

As a subset of a larger public concerned with internet governance issues, the IRP Coalition has also generated a space and provided airplay against dominant discourses within the IGF generation of consultations. I would suggest, on the basis of these provisional findings, that what we are seeing here are multiple publics forming in terms of speaking and address. As a whole they can be taken, albeit with caution, as a larger counterpublic that is voicing an alternative, more holistic, discourse to the ones that have characterized formal agendas and official outcomes of IGF meetings and their precursors. In this sense it is a cautious counterpublic, in that the multistakeholder model is based on achieving consensus above all, eschewing outright controversy and brinkmanship, the sort that has become par for the course in the history of the UN General Assembly, Security Council, and other venues. Ironically, though, this space for diverse voices to be heard without undermining the implied and desired unity of consensual politics belies the intense and subtle struggles over control over the terms of debate, agendas, and larger narratives.

How do these forces of power and resistance operate within the particular modest initiative of the IRP Charter? First, internally, the IRP Charter has to contend with the frustrations and "chilling" effects of consensual models imposed on proceedings for the sake of it. A second aspect is the converse: the political realities of proposing what might be construed, or indeed be emerging "new" rights in light of the pressure under which existing human rights are from being undermined or abused outright. As those UN agencies charged with monitoring human rights abuses alongside the work of major international NGOs such as Amnesty International and Human Rights Watch confront these realities on the ground a project that considers that "the Internet as a new space or domain is considered important enough to write a new charter of rights" (IRP List 2010 op. cit.) underscore the fragility of these international treaties and covenants in principle and practice. In this respect the taking up of rights-based issues for the internet by a direct engagement with the charter project by the UN Special Rapporteur of the Human Rights Council has been a significant success (see La Rue 2011). That said, the charter as the cornerstone, indeed the raison d'être of the IRP Coalition has to contend with how ICT corporations and state-actors have a vested interest in keeping their prerogative in many areas covered by the charter.

Externally, what counts as open consultations, forms of publicity in computer-mediated and evolving arenas for mobilization (direct) or influencing public opinion (as rendered in news media, blogosphere, or campaigns)? In 2011 and into 2012 the caution with which the coalition was proceeding, partly due to lack of financial and human resources to mount a global campaign and partly because the consultation process was consciously kept discrete in order to generate substantive improvements to the charter text itself, started to work against this modus operandi. As a "loose (not registered) group, . . . a global coalition . . . made up of both individuals and various organizations (NGOs, academic institutions, IGOs, businesses, governments) . . . " (IRP List 2010) the IRP Coalition has different priorities. It also has a different sense of the publics it is addressing; an incremental one as opposed to a one-off, intense global coverage whose success is measured at first glance by how many signatures can be gathered. The point of dispute here is that the former approach can be synonymous with a closed-shop process (Solomon cited in Risen 2012) rather than an open consultation.

Two concerns generated the more cautious approach adopted by the coalition, as a voluntary rather than professional campaigning organization. First, the coalition did not see itself as a purely civil society, that is, advocacy undertaking. Rather it saw itself as one looking to strike a balance between the latter priorities and those of business and government, "the Charter is not a civil society document . . . it should not also be a document that enhances the business model of some companies (and so) enhance one right (to) the detriment of other rights" (IRP List 2010). The need for outreach and increasing active participation in the charter project as well as the coalition's active membership itself (rendered in email postings, meeting attendance) was becoming more pressing as the charter in its modestly public version launched at the 2010 Vilnius IGF. It generated commentaries and its own "global" campaign through the Ten Principles into Nairobi IGF in 2011, and then was overtaken by events in the lead up to Baku in 2012. What was apparent at the time and is more striking looking back over the four years of email-based correspondence and offline meetings, outreach events, and corollary rights-based campaigns that started to crystallize in 2012–2013 is the way human rights for the online environment have come to be encapsulated by the trope of "freedom." Freedom construed as "freedom from" (e.g., censorship or prosecution under defamation laws) and freedom construed as "freedom of" (e.g., markets, expression, choice) are, in this respect, not easily reconciled (Mendel et al. 2012; Benedek 2012).

As freedom became a meta-level buzzword in this period *human* rights become subsumed under discussions around other sorts of rights and would-be universal principles within and between the fluid participating formations in the IGF itself. Here the IRP coalition was facing a legitimacy crisis of sorts. Resources and technical difficulties during 2012 underscored that while the IRP Charter had earned its place as a substantive contribution to a growing set of "stories and charters and documents" (IRP List 2011) that had emerged at this time the project was by no means complete. The very real paradox-dilemma here was reconciling the "overarching principle of [social justice, or human rights that is] too abstract to be very useful" (IRP List 2011) for implementation in technical or legal terms given the operational complexity of the internet as a whole let alone its component parts (IRP 2010), but to do so without losing sight of the inherently social focus of the IRP Charter as a counterweight to dominant internet governance discourses. As technical details appear to trump political or normative understandings of the practicalities of how any of the charter's clauses work "in real life" remains a challenge in terms of consciousness-raising within and beyond the IGF setting. Coalition members, and those actively engaged in the drafting process were and still are aware that the "human rights movement is a political movement . . . the greater part of what we appeal to when we appeal to human rights is controversial and contested" (IRP List 2010).

As I have noted in Chapter 2 and with an eye to a further explication in the next chapter, these sorts of resistances from within make such publics in the making complicit in a latter-day iteration of Foucault's *governmentality paradox*; namely one by which populations are being disciplined into a post-Westphalian frame of institutional power known as *multistakeholderism*. How do efforts such as the IRP Charter indicate resistance if they are not to be taken as assimilation, a settling for "as good as it gets"? I would argue that taken together the self-conscious and insubordinate agency of counterpublics looking to temper the seemingly inexorable disciplining of digital governmentality underscores the paradox underlying of the history of liberal polities in which powers that "seek to govern . . . but not too much" (Foucault 2004a, b) suggests that resistance is not futile.

IN CONCLUSION—THE INTERNET IS POLITICAL

No public is universal, even when it wishes to be. (Lewis 2001: 23)

But it is clear that control of our emerging information society should not lie solely with governments and corporations. We can have commercialized, complex technology that is controlled by—and serves the interests of—a few. Or as cooperative ideas about open-knowledge spread, the choice of alternative, human-scale technology that is accessible to many, and controlled from the bottom up. . . . The digital age brings opportunity: . . . Yet it also brings new threats to hard-won civil liberties. (Healy 2012)

The IGF is everything but democracy. It is a place and a game of force and power. (JFC Morfin, Best Bits Email List, 28 August, 2013)

Chapter 2 argued that the internet is ordinary. This shift in mindset is needed in order to take into account the way that everyday, seemingly mundane online practices, communicative cultures, and uses are integral to the geopolitics of the internet in general and the micropolitics of its governance in particular. When considering the technical, legal, and ethical interconnections between (human) rights and the internet in light of burgeoning public and academic debates about the extent of a simmering "internet showdown" (Healy 2012), "hype" (Singh 2012a), or "global battle" (Goldsmith 2012, Mueller 2012, New America Foundation 2012), the politics of the internet intersects with those inherent in mobilization around human rights. Mobilization around this intersection has started to gather momentum in the last two–three years of UN-brokered internet governance consultations, albeit as a latent focal point in the years prior that exercised civil society participants from social movement and advocacy platforms. One reason is down to concerted public awareness campaigns, lobbying, and other sorts of direct and indirect activism within these settings but also further abroad. In this sense recent political events on the ground have combined to generate an increasing awareness of the interconnection between the way some use the internet at the expense of others and the rights to privacy, freedom of expression, cultural diversity, and rights of assembly (to name a few) that are protected under national and international human rights law.

The supraterritorial and computer-mediated dimensions to the "unfolding historical constellation" (Fraser 2007: 8,) in which the internet has evolved and in turn has been a formative element troubles a priori separations between public and private lives, domestic from foreign jurisdictions, and mediated forms of community and identity-formation from those premised on economic or biological determinants and physical proximity. These quantitative and qualitative shifts, some subtle and cumulative, others sudden and dramatic, in where and how people live their lives and how these lives are ordered or governed by others has been shaking up scholarly and policymakers' working assumptions that at the end of the day it is nation-states that do, and should continue to call the shots. This convenient fiction has been useful for those who, while not able to be accredited as political representatives, or state actors so to speak, work closely with the latter to pay for, and thereby have a major say in the running of the cyber-techno-mediascapes of today. The ways in which ordinary people use the internet and these practices have become currency, lifeblood in fact, of internet design and terms of access and use, outstripping existing laws and regulations at the national level.

Over the last two decades at least, the conjuncture of the internet, as an evolving planetary telecommunications system and agglomeration of digitally facilitated communicative practices that are supraterritorial in intent if not in practice, and neoliberal globalization and organized resistance to it have intersected with a number of large-scale realignments of political economic power, social forms, and cultural flows. In the first, the Atlantic west is making way for the Asian-Pacific east. In the second, governments as state actors consciously manage rather than set macroeconomic policy agendas. In the third, cultural artifacts, consumption patterns, and practices of everyday life are created, sustained, and circulated within multiplex local-global flows, which are computer-mediated and contested.

As a transnational collaboration in which the internet is at once the object, means, and medium for this undertaking the IRP Charter process raises some provocative questions for scholars, policymakers, and activists about the form and substance of not only publics in an internet dependent, that is, computer-mediated, world order by also the form and substance of sociopolitical power and its contestation, as both sorts of power relationships, as framing modalities, move in and out of cyberspatial realms of endeavor, persuasion, and dissemination. The IRP Charter's premise is that the UDHR and other covenants are no longer sufficient in explicit terms to incorporate changes, opportunities and threats brought by the increasing embedding of internet media and communications in all facets of life. Neither are national forms of jurisprudence or public or private law sufficient in this view; the design, uses, and access to the internet are also constituted by supraterritorial practices and their implications for accountability (e.g., cloud computing).

As others have already argued, neither the Westphalian state-system (invented in the mid-seventeenth century more or less), aggressive nation-building (mid-nineteenth century), nor worldwide computer-driven telecommunications (mid-twentieth century) have been single determinants in the evolution or *invention* of publics.[33] Publics as already existing and would-be social and discursive formations go hand in hand with the means by which they are organized, articulated, monitored, and then consulted. This occurs by forging national citizenships and delimiting their corollary public opinions in the first two instances or facilitating trans-local, nonproximate connections between once nonconnected groups or communities in the third. Moving up a level, the assumption of custodianship on the part of *intergovernmental* organizations such as the United Nations has long had to contend with the centrifugal power of non-state actors. Transnational corporations, social movements, migrating populations, criminal organizations, and emergent multilateral institutions are capable of undercutting if not overriding even the best intentions of governments organizing themselves into an *international community* to represent "all members of the human family" (UN General Assembly 1948: Preamble).

In view of the last few years of organized mobilization from social actors around internet governance agenda-setting venues at intergovernmental and multilateral organizations, these struggles taking place behind the computer screens of everyday internet access and uses are being won and lost in cyberspace as much as on the ground. This is a shift from social mobilizations, new or old, that aim to meld community-based, national, and international social justice concerns by direct action, face-to-face lobbying, or street-level demonstrations; antiglobalization protests in Seattle, Prague, and Genoa at the turn of this century and antiwar protests in the 1970s and early 2000s are cases in point. Some participant-scholars rejoice at the emergence of the internet as a permissive space for dissent and new forms of community and solidarity. Digitally enabled and facilitated mobilizations and alternative media messages point to defiant publics, crystallizations of discontent and dissent that only make sense by virtue of their computer-mediations. Others are less convinced, seeing the visible fist of corporate rule in the velvet glove of state-sponsored privatization, declining civic engagement at home, and destabilization of social relationships through a US-dominated global information infrastructure. Either the internet is this century's silver bullet to alleviate any number of the planet's woes, from poverty through to economic growth, or a tool of global—digital—domination. In both extremes, a public interest is at stake.

Moving these scholarly debates forward entails working within the digital and embodied interfaces where participants looking to influence agenda-setting, terms of the debate, and eventually strategic decisions on critical aspects of the internet's functioning, access, and terms of use congregate and debate. A look at how the IRP Charter has developed thus far and from close up can throw light on the form, substance, and loci of digital-age governmentality and its various (counter)publics engaging in as well as dissenting from the emplacement of a "triangle, sovereignty-discipline-government, which has as its primary target [a computer-mediated and trans/national] population and as its essential mechanism the apparatuses of security" (Foucault 1991: 102). The IRP Charter case shows how digital-era interventions are being carried out by what we can call for the sake of argument a digital (counter)public working to stake a claim for a future public good. This self-conscious albeit hesitant assumption of working for and speaking to a global public as the object of the exercise, and addressee, is not something more institutionally based, reformist-minded participants in the IRP Coalition would necessarily want to take on. More recent coalition arrivals drawing on younger generations of digital activists have less patience with the reformist, institution-building pace of the IGF.

In this case, we need to reconceive this public as part of a larger constellation; one that operates as a multiplex, multisited and diverse set of publics and, by association, counterpublics. These publics are not consensual by predisposition. They are anchored in local, substate, national, and international frames of reference and realms of day-to-day struggle, compromise, and tactical maneuvering. For multilateral, inclusive in principle, consultations like the WSIS and IGF working practices based on multistakeholder participation, the dominant discourse is one of avoiding open conflict. However, mobilization around human rights and the internet begins from the premise that a wider change is necessary, another internet is possible. These overlapping "digital rights" initiatives, from the IRP Charter, to the Brazilian *Marco Civil*, to the APC *Internet Rights are Human Rights* project, all proceed from the notion that these sorts of changes need time. I would suggest on the basis of these provisional findings that the IRP Charter for all its efforts to mainstream, not offend, to embed itself in preexisting human rights and principles has actually produced a radical document that effectively introduces a new right (cf. Marzouki 2009) despite attempts to avoid doing so. Meanwhile the charter's ethos and articulation of what is at stake has been taken up by UN Human Rights agencies, the wider campaign taken up by larger, well-heeled NGOs, or rising state-actors such as Brazil, major corporations such as Google, and its strategic partners in government and civil society. The next step, moving the IRP Charter up a level (a project called, at time of writing, the "Charter 2.0 Project"), will put pressure on this cautious counterpublic to make its influence felt under the belyingly calm waters of UN consensus-building. This is the task ahead as moves to codify "global internet governance principles" gather force. And in the wake of revelations of the summer of 2013 about US and other government-sanctioned surveillance of ordinary people's web communications at a global level, the task has become even more pressing (Davies, 2013; Franklin 2013b, c). As is the case on the ground with human rights violations, the fledgling recognition that human rights do matter online (UN Human Rights Council 2012) could be all too easily be swept aside in the wake of other priorities.

Paradigm Reboot: Decolonizing Internet Futures

INTRODUCTION

The work for this book was completed in a period dominated by two major themes in critical research on the interrelationship between changes in media and communications and sociopolitical transformation. The first is technological, the effects of the significant inroads made by what is generally known as social media and occurring around the world in less than a decade: social networking sites and microblogs in particular based on largely for-profit platforms that engage and enlist the user to generate content, traffic, and added value in ways that are still being debated and documented. These innovations in the look, accessibility, and effectiveness of computer-mediated communications premised on Web 2.0 designs (see Chapter 3) increasingly predominate in everyday, commercial, and professional communications. They have consolidated a diverse range of variously (in)compatible and (non)interoperable products and services from the precursor generations that characterized the early internet in its heyday—the 1990s.

Today's internet, successively defined by this current generation of commercial integrated platforms of "converging" media, has seen the economic stakes upped as its precursor web-based offerings move up to another level of global coverage and local depth. This spread is accompanied by a comparable shift downwards in size, portability and easy-to-use notions of attractiveness, interconnectedness, linked-up services, and promises of "tailor-made" individuality (Vaidhyanathan 2012) are now part of intense competition for ownership and control of not only the functionalities but also the aesthetics of electronic communications. Here we see the gadgets presented in popular science fiction of 1960s TV shows and recent Hollywood prequel blockbusters such as *Star Trek* (chest-level or wristband communications devices, i.e., people seemingly talking into thin air) or Hollywood versions of science fiction novels such as *Minority Report* (Apple-patented touch-pad movements) on the street. Finding our way, contacting others, and getting information are now condensed down to the size of a hand. The implantation of microelectronics under the human epidermis along with "bionic" or "cyborg" prototypes that can run (as) fast and think (better) than traditional human beings are no longer futurist imaginations. They are real life (Chapters 2 and 3).

The second theme is political. As the euphoria of the Arab Uprisings in 2010–2011 in the Middle East and North African region makes way for the political realities of transitioning from autocratic to more pluralist (viz. democratic) forms of rule, the optimism conveyed by the world's news media and political power-brokers is becoming tempered. Newly won political freedoms in these societies, ongoing civil wars notwithstanding, and ongoing abuses of press freedoms and threats to freedom of speech there and elsewhere are becoming synonymous with how internet freedom is being framed through the prism of antistatist, free market rhetoric in Western societies. Here debates spread across the spectrum of worldviews and ideological differences over how it should be governed, who the watchdogs should be, and who foots the bill for economic growth and technologically enhanced lifestyles. The enormous attention paid to the role played by so-called new media in the overthrow of Ben Ali and Mubarak in Tunisia and Egypt respectively, and ongoing investigations into their real or imagined impact on these and neighboring events (in Iran, Syria, and the Gulf States for instance) notwithstanding, at time of writing, we see that how both (armed) resistance movements and the forces of order make use of media and communications to further their respective ends signal some of the changing modalities of power and resistance in a computer-dependent age.

That technological innovation and successive generations of information and communication technologies and their corollary media industries have played a formative role in political and sociocultural transformation around the world is not a new theme for either protagonists or observers. And neither is the recognition that mobilizing to ensure that affordable and sustainable media and communications are an integral element in policymaking and social justice projects over the long term is never as compelling, never as "sexy" in public relations terms, as is riding the (media) revolutionary bandwagon (Lovink 2012; Barkai 2012; Singh 2012a, b). As many others point out, traditional and emerging media can facilitate the exertion of power as well as facilitate and disseminate forms of resistance (Morozov 2011; Holmes 2007; Mattelart 1994). Hence only history will tell whether the "current revolution in information and communications technologies, may slowly but radically affect who rules, how, and why" (Ronfeldt cited in Ronfeldt and Varda 2008: 2; see Barkai 2012: 18, 20), and not without vigorous scholarly debate, political maneuvering, and activism. Meanwhile the internet, and the cyberspaces it facilitates, has been bought and sold several times over by increasingly powerful corporate agglomerations. On the other hand, governments have started to "wake up" after years of laissez-faire that gave commercial interests a free hand in cornering the market in research and development of the internet's strategic resources, web-based news and entertainment, provision of public services and their accompanying digitalization (e.g., education, healthcare, policing).

Like Rip Van Winkle, government regulators have discovered that things have changed and they no longer call the shots in terms of internet design, access, and use given that these are circumscribed by patented designs and technical standards that have evolved in ad hoc, largely nontransparent, and publicly unaccountable ways. The waxing and waning of political party commitments to free enterprise, global market forces, privatization, and deregulation (viz. neoliberalism) as the sine qua non of economic growth and progress aside, national governments and international governmental organizations have only just started to reconsider their options in a computer-dependent world order. In this new frame of mind some state actors have been flexing their muscles to retain, or regain sovereignty over their media and communications while others are becoming more proactive in the application of either existing or new national and international laws that take the online environment more explicitly into account (OECD 2011; Council of Europe 2012a, b). Within but also countering ongoing commitments to public-private partnerships where commercial operators and service providers bear the financial burden of the internet's civic rollout aside, the "return of the state" after at least a quarter of a century of neoliberal economic orthodoxy has generated a wave of countermanding lobbying and public relations moves on the part of both state and corporate interests.

What links these contradictory dynamics, however, is that these latest technology or media revolutions/internet-age mobilizations have been unfolding in the broader context of a power reshuffle between old and emerging political and economic power blocs, state and nonstate/public and private actors, in the conduct of world affairs that, while they have been branded by the aftermath of the events of 9/11 and military actions undertaken by the Western alliance to win their "global war on terror," also predate the events of 2001. Not only are the underlying premises of surplus value being shaken up by the way we use the internet but also the Anglo-Euro-American axis of technoeconomic power is shifting toward other parts of the world. Yet the global corporations who now own the codes and control access to today's web-based media, namely proprietary software platforms that make up the social networking sites and (micro)blogs officially accessed and used by billions as well as personal computing, reside in the west, the United States in particular. Their owners have a say not just ideologically but in very material terms about the direction the future of the internet's underlying architecture and operations should take, to date based on the Western, Anglo-Euro-American computer protocols that have been used since its inception.

While it is tempting to convert all references to the internet to the web and then both to social media I have not done so, mainly because this would mean conflating terms, collapsing crucial technoeconomic and sociopolitical distinctions. Such a conflation also contributes to a tendency in research on "media and revolution," "the internet and society," "new media cultures" (or any similar phrase) to fall into the trap of overly optimistic—or pessimistic—forms of explanatory determinism. These go hand-in-hand with faulty thinking about the relationship between how a technology is designed, used, and then appropriated or enrolled for diverse and often irreconcilable ends and means that results in ahistorical, teleological, and thereby uncritical analyses. That said, it is hard to resist this temptation to "upgrade" and refer to all media and communications based on computer-mediated networks and their corollary products and services at this time as social media. I have resisted this temptation for two other reasons. The first is that all these latter-day platforms are dependent upon and function as part of the internet; social networking, (micro)blogging, and smartphones with apps galore cannot operate without either the internet or the web applications it facilitates. Both of the latter are not reducible to one another either, and this is more than a technical specification. It is of political economic and sociocultural import, albeit in varying measures. The second reason is that the need to maintain an historical perspective is even more important at this stage in this internet's brief history. Contestations over the narrative—historical and technical as well as cultural—of how contemporary internet media and communications have come to define our world through the ways we use them, and they use us, are gathering momentum. Thinking about old new media is counterintuitive because today's new "new media" have captured the discursive terrain by rendering all precursor (non)computer-mediated communications as somehow not social. This is patently incorrect; even within the short history of the internet as we know it there have been diverse forms of web-based communications, news, and entertainment that have played their part in reconfiguring how individuals and communities form across time and space.

PARADIGM REBOOT

[There is a] place for human experience next to facts. (Vasquez 2006)

I'll next turn to how these three case studies can generate other ways of theorizing media and communications in an internet age on the one hand and, on the other, contested understandings of shifts in power and resistance. Chapter 2 laid out the three conceptual nodes (after the nation-state, publics, and internet governmentality) around which I explore the push and pull between public and privatized forms of power and control as they come up against passive and active forms of resistance. Given relatively little attention in the early years of the web, the digital imaginaries and footprints of how ordinary people reinvent and so practice everyday life as they go online have become both currency and ammunition for mobilizations around the future of the internet. What has changed is that ordinary, nonelite utterances and communicative practices that have to date unfolded below the radar of modern statecraft's compulsion to discipline citizenries—by categorizing, archiving, and persuading bounded populations (Anderson 1991;

Bourdieu 2012; Foucault 2004a, b; Certeau 1984)—are now visible and available online for not only statist agendas.

The visibility and relative accessibility of everyday interactions in cyberspace has been a feature of the social media from the internet's early days (Franklin 2004: 204–206; Rheingold 1994). However, the commercialized platforms that characterize the current generation of social media have shifted this visibility up a level, in terms of quantity and earning power, indexing and archiving dynamics, surveillance and countersurveillance. Running the gauntlet in this context in which the "invention of everyday onlineness," to borrow from Certeau (1984, Chapter 2), arguably redefines what it means to be human, and by association culture and society, points to a reversal of the dualisms that have predominated in critiques of the internet-society nexus. As the next generation of "digital natives" grows up, scholarly and popular debates around which counts more, the online or offline realms, will be given another twist in the face of everyday social realities. In other words:

Hanging out with friends and family increasingly means also hanging out with their technology. While eating, defecating, or resting in our beds, we are rubbing on our glowing rectangles, seemingly lost within the infostream. . . . Never has being disconnected—even if for just a moment—felt so profound. The current obsession with the analog, the vintage, and the retro has everything to do with this fetishization of the offline. (Jurgenson 2012)

As Jurgenson observes there is a paradoxical "disconnect" between the tenor of debates about new social problems and new media, and how people actually go about their everyday lives. Proponents of delinking, in web-saturated societies that is, assume that delinking or unplugging is simply a technical matter when evidence shows that there is a little understood psychoemotional component to being and staying in touch via the internet. Moreover, as they weigh ordinary people's media uses and with that their cumulating digital footprints become a commercial and political strategic resource for incumbent and emerging powers, even knowing whether to delink or how to achieve (or indeed retrieve) some modicum of online anonymity is not knowledge that many users have at their fingertips. This level of intervention in how others monitor and track us online (as is the case in CCTV saturated environments) is not a foregone conclusion, a matter of exercising personal choice, as satisfactory degrees of deletion are beyond most people's control (Rosen 2012). Although we "may never fully log off, . . . this in no way implies the loss of the face-to-face, the slow, the analogue, the deep introspection, the long walks, or the subtle appreciation of life sans screen. We enjoy all of this more than ever before" (Jurgenson 2012). While writing from another, "Google Generation" sensibility about the how conventional sensory and sentient experiences acquire a new allure for those growing up with the web, Jurgenson echoes Haraway's (1990, 1997) points about the hazards of nurturing a false nostalgia for the "paradise lost" of the gendered and ethnic-class power hierarchies that also permeate everyday life on the ground, in meatspace.

These are philosophical and political questions that reach beyond this concluding discussion. The point I want to make here is that taking on board Jurgenson's
observation for the sake of argument, it is not so preposterous a step for critical
analyses to consider that being human, taking part and engaging in the world at
large, in what are increasingly internet-saturated arenas for action implies other
ways to consider power and resistance that do not reify or "fetishize" those premised on physical (territorial) borders and face-to-face forms of communication
and mobilization. Without this recognition we simply see a return of the online
versus offline dichotomy in the literature (Chapters 1 and 2) in another guise.
As Jurgenson goes on to say, the "notion of the offline as real and authentic is a
recent invention, corresponding with the rise of the online. If we can fix this false
separation and view the digital and physical as enmeshed, we will understand that
what we do while connected is inseparable from what we do when disconnected
(Jurgenson 2012). If this observation is empirically viable, and statistics support
this view that people are engaging with each other more and more via smaller and
larger thinking machines linked into the internet (Madden et al. 2012), then fact
has already followed science fiction. According to a 2011 op ed in the *New York
Times* on advances in neurological uses of digital technologies, this increasing
intimacy points how there can be "a cyborg in us all" (Kennedy 2011).

Having a cyborg, or bionic implant, inside a human body is, however, something else from positing cyborgs as a radical re-visioning of the politics of being
human today (Haraway 1990; Franklin 2012c; Hayles 1999). The next three sections reconsider these three conceptual nodes in turn in light of this paradox.

Netizens of the World Unite—We Are All "Cyborgs" Now

In terms of how internet-facilitated social networks trouble organicist understandings of top-down power and bottom-up agency, Nishant Shah thinks through
the conceptual implications of moving away from the Cartesian-Online-offline
dichotomies Jurgenson critiques above. Shah reflects on how it is important to
study cyberspatial practices in terms of changes to how respective practitioners
(see Certeau 1984) are human-avatar-digital hybrids. This is not to dispense with
humanness. Shah like Haraway (1990) is not suggesting (others might, and do) that
not being human is something superior. Rather theirs is a move to recast human
subjectivity, in terms of how users-as-human-cyborgs become transmitters and
objects of power dispositions in cyberspace as it is constituted, and patrolled as
a "practiced place." As the practice of everyday life is constituted increasingly by
how individuals, groups, and communities gather in online arenas, this implies
that political representation, social advocacy, and with these accountability and
legitimacy are no longer confinable to analog notions of "imagined communities"
(Anderson 1991).

How to rethink these conventional understandings in light of web-based imaginings and practices? If internet technologies enable both continuation and departure from existing forms of belonging, of which the nation-state is but one

particular form, then computer-embedded social formations and spaces of belonging, and exclusion let us not forget, have to matter, too, need to be taken into account for theory, research, and policymaking. However, this shift in mindset is a politically and economically charged one given that the way people use the web has outpaced existing legislation and policy agendas that are still rooted in national sovereignty and corporatist models of ownership and control. As Shah argues, taking his cue from Haraway (1990), what has changed is that the practice of everyday life online has been taking place through a process by which

the digital profile—the translated self —comes to stand in for the bodies of the users who not only create the translated self but also mark it with desires and aspirations. The translated self is largely under the control of the physical body. And yet, *there are several ways in which the translated self does not allow for the physical body to emerge as the original, the authentic or the primary self* within the dynamics of [social networking sites]. (Shah 2011, emphasis added)

Shah argues that these translations, to wit cyborg subjectivities, have been raising the commercial and geopolitical stakes. The way people sign up and designate themselves online (e.g., in gaming or virtual worlds, on social networks) and generate new forms of income, along with political and legal challenges to the vested order. What they do and how they organize themselves, or talk to each other online matter for incumbent and emerging powerbrokers. This is because the

digital transactions in which the users within such spaces engage have huge social, economic and cultural purport . . . in the interstices of the different oppositions of the real and the virtual, the physical and the digital, the temporal and the spatial, the biological and the technological. Moreover, the cyborg does not reside simply within the digital domains but becomes an embodied technosocial being, with a material body that enters into other realms of authorship and subjectification. *It is necessary to recognize that the cyborg is not simply a self-authored identity, but is also subject to various other realms of governance.* (Shah 2011: emphasis added)

Shah illustrates this point with the case of the 2006 "Lucknow Gay Scandal" incident in India where four men were prosecuted under the Indian penal code for their activities on a gay dating website that "was looked upon as a physical space where people indulged in 'unnatural sex acts'. The four men were punished, not for anything that they did in public or in the physical world but for their online fantasies" (Shah 2011). This illustrates how, in the Indian context at least, incumbent state powers have started to recognize that the "translated selves" and cyberspatial arenas in which these selves exist and interact can be intercepted and thereby become targets for resharpened forms of disciplining and punishment (Foucault 1984b, c). With commercial interests deploying the same techniques for ostensibly other reasons, this case and others signal how states are moving towards the recognition of online avatars as not only extensions of the self but as more powerful identities than the physical self. The State imagines the users of cyberspace as "real" cyborgs and conceives their online activities, fantasies and role-plays as punishable offences. The State also recognizes their translated selves—their datasets that they authored—as verifiable proof of their existence and actions online. (Shah 2011)

In this respect the genie is out of the bottle.

Publics and/as Counterpublics

We'll turn now to debates about how and where publics, and by association the notion of democratic public spheres, have been morphing in a changing context that sees "translated selves" (Shah 2011 op. cit.) forming within digitally inflected and multisited modalities of power and resistance. Recalling the discussion in Chapter 2 and case study in Chapter 5, Michael Warner's reconceptualization of publics as self-creating and discursively rendered formations of strangers engaging in conversations and with each other consciously as publics (2002) comes into its own in the online environment. What is missing, however, in Warner's exegesis is a fuller account of how these formations unfold and make use of domains that are both parochial and supraterritorial, analog and digital discursive circulations and forms of address. Warner ends his excursion into rethinking publics from a more sociological and culturally inclusive perspective with a caveat about the limits to what he calls their political, namely their "public agency" (2002: 89) in the future. For Warner and this tradition of twentieth century thinkers, it is "difficult to say what such a world would be like. It might need to be one with a different role for state-based thinking; as things stand now it might be the only way a public is able to act is through its imaginary coupling with the state" (2002: 89). Warner goes on to suggest that when "alternative publics," in his exposition these are counterpublics, "are cast as social movements—they acquire agency in relation to the state. They enter the temporality of politics and adapt themselves to the performatives of rational-critical discourse" (ibid.).

In this sense he forecloses on the implications of his argument. By trying to get the genie back in the bottle so to speak he retreats to the position taken by critical theorists in the Habermasian tradition, those who focus on ascertaining the "normative legitimacy and political efficacy of public opinion" (Fraser 2007: 7) within what is still essentially an idealized, Westphalian discursive frame that posits states (for all their limitations) as the bulwark against unfettered capitalism, eliding how states have been the champions of global capital as well as perpetrators of human rights abuses. On the basis of how publics and counterpublics have been forming, addressing each other and distant others online and on the ground around both homelessness issues (Chapter 4) and human rights for the online environment (Chapter 5), it is not possible to agree with either Warner or thinkers like Fraser who contend that in the final analysis it is "hard to associate the notion of efficacious communicative power with discursive spaces that do not correlate with sovereign states" (Fraser 2007: 8). Yet Warner also recognizes this gap between how he conceptualizes self-serving, state-bound publics that double up as audiences, consumer markets, subcultures, or "internet users" on the one hand and those, on the other, that form and then consciously engage as counterpublics in order not to "cede the original hope of transforming, not just policy, but the space of public life itself" (Warner 2002: 89).

While Warner's counterpublics are sexual minorities—"queer publics"—the counterpublics emerging around human/digital rights issues (Chapter 5 around the twinned problems of homelessness and digital divides (Chapter 4), or around free and open-source software (Chapter 3) as a viable alternative to proprietary goods and services, diverge in various directions along whether the primary task is influencing policy or longer term social transformation. First, as is the case in Chapter 4, these differences pan out across different definitions of the problem in hand and then how alternative media are posited and deployed as either a stopgap solution or radical alternative. Second, as is the case in Chapter 5, the tensions between conservationist and transformative motivations are evident around debates over whether revisiting the Universal Declaration of Human Rights for the online environment is the best way to address rights-based issues online. Extensive discussions in the early drafting stages of the Charter of Human Rights and Principles for the Internet pivoted on whether or not access to the internet or indeed the internet itself (however defined) should be construed as a "new right." If so then such a project and its emergence through the activities of various coalitions, alliances, and affiliations would be effectively looking to transform "the space of public life itself" (Warner op. cit.) rather than bolster the status quo (Lipschutz 2005). Definitions become acutely political when change is in the air. A section of the coalition (members of the expert group charged with drafting the charter particularly) adamantly stated that the aim of the exercise was not to posit any new human rights. Others temporized on just this point, while others proceeded to put the notion that access to the internet is a new right at the heart of their global campaigns to promote "internet freedom" (Access 2012).[1]

Despite his own reticence in going "beyond the state" in the final analysis, why Warner's reconceptualization of publics is relevant for this study is that he moves a rather moribund debate forward in two directions nonetheless. The first is continuing to think outside the box of how the historical constellation known as the modern nation-state developed in tandem with its territorialization of citizenries. The second is a move away from behavioralist, survey-dependent notions of publics as the sum total of how opinions are measured. He does this by considering the semantic difference between the "idea of *a* public, as distinct from *the* public as any bounded audience" (2002: 50, original emphasis) as both cultural and political. While his focus is primarily on a "kind of public that comes into being only in relation to texts and their circulation" (2002: 50), his is a continuation of more inclusive, dynamic, and dialogical understandings of publics as practiced-based social formations in a generic sense. Where I would differ is that how any public comes into being can also be apprehended as more than "only" a "space of discourse organized by other than discourse itself" (2002: 50). Even literary media readerships breathe and communicate in more ways than through the written word alone. This is the case increasingly as even as the traditional printed words of discourse as understood in the Warner schematic are now superimposed and enhanced by the multimedia and hypertextualized circulations of web content and the digital footprints their creators leave behind.

An Internet Governmentality Paradox

Now we can move to the wider context in which all three of these case studies have evolved and within which they play their respective parts. Broader questions around "who rules?" and "on what terms?" in a post–Cold War, and arguably post-9/11, context have impacted how nation-states articulate their roles as the incumbent custodians of world order. This is apparent in the form of organizational changes in membership, financing, and political will within the United Nations system. In concert and separately, early twenty-first century state actors have been couching these questions in the idiom of "global governance" for some time albeit with contradictory perspectives on what the main priorities should be (Bøås and McNeill 2004; Gurumurthy and Singh 2012). However, the particular character of internet governance discourses, as not only a multilateral endeavor but also a multistakeholder one, is anchored in the outcomes of the World Summit on the Information Society meetings, hosted by the UN's International Telecommunications Union between 2003 and 2005 in Geneva and Tunis, and the succeeding meetings of the Internet Governance Forum (see Chapter 5). Suffice it to say that with any references to internet governance, then and since, take it as a given that nation-states are not the only ones who can or indeed should make decisions related to how today's media and telecommunications (viz. the internet) works. Whether couched in basic or "enhanced" terms, internet governance as more than the outcome of state-based forms of cooperation relies on the "development and application by Governments, the private sector and civil society, in their respective roles, of shared principles, norms, rules, decision-making procedures, and programs that shape the evolution and use of the Internet" (Working Group on Internet Governance, 2005: 4).

ICT corporations, longstanding strategic partners with cash-strapped and monetarist nation-states, are now taking the lead more aggressively in this undertaking. However the presence and input of the third party mentioned in the above definition—civil society, a relatively new partner and interlocutor in these sorts of international negotiations, is less clear. This situation is not only because of the wide spectrum of activist and advocacy platforms that fall under the rubric of civil society, let alone questions about its representativeness and legitimacy to speak for ordinary people (viz. internet users around the world) as a nominated third stakeholder in these experiments in multistakeholderism at the UN level. As the internet and its (non)regulation becomes increasingly identified with discourses of multistakeholderism, posited as the antidote to state oppression, both corporations and "good-guy" state actors have been increasingly alert and proactive in controlling not only the agenda but also patrolling public debates. Straddling these two poles, at times caught in the crossfire, off-guard, or co-opted by statist or corporatist agendas in this domain, is this third "stakeholder." It is an amalgam of nonconsensual and unequal publics revamped as a consensual, compound noun that represents overlapping and diverging visions of "information and communication societies that are people-centered, inclusive and equitable" (WSIS Civil Society 2003: 2). Who is who, and who is speaking for whom within civil society caucuses, coalitions, and working groups aside, as the WSIS and IGF experience show, full participation at these events does not mean full access or direct influence on key decisions, statements, or agenda priorities. Assuming that these meetings are indeed where key decisions are being molded, and many argue that the WSIS and IGF have been not much more than high-level talk shops, there are more than the rituals of high-level genuflection at stake in the idea that ordinary people can and should organize to have their voice on the record in these settings.

In this respect working toward "enhanced cooperation" in these sorts of global policymaking endeavors makes them an uncomfortable place for "old school" social activists and political revolutionaries. As such civil society participants have had to change their approach, language, and priorities in order to be taken seriously (Franklin 2005a, 2007a). In so doing more than a few have managed to stay upright and carve out and protect their own niche within this evolving institutional ecosystem. Working for and so addressing publics that are not only construed as national citizens, consumers, or shareholders (as is the case for state and corporate actors respectively), civil society participation and representation at such events is a more fluid, less institutionally or legally clear-cut affair accordingly. Ideological differences and huge disparities in resources between smaller civil society (e.g., grassroots) groups and larger international NGOs mean that diversity is not only intrinsic to this third participant but also its driving force. It is also its achilles heel in terms of its own democratic legitimacy, or as some critics note its democratic deficit. If this is so then what does resistance entail for those who have other visions of the internet's future than those promulgated by either their governments or the corporate sector? How would such resistance connect the arcane technical and legal dimensions to running the internet on a day to day basis to more meta-level contestations about the underlying principles that decide on what terms people access and use the web in the first place, shift evidence of (socioeconomic and digital) exclusion from default settings to designs that promote inclusion, or protect human rights online as consistently as they are supposedly promoted and protected offline?

The tradeoff is not only a tactical but also a strategic concern that returns us to how power, and thereby resistance, needs reconceptualizing for digitally inflected domains of thought and action. But it also requires that we reconsider how power is exercised, that is, exerted and reproduced, in a domain presupposed on developing "shared principles, norms, rules, decision-making procedures, and programmes that shape the evolution and use of the Internet" (WGIG 2005: 4).

This definition, the assumption that consensus overrules "dissensus" and that there is a level playing field, is contested in principle and practice. While it has its uses for policy utterances, I would argue within a Foucauldian vein (see Chapter 2) that for critical analysis multistakeholderism as currently practiced around internet governance can be more productively apprehended and so investigated as a computer-mediated—multilateral and transnational—iteration of Foucault's governmentality paradox (Foucault 1991, 2004a, b).

Foucault employs this term as a heuristic for his reconstruction of the rise of the modern nation-state in order to stress the historical contingencies—the disjunctures rather than the inevitability of how this institution came to be. Governmentality, in its best-known formulation, refers to the emergence of a "triangle, sovereignty-discipline-government, which has as its primary target the population and as its essential mechanism the apparatuses of security" (1991: 102). Over time these apparatuses develop techniques by which targeted populations can be better controlled—behaviors regulated and managed—from the cradle to the grave as increasingly centralized powers wield "power over life"; the birth of biopower in Foucault's oft-cited dictum (1984, 2004a). As both the ideas and the institutions underpinning the modern nation-state become entrenched and codified (those of early modern Europe—France—being the case in point), as dispersed populations and forces of order become urbanized and steadily centralized respectively within the geopolitical boundaries of "national sovereignty" populations are positioned, controlled, and then duly act—perform—as national citizens; "the" as opposed to "a" public to all intents and purposes.

The way in which, over time, this tripartite collusion has become both means and ends in itself, with nationally located, citizen-based publics both subjects of, and subjected to these dynamics, makes Foucault's insistence that ordinary people are also complicit in their own domination, coconspirators in the (re)production of these power dispositions, still difficult to swallow. One upshot for analysis is that traditionally clear-cut divisions between "states" on the one hand (top-down power) and "civil society" (where potential resistance and dissent resides) on the other are an over-simplification at best. The interpolation of the "market" (be it global or otherwise) as another autonomous sphere that can be entered and exited at will by such and such "actors" underscores this paradox. If we follow Foucault's point that historical rearrangements of power, agency, and structure over time are coconstitutive (Harding 1998) and that power relations as frozen and mobile hierarchies operate in cumulative but also unpredictable ways, then we can accept that agency—the ability to effect change, or at least articulate noncompliance— does likewise. In any case, resistance does not preexist the historical particularities of emerging "technologies of governmentality" against which it pushes or, as Certeau puts it, resistance both passive and active becomes manifest within but also despite the "grids of discipline" in which ordinary people live (Certeau in Highmore 2002: 66–68).[2]

Rather than a bleak view of the chances to engage in "transforming the space of public life itself" (Warner 2002: 89) this take on whether resistance is, or is not futile (see Chapter 3) disabuses analysts and activists of a certain conceit.

For instance, being granted formal participatory status or being privy to agenda setting in high-level meetings is not ipso facto the exercising of either pure social "agency" or necessarily an expression of legitimate political representation. By the same token, this is not to then claim, as do many opponents to Foucault's take on these matters, that positing the emergence of governmentality as a problematic, ambivalent, and seductive form of institutionalized power and control means that active mobilization against these forces is pointless, nor that engagement from within is a copout. The point for this study is that Foucault's notion stands as both critical precursor and contemporaneous counterpoint to noncritical, functionalist understandings of (global) governance. In the instrumental sense, "governance entails the establishing of institutions; institutions being the rules of the game that permit, prescribe, or prohibit certain actions. . . . Formal organizations are often required to establish, monitor, and enforce rules, as well as to resolve disputes. . . . By altering incentives, governance institutions encourage actors to adopt strategies that overcome collective action dilemmas. Successful collective actions enable actors to cooperate in pursuing their individual and communal goals. . . . However if the benefits and costs are asymmetrical across actors, institutional evolution and change could be conflictual. Institutions are therefore political artifacts (Prakash and Hart 1999: 2).

The difference between this conceptualization and Foucauldian influenced understandings is where the politics are situated. Prakash and Hart imply that organizing collective action and the asymmetry between costs and benefits are separate. If power is productive, all players coconstituent of how and where it is exercised and resisted (see Chapters 1 and 2), then this formulation is rather disingenuous. Moreover it presupposes a consensus based on an idealized notion of level playing fields as if democracy is about everyone agreeing (cf. Laclau and Mouffe 1985; Hardt and Negri 2000; Franklin 2007b). As I noted in the last chapter, visibility in these sorts of consensus-building exercises can be a trap. The formal and substantive enrollment of civil society–based actors in UN-brokered processes such as WSIS and the IGF that set out to be global, transnational, and digitally determined expressions of governance as a consensual act both underscores and pushes at Foucault's original formulation. It underscores it because what makes his conceptualization still so discomforting, particularly for activist communities, is that it stresses how ordinary people are not only complicit in the continuation and reiteration of such power dispositions (there is a payoff) but when they, or groups representing their interests, do swing into action, this agency is "highly constrained" (Lipschutz 2005: 15). Stronger still, given that over time everyday life has become "almost fully internalized within the system of governmentality that constitutes and subjectifies, much of what appears as opposition—by civil society, social movements, etc.—is better understood as integral to governmentality" (Lipschutz 2005: 15). The very media and technologies that are the object of the exercise are also increasingly internalized, and so acting as factors in the processes of socialization and co-optation in turn.

Here I would simply posit that the power redispositions that are currently unfolding around the politics of the internet are tantamount to a twenty-first century form of internet governmentality whereby global populations are being disciplined by the security apparatus of a publicly-privately owned internet. It is too easy nonetheless to then conclude that given these preconditions social actors cannot mount any substantial or self-aware challenge given their enclosure within this power "matrix." As Certeau notes, given these preconditions, the point of engaged research is "to make explicit the systems of operational combination (les combinatoires d'opérations) which also compose a 'culture', and to bring to light the models of action characteristic of users whose status as the dominated element in . . . is concealed by the euphemistic term, consumers" (Certeau in Highmore 2002: 64). There are openings, possibilities for effecting change within, if not despite the larger order of things. Tracing where and how these openings are grasped, missed, or detoured requires a different methodology. In this respect, critics of global governance from within the Foucauldian tradition have paid little attention to how internet media and communications are being enrolled in this process, as well as being engaged as forms of resistance.

One reason for this is that how and where social agency, as a situational or even strategic practice can count beyond its "defaulted" collusion with powers-that-be is undertheorized in Foucault's thought. Foucault, by his own admission, does not deal with the well-worn riposte that follows; if this is so, then what is the alternative? Drawing a distinction between the rigors of critical analysis and the urgency of (in)direct action he neither engages at this level of polemic nor participates in mutual recriminations about what forms of dissent, resistance, or direct action are, or are not politically progressive (Foucault 2004c; Lipschutz 2005: 21, note 7). This silence, while not a policy-prescriptive one, is often a stumbling block for how far governmentality as a critical heuristic can be taken to meet the burgeoning interest in social change and the internet, let alone from the point of view of how resistance is emerging from within this matrix. Overstressing the paradoxical interdependency between the powerbrokers of the internet's technologies of governmentality and their target populations (of "tweeps," "netizens," or "producers") can result in overlooking forms of dissent and activism that are working underground, behind the scenes, and behind our screens in computer-mediated and multilateral settings. These activities and their idioms of dissent and tactical maneuvers take on a fascinating and troubling aspect for those concentrating on confrontational, street-level protests alone.

The rationale for revisiting the governmentality critique in this context is that the ideas, regulatory mechanisms, collaborative practices, and output that purportedly make multistakeholder models for internet governance a global public project, in word and deed, are comprised of offline and online set of practices and outcomes that defy existing legal and theoretical models of—and for—the good society. Yet as civil society participation is being (re)presented as a break from the past at the UN level, held up as best practice in a divided and politically cynical world, this same shift puts a strain on how critical scholars have used Foucault's heuristic to date.

First, governmentality as a critical take on the vexed question of how structure, agency, and power reshape and reconstitute one another at any given is not just a theoretical abstraction. It is one with concrete, practical dimensions to anyone mobilizing dissent or facilitating institutional reform over the longer term. Second, in a postnational frame that is also a digital and transnational one, these dynamics are resolutely multimedia, inseparable from computer-mediated and mobile-connected ways and means of exerting control or resisting it. If this is so, then how established and emerging public discourses around internet futures negotiate what Warner calls the "field of tensions within which any world-making project must articulate itself" (2002: 88) has political import. The ability to convey "different ways of imagining" (Warner 2002: 88) the world with or without the labor-saving devices and communications we have grown accustomed to entails the power dynamics of the capture and recapture of speech (Certeau 1986, 1997b).

IS ANOTHER INTERNET POSSIBLE?

> We stand for a free and open internet. We support transparent and participatory processes for making internet policy and the establishment of five basic principles: Expression: Don't censor the internet. Access: Promote universal access. . . . Openness: Keep the internet an open network. . . . Innovation: Protect the freedom to innovate and create without permission. Don't block new technologies, and don't punish innovators for their users' actions. Privacy: Protect privacy and defend everyone's ability to control how their data and devices are used. (Access 2012)

> Libertarians of the Virtual World . . . we too come from Cyberspace. . . . The Internet . . . is ruled, as are all technologies, not only by the norms and beliefs of its users, but also by the laws and values of the societies in which they live. You allege that government has had no role in the Internet, and for this reason it has no claim to the Internet today, . . . Government labs and government-funded research programs gave birth to the Internet's essential technologies, and government policies continue to guide the development of important Internet innovations today. (Castro 2013)

Let's move back to political realities of "how the internet was won," to borrow from the title of a famous Western. Two scenarios are pertinent as this book comes to a close. First, the two passages cited above point to the increasing polarization of debates about who should control the internet. It is a debate that lines up (predominantly US-based) libertarians, those who maintain that the internet and its cyberspaces have been and should remain unregulated, a government-free zone (Access 2012; Barlow 1996; Rheingold 1994; Kelly 1994), head on with their critics (Castro 2013; Singh 2012a, b). It is a longstanding debate that has been coming back on the boil since the start of the World Summit on the Information Society in 2003, gathering pace toward the end of that decade and start of the next (Frau-Meigs et al. 2012; Gerbner et al. 1993). This is the period in which the internet became not only the means to make revolution, a global platform to make the world a witness of events, but also a means for counterrevolution. It is one in which internet technologies have become increasingly object and subject of this tug of war between advocates of internet freedom and internet governance. The lines of division were already being sharpened as beleaguered governments during the uprisings in the Middle East and North Africa attempted to "pull the plug" by denying citizens access to the internet or mobile phone networks. Other measures included blocking websites, imprisoning bloggers, confiscating mobile phones, and employing "cyberarmies" of online surveillance and disinformation (Barkai 2012; Franklin 2013a; Deibert and Rohozinski 2010).

Other governments facing popular unrest or political dissent, from South Korea through to the United Kingdom, have tried the legal route, for example, draconian changes to defamation laws, introducing real name systems to identify potential dissidents, requiring service providers to give up user data for the same reason (a point underscored to good effect in recent media campaigns of companies such as Google and Microsoft), or increasing police powers to track text messages or access mobile phone data (Song 2012a, b; Mendel et al. 2012). The internet is no longer "just there," access to it something to take for granted. But governments have not been the only perpetrators. Increasingly powerful corporate conglomerates have come under fire for indirect breaches of civil liberties as nonaccountable forms of data retention, prejudicial (and obtuse) terms of use and other sorts of "vendor lock-in" practices, along with the increasing use of automated forms of tracking, tagging, and nonconsensual linking up of people's online practices have gathered pace without informed consent. While governments look to persecute and criminalize in order to assert a semblance of sovereignty in the online environment, corporate web media and service providers—the global brands that dominate the web today—look to seduce and personalize in order to "groom" and consolidate their de facto hold on the hearts, minds, and digital footprints of their "netizens." Chapters Four and Five considered how these contradictory forces affect ordinary internet users in the latter and, in the former, those who through force of circumstance such as homelessness look to connect despite the "denial of access" that comes with disenfranchisement and penury.

The two passages cited at the start of this section also encapsulate divisions within the various communities mobilizing in the internet governance domain at the same time as they point to the ongoing fissures between technoskeptic and technophile analyses of the internet-society-politics nexus more broadly. In this standoff, "freedom" is the operative word, working as an absolute (e.g., the First Amendment of the American Constitution) or relative value (the regulation and limits to freedom in liberal democracies) in the respective rhetoric. These deeper differences acquired a Big Power ideological hue as things came to a head in the lead up to the World Conference on International Telecommunications (WCIT-12) hosted by the International Telecommunications Union (ITU) in December 2012. Following close on the heels of another UN-brokered meeting, the 2012 Internet Governance Forum in Baku, Azerbaijan, the WCIT-12 (dubbed "wicked" by detractors) was ostensibly about revising international telecommunications regulations (ITRs), international treaties from 1988 that clearly predated the internet. Despite all protestations to the contrary from the ITU organizers that the meeting was not about internet governance (Touré in O'Toole 2012), a bloc of governmental delegations led by the United States and the United Kingdom effectively walked out of the negotiations; this was a rerun of a similar walkout in the 1980s from a UNESCO-brokered meeting on media policy (MacBride 1980; Vincent et al. 1999; Frau-Meigs et al. 2012). Well before this meeting however, already present in the IGF meetings the month prior, the ICT corporate sector mounted a successful lobbying offensive and media campaign around the theme of how internet freedom was under threat from undemocratic governments on the one hand and, on the other, the ITU itself; this series of online campaigns presented the factions as wanting to "take over the Internet" (Access 2012).

As is often the case with media campaigns based on hyperbole and appeals to emotions such as fear or recourse to militaristic metaphors by all sides (CDT 2012), there was a grain of truth to these efforts to frame the terms of debate before the meeting took place. The WCIT-12 may not have been about the internet officially; however, in the current technohistoric context, as I have argued (Chapter 2), it is virtually impossible to separate telecommunications from internet communications. This is one reason the US delegation's objections to any attempt by some state actors within the WCIT-12 to assert sovereignty over how their citizens use the phone, (e.g., by claiming the right to be able to monitor telephone conversations), was able to strike a chord. Evoking the specter of totalitarian governments tapping phones and other privacy incursions by mashing up a reanimated Cold War rhetoric (Gurstein 2013; Singh 2012a) with the sense of entitlement assumed by today's "Google Generation" allowed press releases, online campaigns, and public forums to vividly paint the dystopia of an unfree world online (Access 2012; New America Foundation 2012).

It is not possible here to analyze in detail the discursive substance, the political rhetoric, of these campaigns and corollary public debates, nor to go into detail about the substantive legal and technical issues in question. Suffice it to say that these debates crystallized at the intersection, indeed the confluence of changes in the politics, and by association the economics of ownership and control of both the world's telecommunications transmissions infrastructure and the services it carries in tandem with those of the internet. Also crystallizing around this time, as an outcome of successful web campaigns and legwork on the ground in various multilateral consultations that year were diverging positions on the role that "civil society" protagonists need to play in this internet-inflected "war of the worlds."[3]

The second scenario is one that is somewhat less polemicized, albeit unfolding in the same time-space continuum of revved up debates around who runs the internet. I finished writing this book at the same time as UNESCO was hosting an event marking a decade since the first World Summit on the Information Society in 2003. A decade is a very long time in computing terms but less so for multilateral institutions such as the UN. For many internet users today who have grown up with MP3 players, global social networking brands, mobile smartphones, and the broadband connections that make all these devices operational, thinking back to 2003 is comparable to how the post-MTV/CNN generation that grew up with the Walkman/Discman and web of the 1990s regard the days of black and white television. The WSIS + 10 event in Paris in February 2013 underscored the multiple cultural, temporal, and institutional dimensions to this study, the slow burn of multilateral institution building against the emotion and immediacy of online campaigns and political revolutions on the ground.[4]

Continuity and flux, stasis and dynamism, tradition and the reinvention of tradition in terms of how people access and use their media and communications have in this respect a specific sort of timeline, largely dictated by the shelf-life of computerized commodities and their corollary marketing and advertising dynamics. These are also overlaid by daily habits, disinterest in and disuse of newer applications in favor of older ones. The internet also has at this point in time a much shorter lifetime and accompanying historiography than those of the printing press, railways, telephone, and telegraph. But there is a timeline, a "short history" nonetheless, and with this competing historical narratives and discourses of the future. In this respect each of these three case studies have temporal and (cyber)spatial dynamics of their own. The aim here has been to question the theoretical and empirical grounds for the ongoing bifurcation in scholarly debates between optimistic-technophile and pessimistic-technophobe accounts of these shifts. The space between these two extremes, no matter how useful they are for disciplinary or ideological marketing purposes, is where the catch-cry of the turn of the century antiglobalization protests, "another world is possible", can be found.

As the uneven, publicly accessible web, as an operating principle for the Global Internet Infrastructure (Al Gore 1996) is gradually superseded by commercial products and services premised on closed access, the breadth of these three accounts of power, resistance, and the internet from "under the floorboards," metaphorically speaking, highlight how intensifying struggles for ownership and control of the internet's physical and digital architecture go hand in hand with equally intense contestations over the terms of debate for what happens next and which historical narrative frames what we know of the past (Franklin 2011). The narrative, carefully nurtured perception of inbuilt obsolescence, reproduced by popular and academic literature as well as propagated by powerful commercial players, implies that the internet's underlying architecture, along with the web's precursor generations of multifarious user-interfaces (e.g., text-only web pages) and operating protocols, have been tamed—that alternative and nonconformist looks and usages have been rendered docile enough for the "regulation" or "liberation" of the internet by public or private forces working for the public good.

Yet the internet's rapid embedding in all areas of human endeavor still leaves much scholarship flat-footed if not bifurcated between true believers and determined skeptics. One reason for this, I would argue, is a normative ontology that privileges "Real Life"— physically proximate and territorially bound social relations—over and above those manifesting themselves differently, in this case online, in and through cyberspace/s. This organicist notion[5] of proximity underwrites many a polarized debate on the real and imagined impacts of the internet—a synecdoche for sociocultural, political, and economic changes over the last two to three decades. An unease continues to permeate critical views of the internet-society-politics nexus that draw a causal link between information and communication technologies of which the internet is one element, neoliberal globalization, and the erosion of civic engagement as conventionally understood. In this vein but from a more optimist view of what people could do with the internet, critics of the status quo express concern over an emerging hype around the extent to which corporate interests and internet freedom are synonymous belies longstanding alliances between governments and corporate players (viz. public-private partnerships) that infringe upon personal privacy, freedom of expression and of information, and other human rights at home and abroad.

FUTURES

To draw things to a conclusion, here is a brief recapitulation; this book has looked to critically examine more meta-level debates around transnationalism, citizenship, and publics through empirically grounded explorations of how these notions are rendered as human experiences and practices but also as political contestations around who should *not* control the internet. While it is a truism to note that no single agency has complete control over the internet as a whole, this does not mean to say that understanding control in this domain as a shared responsibility, delegated around the internet's distributed network of vested interests is devoid of power contestations that go beyond technolegal specifications. Competing sociocultural norms and values play a formative role at all points. In this sense this study has looked to put people, human experience, back into how the (geo) politics of the internet are being framed. And with that to rethink how "publics" are emerging around general and very specific concerns about the way "business as usual" in the day-to-day running of the internet impacts on politics, culture, and society; but to do so without resorting to media centric, statist, or technophile explanatory paradigms. As the research spans the last decade, at least, of internet applications and uses by ordinary people, as well as political and advocacy elites, the book as a whole provides a closer-up analysis of trends often treated as geographically dispersed relationships, large-scale social networks, or technoeconomic imperatives.

In this context this study has aimed to first provide a fresh way of coming to grips with the ambiguities and glaring power imbalances that link the practice of everyday life online and on the ground with the (geo)politics of the internet. Second, it has aimed to highlight, through three cases, the tensions and contradictions between disparities in access, usefulness, and public provision that exist within internet-dependent societies where digital know-how and want-to are embedded in socioeconomic entitlements. A third thread is to study more closely how incumbent powers (from large software houses to governments to quangos to multilateral institutions) work to dictate the terms of debate, access, and use, or how various actors would have the internet "use" us in other words. This undertaking pivots on four empirical axes. First is the corporate concentration of global ownership and control of the internet's critical resources for commercial gain. Second, there are the competing versions of what sort of internet should be maintained or overhauled, in which state and nonstate actors stake a claim in word and deed. In these competing narratives, and decisions moot and already made, several "alternative" or "other" internets are not only envisaged but also already in operation. These encompass respective visions of to what extent the internet should be market-based and so free from big government (e.g., the United States), market-based yet regulated and so protected from harm (e.g., European Union), state-controlled and harmonious (e.g., China), and obedient (e.g., Russia, Azerbaijan). In these competing alternatives, the distinct albeit interconnected logics or layers that make up the internet's design, access, and use (including content) are all up for grabs. Third, there are the practices of everyday life and ordinary users' habits and preferences that operate as motivators and correctives to these more self-aware vested interests. The fourth axis turns on the issues around democratic and other forms of social and political governance that are premised on internet-embedded forms of explicit sociopolitical "power over" (disciplining, punishment) and implicit forms of socialization and cultural reproduction (persuasion, monitoring, surveillance). These co-opt ordinary people and those in positions of influence into a mutually defined "grid of discipline" and corollary manufacturing of consent in digital settings.

Politicizing the internet has thereby become more necessary than ever. Ironically enough it has become domesticated—normalized and ubiquitous—before many of its most vocal critics have been able to engage effectively with just how political internet access, design, and use have always been. This disconnect between how scholars, politicians, and social activists often speak of the internet and how they—we—actually use its networking capabilities, goods, and services informs and motivates this study. Instead of it appearing as a foreign monolith exerting irrevocable power, positioned uncritically as the sine qua non of all that has changed in the world today, for better or worse (depending on who you read and your own experiences), these case studies show that there is more than one "internet," more than one sort of user-group or set of "user preferences," public formations, spaces, and places at stake and, thereby, more than one set of sociocultural and political economic alternative available in mediatized and computer-programming terms. When taken together we see through these cases where powers look to dominate and others look to resist, or simply exist as online and offline interconnections that are, nevertheless, governed by globally networked computer-mediated communications and information exchange. These studies treat the internet as a socially constructed technology and its politics-culture-society nexus in a more multifaceted, multidisciplinary way than is usually the case.

While these three scenarios are self-contained, indeed warrant book-length treatment in their own right, they are treated here as microcosms of these wider struggles, which are now necessarily (like it or not) unfolding online and on the ground. The intertwining of these domains for thought and action, domination and its resistance, has come about, though the way people, including civic organizations and state agencies, use internet technologies implicates design decisions, and vice versa. Whether all of these are the result of "market push" or "market pull" is another set of debates. These distinct and interconnected loci—online and offline—and their topographies are coconstructed by computer programming's ability to create feedback and work in concert with, but also despite, human intervention. The internet's real and imagined role in each underscores the way in which vested interests imbue it with a comparable role given to other precursor and contemporaneous technologies (e.g., railways, telecommunications, or "mass media") in technoeconomically driven projects to colonize, and ostensibly modernize, underdeveloped parts of the world. This involves not only crafting the internet in their own image or wresting the latter from powerful players, carving out spaces online and off to be able to exist, making do with limited access and opportunities to use the web but also influencing the terms of debate within its national, regional, and increasingly global governance institution-building arenas. In doing so, we can see that what is actually at stake, in-between the policy narratives and lines of code that constitute globally networked computer-mediated communications social realities and imaginaries that are taken for granted and resented in varying degrees, is more than just the one, singular means and ends. In this sense the "internet" is indeed more than the sum of its technical, legal, and sociopolitical parts. As an idea about global interconnectivity (Franklin 2010), it also needs to be understood as a synecdoche of how the world has been changing and how people access this world and see themselves in it.

This is where work on those groups who are less endowed with access, know-how, or want-to in terms of internet connectivity provides another set of insights about what is still possible to date and what options are being squeezed out as the internet becomes not only more commercialized but also more tightly regulated. For the less advantaged within hi-tech societies such as homeless people and many of their civic support networks based on nonprofit organizations or social entrepreneurship, the web throughout its history has been embraced as a place for the voiceless, the invisible to make themselves seen and heard. Either through their own dedicated media, including now online media outlets, or through independent uses of the web and now social media to create a "room of one's own" in cyberspace (to paraphrase Virginia Woolf); for instance through blogs, Facebook pages, or Twitter accounts. Prior to that, these rooms were websites, discussion groups, and email accounts. More than one internet has been at stake, more than one internet has been possible.

Which brings me to my final point: the role of (new) media and corollary communication and information exchange networks in structural transformation, and particularly in terms of righting social injustices, fighting political repression, or combating global poverty among other problems. I will respond by citing the late, great Gil Scott Heron, who penned the 1970s anthem, "The Revolution Will Not Be Televised." In a medley and intermezzo, "A Talk" on the 1974 album, *Midnight Band: The First Minute of a New Day*[6], Scott had this to say to those asking him what he really meant with the phrase "the revolution will not be televised." After noting that the media can be rightly, or wrongly held responsible for exacerbating social divisions along race, class, and gender lines, he goes on to say something that counters interpretations that his is an antediluvian view of the media:

"A lot of times people see battles and skirmishes on TV and they say 'Ah ha the revolution is being televised'. Nah. The *results* of the revolution are being televised. The first revolution is when you *change your mind* about the way you look at things and see that there might be another way to look at it that you have not been shown. What you see later on is the result of that but the *revolution, that change* that takes place will not be televised, it will not be brought to you by . . . (Heron then segues into the original rap, original emphasis as transcribed)

To borrow from this profound understanding of how uses of any media, old, new, or emerging, are symptomatic as well as instruments of domination and resistance, of stasis and change, I end this book by drawing a comparable analogy between Heron's observation and how critical activists and analysts employ internet technologies as the means and medium for revolutionary change and object of critique. What we see here too are the results of changes in the way people have come to see that "there might be another way" to look at things, and certainly to live and articulate these concerns in ways not defined by the ever-tighter grids of disciplines that are being advocated or already put in place by incumbent and new powers. While "we" are all more or less co-opted into the security apparatus of an emergent internet governmentality matrix as "netizens" of the world, this does not presuppose that resistance is futile at all. Indeed, it is more important than ever. However, in an era arguably populated by cyborgs real and imagined, the key thing, as Donna Haraway noted well over twenty years ago (1990), is to know the difference.

CHAPTER 1

1. See in the first instance UN (2000); UN Human Rights Council (2012a, b); and the World Bank (2002). In the second see Lovink (2012); Lievrouw (2011); and Boler (2008) and in the third see Gore (1994); Clinton (2010a, b); and the Council of Europe (2012a, b).

2. Chapter 5 deals with how these two overlapping working principles for running the internet have been the locus—and focal point—for burgeoning power struggles over ownership and control of the internet and corollary media products and services in the first instance and, in the second, over the hearts and minds of consumers or publics—local and global—for whom these products and services are ostensibly designed. For clarity, an explanatory note for how these terms operate here: First, public-private partnerships refer to media and internet-based provisions that private enterprise provides in partnership with governments; contractually, through tax-breaks, or development aid; e.g., the United Nations' Millennium Development Goals lean on this form of private financing of information and communications tools and platforms (UN 2000), as do institutions in OECD countries such as universities, libraries and government departments where strategic services such as email communications are outsourced to private contractors. Public-private partnerships amount to state sponsorship of private finance for infrastructural and service provisions once presided over by telecommunications operators as public services; privatized since the 1990s on the whole and increasingly computerized and/or web-embedded as the internet has developed. Such partnerships are a form of foreign direct investment for cash-strapped economies in the Global South; e.g., in parts of sub-Saharan Africa where microprocessor factories or computer literacy programs in schools are set up by global corporations such as Cisco Systems and Microsoft, and Apple computer manufacturing plants are set up in China. There has been a shift from this bilateral model for setting investment and service provision priorities in recent years towards multilateralism in the form of multistakeholder models which include a third "partner": namely "civil society"; more on this in due course.

3. Methodologically I am following Ulin's argument that social life and research are mutually constitutive, in so far as language is at the center of both in practice (Ulin 1984: 101). Gadamer's approach is to inquire how ethnographically informed modes of research that explore how others see and experience the world around

them requires that researchers, by definition already participating interlocutors, recognize they are involved as more than "just" observers or reporters. In the research field all protagonists "participate mutually" (ibid.: 102) in the unfolding of events and, thereby, contribute to shared and competing sorts of knowledge generated. In the case of internet-embedded practices and struggles over which version of events matters most, for contending parties as well as the analyst, this means unpacking the ways in which this dialectical relationship takes place at any given moment and develops over time, a relationship in which "neither the sender nor the hearer has control over the discourse" (Ulin 1984: 102) despite claims to the contrary. Debates about how establishing, or simply acknowledging that there exist in the world "different visions of what it means to be human" (Ulin 1984: 104, Franklin 2012d) need not however mean dispensing with critical analysis or actions that aim to "reveal [[or combat]] the ideology and domination embedded in normative structures of society" (Ulin 1984: 105). Note 9 below outlines the more practical elements of this rationale.

4. The literature on globalization is too vast, the debates too multiple, to rehearse here. Suffice it to say that this process in which the world is ostensibly getting smaller, the pace of life speeding up with the compaction of social and economic time, at least in terms of the dominant Western historical experience, is as much an idea—a contested discourse about change—as it is a sociocultural fact of life in modern times. For instructive and useful discussions from an interdisciplinary perspective see Appadurai (2002); Harvey (1990); Rupert (2000); Scholte (2000, 2002); and Inda and Rosaldo (2002).

5. In common parlance the internet (or "net") and the web are often used interchangeably even though in technical and historical terms they are distinct and both are specific constellations within a larger set of developments that saw the merging of computing with telephony rechristened information and communication technologies, or ICT (Franklin 2004; 237, Chaudhuri 2012: 334–335). A third term that describes where people go when online, cyberspace, however marks a distinction in disciplinary and analytical sensibilities from these more technical nomenclatures. As Lawrence Lessig states "we can distinguish the Internet from cyberspace . . . . The Internet is a medium of communication. People 'do' things on the Internet [or the web]. Cyberspace by contrast, . . . evokes or calls to life, ways of interaction that were not possible before . . . . Cyberspace communities create a difference in degree that has matured into a difference in kind. There is something unique about the interactions in these spaces. . . ." (Lessig 2006: 83). In and out of favor since William Gibson coined the word (1984), cyberspace is usually used in the singular, as an abstract noun (e.g., Jordan 1999; Deibert and Rohonzinski 2010). As Lessig goes on to argue, cyberspace "is not one place. It is many places. And the character of these many places differs from differences in the people who populate these places. But demographics alone don't explain the variance . . . . Cyberspace in part because the people—who thy are, what their interests are– have changed, and in part because the capabilities provided by the space have changed" (Lessig 2006; 84, 85). Lessig's argument is that these capabilities are constituted by the modalities of "law, the market, norms, and architecture" (Lessig 2006: 340) which enable different sorts of (cyber)spaces as there are, in turn, accessed and perpetuated over time. I too prefer to use this term in the plural based on a phenomenological understanding of space

as dynamic, intersubjective, and socioculturally practiced (Franklin 2004: 54–56, Highmore 2002, Song 2012a, b). Consciously employing the plural form also points to the multiple and polysemous sorts of content, conversations, places, and ways of doing things and being online (encapsulated by the term practices) that allow for inquiries into how "practiced places" come about online (Certeau in Franklin 2004: 165); more on these matters in Chapter 2.

6. It is by definition a translocal-transnational interconnecting technology, or constellation of many technologies that include hardware (machines, devices), tubes, wires and signaling structures (just take a look behind your PC if you still have one or at the closest mobile phone mast), and software—computer programs. By their own admission high-profile figures in the internet's history were able to proceed through state-funded research projects, from Vint Cerf at the US-based Advanced Research Projects Agency Network (ARPANET) facility to Tim Berners-Lee in the UK-Swiss European Organization for Nuclear Research (CERN) consortium (Abbate 2001; Holmes 2007). The internet's origins in the U.S. military's research and development funding in the 1960s makes it an easy target of critiques that would reduce its contemporary popular uses and civic applications to these defense-based applications alone. Since these early days civic uses mean that it has transcended these initial objectives. However these state-funded projects and leading personalities in the early development of both the internet and the web still play a formative role in the internet's underlying operations, policy debates, and incumbent governing bodies, ICANN and the World Wide Web Consortium (W3C) respectively (see Mueller 2002, 2005; Raymond 2001; Stalder 2012); more on these matters in Chapter 3. There are key differences between how these personalities regard its current and future role in society; e.g., the internet is an artifact, a business and nothing more (Cerf 2012).

7. Broadly speaking and without recourse to a fuller exegesis, by the term "critical" I am signaling an ongoing commitment to theory and research that aims to do more than describe or reproduce the political or epistemological status quo, hence evidence of affiliations to theoretical streams anchored in the early twentieth century critical theory of the Frankfurt School, mid-twentieth century critiques of orthodox Marxist politics and theory—including their feminist and postpositivist critical strains, and selective post-modern deconstructions of Western academe's self-appointed authoritativeness (see Borradori 2003). I do not see these divergent streams of thought as necessarily mutually exclusive.

8. The lyrics of the song, "Ac–Cent–Tchu–Ate The Positive (Mister In–Between)" (Johnny Mercer and Harold Arlen) sung by Bing Crosby and the Andrew Sisters; track 13 of The Singing Detective Soundtrack: BBC Records CD 608 (1986).

9. In other words, I will leave aside theoretical debates around the technological or structurally determining factors necessary for ascertaining whether a significant event is transformative one to others; e.g., whether the overthrow of a political leadership is an "event . . . (that) . . . opens up the possibility of an 'entirely new' body politic" (Vazquez 2006: 53, see Fuchs 2012).

10. The research undertaken for each of these three cases is informed by a motivation to empirically ground how practices and their concomitant communities and foundational discourses shape social and political agendas; how people experience, challenge, and create competing narratives and to do so as these unfurl,

in "real time" rather than reconstruct meaning from analysis of their outcomes. It does so through the situational activism of multi-sited ethnographic modes of research (Marcus 1995; Hine 2000; Franklin 2004: 196 passim) to uncover the interinstitutional and intergenerational threads of a continuing story. A fuller methodological exegesis is not feasible in this study however I indicate pertinent points as they arise in each case as well as point to previous work where these practicalities are explicated further. Chapter 3 is a reconstruction of events using secondary sources, corroborated by conversations with insiders and the establishment of statistical indicators about internet and other media uses around the world over the last decade that back up and nuance this narrative with the benefits of hindsight. The bulk of the fieldwork in Chapters 4 and 5 entailed extended and regular periods of participant-observation online and offline, within the fields of action over the last ten years. When not known, I was then granted access primarily as a researcher (Chapter 4), and then as researcher and increasingly participant (Chapter 5). That said, my increasing involvement in decisions and consultations that were the basis of earlier Ford Foundation-funded research into UN consultations, has allowed me a certain purchase on the analysis in Chapter 3. Along with the field notes generated by direct observation over extended (sitting in) and episodic (attending, cowriting submissions, and intervening in summits, meetings) periods of time in the case of street papers (Chapter 4) and UN consultations (Chapter 5) other sorts of data-gathering included interviews (planned and spontaneous), on-the-fly conversations, the analysis of draft documents against final versions, a study of relevant email listserv exchanges where I had access as a working researcher/participant, and website analysis. The fieldwork undertaken in Chapter 5, a mix of online and multi-sited participant-observation whereby I followed, as George Marcus puts it (1995) a particular set of intersecting controversies, debates and protagonists requires an additional note. In this case my gradual shift from relative outsider (newly arrived researcher) to insider (regular observer-participant among many others) underwent another change just prior to going to press. I will discuss this aspect more in Chapter 5 given its implications for how I drew a line in where this part of the story ends. In terms of the research ethics entailed in taking part in as well as researching membership-based conferrals and conversations, I followed the principles of transparency of intent, access requests, and informed consent. For instance in terms of obtaining consent from individuals when citing them anonymously was not sufficient, by (re)declaring my researcher interests at the outset to those in charge of the listserv (former chairs of the Internet Rights and Principles Coalition), online (as candidate for the IRP Coalition Steering Committee in 2009, or engaged in reconstructing the process covered in Chapter 5) where apposite. In most cases, in Chapter 4 particularly, I have anonymized any direct quotes from participants in the New York *BIGNews* Writers' Group as a rule, those who granted me interviews excepted.

11. As such this study is cognisant of retheorizations of Habermasian Public Sphere Theory as a discrete school of thought and methodological predilection for research into the internet-politics-society nexus (see Papacharissi 2010; Fraser 2007; Crack 2008). It does not set out however to intervene directly in these debates in this specific body of theory. That said the findings and analysis are germane to these debates about whether the internet has enhanced or undermined existing public

sphere institutions (e.g., media diversity, freedom of the press, democratic processes). More specifically it takes on board postcolonial critiques of the historical and cultural limitations of ethnocentric understandings of how democracy and the media should work in an ideal world (Habermas 1996 (1968), 2001). See Franklin (2005b).

12. The source for said new data is given as from http://chartbeat.com (accessed February 3, 2013).

13. This is how one new user in my family put it on signing up for their first email account. A word on figures: How internet usages, implying connectivity, are evolving differs if this aggregate figure (of internet usages combined with population statistics) is broken down into either regions, e.g., Asia has double the internet usages of Europe, which is in turn double that of North America (Internet World Stats 2012), or sorts of connectivity and use such as landlines, mobile, or specific online services. These differences feed into different analyses of where the accent or critical mass lies in geographical and geopolitical terms. The key point is that these figures are estimates, commercially and time sensitive. See also ITU (2013); Franklin (2004: 26–27); Center for Law and Democracy (2012).

14. I am borrowing from the title of a Master's degree research module jointly developed and taught with Laurens ten Kate at the University of Humanistics, Utrecht (the Netherlands), 2005–2007.

15. I take the cue here from the catch-cry of political feminism and the women's liberation movement consciously. While this study does not isolate gender power relations as a privileged mode of analysis it draws on previous work (Franklin 2001, 2004, 2005, 2009b) in this vein as well as a postcolonial feminist sensibility for critical research into the technology-culture-society nexus (Franklin 2004; see Wajcman 1991; Youngs 2006; Gurumurthy 2003; Haraway 1997).

16. A transcription of this scene can be found at http://www.whysanity.net/monos/matrix3.html (accessed December 14, 2012). See also http://matrix.wikia.com/wiki/Redpill (accessed December 14, 2012).

17. For instance, it took until 2011 for the (US dominated) International Studies Association to frame its annual convention, held in San Diego, California, around the theme of information and communication technologies (ICT and by implication the internet) as a core theme for international relations theory and research, and until 2012 for positions in "cyberpolitics" to be created in one of the discipline's leading institutions in the United Kingdom. Fortunately, scholars have not waited for these sorts of institutional affirmations to pursue inquiries into these interconnections from the outset. What these tardy recognitions do signal however is the marked disconnect between the rollout of the internet in research and (higher) education across the board on the one hand and, on the other, the relative dearth of curricula around the world that engage the internet and corollary media as not just a "virtual learning" platform but also as an object and field of critical and reflexive inquiry warranting concerted and critical attention.

18. Vint Cerf, a key figure in the development of the internet's foundational computer protocols and vice-president of Google likes to call himself the Internet's Chief Evangelist.

19. Technically these terms mean different things even though they are often used interchangeably. A dilemma is being in the situation of having to choose between two

equally disagreeable or unwanted alternatives, being confronted with a Catch-22 situation in vernacular terms. To speak of a paradox however is to point to something that seems contradictory at first sight but on further reflection contains a core insight if not a grain of truth. The phrase paradox-dilemma rather than paradoxical dilemma is used here not to imply dilemmas that turn out not to be so after all but rather a combination of two distinct sorts of decision-making, analytical registers, and domains for action.

20. Thanks to Jeanette Hoffmann for the phrase "discourses of loss." As noted above, multilateral institutions such as the United Nations or the Council of Europe have been pursuing multistakeholder models for agenda-setting and law-making. The example par excellence is around internet governance consultations that have championed multistakeholderism as an innovation in "who gets to participate in decision-making about internet policy and technology, and how. Since its infancy, the internet has benefited from a lightweight, decentralized, multistakeholder approach to governance that combines targeted government regulation with various formal and informal multistakeholder organizations to help guide its global development" (Llansó 2012). Despite the knockbacks delivered to the reigning neoliberal economic orthodoxy in the wake of the most recent (2008) global economic crisis, this rendition has become a hegemonic discourse for how the internet should be run, one that eschews regulation in preference for "self-regulation," i.e., private enterprise continues to provide the finance and expertise while lobbying for minimal state intervention or legislation around issues such as privacy. This notion is deeply embedded in Anglo-American understandings of best practice for the internet's future development and sustainability. As we will see it is not self-evident in legal terms and has recently come under fire from a number of fronts; highly centralized state actors (e.g., China) and grassroots critics of under-regulated corporate dominance of the internet's critical resources concur in this respect albeit for different reasons that cover a gamut of cultural and ideological differences (Breslow 1991; Brownword 2008; Curran et al. 2012; Dahlberg and Siapiera 2007; Dany 2012).

21. A conventional definition reads for instance as follows; power "is the capacity of an agent or agents to secure specific outcomes through their intervention (or non–intervention) in the course of events . . . . In exercising this capacity the agent implements various kinds of resources" (Thompson 1995: 68). While Foucault was not the first nor will be the last thinker to reconsider notions of power, his critique of narrow definitions of power as the direct exertion of control has had a profound influence on investigations into how "other dimensions of social reality . . . shape how power works. . . ." (Peterson and Runyan 1999: 69). Those other dimensions now include internet technologies (Jordan 1999; Fischbach 2005; Nye 2002; Lessig 2006; Benkler 2006).

22. Thanks to Parminder Jeet Singh for reminding me regularly of this priority.

23. Sloterdijk's metaphor is the Crystal Palace, an enormous glasshouse structure built in 1851 to house the Great Exhibition in London, held at the height of the British Empire; now the name of a south London suburb. The citations from Sloterdijk are the author's translation of the Dutch translation of the German original (2006).

24. One of the most iconic articulations of this view is John Perry Barlow's 1996 Declaration of the Independence of Cyberspace. A more recent articulation is the web-based petition in support of a US-based advocacy campaign around a

Declaration of Internet Freedom in 2012; http://www.internetdeclaration.org/
freedom (accessed January 23, 2013), more on these matters in Chapters 5 and 6.

25. All citations from Fischbach are the author's (loose) translations.

CHAPTER 2

1. As I noted in the last chapter, statistical records of internet penetration and related
   indicators have improved over the last decade in so far as organizations like the ITU
   now take all things internet and mobile into account. According to Internet World
   Stats (2012), the increase in internet use ("penetration") worldwide over the decade
   between 2002 and 2012 increased by over 500%. In that period, the percentage in
   Africa, the Middle East, and Latin America of new users per population increased by
   3,606.7%, 2,639.9%, and 1,310.8% respectively. See also International Telecommunications Union (2013); Mendel et al. (2012); Millward (2012). According to Facebook, the number of users in 2012 stood at one billion, notionally at least one person
   in seven of the world's population has a Facebook account (Vance 2012), most of
   whom are in Brazil, India, Indonesia, Mexico, and the United States in that order.

2. For collections of theory and research, including historical overviews, into the internet's design and uses from the 1990s World Wide Web era and into the Web
   2.0 (i.e., social media) era of today see Shields (1996); Jones (1991); Mandiberg
   (2012), and van Dijck (2013) respectively. Successive generations of web applications are not mutually exclusive however in that many from the early days of the
   web still exist and function, despite the current dominance of Web 2.0 products
   and services that are premised on integrating once separate services (e.g., email
   and weblogs, audio and visual, desktop and mobile phone) onto one platform and
   then housing these online by offering access and services on the web as opposed
   to having the user download the software and store the material onto their own
   system—the principle of cloud computing (O'Reilly 2012: 33, 51). Here too definitions and the historical trajectory of any given software application are also grist
   to the mill of ongoing debates (Everitt and Mills 2009; O'Neil 2009; O'Reilly 2012;
   Searles 2008). For our purposes here the shift lies in the blurring of the separation
   between personal computing goods and services (computers and their software
   packages that then go online) and those based on services offered purely on the
   internet via the web. The latter have shifted the center of gravity from personal
   computing to the web services. Chapter 3 will examine one dimension to this contemporary flux.

3. See the reference to this expression taken from the film *The Matrix* in Chapter 1.

4. To refer to both intergovernmental organizations and multilateral institutions signals
   two distinctions: (1) that what is commonly referred to as the "international state
   system" includes more than nation-states organized in formal organizations such as
   the United Nations; (2) an analytical and historical distinction between these two organizational and ideational forms of supraterritorial, to borrow from Scholte (2000)
   political and economic cooperation, viz. global governance that have emerged over
   the last century (Douglas 1999; Prakash and Hart 1999). The term international organizations no longer captures, if indeed it ever did but that is another set of debates, the
   hybrid and overlapping organizational forms of international and supra-state levels
   of cooperation that currently run, or "frame" the world today, comprised of multilateral, multilevel, and international formations that include and exclude nonstate

actors (e.g., corporate entities, NGOs, financial institutions, scientific advisory committees) in varying measures. The first, older form of international cooperation is comprised of sovereign nation-states with mandates based on United Nations membership. The second, newer organization includes other sorts of membership criteria, wider mandates and ambitions that implicitly recognize that nonstate actors also play a role in international affairs. The line between the two is a shifting one however, waxing and waning according to the fortunes of the United Nations itself, also a multilateral institution in this larger context. As Bøås and McNeill argue organizational differences are but the tip of the iceberg; "the institutions comprising the current multilateral system . . . are particular amalgams of ideas, interests and material power which in turn influence the development of ideas, interests and material conditions" (2004: 4, 6).

5. For example, women were major figures in the history of software programming in the early years of computing (Spiller 2002; Haraway 1990, 1997; Mitter and Rowbotham 1995; Henwood et al. 2001; Wajcman 1991).

6. This refers to gaming communities, hacker networks and those who have populated the web as an alternative viz." Second Life" since the early days as distinct from more organic, spontaneous uptakes by which the web offers opportunities hitherto unavailable on the ground (Franklin 2001, 2003; Karim 2003; Kolko et al. 2000).

7. This borrows from the chapter in Paul Gilroy's *There Ain't No Black in the Union Jack* (Gilroy 2002) entitled "Race is Ordinary." My borrowing of this phrase also implies that race, ethnicity, and gender are also underelucidated elements of these cases and others like them where internet media and communications play a formative, coconstitutive role and not simply an instrumentalist one in how communities form, mobilize to improve their lot (online and on the ground) as well as simply get on with things. See for example Kolko et al. (2000) and Franklin (2004, 2005b, 2007b).

8. Vint Cerf made this comment in one of the many workshops he spoke on at the 2012 Internet Governance Forum in Baku, Azerbaijan. See Cerf (2012).

9. To paraphrase Pierre Bourdieu, also a contemporary of Foucault and Certeau, modern theories of the state implicitly construe the state—as idea, institution, and field of action—as inseparable from understandings of publics and publicness. Hence inherent in all thinking about the state is a notion of public order as a principle. This renders the state as a coconstituent of the ordering of a "space in which the public and the private are in opposition to one another, in which public places are distinct from the domestic ones of ordinary homes, and palaces" (Bourdieu 2012: 24, my translation). The socially constructed quality of states in their physical (judiciaries, legislatures, police forces, armies and so on) and symbolic renditions means in Bourdieu's view, and those of his contemporaries, that while the state is an "illusion" it exists, and exerts power and influence over our lives, in so much as it is believed to exist (Bourdieu 2012: 13, my translation). Within this shared illusion in which the state and the public good are mutually dependent (sociocultural and other differences notwithstanding and not overlooking major ideological changes in the role and reach of state agencies since the 1980s across the Anglo-American-European world) changes in the way states operate as they enroll internet and other computing technologies are thereby intertwined with concomitant changes in the "collective belief" about the future of the "mysterious reality" that is the state (Bourdieu 2012: 13) in

a postneoliberal if not post-Web 2.0 age. See also Braman (2006); Mueller (2010); and Giacomello and Eriksson (2009).

10. Those familiar with Lippmann will note here that he goes on to argue that for this reason there needs to be leadership and governance based on selective and implicitly elite groups, i.e., he was not advocating consultative forms of democracy or "citizen media" in that respect. His is an argument in support of representative government and an independent, professional media.

11. The reference to common unhappiness is taken from Sigmund Freud's observation, based on a psychodynamic understanding of everyday life in which appearances can be deceptive and thereby scientific observation needs to take into account that all is not as it may seem; " But you will see for yourself that much has been gained if we succeed in turning your hysterical misery into common unhappiness" (Breuer and Freud 1895: 305).

12. *The Matrix*, in terms of its plot and dystopian mood lean heavily on precursor cult classics, from HG Wells to more particularly William Gibson, whose collected stories, *Burning Chrome* (Gibson 1984b) and Web 1.0 era novel *Neuromancer* 1984a have been attributed as the founding documents of cyberpunk and the genesis of the term cyberspace; For instance, first as a noun, "It was hot, the night we burned Chrome. Out in the malls and plazas, moths were batting themselves to death against the neon, but in Bobby's loft the only light came from a monitor screen and the green and red LEDs on the face of the matrix simulator. I knew every chip in Bobby's simulator by heart; it looked like your workaday Ono–Sendai VII; the 'Cyberspace Seven,' but I'd rebuilt it so many time that you'd have had a hard time finding a square millimeter of factory circuitry in all that silicon" (Gibson 1984b: 168). Second, as a state of mind or place to be already containing all the ambiguity with which the term has been imbued since: "Cyberspace. A consensual hallucination experienced daily by billions of legitimate operators, in every nation, by children being taught mathematical concepts . . . A graphic representation of data abstracted from the banks of every computer in the human system. Unthinkable complexity. Lines of light ranged in the nonspace of the mind, clusters and constellations of data. Like city lights, receding . . . " (Gibson 1984a; Chapter 2). Other recent cinematic versions in this mood are Source Code, Inception, Minority Report (another adaptation of a Phillip K. Dick story), Pi, and arguably Avatar, along with Hollywood blockbuster adaptations of computer games like Lara Croft and Tron, and the contract signed by film director Duncan Jones in early 2013 to adapt the virtual reality game World of Warcraft for Hollywood.

13. This section draws on Franklin (2010).

14. See Franklin (2001, 2003, 2004, 2005b, 2007b). My thanks to Dong–Hyun Song here for his insights into how Certeau can, and cannot be useful for inquiries into issues of internet governance as they pertain to "cybercontrol" struggles between ordinary internet users, governments, and service providers (Song 2012a, b).

15. Certeau engaged directly with the work of Foucault and Bourdieu, as well as many other thinkers of his generation in some important ways (not always reciprocated in kind). See for instance Certeau's discussion of the limits to Foucault's structuralist tendencies in his collection, Heterologies, (Certeau 1986), and critique of the practice theory of both Foucault and Bourdieu in Chapter 4 of The Practice of Everyday Life (Certeau 1980: 75 passim).

16. The literal translation of the original French title (L'invention du quotidien), is "the invention of everyday life," rendered in the English language editions as "the practice of everyday life" (Franklin 2004: 245, Note 5).

17. Thanks to Joanna Kulesza for this insight.

18. This phrase is one that the Azeri political dissident, Emin Milli, used to good effect at the 2012 Internet Governance Forum in Baku, Azerbaijan (November 2012) in public forums and informal conversation.

19. This phrase is part of a civil society initiative underway at time of writing for the 2013 Bali Internet Governance Forum meeting in September 2013.

CHAPTER 3

1. The terms *web browser* and *search engine* are distinct even if used synonymously. Browser programs are software, that can be downloaded from the internet but usually supplied as a default (i.e., included in the working applications on purchase), developed as specific brands (e.g., Microsoft's Internet Explorer, Apple's Chrome) that allow people to access and navigate their way around the web. Browsers mediate between user and the internet, facilitating access to the web's vast content, goods, and services; the front door by which people enter to find out about what is available online. Search engines are more focused indexing tools (that are accessed via a browser) that can rank, channel, and inform as they "search" the web for specific information, governed by the keywords or phrases entered. Part of the early World Wide Web as a core application, a browser is by definition a more open-ended approach to access hence the more laconic terms, surfing or browsing the web. Search engines are, as their name implies, software codes designed to be more intensive in finding, collating, ranking and listing the content collected. We "search" the web because we want to "find" something specific. Nowadays most users access and use the web via search engines which are effectively high-powered browsers-on-a-mission. To date Google has led the way and the world market in this domain. In September, 2008 Google launched Chrome as its own house-brand browser. At the time Internet Explorer and Mozilla Firefox shared between them over 90% of internet "browsing" activities (49% and 42.6% respectively), already indicating a shift in Microsoft's domination of the browser markets in 2002 (then around 85% more or less). By September 2012, four years later, Google's Chrome had overtaken both with a market share of 44.1% against Firefox (31.8%) and a trailing Internet Explorer (16.1%). By February 2013 Google had consolidated this position to gain 50% of the market, http://www.w3schools.com/browsers/browsers_stats.asp (accessed March 7, 2013).

2. Microsoft has had to work hard to counter accusations of arrogance since it was obliged by law to accommodate others within its operating system. Insiders and pundits put this change of heart and style down to not only the outcome of DOJ v. Microsoft but also the changing commercial, technological and social environment of internet uses and web access in these years. The high profile philanthropy projects of the Bill and Miranda Gates Foundation have also played a role as has a burgeoning unease amongst regulators and pundits about the hazards of cloud-computing dependence in a would be post-Microsoft galaxy. In short Microsoft has morphed from being a gamechanger to having to adapt in order to avoid being assimilated itself (anonymous source).

3. As I noted in Chapters 1 and 2, science fiction—as a popular and serious literary genre—and computers go hand in hand: designers, marketers, scholars, and ordinary viewing publics consume these tropes all the time, from H. G. Wells to Aldous Huxley and into Hollywood they emerge from and contribute to the lexicons in use in the media-ethno-cyberscapes of today's global cultural flows (see Haraway 1990; Franklin 2011; Castells 2002; Shah 2011).

4. Popular science-fiction analogies also abounded in media coverage of the case at the time. For example when referring to the "warp–speed growth" of the corporation (Economist 1998a); in rhetoric from corporate competitors posing as "humanity's defenders" against the "evil empire" of Microsoft (NRC Handelsblad 1997b). During the trial itself, cartoonists made use of popular cultural images, depicting the company as Darth Vader from the Star Wars films, or as Godzilla.

5. *Wikipedia* is as good a place as any for getting the lowdown on popular culture artifacts such as television shows. See http://en.wikipedia.org/wiki/Star_Trek (accessed December 6, 2012) and the database of characters and storylines on the *Star Trek* fansite, http://www.startrek.com/database_article/borg (accessed December 6, 2012).

6. There are many narratives at stake in this reconstruction, a cast of personalities and technical communities who also had a stake, if not very different visions of how the internet and the web should be developed, on whose terms and for what sorts of uses. This version of events has to skate over some of these overlapping narratives. Suffice it to say that the so-called browser wars between Microsoft and its opposition were ones in which individuals, not just emerging and established business interests, played formative roles in developing and advocating "free and open source software" as an alternative to "non-free software" (Stallman 2012) of proprietary branded products. Diverging schools of thought within this larger practitioner community aside, their use of legal avenues were also instrumental in getting the Microsoft antitrust prosecutions around the world. The Linux Operating System and its challenge to Microsoft in the case in point for this chapter. Another, also based on peer-to-peer knowledge exchange and alternative sorts of licensing for end users based on "copyleft" (Lessig 2006; Benkler 2006) within technical (also known as hacker) communities, is the *Samba* suite of programs (http://www.samba.org/samba/). These programs enable users to bypass the need to buy and install Microsoft packages entirely; they are easy to install and use. Assuming of course that people know about these alternatives and are able and willing to go this extra mile. My thanks to Simon Phipps (conversation, February 27, 2013) for reminding me of this undertold dimension to a story where contending ideas of what is meant by "freedom" are paramount. In the case of free software as an ethos: "Think of 'free speech,' not 'free beer.'" (Stallman 2012; see Grassmuck 2002; Tridgell et al. 1997, Raymond 2001 and Chapter 5). Arguments between personalities and institutions still rage, exemplified by distinctions, and overlaps between the *Free Software Foundation* (www.fsf.org) and *Open Source Intiative* (http://opensource.org/).

7. This deregulation—privatization—imperative (*TINA—There Is No Alternative*) is historically contingent; a break in macroeconomic orthodoxy, agenda-setting, and institutional topographies in international settings. Up until the 1970s under the aegis of social democratic, Keynesian economic precepts, such as idea was unthinkable. Telecommunications, energy, water, and transport were regarded as

intrinsically public goods; on the UK and former colonies and in western continental Europe at least—the Soviet/Maoist blocs notwithstanding. With the advent of monetarism and neoliberalism this was all to change. See Bourdieu (1998); Ramonet (2002); McChesney, Wood and Foster (1998); and Schiller (1999).

8. To recall a conceptual premise in this study: Here, technology is treated as socially and historically contingent—"constructed" rather than exogenous to politics, economics, and social mores. As I, and others have argued, this also applies to how information and communication technologies need to be conceptualized. In short, information and communication technologies are what "we" make them. By the same token, once developed, put in place, and used (or not as the case may be) artifacts, systems, and the policy regimes holding these together also impact on who "we" are to become; how people live, communicate, and organize themselves.

9. The stress in these organizational restructurings lay on the notion of *just-in-time* production and distribution, ongoing automation—digitalization—of work processes throughout and organizational "flattening out" by which workforces were drastically reduced. In addition, manufacturing became internationalized—globalized—as multinational—now transnational—corporations shifted factories, and services to low-wage parts of the world. Likewise for the cultural industries: the Hollywood film industry, music majors. newspapers, and television production. Talk of the "new" or "knowledge" economy went hand in hand with these changes; hallmarks of "post-Fordist," "post-industrial," or "postmodern" modes of production in consumer societies. Among the first to be reorganized along these lines were the so-called dinosaurs of public telecommunications operators; victims by necessity of technological imperatives in this climate. In both the United States and Europe, tens of thousands of jobs were scrapped in these sectors.

10. There are various way of measuring and aggregating such figures; more on these indicators in due course. Those compiled by Neilson in November 2012, based on an audience that does not include Asia, Latin America, the Middle East, or Africa (see Millward 2012), rank these companies in terms of "unique audience," percentage of "active reach," and the time spent online with these parent companies' services per person. As of this date Google, Microsoft, and Facebook commanded around 70% and over of these audience ratings, with Yahoo!, Wikimedia (Parent Company of Wikipedia), and Amazon next behind at 51.7%, 38.7%, and 36.5% respectively. Google was head and shoulders ahead in all instances, owner as well of the top rating online video service, YouTube, http://www.nielsen.com/us/en/insights/top10s/internet.html (accessed February 13, 2013). As for social networking sites, increasingly referred to as social media, the top three in February 2013 according to ebizmba.com are Facebook, Twitter, and LinkedIn in that order; http://www.ebizmba.com/articles/social–networking–websites (accessed February 13, 2013). All three are based on the US West Coast, in or close to Silicon Valley, as are Google and Microsoft (Solnit 2013).

11. Take, for example, the development of increasingly smaller processors with ever-increasing capacity, the success of the (Apple pioneered and then Microsoft appropriated) design feature of the "icon" user-interface that quickly put paid to the keystroke operations for word processing (the demise of the 1980–1990s leader, *Word Perfect*, for instance); the development of protocols for enabling computer to computer communications, impossible without with browser and hyper-linking software; the increased speed of glass-fiber and satellite transmissions,

"packet-switching" technologies and such like a the internet moved from its academic-defense establishment homebases into the public domain.

12. For instance, not so long-forgotten names of include *Lycos*, *Geocities*, *Excite.com*, and *Netscape* (Volkskrant September 23, 2007: 7).

13. Using traditional and new digitally sourced mapping techniques *TeleGeography* released a freely accessible (at time of writing) interactive map of the world's submarine communications that consciously draws on older cartographic idioms and sources. The past and the present encapsulated in a version of early modernist cartography that visualizes these ongoing historical asymmetries in connectivity in the material sense; http://blog.telegeography.com/post/42364809478 (accessed February 13, 2013). Its *Global Internet Map* from 2012, using a satellite-age projection underscores these continuities as well as the shift towards the Global South, http://www.telegeography.com/telecom-resources/map-gallery/global-internet-map-2012/index.html (accessed 13 February 2013).

14. In 2008 Bill Gates through his charitable foundation invested heavily in social and research projects; R&D facilities at Cambridge University and in China ($US 80 million); US $100 million in vaccination programs in parts of the global south; $US 20 million for the Seattle Public Library in the United States, and so on. But Microsoft was not alone in its huge marketing budget at the time. In 2000, for instance, CISCO Systems (also a quasi-monopoly in the manufacturing of internet transmission technology—the all important routers and also accused of Borg-like behavior in some quarters) invested around $US 4.5 billion in marketing (Kraaijeveld 2001). Since then, both Microsoft and Google have invested large sums of money into lobbying and a range of public interest campaigns at the national and international level (Becker and Niggemeier 2012; Becker and Rosenbach 2012).

15. Still the only player in the world's browser software market (see Note 1 above), at the end of 2002 when the court ruling was made, the corporation had about $US 43 billion available in ready cash; more than the American trade deficit at the time ($US 40.1 billion). Company profits steadily increased throughout the trial period; 12% in the second quarter of 2002 (Volkskrant 2003e:17, 2003f: 31, 2003g:27). The ability of the corporation to defy, ignore, or simply pay massive fines imposed on it by bodies such as the European Commission or reach workable settlements with agencies such as the US Department of Justice (see Carlile 2008) underscores the breadth of its financial resources, economic clout, and winner-takes-all approach. In 2007–2008 the corporation was still ranked as the world's third largest with a revenue of $US 51.12 billion and its stock-market value set at $US 303 billion. In 2012 Microsoft's revenue was $73.723 billion, with a net income of $16,978: quadrupled since 2000.

16. In "an attempt to clarify just what we mean by Web 2.0," Tim O'Reilly in a piece first published in 2005 (O'Reilly 2012: 32) lists seven features that set Web 2.0 applications apart from its precedents. At the top of the list is the shift to "services, not packaged software" that are designed by "trusting users as co-developers" and "harnessing collective intelligence" in order to offer "software above the single device" (O'Reilly 2012: 51). This is indeed a shift in working practices, business models, and the rights and obligations of those users who are willingly, or by default harnessed into this post–Borg collective intelligence.

17. Over the last century there have been seven major antitrust cases prosecuted in the United States: Standard Oil, American Tobacco, US Steel, IBM, AT&T, Intel, and Microsoft.

18. To pick up from above, and at the risk of getting ahead of the story, Netscape eventually morphed into Mozilla's *Firefox*, able to resume its lead in the global web browser market for a while until it was overtaken by Google Chrome between 2011 and 2012. Google Chrome (48.4%), Firefox (40.3%), and lagging behind Internet Explorer (13.2%) were the three top browsers in early 2013 according to w3schools. com; http://www.w3schools.com/browsers/browsers_stats.asp (accessed February 13, 2013).

19. This refers to an agreement signed in 1994 in the wake of a tied vote in the Federal Trade Commission on the matter, by which the DOJ induced Microsoft to undertake delinking sales and licensing of Windows from its other products. In 2001 the company and the DoJ signed another Consent Decree in order to forego more litigation after three years of slugging it out in the courts. This interim settlement put strict limits to how Microsoft could develop and market its software, requiring it to work with other developers and allow access to its source codes. For the full document set see the US Department of Justice website at http://www.justice.gov/atr/cases/ms_index.htm (accessed May 13, 2013).

20. Access to Microsoft's source code is the deal breaker in this case. Without it other software programs cannot be developed or used effectively for use on MS-based machines and services. All software starts somewhere (Grassmuck 2002:414). Without access to this underlying level of code, no matter how sprightly successive generations of overlaying code may be, all adaptations are basically an unhappy compromise. The Javascript issue, between Sun Microsystems and Microsoft (see below) is another example of the strategic significance the source code is for any feasible commercial collaborations, or compatibility between users using different suppliers. Microsoft's defense pivoted on the notion, widely held, that this is a question of copyright, the corporation's intellectual property and so not for public consumption.

21. Navigator did not come free until Microsoft started to offer Explorer as a "freebie" in 1996. Commercial losses for Netscape were not allayed by a counteroffer as a result of this use of the "free software" principles for commercial ends.

22. Along with other major developers, Microsoft's software is based on the IBM UNIX code; the reason why Microsoft computers installed with Intel processors are rated, at least until 1998, "IBM-compatible." Since the generation of Windows NT and Windows 2000, access to this part of the program—the "Microsoft–DOS shell" was closed off to easy access from the desktop (restricted to "administrator" or with permission). Second, the click-here icons that populate a generically MS desktop (the computer-screen visuals) were acquired from an early collaboration with Apple computers, from Macintosh. The rapid polarization and rhetoric from both companies, and their dedicated followers of ICT fashion, harks back to the subsequent change in Apple's fortunes in the PC sales, trailing its rival for years until its reestablishment as a niche-market, hip and cool global brand in recent years.

23. This partnership was not a happy one, officially ending in 2009. Since its inception in 1983, *America Online*, now rebranded as *AOL* has changed hands and rebranded frequently. Currently headed by former Google executive Tim Armstrong, and according to its (own) Wikipedia entry, the corporation now operates as a "digital media company"; http://en.wikipedia.org/wiki/AOL (accessed 13 February 2013; Lessig 2006: 88–94).

24. Javascript is "a language with which programmers can develop applications for any system; whether that is a PC running on MS Windows, a UNIX server, or an IBM mainframe. Java software is ideal for internet uses and applications in that it doesn't distinguish between different makes of computers or software systems." (Volkskrant 2002b:19; my translation). In this sense Javascript works counterintuitively to the whole modus operandi of Microsoft software; designed to be mutually exclusive. In this sense Javascript's pyrrhic victory over Google in 2012 (see Volkskrant May 8, 2012) underscores how products may come and go but corporate battles for market share in the courtooms but also through their influence over ordinary users' habits (not easy to change but once achieved very profitable) continue. This more recent litigation between Javascript and Google also pivoted on intellectual property rights as proprietary not shareable items (see Benkler 2006, May 2009).

25. This particular cluster was developed in Switzerland by Tim Berners–Lee; the inventor of the World Wide Web by many accounts. Not surprisingly, his consortium of internet software developers, WW3, has been an active opponent to the Microsoft empire (see http://www.w3c.org/). HTTP is the code that governs how websites are linked together—how a user can pass from one to the other. HTML is the computer code that is at the base of web page formatting In so many words, along with internet browsers these codes are—or have been to date the "World Wide Web." Search engines work at the interstices of all three with a cumulative, iterative effect (see Franklin 2007c; Lazuly 2003; Lessig 2006: 145–146).

26. The distinction between open-source and free software on the one hand and proprietary software on the other is not as clearcut as it may seem. Offering free access for ordinary users to open PDF documents in Adobe Acrobat for instance is not the same as computer programmers being able to access its coding if the latter is not openly accessible. Open-source software is defined in its Wikipedia entry as "computer software with its source code made available and licensed with an open source license in which the copyright holder provides the rights to study, change and distribute the software to anyone and for any purpose. Open source software is very often developed in a public, collaborative manner." This is as good a definition as ever: http://en.wikipedia.org/wiki/Open–source_software (accessed March 7, 2013). While not all open source software is "free" (Stallman 2012; Grassmuck 2002: 233) and personality and political differences create diverging schools of thought and practice, the predominate discourse is that a free and open internet, however defined, operates as a "constraint on state power" (Lessig 2006: 139).

27. Note that Mozilla's Firefox is based on Netscape's source code, made available in 1998. Since then Firefox became the Browser of choice for users looking for alternatives to Explorer on principle. As noted above it too has been losing ground lately to Google's Chrome (Volkskrant May 28, 2012). It would take more forensic historical research to ascertain how much of this success was a result of the antitrust ligation, how much the effectiveness of the burgeoning Free and Open Source Software movements at the time, and how much was superior strategizing from competitors.

28. This is the demarcation line between Apple users, by choice and along particular demographic and socioeconomic profiles, and the rest. Here, aesthetics and design cultures mingle with the effect of branding practices. Be that as it may, as I already noted, switching from a MS-based product to join the "Apple community" is a conscious decision to leave the Microsoft collective.

29. See Quintas (1996: 79) and Spiller (2002) for more commentary on what this actually means in ICT uses and applications.

30. For an analysis of the power relations involved standards-setting in international forums, see Hawkins (1996). For all its procedural limitations and contested effectiveness, the main body for international standards-setting, the International Telecommunications Union (ITU) has been under longstanding pressure to streamline its practices, particularly from business lobbies, major ICT corporations, and interest groups such as the Internet Society have made their presence felt here. By contrast the once studied disinterest of major ICT corporations at the UN's *World Summit on the Information Society* (2003–2005) and successor the Internet Governance Forum (2006–present day) did not go unnoticed by grassroots activists and civil society NGOs (Franklin 2005, 2007c). All that changed as corporate and governmental forces mobilized around the 2012 ITU meeting in Dubai, warming up in the preceding Internet Governance Forum in Baku the month prior, to frame the debates and agenda in their terms. At time of writing the fallout, and thought-through analysis of the implications of how major corporate players lobbied and governments such as the United States, United Kingdom, Russia, and China staged various sorts of showdowns and walkouts on the conference floor, upping the ante in doing so, is only starting to emerge. For a high-level UN meeting that was ostensibly "only" about updating longstanding International Telecommunications Regulations (ITRs) to get them up to speed with the technological demands of an internet era the sea shift signaled in the last chapters and its effect on public awareness of these matters. More on this in Chapters 5 and 6.

31. This species, a later plot development, turned out to be able to resist Borg assimilation, able to beat the latter at its own game and, according to one episode in the *Voyager* series, provide leverage for the Federation to negotiate safe passage through Borg territory. More is available on the *Star Trek* Database and Wikipedia, of course; see http://www.startrek.com/database_article/species-8472 and http://en.wikipedia.org/wiki/Species_8472 (accessed February 13, 2013).

32. Microsoft is a significant supplier of software applications for the United Nations; Cisco has donated millions in development projects in sub-Saharan Africa; both and other companies vie for lucrative educational contracts.

33. In 2008, the US league tables of search machines, and their "paid search" revenues from advertising, were basically as follows: Google at the top with 65% of the market, followed by Yahoo! with 21%, and then Microsoft's MSN Search at 7% (Volkskrant, February 2, 2008: 9), though website visits using Yahoo! outstripped Google in July of 2013. Profit margins put Microsoft way out in front (US$ 14.05 billion), followed by Google ($US 4.2 billion), and then by Yahoo (US$ 4.2 billion) with the relative share-values following this last ordering (ibid.). The market share of the latter two differs from country to country; Yahoo! is more popular in China, for instance (Vaidhyanathan 2012: 141–145).

34. Encapsulated at time of writing by the protracted legal battles between Samsung and Apple, also involving Google, around patents for the tablet computer; its shape (e.g., who owns the copyright for a rectangular shaped device) and applications.

35. For instance, *Facebook* users came out massively against the idea of Microsoft attempts to buy out this popular social networking portal; attempts to get Yahoo! via a corporate raider's purchase of a strategic share-interest, Carl Icahn, since the apparent failure of a hostile bid in May of 2008 (Carlile 2008; *Legal Times* 2008; *NZ Herald: Business Herald*, April 25, 2008: 6).

36. In what has become a famous episode in the second *Star Trek* series, *Star Trek: The Next Generation*, Captain Picard is captured, taken on board of the Borg ship, the Cube, and submitted to the Borg's assimilation process. He is rescued by his crew in the nick of time but not before Picard's personality, expertise, and strategic knowledge of his employers, "The Federation," has been appropriated and absorbed by the Borg Collective to become the Borg "Locutus." This double-episode led to an ongoing storyline in which Picard (rescued and then deassimilated) is confronted at regular intervals with the vestiges of his experience as part of the Borg Collective. In the third series, *Star Trek: Voyager*, the Picard-Locutus-Picard metamorphosis is reversed. The crew of the Voyager (under the captainship of Katherine Janeway) have to learn to live with Seven of Nine, a rescued and then rehabilitated Borg. In keeping with a core theme of this sci-fi series, Seven of Nine goes through various stages of learning what being human means (like Spock and Data in previous series).

37. For instance, in the United States the *Free Software Foundation* was set up in 1985, followed closely by the *Free Software Foundation Europe* and other like-minded organizations worldwide; Digital City initiatives such as the Dutch *Digitale Stad* (http://www.dds.nl/) in this era based on not-for-profit premises and notions of cyberspace as a public medium. Bear in mind here that the term "free" was synonymous with "open-source." For more information see Grassmuck (2002: 423 passim), Jordan (1999). Websites anchored in this period and still active at time of writing include http://freie-software.bpb.de/; Chaos Computer Club (http://www.ccc.de/); the Wizards of OS (http://wizards-of-os.org/). See also World-Information.org at http://www.world-information.org/. And the most recent phenomenon, which now has political presence at the European Parliament, in Scandinavia and Germany, the *Pirate Party*; with chapters all around the world and a sizable accumulated Twitter presence based on a broad platform of copyright and patent law reform that does not prosecute peer-to-peer file sharing (or "pirating"), the right to remain anonymous online, the "freedom of information and free exchange of knowledge," http://en.wikipedia.org/wiki/Pirate_party (accessed February 13, 2013).

38. "And there is fear too. The nature of its technology-driven business means that Microsoft's franchise is never secure. There may at any time be lurking out there some new company with an idea cool enough, in the phrase much used by Microserfs, 'to eat our lunch'" (*Economist*, 1998b: 2/4, 1998b).

CHAPTER 4

1. This chapter develops and updates research carried out during a Social Science Research Council Research Fellowship at Columbia University (2002). The initial period was two months spent with the *BIGnews* weekly Writers' Group meetings in midtown Manhattan. I also interviewed a number of people involved in support services and national lobbying, many during the North American National Street Newspaper Association's Annual Conference in Boston (July 19–21, 2002). I'd like to posthumously thank the late Ron Grunberg, editor of *Upward* and *BIGnews* and facilitator-motivator of the *BIGnews* Writers' Group for his hospitality and willingness to answer my questions in recurring visits in the following years. My thanks also to everyone in the Writers' Group in the summer of 2002—Robert, Bryan, Sheri, John, Roger, Don, Haig, Toby, Mark, Vicky—for their insights; these were scintillating discussions (the pizza was great as well). This chapter cannot do justice

to these conversations during the meetings, and in-between. My thanks also to Tim Harris, Michael Stoops, Paula Mathieu, Curly Cohen, and Anitra Freeman, who took the time to speak to me at the Boston NASNA conference of 2002, and since. Also thanks to the Kantlijn writers' group in Amsterdam, who allowed me to sit in on a session in 2003/2004 so providing me with some insight into how these concerns unfold in another geographical and cultural context. To Nadia, the once homeless girl, my thanks for her time and input into this chapter during our long conversation in an inner-city shopping mall in late 2012, and conversations on Twitter and email since.

2. For instance, *Poems from Street Level*, Book 2, which I first accessed it in 2002, then again in 2004, and 2008. At time of writing it was still there: http://www.angelfire. com/poetry/street_writer/ (accessed February 15, 2013). Peaks in mainstream media attention to how homeless internet users are treated as exceptional; part of the "fish riding bikes" genre of reportage as Tim Harris notes (Interview 2012) aside (Dvorak 2009; Cunningham 2009), there are nonetheless some tenacious and savvy applications of all the internet can offer. See for example, the "We are Visible" project by Mark Hovarth as a multimedia photo-video documentary project, http:// invisiblepeople.tv/blog/ (accessed March 24, 2013), the Homeless Guy Blog, http:// thehomelessguy.blogspot.co.uk/ (accessed March 24, 2013), Wandering Scribe, http://wanderingscribe.blogspot.co.uk/ (March 24, 2013), all of whom have been active for a number of years. Amidst the many unpopulated and now stalled pages on the web the longevity of some of these online media for and by homeless users is striking. For example, the documentary photography project based in Budapest, Hungary entitled Saját szemmel/Inside Out has sustained its space at http://www. c3.hu/collection/homeless/ for a decade.

3. My thanks to Tim Harris, director of *Real Change* in Seattle for his insights in two interviews; during the NASNA Conference, Boston, July 2002 and by Skype, in October 2012. Thanks as well to Michael Stoops of the National Coalition for the Homeless (Washington, DC) for two interviews over the same time span, the first in DC in July 2002 and the second by phone in October 2012.

4. Three examples will suffice; Apple's assembly plants in China where recent investigation has revealed poor working conditions that include extremely long working weeks, microprocessor manufacturing in the Mexican maquiladoras that date back to the 1980s, and the dependence of the global electronic markets on precious metals mined in war-torn areas such as the Congo.

5. Anitra Freeman, Writing Workshop with Mark Goldfinger at the NASNA Annual Conference, July 2002.

6. The literature around public perceptions, media representations, and new media opportunities for homeless people is wide-ranging, the largest concentration dating from the 1990s and first decade of the 2000s; e.g., Min (1999), Hodgetts et al. (2008), Lind and Danowski (1991), Power (1999), Lind and Danowski (1991), Guthrie and Dutton (1992), Fooks and Pantazis (1999), Drucker and Grumpert (1997), and Abildgaard (2001).

7. The term "rough sleepers" is officially recognized in United Kingdom nonprofit and governmental agencies concerned with housing. The official definition is "people sleeping, or bedded down, in the open air (such as on the streets, or in doorways, parks or bus shelters), people in buildings or other places not designed for

habitation (such as barns, sheds, car parks, derelict boats, stations or 'bashes')" (UK Government Department for Communities and local Government in WRS 2013; Shelter 2012c). There is a longstanding and diverse literature on these issues. For instance, see Edgar, Doherty, and Meert (2008), Kerr (2003), Kennett and Marsh (1999), Edgar, Doherty, and Meert (2003), Munger (2002), Nunez (1994), Meert et al. (2008), Carey-Webb (1992), Drucker and Grumpert (1997), (Wright 1997), Schneider (2012), and Tosi (2007).

8. These scholarly and public debates wax and wane according to the weather (such as cold winters, hurricanes, or floods) and political moods (such as when immigration or unemployment figures take center stage), the details of which are beyond the scope of this chapter (Passaro 1996; Duneier 1999: 312–317; Wright 1997; Kerr 2003).

9. Physically, homeless people who are sleeping rough in particular are visceral markers of poverty, poor judgment, or bad luck (depending on your view) in the first instance. Those who "demand the street," that is who do not "like to be housed" (comment from *BIGnews* Writers Group meeting July 2, 2002) are exceptions to this rule that astound others combating homelessness, albeit exceptions that generate inordinate media attention. In the second, not having a fixed address in societies where access to services are increasingly linked to location-based (postcodes) and personalized (bank accounts and cards) identifiers in databases denies people access to public libraries, healthcare, and basic financial services to name but a few. One high profile example in the Netherlands was the Tent City of nearly 100 out-processed asylum-seekers that sprang up in an Amsterdam suburb as a protest action, inspired by the Occupy movement, to the hardening of Dutch immigration policy and political debates around multiculturalism. After being removed from their campsite by the local authorities in the winter of 2012–2013, the group was offered shelter in a former church, where they were still residing at time of writing. The residents of the VluchtKerk (Church of Sanctuary) have created their own media space and profile in this time on the web and media outlets such as Facebook, Twitter, local television, and music venues, http://devluchtkerk.nl/en/home (accessed February 14, 2013).

10. There is a whole cartography and mapping of cityscapes entailed here (Certeau 1980, 1984; Wright 1997) and some iconic cases of websites run while on the move in this sense (Civille 1995; Wirth 2012). Writers for street papers who are homeless have a detailed knowledge of where they can access the web: shelters, drop-in centers, and some street paper offices look to provide access for their constituencies as well (Tim Harris, *Real Change*, Seattle, personal conversation at the NASNA Conference, July 19, 2002, interview 2012).

11. Critical studies of whether this intention is met in practice aside (Torck 2001; Schneider 2012; Allen 2009; Butchinsky 2013; Evangelista 2009) this mission is displayed prominently, either on the inside cover of print editions or the online homepage. A note on nomenclature; the more generic term street paper is used here rather than street or homeless newspapers as many of the more established publications move away from print into other formats, into digital or glossy magazine formats, for instance: *The Big Issue*, *The Pavement* magazine in the United Kingdom, and *Real Change* in Seattle are three cases in point. It also follows a preference in this domain to minimize the use of the epithet "homeless," marked by its

pejorative connotations. That said, the majority of publications are printed matter, and it is librarians who have been active in cataloguing these fragile and fast disappearing cultural artifacts.

12. This approach is not just a question of economics, it is also linked to how street papers are part of a politics of writing, voicing, and enacting that looks to make marginalized communities visible, to be seen as "there" (Julia Tripp keynote, "Bring America Home," NASNA Annual Conference, Boston 2002). Sustainability is in this case a substantive ambition, having enough copy and content that is good enough is a constant quest for being legitimate but also for attracting donations and keeping sales up in the face of fierce competition from professional media in an age characterized by financial scarcity (Ron Grunberg interview 2002, Tim Harris interview 2002). That said, being a paper based around homeless issues and sold by primarily homeless vendors in this climate need not mean that there is no hope as some observers and practitioners note that these sorts of media are faring better than their mainstream counterparts (Tim Harris interview 2012).

13. This delicate balance between what vendors invest and what they earn is one that characterizes this self-help business model. Group members noted to me that the minute Ron tried to raise the investment ratio, people disappeared, or rather many vendors would only look to sell just enough copies to finance their immediate needs. Maintaining vendors is an ongoing struggle for street papers generally, not only because this populace is by definition transient and living in precarity but also because there are various legal and social contexts (across the United States but also in other countries) about where street sellers can work, for how long, and under what conditions. In some places street vending is illegal, in others only permissible in certain places. And in general, public appreciation of this undertaking is patchy to put it lightly. My own, very brief, experience taking part in a vendor "sell-off" during the 2002 NASNA conference in Boston underscored this point. I respond now very differently to street paper vendors. A simple life lesson really.

14. Toby Van Buren was one such example. These earnings provided him with an important first step toward some modicum of financial independence, as he himself testifies too in his online autobiography (Van Buren 2006, see Figure 4.3). Others in the writers group reiterated the importance of these earnings to me in this period, a clear improvement from having to beg on the streets. As noted above others have acknowledged Ron's support. Fernanda Cohen has this to say on her blog where she has uploaded sketches of Ron in hospital: "My good friend Ron Grunberg, who published my very first illustration in the NY homeless newspaper *BIGnews* when I was still in college, is going through chemotherapy at Beth Israel Hospital. My sketches will accompany Ron's column, 'New York Blue,' on the treatment for the International Group Of Newspapers" (Cohen 2008). See Figures 4.1, 4.2, and 4.3 for examples of her work.

15. This was taken from the *BIGnews* Writers' Group web page on the website of its umbrella organization, Mainchance, in 2002. This domain name (www.mainchance. org) is no longer in use since the papers folded. However, the organization running the Mainchance Drop-In Center to which *BIGnews* was affiliated at the time, the Grand Central Neighbourhood Social Services Corporation, is still a going concern. Echoes of these publications, under the "Stories" tab, can be heard on the GCNSSC's current website at http://www.grandcentralneighborhood.org/services/

mainchance-drop-in-center/. Both publications were financed by local businesses. When this funding was withdrawn *BIGnews* was unable to continue. Personality conflicts were the last straw as without a homebase for Writers' Group meetings or enough money to pay for production not even voluntary work would not suffice. At the time, moving to a purely online version was an option that Ron Grunberg was considering but circumstances prevented him from seeing this through (Ron Grunberg interview 2004). Ron passed away in 2009.

16. Ron Grunberg made this point in a thread on the Homeless People's Network: December 11, 1998 (Grunberg 1998a). It was still accessible at time of writing. It is a strange sensation to come across the web remains of someone who is deceased. Based on my observations at the time, and since then on trying to retrace his posthumous online presence, Ron Grunberg was a rather desultory web user himself. He maintained the *BIGnews* website mainly with volunteer help, had to have hand-drawn illustrations scanned or photographed for each issue, and was a member of fantasy/science fiction online networks, dabbled in "collabowriting" (see Chapter 5) in literary terms. His main legacy was in the lives he helped (Van Buren 2006; Cohen 2008) and the work he did in the inaugural and since then globally successful Homeless Soccer tournaments around the world, and in keeping *BIGnews* afloat. But there are firm and eloquent traces of Ron in much earlier online forms and forums. One of these was his nickname, GMountain@aol.com, some of the 1990s discussion forums that were the predominant social medium in open cyberspace at the time. While modest and somewhat diffident face to face, Ron was a strong advocate of a holistic, as opposed to a faddish, approach to homelessness and media to empower and advocate on behalf of the poor.

17. Toby Van Buren's autobiography (2006) is online and has full account of Ron and Jeff Grunberg's work to help him get his own place and employment: http://home.earthlink.net/~jromanj/sitebuildercontent/sitebuilderfiles/vanburen-toby-bio-08-01-2006.pdf (accessed November 2, 2012).

18. A comment under the title, NYC: Grand Central Neighborhood—an elaboration that is still available on the Homeless People's Network (Grunberg 1998b).

19. This view was reiterated in various ways during the 2002 NASNA annual conference, from small start up papers to larger more established ones. In this conference for instance all papers represented provided an oral report on the state of their publication, progress and issues around quality and quantity of content.

20. All comments from individuals are referenced here as "Writers Group."

21. This news was something I found out after not hearing back from Ron when I emailed him next. It took some time but eventually the obituary in the 2009 May Bulletin of the International Street Papers Association came to light. Ron's contribution to the lives of individuals (see Van Buren 2006) is part of the subtext of making homelessness as a potent social and political issue visible in cyberspace. As noted above, one contribution Grunberg did make in terms of so-called media worthiness was his work in the early years of the Homeless World Cup series based on getting homeless people to play competitive street football (street soccer to Americans) movement with the New York teams and as part of the international organizing committee. Here Ron's digital footprint is more visible to the naked eye so to speak (Hill 2005). For more on the Homeless World Cup see http://www.homelessworldcup.org/ (accessed March 24, 2013).

22. Despite the limitations to this index where five years of *BIGnews* contents (2001–2005) and covers (included from 2002) are listed (see http://www.philsp.com/homeville/fmi/b24.htm#TOP, accessed March 26, 2013), the cover thumbnails do provide a sense of the aesthetic dimension, in terms of these papers' ambitions to offer more than accounts of being down and out in New York. Online archives are being developed however by other publications such as Real Change (an ongoing project with back issues from 2011 only at time of writing), *The Big Issue* (it has a "covers gallery" from 2011 as well), and the *Pavement Magazine* (United Kingdom) which started up in 2005 has been an online publication, as well as hardcopy, since its inception. All issues from their three editions (London [seventy-six], Scotland [forty-one], the Midlands [twenty-two]) are online. This is a double-edged undertaking though in light of the challenges going digital present for sales, as well as for maintaining homeless vendors at the forefront of the enterprise (Tim Harris interview 2012). A research topic in itself, staying in meatspace or going digital is for street papers is a decision with not only technical and financial but also political dimensions riven by both longstanding dualisms between offline and online worlds and preferred ways of doing things (Stoops interview 2012; Mathieu interview 2002). Homelessness as an issue and its dedicated media, straddles these domains (Howley 2005; INSP 2012). That said, the recognition that "street papers are important independent media sources with historical significance" (INSP Street Paper Archive Project, at http://www.street-papers.org/street-paper-archive/, accessed March 25, 2013) has been a line of continuity from the inception of online services and editions. Online archiving however for publications that are predominately printed matter, and at this scale pivots on whether individual publications have digital versions, and if not how to digitize existing back issues. To illustrate, in 2012 the INSP online archive listed 109 papers, of which 45 (41%) were not hyperlinked. Those that were linked at this time are moreover not always active. Sustaining a digital presence is as much hard work as staying viable on the ground is in this domain.

23. The 2002 NASNA conference in Boston is when the news service idea was launched, its roots in the North American setting is noted deeper in the NASNA website (http://www.nasna.org/about/vision-values/, accessed March 25, 2013). The principle of "how street papers from around the globe are unified under one banner" under the INSP and Street News Service rubrics respectively is foregrounded (http://www.nasna.org/about/ accessed March 15, 2013). The point is that despite marked differences in business models and approach to media and services that "exist to tackle homelessness and poverty" (ibid.) these web-based initiatives have generated sustained interconnections between once diffuse and dispersed projects, providing a transnational public profile in spirit and in kind, a project that is under construction, financially vulnerable to the vagaries of (withdrawn) funding or donations, and dealing with local needs and motivations within a global upturn in homelessness statistics.

24. In 2002 the NASNA website listed around fifty street papers across the United States and Canada. In 2012 there were forty-seven listed as full (thirty-four) or associate members (thirteen). In October, 2012 the INSP website listed 120 members (since then updated to 121). While *The Big Issue* thrives, other papers around the world are struggling to maintain donors, sales, and public support. Amsterdam's *Z!*

magazine is just hanging on, while in a neighboring city, Utrecht, *Straatnieuws* effectively folded in mid-2012. A cooperative venture between the Amsterdam and Utrecht papers that year managed to restart *Straatnieuws*. Decreasing readerships and vendors continue to beset the longer-term viability of street papers around the European Union.

25. There are geographical and generational distinctions here. As Facebook is still the dominant web-based social medium in the United States most established street papers have Facebook pages. Tim Harris at *Real Change* devotes most of his time updating their pages for the organization's 4,700 members, noting that they have not "gone down the Twitter road yet" (Interview 2012). Michael Stoops also notes the role played by the NCH Facebook page (Stoops interview 2012). For those papers listed on the INSP website in October 2012, 125 in total, apart from an email address which all papers listed, two-thirds of these listed a Facebook page (just over 66%), half as many again had a Twitter account (36%) as well. About a third, including most of the German street papers, listed emails only (just under 30%),

26. These points are based on interviews with street paper editors, community organizers, and writers. My thanks too to Daniela Madureira for her input into my thinking here during conversations we had while she was designing a research project into how digitalization is affecting street papers and their mission as social entrepreneurs.

27. At first she tried Google's Blogger template; then moving to Wordpress, Nadia noted sheepishly that the blog was first called "Super Homeless" as an ode to Superman/ Superwoman comics.

28. Determined not to enter into student debt even though getting a university degree is her first wish Nadia is aiming to complete a Legal Executive Diploma, which can open the way to a law degree if work experience goes well. At £500 per annum this is a far more attractive option with the price of university degrees in the UK up to £9,000 per year under the current privatization policies for higher education.

29. For the record, Nadia read this rendition of our conversation on filling me in on the details for why she finally decided to assert her rights to "be forgotten" (Rosen 2012, see Chapter 5) at this point in time. Her reasons are personal and compelling. After some effort and no small amount of personal anxiety the *Huffington Post* complied with her wish to not have her contributions appear online any more.

30. For example; in October 2012 as the new coalition government announced the latest round of austerity measures, the *Volkskrant*—a national daily newspaper in the Netherlands—noted in a side-column that the number of homeless families had risen by a third since 2009 (Volkskrant, October 30, 2012: 13).

31. This point bears some explication because it pertains to the rising number of out-processed refugee populations in homelessness statistics. In the United Kingdom context, to be eligible for emergency or social housing, the first step is whether or not the person is "a United Kingdom citizen who normally lives [there]." If not, then "You may not be eligible for assistance" (Shelter 2013d). This opt-out clause for council housing provision leaves the continuing homelessness of those not eligible for support unaddressed in practice; soup kitchens, emergency shelter, and care is then left to charity. In 2012 the "time-honoured tradition [that] councils have been considered a helping hand of last resort, providing safe secure homes at an affordable price and emergency accommodation for those who find themselves

homeless" (Reeve-Lewis 2012) was effectively done away with in a law change by which applicants have to prove that have not been "made homeless intentionally, through a failure to pay rent or mortgage (as well as other factors)" (Reeve-Lewis 2012).

32. In this archived discussion from an early online networking, Ron Grunberg cites his brother, Jeff, the director of the Grand Central Neighbourhood Services (aka GMountain@aol.com), "NYC: Grand Central Neighbourhood—an elaboration," Homeless People's Network, December 14, 1998: http://hpn.asu.edu/archives/Dec98/0249.html [accessed October 29, 2012].

33. Paula Mathieu (affiliated to *Spare Change* Chicago), personal comment at the North American Street Newspapers' Association's Conference, Boston, July 20, 2002.

34. Paula Mathieu (op. cit.).

CHAPTER 5

1. This comment was one made by Azeri political dissident, Emin Milli, during the 2012 Internet Governance Forum meeting, in Baku, Azerbaijan. This annual meeting was characterized by patchy internet access, reports of hacking and other forms of online privacy breaches, and local activists taking the opportunity of a UN gathering to publicize a ranges of social and political issues in the country, an oil-rich dictatorship. Freedom of expression issues and other human rights abuses in Azerbaijan online and on the ground were forcefully denied by government representatives and supporters in events preceding and during the IGF; events with anti and progovernment supporters that were reminiscent of comparable ones in pre-Arab Spring Tunisia during the final WSIS summit in 2005 (Emin Milli, Wednesday, 16.30: Impact of Internet on Civil Liberties [Civil Rights] in Arab Region [with Azeri bloggers]). Since the IGF left town a number of protesters including Milli have been imprisoned at periodic intervals (Brown 2013, personal conversation, February 27, 2013).

2. Definitions of internet governance itself tend to be circular, focused on the format for how such governance is to be managed if not encouraged (hence a political question). For the sake of argument, in the UN-speak of the Internet Governance Forum itself, more on this shortly, the term amounts to both object and process i.e., "an open and inclusive process, to . . . (discuss) public policy issues related to key elements of Internet governance in order to foster the sustainability, robustness, security, stability and development of the Internet; Facilitate discourse between bodies dealing with different cross-cutting international public policies regarding the Internet and discuss issues that do not fall within the scope of any existing body . . . " (ITU/WSIS 2005b: Paragraph 72).

3. The Internet Society, a prominent interest group that promotes internet access around the world, has been developing a "rough guide" to how the internet runs; circulated in hardcopy, as a laminated poster no less, during the 2012 IGF meeting. Under the heading "no one person, company, organization, or government runs the Internet," they list nine key organizations with direct influence on the decision-making domains that comprise internet governance in the round: operations, policies, "open debate," standards, and services: The Internet Architecture Board (IAB), Internet Corporation for Assigned Names and Numbers (ICANN), Internet Engineering Task Force (IETF), Internet Governance Forum (IGF), Internet

Research Task Force (IRTF), International Organization for Standardization (ISO 3166), Internet Society (ISoc), five Regional Internet Registries (RIRS), and the World Wide Web Consortium (W3C). Six of the nine organizations named are "operational" i.e., technically based so ostensibly distinct from those that concern themselves with policy, "open debate" or services. Along with the Internet Society itself, according to this organigram, the World Wide Web Consortium and the Internet Governance Forum also straddle all these domains. The presence of governments and corporations, and in some cases "civil society," is subsumed under these larger rubrics. An updated version (March 21, 2013) is available at http://www.xplanations.com/whorunstheinternet (accessed March 28, 2013).

4. During the two main WSIS Meetings in 2003 and 2005 (in Geneva and Tunis respectively) parallel meetings were held, WSIS social forums, where local activists and participating NGOs presented alternative programs, and dissenting declarations to those from the official proceedings. In Tunisia, preparatory meetings were punctuated by ad hoc protest actions by pro-government groups (GONGOs)—to be repeated in Baku, Azerbaijan nearly a decade later. WSIS delegates to the 2005 Tunis summit also took part in publicizing demonstrations and rallies in support of political dissidents who were in prison, or on hunger strike, in protest at human right abuses. IGF meetings have been relatively low-key in that respect. However there have been incidents, brief moments of old-school politics as IGF delegates – from civil society, the private sector, and governments lend support to local dissidents publicizing freedom of speech issues on the ground, in Baku in 2012 for instance. As UN hosted meetings however IGF events are held far away from city centers, in remote conference centers where access for and contact with locals is limited, deliberately.

5. This reconstruction is based on what began as ethnographic participant-observation of the IGF, beginning in the third meeting in Hyderabad, 2008. Present at the inaugurations of the Internet Rights and Principles Coalition in the following year at the Sharm el Sheikh IGF my relationship to proceedings leant increasingly towards participatory action research in so far as, like other academics taking part, I became involved in the action as much as observer of what was going on. The material for this case was gathered in these years as my affiliation or rather self-identification to the IGF remained that of an academic (designated as "other" on the registration form) during the time as I served on the IRP Coalition Steering Committee; my research interests and employment made clear in this regard during the nomination and election process. Though I am not the only employed academic in the coalition or the IGF at large nor am I the only one whose research interests encompass either the IGF process as a whole or specific topic areas, what changed as this chapter was being finalized was my role in the IRP Coalition. At the Baku IGF in November 2012 I became co-chair. This case study, as narrative and summation of the original research period has inevitably been colored by this shift to full participation. But the data-gathering and initial reconstruction of the charter-writing process and Ten Principles launch was already written before this change of status, moreover my considering this position, by some months. Access to the mailing list was already granted by previous chairs and my interest in reconstructing the IRP Charter process public knowledge on the list. This change in position does not radically change the conditions of access and informed consent from the outset. Nonetheless this

account is a summation of provisional findings of a research project that has taken on a new dimension hence my focusing on the period up until my (unexpected) change in role. Future work will thereby take this into account. At this point I would like to thank Max Senges, Lisa Horner, and Dixie Hawtin all former coalition (co-) chairs, for their input into my thinking, and opportunity to be part of the coalition's early days. Thanks as well to Matthias Kettemann my current co-chair, Meryem Marzouki, Tapani Tarvainen, Parminder Jeet Singh, Minda Moreira, Keith Hubbard, Robert Bodle, Lee Hibbard, Andrew Puddephatt, Thomas Schneider, Wolf Ludwig, and many others for their invaluable input into getting the coalition back on its feet in late 2012 and ongoing debates about the big, and minute politics of the internet. This version of events is open to correction, criticism, and additional information, for it is after all a narrative in the making.

6. See Notes 2 and 20 in Chapter 1.

7. This chapter was completed as the first meeting of the "WSIS + 10" review period, hosted by the UNESCO in 2013 and ITU in 2015, at the same time as the UN Millennium Development Goals come up for review (ITU/WSIS 2005b: Paragraph 111).

8. This phrase was the title of a keynote address from Ron Deibert delivered at a public debate hosted by the Dutch Scientific Council for Government Policy (The Hague, November 22, 2012), available at http://www.youtube.com/watch?v=27dU6lseHT8 (accessed March 28, 2013).

9. See note 5 above for how my role changed from observing researcher to a more fully immersed participatory role.

10. The term "human rights" features thirty times in the first document and twice only in the second; once in fact as the second time is a repetition. These sorts of enumerations are only a part of the story in terms of contested narratives around how human rights and internet governance are or should be linked in practice but in internet-based settings where keyword searches and automated indexing constitute visibility and significance, this difference in frequency is striking (see Rogers 2000, Franklin 2007a).

11. The inclusion of web conferencing tools as part of the rollout of remote participation opportunities during IGF meetings has gathered momentum since the 2010 IGF in Vilnius. Here too, meatspace meetings and interventions are increasingly supplemented by remote participation from those attending by virtual means. The IGF is thereby a multisited event in theory and practice. How remote participation enhances proceedings, generates another dimension to the written and now audio record of these meetings is another topic, as are the power differentials for those participating from less well resourced parts of the world.

12. The first round of IGF meetings (2006–2010) kicked off in Athens (2006), then Rio de Janeiro, Hyderabad, Sharm El Sheikh, and Vilnius respectively. The second round (2011–2015) of meetings have been held to date in Nairobi, Baku, and Bali. The two main summits of the IGF's precursor consultative exercise, the WSIS, took place in Geneva (2003) and Tunis (2005). These larger events were the climax of the previous year's preparatory meetings on the ground (Geneva as the default home-base) and numerous online consultations.

13. Based on a UN mandate, the 2005 Tunis Agenda (ITU/WSIS 2005: Article 72) that was one of the outcomes of the WSIS the IGF is by its own admission "The Internet

Governance Forum is an open forum which has no members" (IGF 2011). It also has no recommendation-making accreditation or structural funding, so its existence depends on the UN General Assembly and the depth of the host country's pockets as well as those of UN member states and other donors, from industry and intergovernmental organizations amongst others: see http://www.intgovforum.org/cms/funding (accessed February 22, 2013). The IGF is structured around a Geneva-based Secretariat and a Multistakeholder Advisory Group, the MAG. The Secretariat is comprised of UN employees and the MAG of "stakeholders" from industry, governments, academe and the "technical community." Participation in any of the IGF annual events, or preparatory meetings, is based on registering oneself as private sector, government, or civil society. Registration is free, credentials based on passport and other identity parameters entered online and confirmed by return email. Gaining access to the respective forums entails their own identity and security checks at the border and entrance to the IGF venue in the host country. The UN provides the security and legal cover for these events wherever they are held. In short the IGF has loosened up the procedures by which people, as individuals or groups, can take part from its predecessor the WSIS, where diplomatic credentials and official accreditation as a participating organization restricted access.

14. First-timers to the IGF meetings noted its convivial atmosphere as markedly different from other UN events, as well as the different atmosphere created when delegates are not from one particular sector. Rubbing shoulders with governmental representatives or corporate executives does provide a different feel to a trade fair or academic conference. It does not, however, divest the gathering from other sorts of power dispositions such as diplomatic protocol, or agenda-setting. Getting in the door is but a start (Dany 2012; Flyverbom 2011; Franklin 2005, 2007a).

15. Within those taking part in IGF meetings as civil society participants, current concerns center on how to keep the momentum going in the face of increasing alarm over the "chilling effect" of corporate and government strategies for the future internet; increased surveillance, censorship, and commodification of the publicness of internet access and uses. Efforts currently focus on various organizational hubs; UN agencies concerned with the stewardship of the WSIS (the ITU and UNESCO), the plenary IGF meetings, and regional spinoffs (in South America, Europe, South Pacific, and India for instance). Concerted interventions at ICANN meetings, and a number of European-based gatherings, the European Dialogue of Internet Governance (EuroDIG), and meetings sponsored by the Council of Europe are also key arenas where activists, academics, and governmental representatives rub shoulders with each other, and corporate players (from Microsoft to Google).

16. See (http://www.intgovforum.org/cms/dynamiccoalitions, accessed March 28, 2013).

17. Thanks to Allon Bar for this turn of phrase.

18. The charter itself is available on http://internetrightsandprinciples.org/site/charter/ (accessed February 17, 2013).

19. This was not a foregone conclusion as even in its short lifespan the IGF has seen many dynamic coalitions come and go. The IRP coalition itself was an amalgam of two others, the Internet Bill of Rights and Freedom of Expression coalitions who opted to consolidate their energies in the IRP Coalition (personal conversation, Ben Wagner February 2013). In addition the IRP coalition's website, already a

production of voluntary labor and goodwill (see Chapter 4 for other examples), was hacked in early 2012 which rendered it useless. In November of that year during the Baku IGF meeting the mailing list went offline (the last email was one I actually sent to the list about human rights abuses in Azerbaijan), the mailing list archives became inaccessible for reasons as yet unclear, and password access to the administrator interface for the hosting service unclear as former chairs and website moderators (also voluntary and ad hoc labor) liaised to reestablish access. The whole process of getting the coalition back on the road in digital and web-based terms took nearly three months as without the mailing list or access/ownership of the domain name there was no coalition as such. Reestablishing a list based on archives kept on various people's computers and technical assistance from specialists in the coalition, and the labor of completely rebuilding the website was a major milestone in the beginning of 2013.

20. In principle and for the sake of argument I am following the line that while social, economic, political and civil rights are distinctive types of rights it does not "serve the human rights discourse to differentiate between 'civil rights' and 'human rights'" (IRP list 2012), hence human rights can serve as the overarching rubric for various sorts of rights and their legal instruments. This is a bone of contention within the coalition (i.e., around the distinction between rights and principles in theory and in practice) as well as debates at large that pit technical understandings of access to the internet for instance against social and political ones (IRP list 2012; Cerf 2012). The inclusion of "human" in emerging projects focusing on "internet rights and principles" within the IGF at least is thereby a political point. This argument is a substantial dimension to the IRP Coalition since its inception and deserves its own treatment. In pragmatic terms I would argue that while human rights need to be regarded as core principles for internet governance (hence the IRP Charter) laying the stress on internet principles alone need not imply human rights are fully accorded their place (see OECD 2011).

21. The Portuguese language website for the Marco Civil is http://culturadigital.br/marcocivil/ (accessed February 17, 2013). An English language edition and translation of the Marco Civil's ten principles (an inspiration for the coalition's own version for its charter) can be found on the organizing committee's website (CGI.br 2009).

22. In particular Wolfgang Benedek, Meryem Marzouki, Dixie Hawtin, and Rikke Jørgensen. It is worth noting that members of said-Expert Group were uneasy about this status; " I don't consider myself an expert" as one member noted on several occasions in listserv discussions.

23. Other contemporaneous declarations include the Internet Blueprint, a US-Focused statement from Public Knowledge; http://internetblueprint.org/; The Web Kids Manifesto; http://kuriouswax.com/we-the-web-kids-a-manifesto/; A Communications Bill of Rights for Disabled communities; http://www.asha.org/NJC/bill_of_rights.htm; The Madrid Privacy Declaration; http://thepublicvoice.org/madrid-declaration/endorsement/default.php; Jeff Jarvis's Bill of Rights in Cyberspace; http://buzzmachine.com/2010/12/10/bill-of-rights-in-cyberspace-amended-2/; a Consumers' Privacy Bill of Rights; http://www.consumerismcommentary.com/privacy-bill-of-rights/, and so on

24. Namely those covenants under the rubric of the International Bill of Rights: the Universal Declaration of Human Rights (1948), International Covenant on Civil

and Political Rights (1966), and the International Covenant on Economic, Social and Cultural Rights (1966).

25. All citations from the IRP Coalition mailing list have been anonymized, the year of posting only noted for that reason.

26. The lack of clarity in terms of how the charter's rendition of the UDHR applies specifically to the internet in the first draft drew comment from initial presentations on the ground and online. In the first instance, legal experts, this case as part of an audience for a presentation I gave at the Edinburgh Law School in 2010, noted how the initial table of contents lacked concrete, explicit references to the internet in general or the online environment in particular. In the second that respective clauses created untenable contradictions in definitional and legal terms. In the third, that all these rights and obligations are already covered in public, private, or international jurisprudence.

27. The material presented here calls for more extended analysis in terms of the explicit content of the eventual charter from a legal and political perspective and debates arising. The shape and dynamics of the online debates around these clauses, how differences were settled compromises reached take us into the realm of what Hauser calls "vernacular rhetoric" (Hauser 1999). The interpersonal, intra-coalition disputes and positions taken are another line of inquiry. In short, this section is but a snapshot.

28. See United Nations Documentation—Research Guide: Human Rights, http://www.un.org/Depts/dhl/resguide/spechr.htm. For a quick comparison see the UDHR, http://www.un.org/en/documents/udhr/.

29. As an early FAQ document, written as a guideline to introduce the charter to the unfamiliar explains, the writing evolved along three conscious paths: "A. The Charter of Human Rights and Principles for the Internet (formerly 'section 1' of the Charter): this document outlines how human rights should be interpreted to apply to the Internet. The document is being developed through a thorough assessment of what is needed to respect, protect and fulfil human rights on the Internet. : B. Implementation Guidelines for Specific Actors and Technologies (formerly 'section 2' of the Charter): Whereas the Charter outlines how human rights apply to the Internet, this document drills down to detail what freedoms Internet users have and how these goals can be achieved in practice. It outlines the actions required of each different sector, whether it be governments, search engines, telecommunications companies, software developers, users etc. in order to fulfil those goals: C Explanatory Notes (Sources of Rights and Principles for the Internet): this document explains the interpretations which are presented in the Charter, and outlines the legal status of each provision. As a fast developing area of law, some of our interpretations are already hard law, others are soft law, and some are based on our own understanding of what human rights mean online. This document will clarify the status of each Charter provision under International law and will outline all supportive documents including International, regional and national law and regulation, and standards set by civil society and other relevant institutions" (FAQ notes compiled by Lisa Horner, IRP Coalition Chair, January 2011).

30. Within UN consultations, in the EU and parts of Latin America several threads to the IRP Charter bear mentioning. In particular; (i) The Communication Rights for the Information Society campaign's declaration dating from the WSIS summit entitled Communication Rights at http://www.crisinfo.org/; (ii) The Association for

Progressive Communications and their precursor Bill of Rights for the Internet, currently rolled out into their Internet Rights Charter and a source document for the IRP Charter (Benedek 2012) http://www.apc.org/en/node/5677/; as noted already, the ten principles developed during the Brazilian Marco Civil process inspired and informed the IRP Charter drafting process in 2010; (iii) At this time, an Internet Rights Declaration by Chinese intellectuals in 2010 provided a public impetus to the early drafting stages; http://underthejacaranda.wordpress.com/2009/10/08/internet-human-rights-declaration/, (iv) Digital Civil Rights in Europe (EDRI) is a coalition that has also been an active member, and promoter of the Charter; http://www.edri.org/edrigram/number9.7/10-internet-principles-rights.

31. It bears underscoring that the charter itself is a contested document even within the coalition; at all points in the drafting and then eventual launch of the full charter and the Ten Principles, every clause was subjected to intense, and at times fierce debate. Hence this account is not to suggest that the process was comparable to a campfire experience. Debates still rage, outwardly and under the surface about the role the charter itself has to play for the IGF at large as the latter embarks on a project of establishing a set of universal principles for Internet Governance (also contested) and moreover for specific rights-based projects of coalition member organizations. Either it is a document with high ambitions and legal "teeth," or it is a "matrix or the main material from which different kinds of initiatives could originate," or an "open-source document to inspire other, maybe more limited and binding initiatives," or an "elaborated, internally consistent . . . Talmudic . . . document," or it is simply one of many other attempts that "will face being superseded or bypassed." In this sense there are coalition members who advocate the "this is as good as it gets approach" namely that as an "open-source process" (see Chapter 3) if the charter and its coalition can become established as the "definitive space for the discussion, exploration, and collation of rights issues. . . . it [the Charter] could live forever or at least for a long, long time" (IRP list 2011).

32. The trade union movement, women's movement, civil rights movements, student protests, indigenous land-rights movements, and successive antiwar demonstrations targeting local and national decisions yet with international repercussions are cases in point for twentieth/twenty-first century memories.

33. Here I borrow from Eric Hobsbawm (1983: 1).

CHAPTER 6

1. The Expert Group drafting the first version of the charter comprised legal experts, EU-lobbyists, as well as activists. In the latter case, institutional reformism and activism resided in the same person. For tactical treasons it was agreed that any hint of the project being one about new rights had to be avoided. First, this move was seen as jeopardizing the charter's standing and sustainability with the international human rights community (viz. a subsection of a wider public to all intents and purposes). Second, in order to be taken seriously to work within the existing "rational-political discourses" (Warner op. cit.) of international human rights institutions.

2. See Lipshutz (2005) for whom the conflation of the market and the political is a key issue in analytical and practical terms. See also Prakash and Hart (1999), Bøås and McNeill (2004), and Hardt and Negri (2000) for different angles on how to rework Foucault's ideas. Apart from the latter, methodical consideration of how ICT and/

or the internet are imbricated in both analysis and conclusions drawn is patently absent.

3. Along with the United States and the United Kingdom, Canada, Costa Rica, the Czech Republic, Denmark, Egypt, Kenya, the Netherlands, New Zealand, Poland, Qatar, and Sweden refused to sign the draft treaty; those who did sign included Russia and China. The polemic that was unleashed in the blogosphere and technology rubrics of the world's major news outlets before, during, and after the meeting runs the gamut of pro- and anti-regulation ideologies, pitting advocates of free enterprise and self-regulation (e.g., Google and Microsoft and US-based lobby groups) against those supporting governmental regulation. Along this spectrum a range of political and academic commentators and internet governance pundits debated whether this was a storm in a teacup, a rendering of Cold War politics in a digital age form, or an auguring of more serious standoffs to come (Mueller 2012; Goldsmith 2012; Becker and Reißmann 2012; O'Toole 2012; Gurstein 2013).

4. Entitled Towards Knowledge Societies for Peace and Sustainable Development: First WSIS + 10 Review Event, this UNESCO hosted event (February 25–27, 2013) was the first review of the World Summit on the Information Society; in 2013 marking ten years since the first WSIS meeting in Geneva. The second event, hosted by the ITU will take place in 2015 to mark ten years since the last WSIS meeting in Tunis (2005). 2015 is also when the Millennium Developments Goals are due to culminate (UN 2000).

5. Thanks to Yanaika Zomer for this expression.

6. Gil Scott-Heron, Brian Jackson, and the Midnight Band, Midnight Band: The First Minute Of A New Day, Arista—AB 4030, Arista—A 4030, Arista—AL5–8154, recorded live at New York University in 1974.

LITERATURE LIST

Abbate, Janet, 2001, *Inventing the Internet*, Boston: MIT Press.

Abildgaard, 2001, "Down and Out in Budapest and Vollsmose," *Art India* magazine, April 2001, http://www.c3.hu/collection/homeless/store/artindia.html.

Abraham, Sunil, 2012, "Sense and Censorship," Centre for Internet and Society, January 31, 2012, http://cis-india.org/internet-governance/sense-and-censorship.

Access, 2012, *Declaration of Internet Freedom* Campaign, Accessnow.org, https://www.accessnow.org/page/s/internetdeclaration (accessed February 22, 201).

Access, 2013, "Tell the ITU: The Internet Belongs to Us!" *Access: Campaigns*, https://www.accessnow.org/page/s/itu (accessed February 22, 2013).

Allen, Mike, 2009, "The Political Organisation of People Who Are Homeless: Reflections of a Sympathetic Sceptic," *European Journal of Homelessness*, vol. 3, December: 289–299.

Amelrooy, Peter van, 2003, "Knokken tegen de Taliban van internet," de Volkskrant, Amsterdam: de Volkskrant, January 9, 2003: 18.

Ammelrooy, Peter van, "Slimme huid vervangt electrode," *de Volkskrant*, August13, 2011: 33.

Anderson, Benedict, 1991, *Imagined Communities: Reflections on the Origin and Spread of Nationalism*, rev. ed., London/New York: Verso Books.

Ansley, Francis, 2002, "Who Counts? The Case for Participatory Research" in *Labouring Below the Line: The New Ethnography of Poverty, Low-Wage Work, and Survival in the Global Economy*, FrankMunger (ed.), New York: Russell Sage Foundation, 245–270.

Appadurai, Arjun, 2002, "Disjuncture and Difference in the Global Cultural Economy," in *The Anthropology of Globalisation: A Reader*, J. X. Inda and R. Rosaldo (ed.), MA/Oxford UK: Blackwell Publishers, 27–47.

Arellano, Lucy, 2004, "Street Paper Profile: New York City's BIGNews and Upward," Street Papers Focus Group: Spring 2004 Case Studies, Seattle: Washington University, http://depts.washington.edu/stnews/arrelano.html (accessed October 29, 2012).

Arthur, Charles, 2012, "Internet Remains Unregulated after UN Treaty Blocked," *The Guardian*, December 14, 2012, http://www.guardian.co.uk/technology/2012/dec/14/telecoms-treaty-internet-unregulated?CMP=twt_fd (accessed February 22, 2013).

Arthur, Charles, 2013, "Google Cleared of Search Results Bias after Two-year US Investigation," *The Guardian*, January 4, 2013, http://www.guardian.co.uk/technology/2013/jan/03/google-cleared-search-bias-investigation?CMP=twt_gu (accessed February 13, 2013).

Aslama, Minna, and Philip M. Napoli (eds.), 2010, *Communications Research in Action: Scholar-Activist Collaborations for a Democratic Sphere*, New York: Fordham University Press.

Association of Progressive Communications, 2012, *Going Visible: Women's Rights On The Internet*, APC-Women's Rights Programme Report to Addressing Inequalities: The Heart of the Post-2015 Development Agenda and the Future We Want for All, Global Thematic Consultation, UN Women/Unicef, October 2012, http://www.worldwewant2015.org/file/287493/download/311684 (accessed February 18, 2013).

Baban, F., and F. Keyman, 2008, "Turkey and Postnational Europe: Challenges for the Cosmopolitan Political Community," *European Journal of Social Theory*, vol. 11, no. 1: 107–124.

Bakardjieva, Maria, 2005, *The Internet in Everyday Life*, London: Sage Publications.

Bankston, Kevin, 2012, "This Week: CDT at the 2012 Internet Governance Forum," Center for Democracy and Technology, November 5, 2012, https://www.cdt.org/blogs/kevin-bankston/0511week-cdt-2012-internet-governance-forum (accessed February 17, 2013).

Barbrook, Richard, 2006, *The Class of the New*, Mute, www.theclassofthenew.net (accessed February 13, 2013).

Darkai, Moran, 2012, *Revolution: Share! The Role of Social Media in Pro-Democratic Movements*, Wilfried Rütten (ed.), European Journalism Centre, http://www.ejc.net/revolution_share/ (accessed September 14, 2012).

Barlow, John Perry, 1996, A *Declaration of the Independence of Cyberspace*, February 8, 1996, https://projects.eff.org/~barlow/Declaration-Final.html (accessed January 3, 2013).

Barrickman, Nick, 2012, "Homelessness, Social Misery on the Rise in US Capital," *World Socialist Website*, August 30, 2012, http://www.wsws.org/articles/2012/aug2012/dcho-a30.shtml (accessed October 26, 2012).

Barron's Business Guides, 1995, *Dictionary of Computer Terms*, 4th ed., New York: Barron's Educational Series Inc.

Basch, L., N. Glick Schiller, and C. Blanc-Szanton, 1994, *Nations Unbound: Transnational Projects, Postcolonial Predicaments and Deterritorialised Nation-States*, New York: Gordon and Breach.

Bauer, Johannes, 1994, "The Emergence of Global Networks in Telecommunications: Transcending National Regulation and Market Constraints," *Journal of Economic Issues*, vol. 28, no. 2, June 1994: 391–402.

BBC News, 2010, "Internet access is 'a fundamental right'", March 8, 2010, http://news.bbc.co.uk/2/hi/technology/8548190.stm (accessed January 3, 2013).

Becker, Sven, and Stefan Niggemeier, 2012, "Google's Lobby Offensive. Internet Giant Builds Web of Influence in Berlin," Christopher Sultan (transl.), *Spiegel Online International*, September 25, 2012, http://www.spiegel.de/international/business/how-google-lobbies-german-government-over-internet-regulation-a-857654.html (accessed December 4, 2012).

Becker, Sven, and Ole Reißmann, 2012, "ITU–Gipfel in Dubai Kalter Krieg ums Internet," *Spiegel Online: Netzwelt*, December 3, 2012, http://www.spiegel.de/netzwelt/netzpolitik/itu-gipfel-in-dubai-kalter-krieg-ums-internet-a-870571.html (accessed December 3, 2012).

Becker, Sven, and Marcel Rosenbach, 2012, "Net Neutrality? Google Prods Users to Fight Copyright Law," *Spiegel Online International*, December 3, 2012, http://www.spiegel.

de/international/business/google-encourages-users-to-join-campaign-against-copyright-draft-law-a-870590.html (accessed December 4, 2012).

Beer, Patrice de, 1998, "*Apple et AOL témoignent des pressions exercées sur eux par Micro-soft*," *Le Monde*, France, November 3, 1998:18.

Behr, Rafael, 2009, "The Web Has Limits to Its Freedoms after All," Focus: Special Report, *The Observer*, January, 17, 2010: 23.

Benedek, Wolfgang, 2012, *Discussion paper mapping-out issues regarding a Compendium of Rights of Internet Users*, Council of Europe: Committee of Experts on Rights of Internet Users (MSI-DUI), MSI-DUI (2012)03, July 25, 2012, http://www.coe.int/t/dghl/standardsetting/media/MSI-DUI/MSI-DUI%282012%2903E_Discussion%20Paper%20%28W%20%20Benedek%29.asp#TopOfPage (accessed January 3, 2013).

Bénilde, Marie, 2007, "On achète bien les cerveaux. La publicité et les medias," *Le Monde Diplomatique,* July 2007, at http://www.monde-diplomatique.fr/2007/07/DIVRY/14977.

Benkler, Yochai, 2006: *The Wealth of Networks: How Social Production Transforms Markets and Freedom*, New Haven: Yale University Press.

Berkowitz, Elana, 2003, "Urban Legend: Ron Grunberg: Homeless Soccer Takes Off," *City Limits*, August 15, 2003, http://www.citylimits.org/news/articles/2973/urban-legend-ron-grunberg (accessed October 29, 2012).

Bernstein, Nina, 2002, "Once Again, Trying Housing as a Cure for Homelessness," *New York Times*, http://nationalhomeless.org.housing.nyt123.html (accessed June 23, 2002).

Best Bits, 2012, "Statement of Civil Society Members and Groups Participating in the 'Best Bits' Pre–IGF Meeting at Baku in 2012," *Best Bits 2012, Baku Azerbaijan*, http://bestbits.igf-online.net/statement/ (accessed February 17, 2013).

Bingham, R. D., Roy E. Green, and S. B. White (eds.), 1987, *The Homeless in Contemporary Society*, London: SAGE Publications.

Blankesteijn, Herbert, 2002, "Ik klik en accepteer!," *NRC Handelsblad*, October 14, 2002: 12.

Blonk, H. C. van der, 1995, "Monopolie en Macht in de Personal Computer Industrie," *Amsterdams Sociologische Tijdschrift*, jrg. 22, 3, December 1995: 488–511.

Blum, Andrew, 2012, *Tubes: A Journey to the Centre of the Internet*, New York: Harper Collins.

Bøås, Morten, and D. McNeill (eds.), 2004, *Global Institutions and Development: Framing the World?*, New York: Routledge.

Boler, Megan (ed.), 2008, *Digital Media and Democracy: Tactics in Hard Times.* Cambridge, MA: MIT Press.

Borradori, Giovanna, 2003, *Philosophy in a Time of Terror: Dialogues with Jürgen Habermas and Jacques Derrida*, Chicago: University of Chicago Press.

Bourdieu, Pierre, 1998, "*L'essence de Néoliberalisme*" *Le Monde Diplomatique*, Paris, March 1998.

Bourdieu, Pierre, 2012, *Sur l'État: Cours au Collège de France 1989–1992*, Paris: Raisons d'agir/Seuil.

Braman, Sandra, 2006, *Change of State: Information, Policy, and Power.* Cambridge, MA: MIT Press.

Breslow, Harris, 1991, "Civil Society, Political Economy, and the Internet" in *Virtual Culture: Identity and Communication in Cybersociety*, Steven G. Jones (ed.), London: SAGE Publications, 236–257.

Breuer, Joseph, and Sigmund Freud, 1895, Studies in Hysteria, Eastford, CT: Martino Fine Books.

Bright, Peter, 2011, "Microsoft Buys Skype for $8.5 Billion. Why, Exactly?" Wired, May 10, 2011, http://www.wired.com/business/2011/05/microsoft-buys-skype-2/ (accessed February 13, 2013).

Brousseau, Eric, Meryem Marzouki, and Cécile Méadel (eds.), 2012, Governance, Regulations and Powers on the Internet, Cambridge, UK: Cambridge University Press.

Brown, Deborah, 2013, "Amid Crackdown in Azerbaijan, Blogger Gets the Harshest Sentence," Access Blog, January 30, 2013, https://www.accessnow.org/blog/2013/01/30/amid-crackdown-in-azerbaijan-blogger-gets-the-harshest-sentence (accessed February 21, 2013).

Brownsword, Roger, 2008, Rights, Regulation and the Technological Revolution, New York: Oxford University Press.

Burke, Peter, and Asa Briggs, 2009, A Social History of the Media: From Gutenberg to the Internet, 3rd ed. Oxford, UK: Polity Press.

Business Week, 1999a, "Telecom's New Giants," European ed., May 3, 1999: 24–27.

Business Week, 1999b, "A Wiser Bull? American News," Business Week, May 3, 1999: 98–101.

Butchinsky, Chantal, 2013, "Sources of Stigma: Researching Street Homelessness— Interviews and Participant Observation," Academic.edu, http://www.academia.edu/351960/Sources_of_Stigma_Researching_Street_Homelessness_-_Interviews_and_Participant_Observation (accessed March 18, 2013).

Calhoun, Craig, and Michael McQuarrie, 2012, "The Reluctant Counterpublic." In The Roots of Radicalism: Tradition, the Public Sphere, and Early Nineteenth-Century Social Movements. Craig Calhoun (ed.), Chicago: University of Chicago Press: 152–181.

Cammaerts, Bart, 2008, "Critiques on the Participatory Potentials of Web 2.0," Culture, Communication and Critique, vol. 1, issue 4: 358–377.

Carlile, 2008, New Zealand Herald: Business Herald, April 25, 2008: 6.

Castells, Manuel, 1996, The Rise of the Network Society, the Information Age: Economy, Society and Culture, vol. 1, Oxford, UK: Blackwell Publishers.

Castells, Manuel, 2002, The Internet Galaxy: Reflections on the Internet, Business, and Society, New York: Oxford University Press.

Castells, Manuel, 2012, Networks of Outrage and Hope: Social Movements in the Internet Age, London: Polity Press.

Castro, Daniel, 2013, "A Declaration of the Interdependence of Cyberspace," Opinion: Computerworld, February 8, 2013, http://www.computerworld.com/s/article/9236603/A_Declaration_of_the_Interdependence_of_Cyberspace?taxonomyId=167&pageNumber=1 (accessed February 22, 2013).

Centre for Democracy and Technology, 2012, "ITU Move to Expand Powers Threatens the Internet: Civil Society Should Have Voice in ITU Internet Debate," Background Paper, Center for Democracy and Technology, March 19, 2012, https://www.cdt.org/files/pdfs/CDT-ITU_WCIT12_background.pdf (accessed February 22, 2013).

Center for Law and Democracy, 2011, Commentary on the Charter of Human Rights and Principles for the Internet, version 2, October 2011, http://www.law-democracy.org/wp-content/uploads/2011/10/Charter-Commentary.pdf (accessed February 18, 2013).

Center for Law and Democracy, 2012, A Truly World-Wide Web: Assessing the Internet from the Perspective of Human Rights, April 2012, http://www.law-democracy.org/wp-content/uploads/2010/07/final-Internet.pdf (accessed February 18, 2013).

Centrepoint, 2010, The Changing Face of Youth Homelessness: Trends in Homeless Young People's Support Needs, report published by Centrepoint, UK, http://www.centrepoint.

org.uk/media/11287/the_changing_face_of_youth_homelessness_-_final_report.pdf (accessed March 31, 2013).

Cerf, Vint, 2012, "Internet Access is not a Human Right," *New York Times,* January 4, 2012: http://www.nytimes.com/2012/01/05/opinion/internet-access-is-not-a-human-right.html?_r=1.

Certeau, Michel de, 1980, *L'invention du quotidien: 1 arts de faire,* Paris: Union Générale d'Editions.

Certeau, Michel de, 1984, *The Practice of Everyday Life,* Steven Rendall (trans.), Berkeley: University of California Press.

Certeau, Michel de, 1986, *Heterologies: Discourse on the Other,* Brian Massumi (trans.), Minneapolis: University of Minnesota Press.

Certeau, Michel de, 1991, "Travel Narratives of the French to Brazil: Sixteenth to Eighteenth Centuries," *Representations* Special Issue: *The New World,* no. 33, Winter 1991: 221–226.

Certeau, Michel de (with Luce Giard), 1994 (1983), "L'Ordinaire de la Communication," report for the French Ministry of Culture, Paris: Dalloz, reprinted in *La Prise de Parole et Autres Écrits Politiques,* Luce Giard (ed.), Paris: Éditions de Seuil: 165–224.

Certeau, Michel de, 1997a, *Culture in the Plural,* Minneapolis: University of Minnesota Press.

Certeau, Michel de, 1997b, *The Capture of Speech and Other Writings,* Minneapolis: University of Minnesota Press.

CGI.br (Brazilian Internet Steering Committee), 2009, *Resolution CGI.Br/RES/2009/003/ P—Principles for the Governance and Use of the Internet,* CGI.br—Regulations, http://www.cgi.br/english/regulations/resolution2009-003.htm (accessed February 17, 2013).

Champlin, Dell, and Paulette Olson, 1994, "Post-Industrial Metaphors: Understanding Corporate Restructuring and the Economic Environment of the 1990s," *Journal of Economic Issues,* vol. 28, no. 2, June 1994: 449–459.

Chaudhuri, Anindya, 2012, "ICT for Development: Solutions Seeking Problems?" *Journal of Information Technology,* vol. 27, no. 4, December 2012: 326–338.

Civille, Richard, 1995, "The Internet and the Poor," in *Public Access to the Inter*net, Brian Kahin and James Keller (eds.), Cambridge, MA: MIT Press: 175–207.

Clapham, Andrew, 2007, *Human Rights: A Very Short Introduction,* New York: Oxford University Press.

Clifford, James, 1997, *Routes: Travel and Translation in the Late Twentieth Century,* Cambridge, MA: Harvard University Press.

Clinton, Hillary Rodham, 2010a, *Internet Freedom,* speech delivered at the Newseum in Washington, DC, January 21, 2010, http://www.foreignpolicy.com/articles/2010/01/21/internet_freedom?page=full (accessed January 2, 2013).

Clinton, Hillary Rodham, 2010b, "Remarks on Innovation and American Leadership to the Commonwealth Club," San Francisco, CA, October 15, 2010, http://www.state.gov/secretary/rm/2010/10/149542.htm (accessed January 2, 2013).

Cohen, Fernanda, 2008, *Fernanda Cohen Blog*: May 2008, http://fernandacohen.com/blog/2008/05/may-2008/ (accessed March 25, 2013).

Coleman, Lara Montesinos, and Karen Tucker (eds.), 2012, *Situating Global Resistance: Between Discipline and Dissent,* London/New York: Routledge.

Comenetz, Jacob, "Innovating Public Diplomacy For a New Digital World," *Washington Diplomat,* July 27, 2011, http://www.washdiplomat.com/index.php?option=com_content&id=7955:innovating-public-diplomacy-for-a-new-digital-world&Itemid=428.

Couldry, Nick, 2012, *Media, Society, World: Social Theory and Digital Media Practice*, Oxford: Polity Press.

Council of Europe—Committee of Ministers, 2012a, "Extract from Committee of Ministers' document CM (2012)911," *Council of Europe: Media—Freedom of Information and Expression*, http://www.coe.int/t/dghl/standardsetting/media/MSI-DUI/MSI-DUI_ToR%20EN%20%28final%29.asp#P1_58 (accessed February 15, 2013).

Council of Europe—Committee of Ministers, 2012b, Internet Governance: Council of Europe Strategy 2012–2015, CM Documents, CM(2011)175 final, March 15, 2012, https://wcd.coe.int/ViewDoc.jsp?Ref=CM%282011%29175&Ver=final&Language=1 anEnglish&Site=CM&BackColorInternet=C3C3C3&BackColorIntranet=EDB021& BackColorLogged=F5D383 (accessed January 2, 2013).

Cowhey, Peter F., and Jonathan D. Aronson, 2009, *Transforming Global Information and Communication Markets: The Political Economy of Innovation*, Cambridge, MA: MIT Press.

Crack, Angela M., 2008, *Global Communication and Transnational Public Spheres*, New York: Palgrave Macmillan.

Cubitt, Sean, 1997, *Digital Aesthetics*, London: Lon Publications.

Cunningham, Kendra, 2009, "Homeless Folks Getting Reconnected through Facebook, Twitter," *Switched*, June 4, 2009, http://www.switched.com/2009/06/04/homeless-folks-getting-reconnected-through-facebook-twitter/ (accessed October 26, 2012).

Curran, James, Natalie Fenton, and Des Freedman, 2012, *Misunderstanding the Internet*, New York: Routledge.

Dabu, Christl, 2002, "Bridging the Digital Divide," *Digital Journal Magazine*, Article RA 2083, http://www.digitaljournal.com/news/?articleID=2083 (Accessed February 18, 2002).

Dahlberg, Lincoln, and Eugenia Siapiera (eds.), 2007, *Radical Democracy and the Internet: Interrogating Theory and Practice*. New York: Palgrave Macmillan.

Dany, Charlotte, 2012, *Global Governance and NGO Participation: Shaping the information Society in the United Nations*, New York: Routledge.

Davidson, B. M. 2001, "Homeless People and the Internet," http://cmtk3.webring.org/l/rd?ring=streetring;id=2;url=http%3A%2F%2Fbmdavidson.tripod.com%2Findex. html.

Davies, Simon (The Privacy Surgeon), 2013: "Analysis: Eight global repercussions from the PRISM disclosures," June 25, 2013, http://www.privacysurgeon.org/blog/incision/analysis-eight-global-repercussions-from-the-snowden-affair/ (accessed July 15, 2013).

Dayan, Daniel, 2001, "The Peculiar Public of Television." *Media, Culture and Society*, vol. 23, no. 6: 743–765.

Deibert, Ronald J., 2000, "International Plug'n Play? Citizen Activism, the Internet, and Global Public Policy," *International Studies Perspectives*, vol. 1, no. 3, December: 255–272.

Deibert, Ronald J., 2008, "Black Code Redux: Censorship, Surveillance, and the Militarization of Cyberspace," in *Digital Media and Democracy: Tactics in Hard Times*, Megan Boler (ed.), Cambridge, MA: MIT Press: 137–163.

Deibert, Ronald J., and Rafal Rohozinski, 2010, "Risking Security: Policies and Paradoxes of Cyberspace Security," *International Political Sociology*, 4: 15–32.

De Kock, Leon, 1992, "Interview with Gayatri Chakravorty Spivak: New Nation Writers Conference in South Africa," *ARIEL: A Review of International English Literature*, vol. 23, no. 3: 29–47, http://ariel.synergiesprairies.ca/ariel/index.php/ariel/article/viewFile/2505/2458 (accessed November 2, 2012).

Desjarlais, Robert R., 1997, *Shelter Blues: Sanity and Selfhood among the Homeless*, Philadelphia: University of Pennsylvania Press.

Dick, Phillip K., [1968] 2000, *Do Androids Dream of Electric Sheep?* Oxford: Oxford University Press.

Dijck, José van, 2013, *The Culture of Connectivity: A Critical History of Social Media*, New York: Oxford University Press.

Dimaggio, Paul J., and Ezster Hargattai, 2001, "From the 'Digital Divide' to 'Digital Inequality': Studying Internet Use as Penetration Increases," Working Paper 19, Center for Arts and Cultural Policy Studies, Woodrow Wilson School, Princeton, NJ.

Dordick, Gwendolyn A., 1997, *Something Left to Lose: Personal Relations and Survival among New York's Homeless*, Philadelphia: Temple University Press.

Douglas, Ian R., 1999, "Globalization as Governance: Toward an Archaeology of Contemporary Political Reason" in *Globalization and Governance* A. Prakash and J. A. Hart (ed.)., New York: Routledge, 134–160.

Drache, Daniel, 2008, *Defiant Publics: The Unprecedented Reach of the Global Citizen.* Cambridge, UK: Polity Press.

Drake, William J., 2001, "Communications," in *Managing Global Issues: Lessons Learned*, P. J. Simmons and Chantelde Jonge Oudraat (eds.), Washington, DC: Carnegie Endowment for International Peace, 25–74.

Drucker, Susan J., and Gary Grumpert (eds.), 1997, *Voices in the Street: Exploration in Gender, Media, and Public Space*, Cresskill, NJ: Hampton Press.

Duffy, Peter, 2000, "New Yorkers & Co.: Keeping the Faith in Boom Times," *New York Times Archives*, October 8, 2000, http://www.nytimes.com/2000/10/08/nyregion/new-yorkers-co-keeping-the-faith-in-boom-times.html?pagewanted=all&src=pm (accessed March 25, 2013).

Duneier, Mitchell, 1999, *Sidewalk*, New York: Farra, Straus and Giroux.

Dvorak, Phred, 2009, "On the Street and On Facebook: The Homeless Stay Wired," *The Wall Street Journal: Europe Edition*, May 30, 2009, http://online.wsj.com/article/SB124363359881267523.html#articleTabs%3Darticle (accessed March 25, 2013).

Dyer-Witheford, N., 1999, *Cyber-Marx: Cycles and Circuits of Struggle in High Technology Capitalism*, Urbana-Champaign, IL: University of Illinois Press.

Economist, The, 1995, "Survey: Telecommunications," *The Economist*, September 30, 1995: 5–40.

Economist, The, 1997, "A Survey of Communications: A Connected World," *The Economist*, September 13, 1997: 3–42.

Economist, The, 1998a, "Microsoft's Contradiction," from *The Economist* Print Edition, January 29, www.economist.com.

Economist, The, 1998b, "Play Nicely or not at All," from *The Economist* Print Edition, May 21, www.economist.com.

Economist, The, 1999a, "Pricks and Kicks," from *The Economist* Print Edition, August 12, www.economist.com.

Economist The, 1999b, "Survey 20th Century: On the yellow brick road," *The Economist*, September, 11.

Economist The, 2000, "Winternet," *The Economist* Print Edition, June 29, www.economist.com.

Economist The, 2012, "Internet Regulation: A Digital Cold War?" December 14, http://www.economist.com/blogs/babbage/2012/12/internet-regulation?fsrc=scn/tw_ec/a_digital_cold_war_ (accessed December 14, 2012).

Edgar, Bill, Joe Doherty, and Henk Meert, 2003, *Review of Statistics on Homelessness in Europe*, European Directory on Homelessness, European Federation of National Organizations Working with the Homeless (FEANTSA), Brussels: Belgium.

Edkins, Jenny, 2008, "Why Do We Obey?," in *Global Politics: A New Introduction*, Jenny Edkins and Maja Zehfuss (eds.), London, New York: Routldege, 123–146.

Eschle, C., and B. Maiguashca (eds.), 2005, *Critical Theories, International Relations and the "Anti-Globalization Movement": The Politics of Global Resistance*, New York: Routledge.

European Commission, 1997, *Building the European Information Society for Us All*, Final policy report of the high-level expert group, Directorate General for Employment, Industrial Relations and Social Affairs, Brussels: European Commission Directorate General III, Industry.

Evangelista, Guillem Fernàndez, 2010, "Poverty, Homelessness and Freedom: An Approach from the Capabilities Theory," *European Journal of Homelessness*, vol. 4, December 2010: 189–2002.

Everitt, Dave, and Simon Mills, 2009, "Cultural Anxiety 2.0," *Media, Culture and Society*, vol. 31, no. 5: 749–768.

Farivar, Crrus, 2011, *The Internet of Elsewhere*, New Brunswick, NJ: Rutgers University Press.

FEANTSA, 2010, *Changing Faces: Homelessness Among Children, Families and Young People*, Homeless in Europe Magazine, Autumn, http://www.feantsa.org/IMG/pdf/homeless_in_europe_autumn2010_en_final.pdf.pdf (accessed February 14, 2013).

FEANTSA, 2012a, *ETHOS—European Typology of Homelessness and Housing Exclusion*, http://www.feantsa.org/IMG/pdf/en.pdf (accessed February 14, 2013).

FEANSTA, 2012b, "About Us," http://www.feantsa.org/spip.php?article120&lang=en (accessed February 14, 2013).

Federal Trade Commission, 2013, "Google Agrees to Change Its Business Practices to Resolve FTC Competition Concerns in the Markets for Devices like Smart Phones, Games and Tablets, and in Online Search," *Federal Trade Commission: News*, January 3, http://ftc.gov/opa/2013/01/google.shtm (accessed February 13, 2013).

Feenberg, Andrew, 1999, *Questioning Technology*, London: Routledge.

Feld, Harold, 2012, "Shutting Down the Phone System Gets Real: The Implications of AT&T Upgrading to an All IP Network," *Public Knowledge: Policy Blog*, November 13, 2012: http://www.publicknowledge.org/blog/shutting-down-phone-system-gets-real-implicat (accessed December 26, 2012).

Fenton, Natalie, 2008, "Mediating Solidarity,"*Global Media and Communication*, vol. 4, no. 1: 37–57.

Fischbach, Rainer, 2005, *Mythos Netz: Kommunikation Jenseits von Raum und Zeit?* Zürich: Rotpunktverlag.

Fiske, John, 1999 (1991), "For Cultural Interpretation: A Study of the Culture of Homelessness," in *Reading the Homeless: The Media's Image of Homeless Culture*, Eungjun-Min (ed.), London: Praeger Publishers, 1–22.

Fitzpatrick, Suzanne, 2000, *Young Homeless People*, New York: St., Martin's Press.

Flyverbom, Mikkel, 2011, *The Power of Networks: Organizing the Global Politics of the Internet*. Cheltenham, England: Edward Elgar Books.

Fooks, Gary, and Christina Pantazis, 1999, "The Criminalisation of Homelessness, Begging and Street Living," in *Homelessness: Exploring the New Terrain*, Patricia Kennett and Alex Marsh (eds.), Bristol, UK: The Policy Press, 123–160.

Foremski, Tom, 1999, "Gearing up for the next Generation of IT systems," *Financial Times*, Information Supplement, June 2: 11.

Forrest, Ray, 1999, "The New Landscape of Precariousness" in *Homelessness: Exploring the New Terrain*, Patricia Kennett, and Alex Marsh (eds.), Bristol, UK: The Policy Press: 17–36.

Foster, John Bellamy, and Robert W. McChesney, 2011, "The Internet's Unholy Marriage to Capitalism," *Monthly Review*, vol. 62, issue 10, http://monthlyreview.org/2011/03/01/the-internets-unholy-marriage-to-capitalism#en2.

Foucault, M., 1984a, "Interview: Polemics, Politics and Problematizations," interview with Paul Rabinow, http://foucault.info/foucault/interview.html (accessed November, 24, 2012).

Foucault, Michel, 1984b [1975], "Panopticism," in The Foucault Reader: An Introduction to Foucault's Thought, Paul Rabinow (ed.), London: Penguin Books, 206–213.

Foucault, Michel, 1984c, "Truth and Power," in *The Foucault Reader: An Introduction to Foucault's Thought*, Paul Rabinow (ed.), London: Penguin Books, 51–75.

Foucault, Michel, 1991 [1978], "Governmentality," in *The Foucault Effect: Studies in Governmentality with two Lectures and an Interview with Michel Foucault*, G. Burchell, C. Gordon, and P. Miller (eds.), Chicago: University of Chicago Press, 87–104.

Foucault, M., 2004a, "Naissance de la biopolitique," *Cours au Collège de France*, 1978–1979, *Dits et Ecrits*, Paris: Gallimard, 79.

Foucault, M., 2004b, "Sécurité, Territoire, Population," *Cours au Collège de France*, 1977–1978, *Dits et Ecrits*, Paris: Gallimard, 119.

Franklin, M. I., 2001, "InsideOut: Postcolonial Subjectivities and Everyday Life Online," *International Feminist Journal of Politics*, vol. 3, no. 3, November 2001: 387–422.

Franklin, M. I., 2002, "Reading Walter Benjamin and Donna Haraway in the Age of Digital Reproduction," *Information, Communication and Society*, vol. 5, no. 4: 591–624.

Franklin, M. I., 2003, " 'We are the Borg': Microsoft and the Power Struggle for Control of the Internet," in *Digitaal contact: het net van de begrensde mogelijkheden*, Jeroen de Kloet, Suzanne Kuik, and Giselinde Kuipers (eds.), Amsterdams Sociologisch Tijdschrift, AST-Thema, vol. 30: 223–253.

Franklin, M. I., 2004, *Postcolonial Politics, the Internet, and Everyday Life: Pacific Traversals*, New York: Routledge.

Franklin, M. I., 2005a, *Gender Advocacy at the World Summit on the Information Society: Preliminary Observations*, Research Report completed for the Ford Foundation, http://www.genderit.org/content/gender-advocacy-world-summit-information-society (accessed December 3, 2012).

Franklin M. I., 2005b, "Keeping Public Cyberspace Open: Lessons from the Pacific Islands," *Pacific Journalism Review*, vol. 11, no. 1: 60–88).

Franklin, M. I, 2007a, "NGO's and the 'Information Society': Grassroots Advocacy at the UN—a cautionary tale," *Review of Policy Research*, vol. 24, no. 4, July 2007: 309–330.

Franklin, M. I., 2007b, "Democracy, Postcolonialism, and Everyday Life: Contesting the 'Royal We' Online," in *The Internet and Radical Democracy: Exploring Theory and Practice*, Lincoln Dahlberg and EugeniaSiapera (eds.), London: Palgrave Macmillan, 168–190.

Franklin, M. I., 2009a, "Who's Who in the "Internet Governance Wars": Hail the Phantom Menace?" in *Who Controls the Internet? Beyond the Obstinacy or Obsoleteness of the State*, GiampieroGiacomello and Johan Eriksson (eds.), *International Studies Review*, vol. 11, issue 1, March 2009: 221–226.

Franklin, M. I., 2009b, "Sex, Gender, and Cyberspace," in *Global Gender Matters: A Feminist Introduction to International Relations*, Laura Shepherd (ed.). New York, Routledge, 328–349.

Franklin, M. I., 2010, "Digital Dilemmas: Transnational Politics in the 21st Century," *Brown Journal of World Affairs*, vol. 16, issue 11: 67–85.

Franklin, M. I., 2011, "Decolonising the Future: Not to Go Where Cyborgs Have Gone Before?" in *Interoperabel Nederland*, Nico Westpalm van Hoorn, Peter Waters, and Pieter Wisse (eds.), Dutch Ministry of Economic Affairs, Den Haag: The Netherlands, 4–22, http://www.forumstandaardisatie.nl/fileadmin/os/publicaties/01.1_Franklin.pdf (accessed March 1, 2013).

Franklin, M. I, 2012c, "Being Human and the Internet: Against Dichotomies," *Journal of Information Technology: Organization, Management, Information and Systems*, vol. 27, no. 4, December 2012: 315–318.

Franklin, M. I, 2013a, "How Does the Way We Use the Internet Make a Difference?" *Global Politics: A New Introduction*, 2nd ed., Maja Zehfuss and Jenny Edkins (eds.). New York: Routledge, 176–199.

Franklin, M. I., 2013b, "Like It or Not, We Are All Complicit in Online Snooping," *The Conversation*, June 20, 2013; http://theconversation.com/like-it-or-not-we-are-all-complicit-in-online-snooping-15219 (accessed July 15, 2013).

Franklin, M. I., 2013c, "Human rights on the internet: online, you have rights too," *The Guardian: Media Network*, July 17, 2013; http://www.theguardian.com/media-network/media-network-blog/2013/jul/17/human-rights-internet-online (accessed 1 August, 2013).

Fraser, Nancy, 2005, "Reframing Justice in a Globalizing World," *New Left Review*, 36, November–December 2005: 69–88.

Fraser, Nancy, 2007, "Transnationalizing the Public Sphere: On the Legitimacy and Efficacy of Public Opinion in a Post–Westphalian World," in *Theory, Culture, and Society*, vol. 24, no. 4: 7–30.

Frau-Meigs, Divina, Jérémie Nicey, Michael Palmer, Julia Pohle, and Patricio Tupper (eds.), 2012, *From NWICO to WSIS: 30 Years of Communication Geopolitics*, Chicago: Intellect.

Freedman, Des, 2008, *The Politics of Media Policy*, Cambridge. UK: Polity Press.

Freeman, Anitra, 2002, *Real Change*, Seattle, interview with author at the Annual Conference of the North American Street Newspapers Association (NASNA), Boston, July18, 2002.

Friedman, Yona, 2000 [1975], *Utopies Réalisables*, Paris: Éditions de l'éclat.

Fuchs, Christian, 2007, *Internet and Society: Social Theory in the Information Age*, New York: Routledge.

Fuchs, Christian, 2012, "Some Reflections on Manuel Castells' Book Networks of Outrage and Hope: Social Movements in the Internet Age," *Triple C: Cognition, Communication, Cooperation*, vol. 10, no 2 : 775–797.

Gaiser, Ted J., and Anthony E. Schreiner, 2009, *A Guide to Conducting Online Research*, London: SAGE Publications Ltd.

Gerbner, George, Hamid Mowlana, and Kaarle Nordenstreng (eds.), 1993, *The Global Media Debate: Its Rise, Fall, and Renewal*, Norwood, NJ: Ablex Publishing Corporation.

Giacomello, Giampiero, and Johan Eriksson (eds.), 2009, "Who Controls the Internet? Beyond the Obstinacy or Obsoleteness of the State," Review Forum: *International Studies Review*, vol. 11, issue 1, January: 205–230.

Giard, Luce, 1994, "Par quoi demain déjà se donne à naître," in *La Prise de Parole et autres écrits politiques*, Michel de Certeau. Paris: Éditions du Seuil: 7–26.

Gibson, William, 1984a, *Neuromancer*, New York: Ace Books, http://project.cyberpunk. ru/lib/neuromancer/ (accessed December 24, 2012).

Gibson, William, 1984b (1982), *Burning Chrome*, New York: Ace Books.

Gilroy, Paul, 1993, *The Black Atlantic: Modernity and Double Consciousness*. Cambridge: Harvard University.

Gilroy, Paul, 2002, *There Ain't No Black in the Union Jack*, 2nd ed., London/New York: Routledge.

Gilroy, Rose, and Roberta Woods (eds.), 1994, *Housing Women*, London/New York: Routledge.

Glasser, Irene, 1994, *Homelessness in Global Perspective*, New York/Toronto: G.K. Hall & Co.

Glasser, Irene, and Rae Bridgman, 1999, *Braving the Street: The Anthropology of Homelessness*, New York/Oxford: Berghahn Books.

GlobalVoices, 2012, "Brazil: Will the Pioneering Internet Bill of Rights Pass?," Global Voices Online, August 6, 2012, http://globalvoicesonline.org/2012/08/06/brazil-internet-bill-of-rights-marcocivil/ (accessed February 13, 2013).

Golden, Stephanie, 1992, *The Women Outside: Meanings and Myths of Homelessness*, Berkeley: University of California Press.

Goldsmith, Jack, and Tim Wu, 2006, *Who Controls the Internet? Illusions of a Borderless World*. New York: Oxford University Press.

Goldsmith.Jack, 2012, "WCIT 2012: An Opinionated Primer and Hysteria Debunker," *Lawfare: Hard National Security Choices*, http://www.lawfareblog.com/2012/11/wcit-12-an-opinionated-primer-and-hysteria-debunker-2/#more-10219 (accessed November 30, 2012).

Google, 2012, *Investor Relations: Code of Conduct*, available at http://investor.google.com/corporate/code-of-conduct.html (accessed December 6, 2012).

Gore, Al, 1994, Remarks prepared for delivery by US Vice President Al Gore, World Telecommunication Development Conference, Buenos Aires, March 21, 1994: http://www.itu.int/itudoc/itu-d/wtdc/wtdc1994/speech/gore.txt.

Gore, Al, 1996, "Policy Commentary: Bringing Information to the World: The Global Information Infrastructure," *Harvard Journal of Law and Technology*, vol. 9, no. 1, Winter 1996: 1–9.

Grassmuck, Volkmer, 2002, *Freie Software: zwischen privat- und gemeineigentum: themen und materialen*, Bonn, Duitsland: Bundeszentrale für politische Bildung.

Green, Norma Fay, 1998, "Chicago's StreetWise at the Crossroads: A Case Study of a Newspaper to Empower the Homeless in the 1990s," *Print Culture in a Diverse America*, James P. Danky and Wayne A. Wiegand (eds.). Urbana: University of Illinois Press, 34–55.

Greene, David, 1998, "America's First Homeless Newspaper Folds," Bronx News: New York Community Media Alliance, Edition 304, January 17, 2008, http://www.indypressny.org/nycma/voices/304/briefs/briefs/ (accessed October 26, 2012).

Greve, Georg, 2002, Vorworte, in *Freie Software: zwischen privat- und gemeineigentum: themen und materialen*, Volkmer Grassmuck (ed.), Bonn, Duitsland: Bundeszentrale für politische Bildung, 13–15.

Grunberg, Ron, 1998a, Posting on the *Homeless People's Network*: December 11, 1998, http://hpn.asu.edu/archives/Dec98/0206.html (accessed October 29, 2012).

Grunberg, Ron, 1998b, "NYC: Grand Central Neighborhood—an Elaboration," posting on the *Homeless People's Network*, December 14, 1998, http://hpn.asu.edu/archives/Dec98/0249.html (accessed October 29, 2012).

Grunberg, Ron, 2002, editor of *BIGnews* and *Upwards!*, interview with author at the Annual Conference of the North American Street Newspapers Association (NASNA), Boston 2002, July 19, 2002.

Grunberg, Ron, 2004, editor of *BIGnews* and *Upwards!*, interview with author, Mainchance Drop-in Center, New York, July 23, 2004.

Guardian, The, 1999, "Judge Rules Microsoft Is Monopoly," *The Guardian*, 6 November: 27.

Guilhot, Nicolas, 2005, *The Democracy Makers: Human Rights and the Politics of Global Order*, New York: Columbia University Press.

Gurstein, Mike, 2013, "Civil Society and the Emerging Internet Cold War: Non–Alignment and the Public Interest," *Blog: Gurstein's Community Informatics*, February 11, 2013, http://gurstein.wordpress.com/2013/02/11/civil-society-and-the-emerging-internet-cold-war-non-alignment-and-the-public-interest/ (accessed February 22, 2013).

Gurumurthy, Anita, 2003, "A Gender Perspective to ICTs and Development: Reflections toward Tunis," Heinrich Böll Foundation, http://www.worldsummit2003.de/en/web/701.htm (accessed March 31, 2013).

Gurumurthy, Anita, 2013, *"What Went Wrong?" Anita Gurumurthy's statement at the closing ceremony of WSIS plus 10 review*, Gender IT.org, http://www.genderit.org/sites/default/upload/wsis__10_closing_statement_by_anita_g.pdf (accessed March 26, 2013).

Gurumurthy, Anita, and Parminder Jeet Singh, 2012, "Reclaiming Development in the Information Society," *In Search of Economic Alternatives for Gender and Social Justice: Voices from India*, C. Wichterich (ed.), WIDE/ITforChange, Bangalore, India.

Guthrie, K. Kendall, and William H. Dutton, 1992, "The Politics of Citizen Access Technology: The Development of Public Information Utilities in Four Cities," *Policy Studies Journal*, vol. 20, issue 4, Winter: 574–597.

Habermas, Jürgen, 1996 [1968], "Technology and Science as 'Ideology'" in *The Habermas Reader*, W. Outhwaite (ed.), Cambridge UK: Polity Press: 53–65.

Habermas, Jürgen, 2001, *The Postnational Constellation: Political Essays*, Boston: MIT Press.

Hakken, David, 2003, *The Knowledge Landscapes of Cyberspace*, London: Routledge.

Hall, Stuart, 1996, "New Ethnicities" in *Stuart Hall: Critical Dialogues in Cultural Studies*, David Morley and K-H. Chen (eds.). London/New York: Routledge: 441–449.

Hamelink, Cees J., 1998, "The People's Communication Charter," *Development in Practice*, vol. 8, no. 1, February 1998: 68–74.

Handler, Joel F., 2002, "Commentary—Quiescence: The Scylla and Charybdis of Empowerment," in *Labouring Below the Line: The New Ethnography of Poverty, Low-Wage Work, and Survival in the Global Economy*, Frank Munger (ed.), New York: Russell Sage Foundation, 271–289.

Hansen, Lene, and Helen Nissenbaum, 2009, "Digital Disaster, Cyber Security, and the Copenhagen School," *International Studies Quarterly*, vol. 53, issue 4: 1155–1175.

Haraway, Donna J., 1990, "A Manifesto for Cyborgs: Science, Technology, and Socialist Feminism in the 1980's," in *Feminism/Postmodernism*, L. Nicholson (ed.), London/New York: Routledge,190–233.

Haraway, D. J. 1992, "The Promises of Monsters: A Regenerative Politics for Inappropriate/d Others," in *Cultural Studies*, L. Grossberg, C. Nelson, and P. A. Treichler (eds.), New York/London: Routledge: 295–337.

Haraway, Donna, J., 1997, *Modest_Witness@Second_Millennium.FemaleMan©_ Meets_ OncoMouse™: Feminism and Technoscience*, New York/London: Routledge.

Haraway, Donna J., 2003, *The Companion Species Manifesto: Dogs, People, and Significant Otherness*, Chicago: Prickly Paradigm Press.

Harding, Sandra, 1998, *Is Science Multicultural? Postcolonialisms, Feminisms, and Epistemologies*, Bloomington: Indiana University Press.

Hardt, Michael and Antonio Negri, 2000, *Empire*, Boston: Harvard University Press.

Harmon, Amy, 1998, "De missie van de Microsofties," NRC Handelsblad, May 30, 1998: Z6.

Harris, Tim, 2002, director and founder of *Real Change*, Seattle, interview with author at the Annual Conference of the North American Street Newspapers Association (NASNA), Boston, July 18, 2002.

Harris, Tim, 2012, executive director and founder of *Real Change*, Seattle, Skype interview with author, October 31, 2012.

Harrison, Malcolm, 1999, "Theorising Homlessness and 'Race,'" in *Homelessness: Exploring the New Terrain*, Patricia Kennett and Alex Marsh (eds.), Bristol, UK: The Policy Press, 101–122.

Hartman, Chester W., 2002, *Between Eminence and Notoriety: Four Decades of Radical Urban Planning*, New Brunswick, NJ, Centre for Urban Policy Research.

Harvey, Brian, 1999, "Models of Resettlement for the Homeless in the European Union," in *Homelessness: Exploring the New Terrain*, Patricia Kennett and Alex Marsh (eds.), Bristol, UK, The Policy Press, 267–292.

Harvey, David, 1990, *The Condition of Postmodernity: An Enquiry into the Origins of Cultural Change*, Cambridge, MA/Oxford, UK: Blackwell.

Harvey, David, 2005, *A Brief History of Neoliberalism*, New York/London: Oxford University Press.

Hauser, Gerard A., 1999, *Vernacular Voices: The Rhetoric of Publics and Public Spheres*, Columbia, South Carolina: University of South Carolina Press.

Hawkins, Richard, 1996, "Standards for Communication Technologies: Negotiating Institutional Biases in Network Design," in *Communication by Design: The Politics of Information and Communication Technologies*, Robin Mansell and Roger Silverstone (eds.), New York: Oxford University Press: 157–186.

Hawtin, Dixie, 2011, "Internet Charters and Principles: Trends and Insights" in *Global Information Society Watch 2011*, South Africa: APC and Hivos: 51–54.

Hayles, Katherine, 1999, *How We Became Posthuman: Virtual Bodies in Cybernetics, Literature and Informatics*. Chicago: University of Chicago Press.

Healy, Hazel, 2012, "Internet showdown: Why Digital Freedom Matters—to Us All," *New Internationalist*, December, issue 458, http://newint.org/features/2012/12/01/open-source-digital-freedom-keynote/ (accessed February 18, 2013).

Henwood F., G. Hughes, H. Kennedy, N. Miller, and S. Wyatt, 2001, "Cyborg Lives in Context: Writing Women's Technobiographies," in F. Henwood, H. Kennedy, and N. Miller (eds.), *Cyborg Lives: Women's Technobiographies*, York: Raw Nerve Books, 11–34.

Highmore, Ben (ed.), 2002a, *The Everyday Life Reader*. London/New York: Routledge.

Highmore, Ben, 2002b, *Everyday Life and Cultural Theory: An Introduction*. London/New York: Routledge.

Highmore, Ben (ed.), 2003, *The Certeau Reader*, Oxford: Blackwell Publishers.

Hill, Matt, 2005, "For New York's Homeless, A Chance to Reach Their Goals," Healthy Living NYC, August 6, 2005, http://www.healthylivingnyc.com/article/162 (accessed March 24, 2013).

Hine, Christine, 2000, *Virtual Ethnography*. London: SAGE publications.

Hislop, Dominic, 1998, "Homeless Project" in *Border Economies*, http://www.moneynations.ch/topics/border/text/hislop.htm (accessed July 16, 2013).

Hobsbaum, Eric, 1983, "Introduction: Inventing: 1.14Traditions," in *The Invention of Tradition*, Eric Hobsbaum and Terence Ranger (eds.), Cambridge, UK: Cambridge University Press: 1–14.

Holmes, Brian, 2007, "Future Map or How the Cyborgs Learned to Stop Worrying and Learned to Love Surveillance," in the *Continental Drift: The Other Side of Neoliberal Globalization* Blog, http://brianholmes.wordpress.com/2007/09/09/future-map/ (accessed April 22, 2009).

Horkheimer, M., and T. W. Adorno, 2002 [1944], *Dialectic of Enlightenment: Philosophical Fragments*, E. Jephcott (trans.), Stanford, CA: Stanford University Press.

Hovarth, Mark, 2012, "Adventures of a Once Homeless Girl: Nadia Gomos," *Huffington Post*: The Blog, July 22, 2012, http://www.huffingtonpost.com/mark-horvath/a-once-homeless-girl_b_1693612.html?utm_hp_ref=impact (accessed March 31, 2013).

Howley, Keith, 2005, *Community Media: People, Places, and Communication Technologies*, New York: Columbia University Press.

Inda, Jonathan Xavier, 2000, "A Flexible World: Capitalism, Citizenship, and Postnational Zones," PoLAR, vol. 23, no. 1: 86–102.

Inda, Jonathan Xavier, and R. Rosaldo, 2002, "Introduction: A World in Motion," in *The Anthropology of Globalisation: A Reader*, J. X. Inda and R. Rosaldo (eds.), Oxford, UK: Blackwell Publishers, 1–36.

INSP, 2012, "World's First Digital Street Paper Launches in UK," INSP News Service, October 24, 2012, http://www.streetnewsservice.org/news/2012/october/feed-352/world%E2%80%99s-first-digital-street-paper-launches-in-uk.aspx (accessed February 15, 2013).

International Service for Human Rights (ISHR), 2011, "Special Rapporteur on Freedom of Expression Discusses Internet Access with General Assembly," November 11, 2011, http://www.ishr.ch/general-assembly/1198-special-rapporteur-on-freedom-of-expression-slams-use-of-sophisticated-tactics-to-censor-internet-co?utm_source=IS HR+Publications+and+News&utm_campaign=d93829efb3-RSS_Email_Campaign_General_Assembly&utm_medium=email (accessed February 17, 2013).

International Telecommunications Union, 2013, *ICT Data and Statistics*, http://www.itu.int/ti/industryoverview/index.htm (accessed March 14, 2013).

Internet Governance Forum, 2008, *Chairman's Summary*, Third Meeting of the United Nations Internet Governance Forum, Hyderabad, India, December 3–6, 2008, http://www.intgovforum.org/cms/2008-igf-hyderabad (accessed January 7, 2013).

Internet Governance Forum, 2011, *What Is the Internet Governance Forum?* Background Note: Internet Governance Forum: Nairobi, September 23–27, 2011, http://www.intgovforum.org/cms/2011/press/Backgrounder_What_is_IGF_final.doc (accessed February 22, 2013).

Internet Rights and Principles Coalition, 2013a, homepage, http://internetrightsandprinciples.org/ (accessed March 23, 2013).

Internet Rights and Principles Coalition, 2013b, "Unesco Wsis + 10: Report From The IRP Coalition Session 51," IRP Coalition Homepage, http://internetrightsandprinciples.org/site/unesco-wsis-10-report-from-the-irp-coalition-session-51/ (accessed April 2, 2013).

Internet World Stats, 2012, *Internet Usage Statistics—The Internet Big Picture: World Internet Users and Population Stats*, http://www.internetworldstats.com/stats.htm (accessed November 30, 2012).

Introna, Lucas D., and Helen Nissenbaum, 2000, "Shaping the Web: Why the Politics of Search Engines Matter," *The Information Society*, vol. 16, no. 3: 169–186.

Iosifidis, Petros, 2011, *Global Media and Communication Policy*. London/New York: Palgrave Macmillan.

ITU/WSIS, 2003a, *Declaration of Principles: Building the Information Society: A Global Challenge in the new Millennium*, Document WSIS-03/GENEVA/DOC/4-E, 2003, http://www.itu.int/wsis/docs/geneva/official/dop.html (accessed March 29, 2013).

ITU/WSIS, 2003b, *Plan of Action*, Document WSIS-03/GENEVA/DOC/5-E, December 2003, http://www.itu.int/wsis/docs/geneva/official/poa.html (accessed March 29, 2013).

ITU/WSIS, 2005a, *Political Chapeau/Tunis Commitment*, http://www.itu.int/wsis/docs2/pc2/off3.html (accessed March 29, 2013).

ITU/WSIS, 2005b, *Tunis Agenda for the Information Society*, WSIS-05/TUNIS/DOC/6 (Rev. 1)-E, November 18, 2005, http://www.itu.int/wsis/docs2/tunis/off/6rev1.html (accessed February 22, 2013).

Jameson, Fredric, 1984, "Postmodernism or the Cultural Logic of Late Capitalism," in *New Left Review* 146: 53–93.

Jameson, Fredric, 2005, *Archaeologies of the Future: The Desire Called Utopia and Other Science Fictions*. London/New York: Verso.

Jole, Francisco van, 1998, "De ongrijpbare vijand van Microsoft," in de Volkskrant, Amsterdam, The Netherlands, November 4, 1998: 35.

Jole, Francisco van, 2004, "*Lente op internet*," de Volkskrant, Amsterdam, The Netherlands, March 6: 1M.

Jones, Steven G., 1991, "The Internet and its Social Landscape," in *Virtual Culture: Identity and Communication in Cybersociety*, Steven G. Jones (ed.), London: SAGE Publications, 7–35.

Jongeneel, Christian, 1998, "*Software kan wel een keurslijf gebruiken*," in de Volkskrant, Amsterdam, The Netherlands, October 31: 5W.

Jongeneel, Christian, 2003, "Slimme virussen komen eraan," de Volkskrant, Amsterdam, The Netherlands, February 8: 3W.

Jordan, Tim, 1999, *Cyberpower*, London/New York: Routledge.

Jørgensen, Rikke F (ed.), 2006, *Human Rights in the Global Information Society*, Cambridge, MA: MIT Press.

Jurgenson, Nathan, 2012, "The IRL Fetish," *The New Inquiry*, June 28, http://thenewinquiry.com/essays/the-irl-fetish/ (accessed December 3, 2012).

Kahin, Brian, and James Keller (eds.), 1996, *Public Access to the Internet*, Cambridge, MA: MIT Press.

Kahn, R., and Douglas Kellner, 2007, "Globalization, Technopolitics, and Radical Democracy," in *Radical Democracy and the Internet: Interrogating Theory and Practice*, L. Dahlberg and E. Siapera (eds.), London/New York: Palgrave Macmillan, 17–36.

Karim, Karim H., 2003, "Mapping Diasporic Mediascapes," in *The Media of Diaspora*, K. H. Karim (ed.), London/New York: Routledge, 1–17.

Kehoe, Louise, 1999, "Microsoft raises the stakes in global software contest," Financial Times Survey: Information Technology, *Financial Times*, 11.

Kelly, K., 1994, *Out of Control: The New Biology of Machines, Social Systems, and the Economic World*, New York: Addison-Wesley Publishing.

Kennedy, Pagan, 2011, "The Cyborg in Us All," *New York Times Magazine*, September 14, 2011, http://www.nytimes.com/2011/09/18/magazine/the-cyborg-in-us-all.html?_r=0 (accessed March 17, 2013).

Kennett, Patricia, 1999, "Homelessness, Citizenship and Social Exclusion," in *Homelessness: Exploring the New Terrain*, Patricia Kennett and Alex Marsh (eds.), Bristol, UK: The Policy Press, 37–60.

Kennett, Patricia, and Alex Marsh, (eds.), 1999, *Homelessness: Exploring the New Terrain*, Bristol, UK: The Policy Press.

Kennett, Patricia, and Alex Marsh, 1999, "Exploring the New Terrain," in *Homelessness: Exploring the New Terrain*, Patricia Kennett and Alex Marsh (eds.), Bristol, UK: The Policy Press, 1–16.

Kern, Rafael, 2012, "Marco Civil: Old Politics Strikes Back," *Access* Blog, November 29, 2012, https://www.accessnow.org/blog/2012/11/29/marco-civil-old-politics-strikes-back (accessed December 14, 2012).

Kerr, Daniel, 2003, "'We Know What the Problem Is': Using Oral History to Develop a Collaborative Analysis of Homelessness from the Bottom Up," *The Oral History Review* vol. 30, no. 1: 27–45.

Keulemans, Maarten, 2011, Bureaucomputers en laptops verdwijnen, interview with Djam Khoe in: De Volkskrant, Amsterdam, The Netherlands, July 26, 2011: 14.

Kilbourn, R. J. A., [2000] 2008, "Re-Writing 'Reality': Reading *The Matrix*" in *Cultural Studies: An Anthology*, M. Ryan and H. Musiol (eds.), Mulden, MA/Oxford, UK: Blackwell Publishing, 1034–1043.

Kleinsteuber, Hans J. (ed.), 1996, *Der "Information Superhighway": Amerikanische Visionen und Erfahrungen*, Germany: Westdeutscher Verlag.

Knebel, Patricia, 2011, "Brazil: Congress Debates Civil Rights Framework for the Internet," *Infosurhoy.com*, October 5, 2011, http://infosurhoy.com/cocoon/saii/xhtml/en_GB/features/saii/features/main/2011/10/05/feature-01 (accessed February 17, 2013).

Knipfel, Jim, 2000, "Teaching the Homeless to Fish," *New York Press*, August 8, 2000, http://nypress.com/teaching-the-homeless-to-fish/ (accessed October 29, 2012).

Kolko, Beth, Lisa Nakamura, and G. B. Rodman, 2000, *Race in Cyberspace*, New York/London: Routledge.

Kraaijeveld, Kees, 2001, "*Wij zijn CISCO: verzet is zinloos*" in Volkskrant Magazine, no. 82, March 24, 2001, de Volkskrant, Amsterdam, The Netherlands: 46–53.

Kramer, Eric Mark, and Lee Soobum, 1991, "Homelessness: The Other as Object:" in *Reading the Homeless: The Media's Image of Homeless Culture*, Eungjun Min (ed.), Westport, CT/London: Praeger Publishers: 135–158.

Kuhn, Thomas, 1962, *The Structure of Scientific Revolutions*. Chicago: University of Chicago Press.

Küpfer, Sandra, 1998, "We worden niet dommer maar slimmer: Gesprek met cyberdelicus Douglas Rushkoff," NRC Handelsblad, Cultureel Supplement, February 27, 1998: CS3.

Kushnick, Bruce, 2012, "'Internet Freedom'? AT&T's Verbal Jujitsu to Close Down Telecommunications in America," *Huffington Post*, September 10, 2012, http://www.huffingtonpost.com/bruce-kushnick/internet-freedom-att_b_1869358.html (accessed December 26, 2012).

Laclau, Ernesto, and Mouffe Chantal, 1985, *Hegemony and Socialist Strategy: Towards a Radical Democratic Politics*, London/New York: Verso.

Lacroix, Guy, 1998, *"Cybernétique et Société Norbert Wiener ou les déboires d'une pensée subversive"* in Terminal No. 61, Paris, l'Harmattan.

Landzelius, Kyra (ed.), 2006, *Native on the Net: Indigenous and Diasporic Peoples in the Virtual Age*. London/New York: Routledge.

La Rue, Frank, 2011, *Report of the Special Rapporteur on the Promotion and Protection of the Right to Freedom of Opinion and Expression*. Human Rights Council: UN General Assembly, A/HRC/17/27, May 16, 2011, http://www2.ohchr.org/english/bodies/hrcouncil/docs/17session/A.HRC.17.27_en.pdf (accessed February 15, 2013).

Latour, Bruno, 1988, *Science in Action: How to follow Scientists and Engineers through Society*, Boston: Harvard University Press.

Latour, Bruno, 2007, "Beware, your imagination leaves digital traces," *Times Higher Literary Supplement*, April 6, 2007, http://docs.google.com/View?docid=ad6vvc428w8_103gzv2fdgf (accessed April 23, 2009).

Latour, Bruno, 2012, "Avoir ou ne pas avoir de réseau: that's the question" in *Débordements: Mélanges offerts à Michel Callon*, Madeleine Akrich et al. (eds.), Paris: Presses de l'Ecole des Mines, 2010: 257–268.

Lazuly, P., 2003, "Le monde selon Google," *Le Monde diplomatique*, November, 2003: http://www.monde-diplomatique.fr/2003/10/LAZULY/10471 (accessed March 31, 2013).

Le Crosnier, H., 2008, "Mouvements tectoniques sur la Toile," in *Le Monde Diplomatique*, March 2008: http://www.monde-diplomatique.fr/2008/03/LE_CROSNIER/15673 (accessed March 31, 2013).

Lefebvre, Henri, 1991 (1947), *The Critique of Everyday Life*, vol. 1, John Moore (trans.), London: Verso.

Lemos, A., 1996, "The Labyrinth of Minitel," in Rob Shields (ed.), *Cultures of Internet: Virtual Spaces, Real Histories, Living Bodies*, London, Thousand Oaks, New Delhi: SAGE Publications: 33–48.

Lenin, Vladimir Ilyich, 1902, "What Is to Be Done? Burning Questions of our Movement," in *Lenin's Collected Works*, vol. 5, Joe Fineberg and George Hanna (trans.), Foreign Languages Publishing House, 1961, Moscow: 347–530.

Lessig, Lawrence, 2006, *Code and Other Laws of Cyberspace, Version 2.0*, New York: Basic Books.

Lewis, Justin, 2001, *Constructing Public Opinion: How Political Elites Do What They Like and Why We Seem to Go Along With It*, New York: Columbia University Press.

Lievrouw, Leah, 2011, *Alternative and Activist Media*, Oxford UK: Polity Press.

Ligtenberg, Lucas, 1998, "Onbedoelde gevolgen van deregulering," *NRC Handelsblad*, woensdag, June 20, 1998: 18.

Lind, Rebecca Ann, and James A. Danowski, 1991, "The Representation of the Homeless in U.S. Electronic Media: A Computational Linguistic Analysis" in *Reading the Homeless: The Media's Image of Homeless Culture*, Eungjun Min (ed.), Westport, CT/ London, Praeger Publishers: 109–120.

Lippmann, Walter, 1993 [1927] *The Phantom Public*. New Brunswick, NJ: Transaction.

Lipschutz, Ronnie D., 2005, *Globalization, Governmentality and Global Politics: Regulation for the rest of us?*, with James K. Rowe. London/New York: Routledge.

Llansó, Emma, 2012, "ITU: Internet Governance or Just Governing the Internet?" Centre for Democracy and Technology, June 28, 2012: https://www.cdt.org/blogs/emma-llanso/2806itu-internet-governance-or-just-governing-internet (accessed December 6, 2012).

Lovink, Geert, 2003, *Dark Fiber: Tracking Critical Internet Culture*, Boston: MIT Press, 2003.

Lovink, Geert, 2012, *Networks without a Cause: A Critique of Social Media*. Oxford UK: Polity Press.

Lunenfeld, Peter (ed.), 2000, *The Digital Dialectic: New Essays on New Media*. Cambridge, MA: MIT Press.

Lüthje, Boy, 1997, "*Transnationale Dimensionen der 'network revolution'*" in *Europsische Telekommunikation im Zeitalter der Deregulierung: Infrastruktur im Umbruch*, edited by Jossef Esser, Boy Lüthje, Roland Noppe, Duitsland: Westfslisches Dampfboot: 36–77.

MacBride, Sean, (ed.), 1980, *Many Voices, One World: Towards a New more just and more efficient world information and communication order*, report by the International Commission for the Study of Communication Problems, UNESCO, 1980.

Madden, Marion, Sandra Cortesi, Urs Gasser, Amanda Lenhart, and Maeve Duggan, 2012, "Parents, Teens, and Online Privacy" Report for the *Pew Internet and American Life Project*, November 20, 2012, http://www.pewinternet.org/Reports/2012/Teens-and-Privacy/Summary-of-Findings.aspx (accessed November 30, 2012).

Madrigal, Alexis C., 2012, "Dark Social: We Have the Whole History of the Web Wrong," *The Atlantic*, October 12, 2012, http://www.theatlantic.com/technology/archive/2012/10/dark-social-we-have-the-whole-history-of-the-web-wrong/263523/ (accessed October 12, 2012).

Maggio, J., 2007, "Can the subaltern be heard?: Political Theory, Translation, Representation, and Gayatri Chakravorty Spivak," *Alternatives: Global, Local, Political*, October: 419–443.

Mandiberg, Michael, (ed.), 2012, *The Social Media Reader*, New York and London: New York University Press.

Manière de voir, 1995, *Médias et contrôle des esprits*, no. 27, August, Paris, France: *Le Monde Diplomatique*.

Manière de voir, 1996, *Internet: l'extase et l'effroi*, Hors-Série, October. Paris, France: *Le Monde Diplomatique*.

Mansell, Robin, and Roger Silverstone (eds.), 1996, *Communication by Design: The Politics of Information and Communication Technologies*, New York: Oxford University Press.

Mansell, Robin, and U. Wehn, 1998, *Knowledge Societies: Information Technology for Sustainable Development*, United Nations/Oxford: Oxford University Press.

Marcus, George E, 1995, "Ethnography in/of the World System: The Emergence of Multi–Sited Ethnography" in Annual Review of Anthropology, vol. 24: 95–117.

Marres, Noortje, and Richard Rogers, 2005, "Recipe for Tracing the Fate of Issues and Their Publics on the Web," in *Making Things Public*, Bruno Latour and Peter Weibel (eds.), Karlsruhe/Cambridge: ZKM/MIT Press.

Marzouki, Meryem, 2009, Privacy Issues with EU Law Enforcement Cooperation Developments, European Digital Rights statement at the *Public Voice Conference: Global Privacy Standards in a Global World*, November 3, 2009, Madrid, Spain, http://www.edri.org/files/Presentation_Meryem_EDRi_civil_society.pdf (accessed March, 23 2010),

Maslow, A. H., 1943, "A Theory of Human Motivation," *Psychological Review*, 50: 370–396.

Mathieu, Paula, 2002, interview with author at the Annual Conference of the North American Street Newspapers Association (NASNA), Boston, 2002.

Mattelart, Armand, 1994, *Mapping World Communication: War, Progress, Culture*, Minneapolis: University of Minnesota Press.

Mattelart, Armand, 1995, *"Une éternelle promesse: les paradis de la communication"* in *Le Monde Diplomatique*, Paris, France: Le Monde Diplomatique, November 1995: 4–5.

Mattelart, Armand, 2007, "Le champ de la communication: Qui contrôle le concepts?" in *Le Monde Diplomatique*. Paris: Le Monde Diplomatique. vol. 54. no. 641. August: 23.

Mattelart, Armand, and Costas Constantinou, 2008, *Communications/excommunications: an interview with Armand Mattelart*. Fifth Estate Online: http://www.fifth-estate-online.co.uk/comment/Mattelart-intervie%5B1%5D.pdf (accessed December 1, 2012).

May, Christopher, 2009, *The Global Political Economy of Intellectual Property Rights, 2nd edition: The New Enclosures*, London/New York: Routledge,

McChesney, R., E. Wood, and J. Foster (eds.), 1998, *Capitalism and the Information Age: The Political Economy of the Global Communication Revolution*, New York: Monthly Review Press.

McHaffie, Patrick, 1997 "Decoding the globe: globalism, advertising, and corporate practice" in *Environment and Planning D: Society and Space* 1987, vol 15: 73–86,

McLuhan, Marshall, 2001 (1964), *Understanding Media: The Extensions of Man*, London/ New York: Routledge.

McLuhan, Marshall, and Bruce R. Powers, 1989, *The Global Village: Transformations in World Life and Media in the 21st Century*, Oxford: Oxford University Press.

McLuhan, Marshall, and Quentin Fiore, 1967, *The Medium Is the Massage: An Inventory of Effects*, New York: Bantam Paperbacks.

Meert, Henk, and Karen Stuyck, 2008, "Homelessness, Post-Fordist Solidarity and Disciplining Urbanism," *In My Caravan I Feel like Superman: Essays in Honour of Henk Meert 1963-2006*, Joe Doherty and Bill Edgar (eds.), FEANTSA and Centre for Housing Research, St. Andrews: Scotland, 145–169.

Meert, Henk, Karen Stuyck, Pedro José, Cabrera Evelyn, Dyb Masa, Filipovic Györi, Péter Ilja Hradecký, Marie Loison, and Roland Mass, 2008, "The Changing Profiles of Homeless People: Conflict, Rooflessness and the Use of Public Space," *In My Caravan I Feel like Superman: Essays in Honour of Henk Meert 1963-2006*, Joe Doherty and Bill Edgar (eds.), FEANTSA and Centre for Housing Research, St. Andrews: Scotland, 170–206.

Melber, Ari, 2012, "Why Graph Search Could Be Facebook's Largest Privacy Invasion Ever," *The Nation*, January 27, http://www.thenation.com/blog/172459/

why–graph–search–could–be–facebooks–largest–privacy–invasion–ever# (accessed February 10, 2013).

Mendel, Toby, Andrew Puddephatt, Ben Wagner, Dixie Hawtin, and Natalia Torres, 2012, *Global Survey on Internet Privacy and Freedom of Expression*, UNESCO Series on Internet Freedom, Paris: UNESCO.

Mendoza, Nicolás, 2011, "A Tale of Two Worlds: Apocalypse, 4Chan, WikiLeaks and the Silent Protocol Wars," in *Radical Philosophy*, no. 166, March/April: 2–8.

Michael, Kilburn, 1996, "Spivak, Gayatri Chakravorty: Glossary of Key terms in Spivak's work," in *Postcolonial Studies@ Emory: Critics and Theorists*, http://postcolonialstudies. emory.edu/gayatri-chakravorty-spivak/ (accessed February 14, 2013).

Mickey, Z., 2006, "Street News and NYC's Homeless: An Interview with John 'Indio' Washington," January 31, *Monthly Review Zine*, http://mrzine.monthlyreview. org/2006/mickeyz310106.html (accessed March 25, 2013).

Miller, Daniel, and Don Slater, 2000, *The Internet: An Ethnographic Approach*, Oxford: Berg.

Millward, Stephen, 2012, "Now With Over 1 Billion Netizens, This Is How Asia Is Social and Mobile in 2012," *TechinAsia*, http://www.techinasia.com/asia-social-mobile-infographic-2012/ (accessed November 30, 2012).

Min, Fungjun, (ed.), 1999, *Reading the Homeless: The Media's Image of Homeless Culture*, London: Praeger Publishers.

Minton, Anna, 2006, *What Kind of World Are We Building? The Privatization of Public Space*, Report for RICS, http://www.annaminton.com/Current_Projects.htm (accessed October 29, 2012).

Miriri, Duncan, 2011, "Europe plans charter to safeguard Internet users," Reuters, September 27, 2011, http://www.reuters.com/article/2011/09/27/us-internet-governance-europe-idUSTRE78Q3RP20110927 (accessed February 17, 2013).

Mitter, Swasti, and Sheila Rowbotham (eds.), 1995, *Women Encounter Technology*. London/New York: Routledge and UNU Press.

Morozov, Evgeny, 2011, *Net Delusion: The Dark Side of Internet Freedom*, Philadelphia, PA: Perseus Books.

Mueller, Milton, 2002, *Ruling the Root: Internet Governance and the Taming of Cyberspace*, Boston MA: MIT Press.

Mueller, Milton, 2010, *Networks and States: The Global Politics of Internet Governance*, Boston MA: MIT Press.

Mueller, Milton, 2012, "Threat analysis of WCIT part 2: Telecommunications vs. Internet," *Internet Governance Project*, June 7, 2012, http://www.internetgovernance. org/2012/06/07/threat-analysis-of-wcit-part-2-telecommunications-vs-internet/ (accessed November 30, 2012).

Munger, Frank, (ed.), 2002, *Labouring Below the Line: The New Ethnography of Poverty, Low-Wage Work, and Survival in the Global Economy*, New York: Russell Sage Foundation.

Munger, Frank, 2002, "Conclusion: Democratising Poverty," in *Labouring Below the Line: The New Ethnography of Poverty, Low-Wage Work, and Survival in the Global Economy*, Frank Munger (ed.), New York: Russell Sage Foundation, 290–312.

Munger, Frank, 2002, "Identity as a Weapon in the Moral Politics of Work and Poverty," in *Labouring Below the Line: The New Ethnography of Poverty, Low-Wage Work, and Survival in the Global Economy*, Frank Munger (ed.), New York: Russell Sage Foundation, 1–28.

Murray, Andrew, 2010, "A Bill of Rights for the Internet," *The IT Lawyer Blog*, October 21, http://theitlawyer.blogspot.de/2010/10/bill-of-rights-for-internet.html (accessed February 17, 2013).

Musiani, Francesca, 2009, "The Internet Bill of Rights: A Way to Reconcile Natural Freedoms and Regulatory Needs?" *SCRIPTed–A Journal of Law, Technology and Society*, vol. 6, issue 2, August, http://www.law.ed.ac.uk/ahrc/script–ed/vol6–2/musiani.asp (accessed March 31, 2013).

NASNA (North American Street Newspaper Association), 2013, *Home: What Is NASNA?* http://www.nasna.org/ (accessed March 24, 2013).

NASNA, 2013b, *Vision and Values*, http://www.nasna.org/about/vision–values/ (accessed March 24, 2013).

National Alliance to End Homelessness, 2013, *About Homelessness: Snapshot of Homelessness*, http://www.endhomelessness.org/pages/snapshot_of_homelessness (accessed February 15, 2013).

National Coalition for the Homeless (NCH), 2002, "Poverty vs. Pathology: What's 'Chronic' About Homelessness?," http://nationalhomeless.org/publications/chronic/full.html (accessed February 14, 2013).

National Coalition for the Homeless (NCH), 2003, "Illegal to be Homeless: The Criminalization of Homelessness in the United States," Report from the National Coalition for the Homeless and the National Law Center on Homelessness and Poverty, http://www.nationalhomeless.org/publications/crimreport/index.html (accessed February 14, 2013).

National Coalition for the Homeless (NCH), 2009a, "Foreclosure to Homelessness 2009: the Forgotten Victims of the Subprime Crisis," Report for the National Coalition for the Homeless, http://nationalhomeless.org/publications/index.html (accessed February 14, 2013).

National Coalition for the Homeless (NCH), 2009b, "How many People Experience Homelessness?" *Fact Sheets*, National Coalition for the Homeless, http://nationalhomeless.org/factsheets/How_Many.html (accessed February 14, 2013).

National Coalition for the Homeless (NCH), 2009c, "Who Is Homeless?" Fact Sheets: National Coalition for the Homeless, http://nationalhomeless.org/factsheets/who.html (accessed Febuary 14, 2013).

National Coalition for the Homeless (NCH), 2012, *Hate Crimes against the Homeless Violence Hidden in Plain View*, January 2012, www.nationalhomeless.org/publications/hatecrimes/hatecrimes2010.pdf (accessed July 16, 2013).

Naughton, John, 2010, "The Future of Facebook," *The Observer*, March 14, http://www.guardian.co.uk/technology/2010/mar/14/facebook-john-naughton-the-networker (accessed March 23, 2010).

New America Foundation, 2012, "Who Should Govern the Internet?" *Future Tense*, November 29, 2012, http://newamerica.net/events/2012/who_should_govern_the_internet (accessed December 6, 2012).

New Relic Blog, 2012, "Browser Wars: A New Installment of our Ongoing Series on Browser Speed," http://blog.newrelic.com/2012/11/06/browser–wars–a–new–installment–of–our–ongoing–series–on–browser–speed/?utm_source=BLOG&utm_medium=content&utm_content=110612&utm_campaign=RPM&utm_term=WhichOneIstheFastest&mpc=CN–BLOG–RPM–EN–100–BrowserWars–WhichOneIstheFastest (accessed November 30, 2012).

Nightingale, Carl H., 2002, "Looking For Stories of Inner–City Politics: From the Personal to the Global," in *Labouring Below the Line: The New Ethnography of Poverty, Low-Wage Work, and Survival in the Global Economy*, Frank Munger (ed.), New York: Russell Sage Foundation, 111–121.

NRC Handelsblad, 1996, *"Drieduizend banen weg bij mijlardenfusie Babybells*," April 23, 1996, The Netherlands: 18.

NRC Handelsblad, 1997a, "Een software oorlog," in *Dossier Microsoft*, NRC Handelsblad, February 5, http://retro.nrc.nl/W2/Lab/Microsoft/970225eco.html (accessed December 6, 2012).

NRC Handelsblad, 1997b, "Hegemonie Microsoft moeilijk te doorbreken," in *Dossier Microsoft*, NRC Handelsblad, November 20, http://retro.nrc.nl/W2/Lab/Microsoft/971120eco.html (accessed December 6, 2012).

NRC Handelsblad, 1997, "Microsoft op zere tenen," *Dossier Microsoft*, NRC Handelsblad, December 31, 1997: http://retro.nrc.nl/W2/Lab/Microsoft/971231eco.html (accessed December 6, 2012).

NRC Handelsblad, 1998, *"Slag voor KPN Telecom: Alliantie van BT en AT&T in telecom*," July 27, The Netherlands: NRC Handelsblad, 9.

NRC Handelsblad, 1999, "Goliath Gates," in *Dossier Microsoft*, NRC Handelsblad, November 8, http2012://retro.nrc.nl/W2/Lab/Microsoft/991108b.html (accessed December 6, 2012).

NRC Handelsblad, 2000, *Dossier Microsoft*, 1 NRC Handelsblad, August 2, http://retro.nrc.nl/W2/Lab/Microsoft/inhoud (accessed December 6, 2012).

NRC Handelsblad, 2002a, "Rechter VS geeft Microsoft gelijk," November 2: 1.

NRC Handelsblad, 2002b, "Overheid wil pc bevrijden," NRC Handelsblad: Economie, November 21, http://archief.nrc.nl/index.php/2002/November/21/Economie/15/Overheid+wil+pc+bevrijden/check=Y (accessed December 6, 2012).

Nunez, Ralph da Costa, 1994, *The New Poverty: Homeless Families in America*, New York/London: Insight Books, Plenum Press.

Nye, Joseph S., Jr., 2002, "The Information Revolution and American Soft Power," *Asia Pacific Review*, vol. 9, no. 1, May 2002: 60–76.

OECD, 1997, "Special Issue on Information Infrastructures," *STI Review*, vol. 1997, issue 1, http://www.oecd-ilibrary.org/science-and-technology/sti-science-technology-and-industry-review/volume-1997/issue-1_sti_rev-v1997-1-en (accessed February 10, 2013).

OECD, 2000, *Information Technology Outlook 2000: ICTs, E-commerce and the Information Economy*, Paris: OECD.

OECD, 2001, *Understanding the Digital Divide*, Paris: OECD.

OECD, 2011, *OECD Council Recommendation on Principles for Internet Policy Making*, December 13, Paris: OECD, www.oecd.org/internet/ieconomy/49258588.pdf (accessed March 28, 2013).

Ogles, Jacob, 2006, "Laptops Give Hope to the Homeless," WIRED, June 26, http://www.wired.com/science/discoveries/news/2006/06/71153 (accessed October 26, 2012).

Olesen, Thomas (ed.), 2010, *Power and Transnational Activism*, London: Routledge.

O'Neil, Mathieu, 2009, *Cyberchiefs: Autonomy and Authority in Online Tribes*, New York/London: Pluto Press.

Ong, Aihwa, 1999, *Flexible Citizenship: The Cultural Logics of Transnationality*, Durham, NC: Duke University Press.

O'Reilly, Tim, 2012, "What Is Web 2.0? Design Patterns and Business Models for the Next Generation of Software," in *The Social Media Reader*, Michael Mandiville (ed.), New York: New York University Press, 32–50.

O'Toole, Thomas, 2012, "ITU's Toure: WCIT Talks Are Not About Internet Governance," Bloomberg BNA: E-Commerce and Tech Law Blog, September 11, http://www.bna.com/itus-toure-wcit-b17179869586/ (accessed February 22, 2013).

Papacharissi, Zizi A., 2010, *A Private Sphere: Democracy in a Digital Age*, Oxford, UK: Polity Press.

Passaro, Joanne, 1996, *The Unequal Homeless: Men on the Streets*, Women in Their Place, New York/London, Routledge.

Pavement, The, 2013, *Rights Guide for Rough Sleepers*, London: Housing Justice, http://www.thepavement.org.uk/pdfs/rights-guide.pdf (accessed March 18, 2013).

Peterson, V. S., and Runyan, A. S., 1999, *Global Gender Issues*, 2nd ed., Dilemmas in World Politics Series, Oxford: Westview Press.

Pfeffer, Rachel, 1997, *Surviving The Streets: Girls Living on their Own*, New York: Garland Publishing.

Power, Gerard, 1999, "Media Image and the Culture of Homelessness: Possibilities for Identification" in Reading the Homeless: The Media's Image of Homeless Culture, Eungjun Min (ed.), London: Praeger Publishers: 65–84.

Prakash, Aseem, and Jeffrey A. Hart, 1999, "Globalization and Governance: An Introduction," in *Globalization and Governance*, Aseem Prakash and Jeffrey A. Hart (eds.), London/New York: Routledge, 1–24.

Price, Emily, 2012, "Austin's Homeless Become Controversial Wi–Fi Hotspots During SXSW [VIDEO]," Mashable.com, March 12, http://mashable.com/2012/03/12/homeless-hotspots-sxsw/?replytocom=18055403 (accessed December 12, 2012).

Public Voice Coalition, 2009, *The Madrid Privacy Declaration: Global Privacy Standards for a Global World*, 3 November, http://thepublicvoice.org/madrid-declaration/ (accessed March 23, 2010).

Quintas, Paul, 1996, "Software by Design," in *Communication by Design: The Politics of Information and Communication Technologies*, R. Mansell and R. Silverstone (eds.), Oxford: Oxford University Press: 75–102.

Raymond, Eric S., 2001, *The Cathedral and the Bazaar: Musings on Linux and Open Source by an Accidental Revolutionary*, Sebastopol, CA: O'Reilly Media.

Reeve-Lewis, Ben, 2012, "New homeless rules a 'profound and astonishing' shift in housing policy," *The Guardian*, October 26, http://www.guardian.co.uk/housing-network/2012/oct/26/council-homelessness-rules-housing-policy?CMP=twt_gu (accessed October 26, 2012).

Rheingold, Howard, 1994, "A Slice of Life in My Virtual Community," in Linda Harasim (ed.), *Global Networks: Computer Networks and International Communication*, Cambridge, MA: MIT Press, 57–80.

Richardson, James, 2010, "Food or Facebook for America's Homeless?," *Huffington Post*, December 17, http://www.huffingtonpost.com/james-richardson/food-or-facebook-for-amer_b_798179.html (accessed October 26, 2012).

Risen, Tom, 2012, "Copyright Driving US Internet Freedom Debate," *The Netizen Project*, July 20, http://netizenproject.org/2012/07/20/copyright-driving-us-internet-freedom-debate/ (accessed February 18, 2013).

Rogers, Richard (ed.), 2000, *Preferred Placement*, Maastricht: Jan van Eyck Akademie Editions.

Ronfeldt, D., and Varda, D., 2008, *The Prospect for Cyberocracy (Revisited)*, http://opensiuc.lib.siu.edu/cgi/viewcontent.cgi?article=1024&context=pn_wpShapiro (accessed September 14, 2012).

Rosen, Jay, 2012, "The People Formally Known as the Audience," in *The Social Media Reader*, Michael Mandiville (ed.), New York: New York University Press, 13–23.

Rosen, Jeffrey, 2012, "The Right To Be Forgotten," *Stanford Law Review*, February 13, 64. Stan. L. Rev. Online 88, http://www.stanfordlawreview.org/online/privacy-paradox/right-to-be-forgotten (accessed December 1, 2012).

Rosenfeld, Jona M. (ed.), 2000, *Artisans of Democracy: How Ordinary People, Families in Extreme Poverty, and Social Institutions become Allies to Overcome Social Exclusion*, Lanham, MD: University Press of America.

Ross, Andrew, 1995 (1997), "Science Backlash on Technoskeptics: 'Culture Wars' Spill Over," *The Nation*, October 2, http://www.thomson.com/routledge/cst/ross.html.

Rott, Nathan, 2010, "Homeless Man in D.C. Uses Facebook, Social Media to Advocate for Others Like Him," *Washington Post*, December 13, http://www.washingtonpost.com/wp-dyn/content/article/2010/12/12/AR2010121203509.html (accessed October 26, 2012).

Rupert, M., 2000, *Ideologies of Globalization: Contending Visions of a New World Order*, London/New York: Routledge.

Rushkoff, Douglas, 2001, "Virtuelles Marketing," in *Cyberhypes, Möglichkeiten und Grenzen des Internet*, Rudolf Maresch and Florian Rötzer (eds.), Frankfurt am Main, Edition Suhrkamp, 102–122.

Rushkoff, Douglas, 2010, *Program or Be Programmed: Ten Commandments for a Digital Age*, New York: OR Books.

Sachs, W., (ed.), 1993, *The Development Dictionary: A Guide to Knowledge as Power.* London: Zed Books.

Sackmann, Chris, and McKay, Stephen, 2003, "BIG News/Upward," Street Paper Focus Group: Spring 2003 Case Studies, Washington University: Seattle, http://depts.washington.edu/stnews/bignews.html (accessed October 29, 2012).

Sahlin, Ingrid, 2008, "Urban Definitions of Places and People," *In My Caravan I Feel like Superman: Essays in honour of Henk Meert 1963–2006*, Joe Doherty and Bill Edgar (eds.), FEANTSA and Centre for Housing Research, St Andrews: Scotland, 101–126.

San Francisco Chronicle, 2011, "Ted Williams, Homeless Internet Sensation, Offered Job by Cavaliers," January 5, http://www.sfgate.com/sports/article/Ted-Williams-Homeless-Internet-Sensation-2385329.php (accessed October 26, 2012).

Sassen, Saskia, 2002, "Commentary—Deconstructing Labour Demand in Today's Advanced Economies: Implications for Low–Wage Employment" in *Labouring Below the Line: The New Ethnography of Poverty, Low-Wage Work, and Survival in the Global Economy*, Frank Munger (ed.), New York: Russell Sage Foundation, 73–94.

Schiller, Dan, 1999, *Digital Capitalism: Networking the Global Market System*, Cambridge, MA: MIT Press.

Schmitz, Rob, 2010, "Former Homeless Man's Videos Profile Life On Street," *NPR Blog*, March 6, 2010, http://www.npr.org/templates/story/story.php?storyId=124356908 (accessed February 15, 2013).

Schneider, Barbara, 2012, "Blogging Homelessness: Technology of the Self or Practice of Freedom?" paper presentation: *Applying Foucault's Technologies of the Self to Web 2.0:*

Communication, Self and Online Community Panel: International Communications Association's Annual Conference, May 24–28, Phoenix.

Scholte, Jan–Aart, 2000, *Globalization: A Critical Introduction*, New York: St. Martins Press.

Scholte, Jan–Aart, 2002, "What is Globalization? The Definitional Issue—Again," *CSGR Working Paper*, no. 109/02, December. Coventry: University of Warwick, http://www2.warwick.ac.uk/fac/soc/csgr/research/workingpapers/2002/wp10902.pdf (accessed February 12, 2013).

Searles, Doc, 2008, "Understanding Infrastructure," *Linux Journal*, April 19, http://www.linuxjournal.com/content/understanding–infrastructure (accessed January 29, 2013).

Sennett, Richard, 2012, *Together: The Rituals, Pleasures, and Politics of Cooperation*, New Haven: Yale University Press.

Shachtman, Noah, 2009, "He Hacks by Day, Squats by Night," *Wired*, June 6, 2002, http://www.wired.com/culture/lifestyle/news/2002/03/50811 (accessed October 26, 2012).

Shah, Nishant, 2011, "Material Cyborgs, Asserted Boundaries," Centre for Internet and Society Blog, November7, http://cis–india.org/internet–governance/front–page/material–cyborgs–asserted–boundaries (accessed December 3, 2012).

Shapiro, Andrew L., 1999, *The Control Revolution: How the Internet is Putting Individuals in Charge and Changing the World We Know*, New York: Public Affairs—Perseus Books.

Shapiro, Michael J., 2004, *Methods and Nations: Cultural Governance and the Indigenous Subject*, London/New York: Routledge.

Sharples, Carinya, 2012, "How to Make the Homeless Visible," *The Guardian*, July 24, http://www.guardian.co.uk/society/2012/jul/24/homeless–visible–camera–video (accessed October 29, 2012).

Shelter, 2012, "Homeless Families in B&B's on the Rise," *Shelter News—Previous Years*, December 6, http://england.shelter.org.uk/news/previous_years/2012/december_2012/homeless_families_in_b_and_bs_on_the_rise (accessed February 14, 2013).

Shelter, 2013a, "Rising Rents leave a Generation Caught in the 'rent Trap'," *Shelter—News*, January 31, http://england.shelter.org.uk/news/january_2013/rising_rents_leave_a_generation_in_the_rent_trap (accessed February 14, 2013).

Shelter, 2013b, "Housing Costs Cause Stress and Depression for Millions," *Shelter—News*, January 17, http://england.shelter.org.uk/news/january_2013/housing_costs_cause_stress_and_depression_for_millions.

Shelter 2013c, *Homelessness: What is Homelessness?*, http://england.shelter.org.uk/get_advice/homelessness/what_is_homelessness (accessed February 15, 2013).

Shelter 2013d, *Downloads and Tools: Emergency housing rights checker*, http://england.shelter.org.uk/get_advice/downloads_and_tools/emergency_housing_rights_checker (accessed October 13, 2012).

Shields, Rob (ed.), 1996, *Cultures of Internet: Virtual Spaces, Real Histories, Living Bodies*, London: SAGE Publications.

Singh, J. P., 2012, "Towards Knowledge Societies in UNESCO and Beyond," in *From NWICO to WSIS: 30 Years of Communication Geopolitics*, Divina Frau-Meigs, Jérémie Nicey. MichaelPalmer, Julia Pohle, and Patricio Tupper (eds.), Bristol UK/Chicago: Intellect: 153–162.

Singh, Parminder Jeet, 2012a, "Hyping One Threat to Hide Another," *The Hindu*, November 28: http://www.thehindu.com/opinion/lead/hyping-one-threat-to-hide-another/article4140922.ece (accessed November 30, 2012).

Singh, Parminder Jeet, 2012b, "A false consensus is broken," *The Hindu*, 21 December, http://www.thehindu.com/opinion/lead/a-false-consensus-is-broken/article4222688.ece (accessed December 21, 2012).

Singh, Parminder Jeet, 2012c, *A Development Agenda in Internet Governance*, paper delivered to the Geneva South Centre, IT For Change, http://www.itforchange.net/ITfC_South_Centre_2012 (accessed February 17, 2013).

Sloterdijk, Peter, 2006, *Het kristalpaleis: een filosofie van de globalisering*, transl. Hans Driessen, Amsterdam: Uitgeverij Boom.

Smith, Rhona K. M., 2012, *Textbook on International Human Rights*, 5th ed., Oxford: Oxford University Press.

Solnit, Rebecca, 2013, "Diary: Google Invades," *London Review of Books*, vol. 35, no. 3, February 7: 34–35.

Song, Dong-Hyun, 2012a, "Power Struggles in Korean Cyberspace and Korean Cyber Asylum Seekers," *Cultural Policy, Criticism and Management Research*, no. 5, http://culturalpolicyjournal.org/past-issues/issue-no-5/power-struggles-in-korean-cyberspace/.

Song, Dong-Hyun, 2012b, Power Struggles in Korean Cyberspace and Korean Cyber Asylum Seekers. Doc. thesis, Goldsmiths, University of London, http://eprints.gold.ac.uk/8052/ (accessed July 16, 2013).

Souza, Carlos Affonso, 2012, "What's holding back Marco Civil, Brazil's internet bill of rights?," *Access Policy Team: Access Blog*, September 27, https://www.accessnow.org/blog/092712-whats-holding-back-marco-civil-brazils-internet-bill-of-rights/ (accessed February 17, 2013).

Spiller, Neill, 2002 (ed.), Cyber_Reader: Critical Writings for the Digital Era, London/New York: Phaidon Press.

Spivak, Gayatri, 1985, "Can the Subaltern Speak? Speculations on Widow-Sacrifice," *Wedge* 7–8 (Winter–Spring): 120–130.

Stalder, Felix, 2012, "Between Democracy and Spectacle: The Front–End and Back–End of the Social Web," in *The Social Media Reader*, Michael Mandiberg (ed.), New York: New York University Press: 242–256.

Stallabrass, Julian, 1995, "Empowering Technology: The Exploration of Cyberspace," in *New Left Review*, no. 211, May/June: 3–33.

Stallman, Richard, 2012 "GNU Operating System: Why Open Source misses the point of Free Software," *Free Software Foundation: Philosophy*, http://www.gnu.org/philosophy/open-source-misses-the-point.html (accessed March 7, 2013).

Standage, Tom, 1998, *The Victorian Internet: The Remarkable Story of the Telegraph and the Nineteenth Century's On-Line Pioneers*, New York: Berkley Books.

Stielstra, Theo, 2002, "Google geeft smoelende sites geen kans," de Volkskrant, Amsterdam, The Netherlands, December 5: 18.

Stoops, Michael, 2002, coordinator, NCH Street Newspapers Project, National Coalition for the Homeless (NCH), interview with the author, Washington DC, July 12, 2002.

Stoops, Michael, 2012, director of community organizing, National Coalition for the Homeless (NCH), Washington, DC, telephone interview with the author, August 15, 2012.

Stringer, Lee, 1998, *Grand Central Winter: Stories from the Street*, New York: Seven Stories Press.

Suri, Sanjay, 2008, "Media: Against Giant Odds, A Touch of Triumph," *Inter Press Service*, June 27, http://www.ipsnews.net/2008/06/media-against-giant-odds-a-touch-of-triumph/ (accessed October 29, 2012).

Swithinbank, Tessa, 2001, *Coming Up From the Streets: The Story of The Big Issue*. London: Earthscan.

Taglang, Kevin, 2001, A Low-Tech, Low-Cost Tool for the Homeless, *Digital Divide Network*, December 10, 2001; http://web.archive.org/web/20031224221827/http://www.digitaldividenetwork.org/content/stories/index.cfm?key=204 (accessed 1 August 2013).

Taylor, Paul, 1999a, "The Struggle for Survival in an IT-Dominated World," *Financial Times Survey: Information Technology, Part One*, March 3, I–XII.

Taylor, Paul, 1999b, "Linux Takes on the Software Giant," *Financial Times, Financial Times Survey: Information Technology*, June 2: I.

Thompson, John B., 1995, *The Media and Modernity: A Social Theory of the Media*, Cambridge/Oxford: Polity Press.

Tomlinson, John, 1999, *Globalization and Culture*, Cambridge/Oxford: Polity Press.

Torck, Danièle, 2001, "Voices of homeless people in street newspapers: a cross-cultural exploration," *Discourse and Society*, vol. 12, no. 3: 371–392.

Tosi, Antonio, 2007, "Homelessness and the Control of Public Space—Criminalising the Poor?" *European Journal of Homelessness*, vol. 1, December: 225–236.

Toulouse, C., and Timothy W. Luke (eds.), 1998, *The Politics of Cyberspace*, New York/London: Routledge.

Trebing, Harry M., 1994, "The Networks as Infrastructure—The Reestablishment of Market Power," in Journal of Economic Issues, vol. 28, no. 2, June, 379–389.

Tridgell, Andrew, and the SambaTeam, 1997, *A History of Samba written in 1994: A Bit of History and a Bit of Fun*, June 27, http://www.rxn.com/services/faq/smb/samba.history.txt (accessed March 7, 2013).

Turkle, Sherry, 2011, *Alone Together: Why We Expect More from Technology and Less from Each Other*. New York: Basic Books, http://www.amazon.com/Alone-Together-Expect-Technology-Other/dp/0465010210 - reader_0465010210.

UCL (University College London) CIBER Group, 2008, *Information Behaviour of the Researcher of the Future*, London: University College London, CIBER Briefing paper, 9, http://www.jisc.ac.uk/media/documents/programmes/reppres/gg_final_keynote_11012008.pdf (accessed November 30, 2012).

Ulin, Robert C., 1984, *Understanding Cultures: Perspectives in Anthropology and Social Theory*, Austin: University of Texas Press.

UN General Assembly, 1948, Universal Declaration of Human Rights, http://www.un.org/en/documents/udhr/ (accessed July 15, 2013).

UN General Assembly, 2000, *Millennium Development Goals*, http://www.un.org/millenniumgoals/ (accessed December 12, 2012).

UNESCO 2013a, "WSIS + 10: Towards Inclusive Knowledge Societies for Peace and Sustainable Development," 1st WSIS Review meeting, February 25–27, 2013, http://www.unesco.org/new/en/communication–and–information/flagship–project–activities/unesco–and–wsis/wsis–10–review–meeting/ (accessed December 12, 2012).

UNESCO 2013b, *Final Recommendations—First WSIS + 10 Review Event: Towards Knowledge Societies for Peace and Sustainable Development*, http://wa2.www.unesco.org/new/typo3temp/pics/d9d8ff7cd1.gif (accessed March 24, 2013).

United Nations Human Rights Council, 2012, *Resolution A/HRC/RES/20/8: Promotion and protection of all human rights, civil, political, economic, social and cultural rights, including the right to development*, UN General Assembly: OHCHR, http://ap.ohchr.org/documents/dpage_e.aspx?si=A/HRC/RES/20/8 (accessed February 27, 2013).

US Department of State, 2012, *21st Century Statecraft*, http://www.state.gov/statecraft/ overview/ (accessed January 2, 2013).

Vaidhyanathan, Siva, 2012, *The Googlization of Everything (and why we should worry)*, Berkeley: University of California Press.

Van Aelst, P., and S. Walgrave, 2003, "New Media, New Movements? The Role of the Internet in Shaping the 'Anti–Globalization' Movement," in *Information, Communication and Society*, vol. 5, no. 4, 2002: 465–493.

Van Buren, Toby, 2006, *Autobiography—Tobias (Toby) Van Buren—08/01/2006*; http:// home.earthlink.net/~jromanj/sitebuildercontent/sitebuilderfiles/vanburen-toby-bio-08-01-2006.pdf (accessed July 15, 2013).

Vance, Ashlee, 2012, "Facebook: The Making of 1 Billion Users," *Business Week*, October 4, http://www.businessweek.com/articles/2012-10-04/facebook-the-making-of-1-billion-users (accessed February 1, 2013).

Vázquez, Rolando, 2006, "Thinking the Event with Hannah Arendt,"*European Journal of Social Theory*, vol. 9, no. 1: 43–57.

Vertovec, Stephen, 1999, "Conceiving and researching transnationalism," *Ethnic and Racial Studies*, vol. 22, no. 2: 447–462.

Vincent, Andrew, 2010, *The Politics of Human Rights*. Oxford, UK: Oxford University Press.

Vincent, R. C., K. Nordenstreng, and M. Traber (eds.), 1999, *Towards Equity in Global Communication: MacBride Update*. Cresskill, NJ: New Hampton Press.

Vise, David A., 2005, *The Google Story*, Oxford: Pan McMillan.

Volkskrant, de, 1998, "*Brussel gaat alliantie BT met AT&T onderzoeken*," Amsterdam, The Netherlands, December 8: 17.

Volkskrant, de, 2002a, "In spaghettiwestern met Microsoft verliest de klant," Amsterdam, The Netherlands, November 4.

Volkskrant, de, 2002b, "rechtbank dwingt Microsoft weer tot inbouw van Java," Amsterdam, The Netherlands, December 29: 19.

Volkskrant, de, 2003a, "Microsoft schikt met consumenten Californië," Amsterdam, The Netherlands, January 13: 6.

Volkskrant, de, 2003b, "Wantrouwen brengt man van 106 miljard ten val," Amsterdam, The Netherlands, March 14: 16.

Volkskrant, de, 2003c, "Intel," Amsterdam, The Netherlands, January 15: 16.

Volkskrant, de, 2003d, "overheden mogen kroonjuwelen van Microsoft betasten," Amsterdam, The Netherlands, January 16: 17.

Volkskrant, de, 2003e, "Microsoft," Amsterdam, The Netherlands, January 17: 17.

Volkskrant, de, 2003f, "Mineurstemming door IBM en Microsoft," Amsterdam, The Netherlands, January 8: 31.

Volkskrant, de, 2003g, "Dollar daalt fors handelstekort in VS," Amsterdam, The Netherlands, January 18: 31.

Volkskrant, de, 2012, "Daklozenopvang kan groei niet aan," October 30, 2012: 13.

Waal, Martijn de, 1998, "*Zweetvoeten.com en de strijd om Internet*," in de Volkskrant, Amsterdam, The Netherlands, 14 March, 55.

Wajcman, Judy, 1991, *Feminism Confronts Technology*, Cambridge, UK: Polity Press.

Walters, William, 2012, *Governmentality: Critical Encounters*, London/New York: Routledge.

Warner, Michael, 2002, "Publics and Counterpublics," *Public Culture*, vol. 14, no. 1, Winter: 49–90.

Warschauer, Mark, 2002, "Reconceptualising the Digital Divide," *First Monday*, vol. 7, no. 7, http://firstmonday.org/htbin/cgiwrap/bin/ojs/index.php/fm/article/view/967/888 (accessed March 18, 2013).

Watson, Sophie, 1999, "Home Is Where the Heart Is: Engendering Notions of Homelessness" in *Homelessness: Exploring the New Terrain*, Patricia Kennett and Alex Marsh (eds.), Bristol, UK: The Policy Press, 81–100.

Weberman, D., 2001, "The Matrix Simulation and the Postmodern Age," in *The Matrix and Philosophy: Welcome to the Desert of the Real*, W. Irwin (ed.). Chicago: Open Court, 225–239.

Wikipedia, 2013, *Internet Governance*, http://en.wikipedia.org/wiki/Internet_governance (accessed July 15, 2013).

Wilson, Samuel M., and Leighton C. Peterson, 2002, "The Anthropology Of Online Communities,"*Annual Review of Anthropology*, vol. 31: 449–467.

Winkelstein, Julie Ann, and Edwin-Michael Cortez, 2010, "How and Why Public Libraries Can, Should and Do Facilitate the Use of the Internet by the Homeless: A Look at the Programs, Barriers and Political Climate," paper presented at *BOBCATSSS 2010: Bridging the digital divide: libraries providing access for all?* Parma, Italy, January 25–27, http://hdl.handle.net/1889/1275 (accessed March 26, 2013).

Winokur, M., 2003, "The Ambiguous Panopticon: Foucault and the Codes of Cyberspace," Article a24, *ctheory.net*, March 13, http://www.ctheory.net/articles.aspx?id=371 (accessed November 6, 2008).

Wirth, Anne-Juliane, 2012, "'Ich will ihnen eine Stimme geben': Helmut Richard Brox ist obdachlos—und engagiert sich,"*Strassenfeger: Soziale Strassenzeitung*, no. 18, August: 4–5.

Working Group on Internet Governance, 2005, *Report of the Working Group on Internet Governance*, Château de Bossey, June 2005, www.wgig.org/docs/WGIGREPORT.pdf (accessed February 21, 2013).

World Bank, 2002, *The Right to Tell: The Role of Mass Media in Economic Development*, WBI Development Studies, Washington D.C.: The International Bank for Reconstruction and Development/The World Bank.

Wouters, Paul, Anne Beaulieu, Andrea Scharnhorst, and Sally Wyatt (eds.), 2012, *Virtual Knowledge: Experimenting in the Humanities and the Social Sciences*, Cambridge, MA: MIT Press.

Wright, Talmadge, 1997, *Out of Place: Homeless Mobilizations, Subcities, and Contested Landscapes*, Albany, NY: State University of New York Press.

WRS: Women Rough Sleepers Who Suffer Violence, 2013, *Project Overview: What Are Women Rough Sleepers?* http://www.womenroughsleepers.eu/content/project-overview (accessed March 18, 2013).

WSIS Civil Society Caucus, 2003, *Shaping Information Societies for Human Needs*. Civil Society Declaration Unanimously Adopted by the WSIS Civil Society Plenary on December 8, 2003, http://www.itu.int/wsis/docs/geneva/civil-society-declaration.pdf (accessed March 17, 2013).

WSIS Civil Society Caucus, 2005, *Civil Society Declaration: Much More Could have been Achieved*, Document WSIS-05/TUNIS/CONTR/13-E, December 2005 18, http://www.itu.int/wsis/docs2/tunis/contributions/co13.doc (accessed March 17, 2013).

Wyatt, Sally, G. Thomas, and T. Terranova, 2002, "They came, they surfed, they went back to the beach: Conceptualising use and non–use of the Internet," in *Virtual*

Society? Technology, Cyberpole, Reality, Steve Woolgar (ed.), Oxford: Oxford University Press, 23–40.

Youngs, Gillian, 2006, *Global Political Economy in the Information Age: Power and Inequality*, London/New York: Routledge.

Žižek, Slavoj, 2003 [2001], "A Holiday from History and Other Real Stories" reprinted in *Dial H-I-S-T-O-R-Y* by Johan Grimpnprez, Belgium-France, 68 min, DVD NTSC, 2003 after the original Digital Betacam, 1997, Brussels: Argos Editions, DVD booklet.

Žižek, Slavoj, 2006, *The Parallax View*, Cambridge, MA: MIT Press.